The Penguin Interdisciplinary Readings represent an attempt to come to grips with one of the most important areas of study in the Social Sciences today. Although each of the disciplines in the social sciences has made great advances during the past twenty years there is a danger that they will simply continue to pursue, in greater and greater detail the specialized methods which each of them has evolved. Although this kind of specialized work is necessary, and indeed highly desirable, students of society have become more and more aware of its inherent limitations. The reality of any social situation is that a number of events take place each of which may have economic, political, sociological and other dimensions; each situation has its historical setting and its own psychological components. Individual disciplines abstract from these events selecting the data which seem relevant to their own assumptions, and elaborating explanations within their own theoretical framework. However, if it is argued that only a partial understanding of the nature of social reality can emerge from such specialized approaches, what are the alternatives?

In the present state of development of the social sciences, there is certainly no integrating theory which can neatly fit together all the pieces to provide a 'complete' picture, if indeed such a complete picture is theoretically possible. Advocates of a holistic social science who reject the fragmented approach of individual disciplines and wish to replace them with a 'global' study of society in all its aspects, simply finish up with a randomly chosen collection of facts. The other alternative is to acknowledge that the study of society must begin by applying the varied techniques of the individual disciplines to 'specific problems' existing in the real world. Such 'problems' may be narrowly conceived or they may be extremely broad in scope. Nevertheless, the existence of a problem to be studied provides the focus for the bringing together of the methods and data of the various disciplines, even if the immediate result is merely to demonstrate how those methods and conclusions conflict, and how each of the disciplines, in pursuing its own particular academic aims, may fail to illuminate the central core of the problem. It is only through such a problem-oriented approach that the beginnings of an integrated social science might emerge.

The books of Readings grew out of the development at the University of Kent of a number of interdisciplinary courses based upon this view of the present state of the social sciences. Each course will attempt to take a particular area or problem in the social sciences and bring to bear upon it the work which has been done in a number of different disciplines. The first volumes in this series are therefore edited by members of the Faculty of Social Sciences at the University of Kent, based upon the courses which they are preparing, but future volumes in the series will be prepared by a wide range of authors, and it is also intended to produce a series of original texts dealing with specific problems in an interdisciplinary way.

Each volume of Readings, therefore, is an attempt by an individual to take a particular problem and to draw from the literature of the subjects concerned those contributions which would seem most likely to illuminate the present state of knowledge in the social sciences relating to that problem, and also to provide the basis for a more integrated understanding of this particular piece of social reality. For each of the editors the selection of the readings must be in one sense a very personal selection, based upon his conception of the nature of the problem, of what is important to the understanding of that problem, and of how the various elements of the different disciplines might eventually be combined to provide such an understanding. Each editor has produced a fairly lengthy introduction which attempts to set his particular choice of materials within the context of the current state of the debate in the disciplines concerned.

If our view of the best way to make progress in the study of the social sciences is correct, this series might provoke the kind of interdisciplinary research, both by groups and by individuals, which may help to make our understanding of the nature of society both more satisfying academically, and more fruitful as a basis for future policy.

M. J. C. Vile

Underdevelopment and Development

The Third World Today

Selected Readings

Edited by Henry Bernstein

Penguin Books

Penguin Books Ltd, Harmondsworth,
Middlesex, England
Penguin Books Inc., 7110 Ambassador Road,
Baltimore, Md 21207, USA
Penguin Books Australia Ltd,
Ringwood, Victoria, Australia

First published 1973
This selection copyright © Henry Bernstein, 1973
Introduction and notes copyright © Henry Bernstein, 1973
Copyright acknowledgement for items in this volume
will be found on page 381

Made and printed in Great Britain by
Richard Clay (The Chaucer Press) Ltd, Bungay, Suffolk
Set in Monotype Times

For some young Turks

Contents

Introduction:
Development and the Social Sciences

While economists took the sociology out of political economy, sociologists took out the economy.
R. Frankenberg (1967, p. 49)

An adequate understanding of the new countries of the 'third world' demands that one pursue scientific quarry across any fenced-off academic field into which it may happen to wander.
C. Geertz (1963, p. xviii)

I

The idea of development as the progressive transformation of society begins to assume a modern form in the writings of the 'founding fathers' of social science. The theories of the political economists and evolutionary sociologists of the late eighteenth and nineteenth centuries were shaped in the context of radical social change in Europe. In the period since the end of the Second World War, development has become a slogan of global aspiration and effort. The issues of underdevelopment and development have gained a specific and dramatic focus from a context that includes the demise of classic European imperialism, and the conflicting claims of rival socio-economic systems.

A strategic contrast with many earlier conceptions is the emphasis on conscious action to effect large-scale change in a desired direction, utilizing in a centralized or at least co-ordinated way the resources available to given political units. The aspiration to change, and institutional means for achieving it, are central to present day conceptions of development. Policy for development is a major preoccupation of the governments of poor countries; help is promised by those of rich countries. Research on development and the channelling of resources – investment capital, equipment, skilled personnel and know-how – have become the functions of specially created agencies.

This much is common knowledge. Indeed the movement for development embodies a value judgement with which few would disagree: the desirability of overcoming malnutrition, poverty and disease which are the most immediate and widespread aspects of human suffering. In positive terms some advocate a commitment to development that transcends the limiting terms of economic growth to embrace such features of social justice as equality of opportunity, full employment, generally available social services, equitable distribution of income and basic political freedoms (see for example, Seers, 1969).

In these terms a broad consensus may be discernible, but such an agreement on desired ends does not necessarily take us far in understanding the realities of the contemporary world. Statements issuing from politicians and planners, bankers and businessmen, academics and experts of many descriptions, point to a wide variety of assumptions, interests and concerns, as well as actual proposals. The issues of development in the Third World have political ramifications of far-reaching significance; not surprisingly their consideration entails intellectual controversy. The naive plea that the brutal data of human deprivation on such a scale should somehow be 'above' politics displays both a wilful disregard of the nature of entrenched inequality and a denial of the materials from which politics might be created. The same is true of the technocratic approach which sees the achievement of development as dependent on the abstract rationality of techniques of forecasting, allocation and appraisal, free from the 'interference' of politics. Both views – misconstrued assertions on behalf of the qualities of 'heart' and 'mind' – are grossly inadequate to the extreme responsibilities of effective analysis and action that have to be faced.

To pursue the meaning of development therefore is not to initiate an exercise in semantics but is a necessary first step in thinking clearly about the range of situations, problems and possibilities subsumed in the uses of the term. Modes of definition embody particular assumptions and concerns and give rise to particular methods and uses. It is one of the peculiarities of social science that its concepts and the activities of its practitioners themselves enter the field of study. Nowhere is this more true than in development studies where the most pressing of human needs and the conceptions of the development professional – academic, consultant, planner and administrator – confront each other.

This is not the place to attempt a systematic review of theories of development in the various social science disciplines. The purpose is rather to indicate in the light of some central questions the general basis of an approach to the interdisciplinary problem. This is necessarily a preliminary and tentative undertaking. By restricting discussion to a protected corner called the 'philosophy of social science', questions of theory and method may be treated with formal elegance and precision but it is less important to preserve these qualities than to assess the usefulness of different perspectives in analysis, in indicating how to frame the questions we need to ask as well as how we might go about answering them.

II

Two aspects of the orientation employed here should be made explicit at the start:

1 Development is understood in a broad economic sense

This apparent violation of the interdisciplinary commitment becomes superficial once it is stressed that social development is inseparable from economic development, and secondly that the latter cannot be left to the attention of economists alone. As Professor Penrose observed in a book review several years ago (1968) – 'It is, of course, common for economists to note the importance of (non-economic) considerations, but usually only to ignore them.' On the other hand, the other social sciences are relevant to the extent that they illuminate the fully social nature of economic development, a quality that cannot be claimed automatically for the contributions of sociologists and political scientists.

2 The perspective adopted is a historical one

The use of such a perspective goes beyond the notion of 'historical background' to the *theoretical comprehension of development and underdevelopment as historical processes*, that is to say, as opposed to static conditions or processes embodying a non-historical conception of time and movement (as in systems theory for example). It follows that the study of society and that of history cannot be pursued separately. The subject matter of the specialized domains of social science – 'the' economic, 'the' political, 'the' sociological and 'the' psychological – are inextricably related in reality. A consciousness of the historical nature of this reality and a commitment to its theoretical elucidation can cut across the professional boundaries as the basis of an interdisciplinary approach.

III

First, it is useful to note a distinction between economic growth and development. This has been defined rather formally in terms of 'changes in the value of economic parameters in given institutional conditions . . . (and) changes in the value of economic parameters (which) are accompanied or even preceded by institutional change' (Wilber, 1969, p. 8). A supplementary formulation is that 'growth is a quantitative process, involving principally the extension of an already established structure of production, whereas development suggests qualitative changes, the creation of new economic and non-economic structures' (Dowd, 1967, p. 153). The two statements draw attention to the kind of change with which we are concerned, and especially the encompassing nature of development with respect to the economic and the non-economic – a continuing distinction symptomatic of the interdisciplinary problem.

At two extremes (though habitual ones) of theoretical and empirical expression, economics has failed to confront the density of development as a social process and the range of its historical possibilities. As the authors of an authoritative theoretical survey concluded – 'The variety of growth models is very great and with ingenuity can evidently be almost indefinitely enlarged. This is largely due to the rather extreme level of abstraction employed and the very artificial nature of the problems considered.' (Hahn and Mathews, 1967, p. 110). The inadequacy of the method of abstracting and manipulating a few variables in pristine isolation, is matched by the technical and conceptual strains on growth statistics and the (often politically motivated) uses to which they are put.[1]

Other aspects of economic theory, and social science theories

1. In discussing American practices, and the United States has statistical resources far superior to those of underdeveloped countries, a leading authority stressed that *'Precise uses of "growth rates" are entirely inadmissible, whether for comparing different countries or short periods of the same country.* Their computation is largely arbitrary. The concept itself, is vague and unreliable' (Morgenstern, 1963, p. 300 – author's italics).

Apart from the basic unreliability of many statistics, the point has been well made that the kinds of aggregates used often conceal more than they reveal. The need for disaggregation is a central theme of the two books on planning from which Readings 11 and 13 are taken. In the former Griffin and Enos provide some illuminating examples of the caution with which statistics must be used, both at the technical level (procedures of calculation) and the theoretical level (assumptions and inferences).

in general, have been found wanting in face of the challenge to their competence presented by contemporary underdevelopment, that is to say, by situations which represent very different historical conditions from those with which Western social science has been primarily concerned and by which it has been shaped.[2] Some of the central theoretical problems, as distinct from merely ethnocentric and chauvinist prejudices, stem from a tradition of model-building which centres on closed systems employing self-regulating mechanisms (such as market forces) to maintain equilibrium. Reinhard Bendix has offered a poignant comment on the centrality of equilibrium as an organizing concept:

[. . .] the dominant experience of our generation appears to be that the unanticipated repercussions of European expansion were effective enough to undermine or destroy social frameworks (of traditional societies) but often not nearly effective enough to provide structural alternatives. To future historians it may appear as a touching if minor irony that an organic conception of society based on the idea of equilibrium is one of the major intellectual perspectives of our time (Bendix, 1969, p. 360).

In the 1950s Gunnar Myrdal pointed to some of the ways in which the prevailing assumptions of economic theory precluded an adequate understanding of underdevelopment, and hence effective action to overcome it. The equilibrium postulate, he argued, is irrelevant to the imperatives of rapid development while market forces, rather than having a positive distributive and stimulating effect, in fact sustain and even intensify existing unequal relationships.[3] Myrdal's notion of cumulative and circular causation represents an early attempt to characterize underdevelopment in dynamic and relational terms, as opposed to viewing it merely as a static condition of backwardness (see pp. 25–7 below). His stress on the totality of the process of development emphasized the need to transcend the conventional segregation of economic and 'non-economic' factors (Myrdal, 1957).

2. Relevant here is the well-known article by Seers (1963), reprinted in Martin and Knapp (1967), where the debate is taken up by Myint.

3. The analogous sociological theory of development by 'diffusion' is trenchantly criticized by Frank (1969b). The question of technology is a highly salient theme for the consideration of this and related issues, as Vaitsos (Reading 18) illustrates.

The assumption of perfect competition (and its advantages), has long failed to reflect the reality of capitalist development if indeed it ever did. Clairmonte (1960) provides a useful discussion in the light of an historical perspective on underdevelopment.

Typically, orthodox economic theory has proceeded by ignoring factors other than those rigidly defined as economic – by treating them as residual as the term 'non-economic' implies, or by holding them 'constant',[4] or by assuming the social and institutional conditions of the particular experience of development it itself reflects. On the other hand, the theories of sociologists and political scientists have projected a model of Western society as paradigmatic of the state of being modern or developed, while tending to ignore the problematic economic dimension of Third World 'modernization'.[5] However it is precisely the failure of previous 'attested' modes of development to reproduce themselves in the Third World that defines contemporary conceptions of underdevelopment.

IV

The need for an interdisciplinary approach is widely recognized – 'it is obvious that any effort to treat development in economy, polity and society as separate processes simply makes little sense' (Lipset, 1969, p. xiii). However, the interdisciplinary ideal has not been matched by practice.[6] Lipset observed that while the emergence of development as a special area of social science interest encouraged the aim of interdisciplinary cooperation, this initial impulse has been vitiated by disillusionment with the performance of the underdeveloped countries – a sadder comment on the prescriptive models of development and modernization employed than he seems to realize (Lipset, pp. xii, xiv).

It is clear that the construction of a viable interdisciplinary strategy requires explicit methodological premises; it cannot be assumed to emerge from simply pooling the contributions of

4. '[. . .] in dealing with historical processes one cannot always proceed as if all other things remained equal; for often they do not, and it is the change in those "other things" which is crucial' (Hoselitz, 1965, p. 183).

5. For example, by locating (or losing) economic development in a very abstract schema of social change viewed as differentiation, and/or by focusing on such questions as new forms of social integration *attendant* on economic development (Bernstein, 1971, 1972).

6. An example of the very shallow nature of some conceptions of 'interdisciplinary integration' is provided by Röling (1966) who argues that development in the Third World depends on changing the behaviour of its people to conform with that assumed in economic theory. The role of sociology accordingly is to study the means by which this may be achieved!

different disciplines. An economist has posed the problem in these terms:

The fundamental problem . . . is that the social sciences are linked by a common subject matter rather than a common theory – where disciplines operate in generally different fields but are linked by dependence on a common theoretical base (as, say, biochemistry and mechanical engineering depend on a common stock of ideas about molecular and atomic structure) the problem of joint application is much less than where the disciplines operate in the same problem field but with different intellectual bases (for example, biochemistry and psychiatry) (Cumper, 1968, p. 248).

This statement points to two related issues. One concerns what may be termed an optional interdisciplinary approach. For some purposes co-operation between disciplines (joint application) is deemed appropriate, say in the discussion of land reform or the formation of an industrial labour force, while for other purposes it is not, for example, in the analysis of capital flows (which belongs to economics 'proper') or of belief systems (which belongs to to sociology or anthropology 'proper').[7] To establish any procedure (other than an *ad hoc* one) for deciding what is appropriate it is necessary to have criteria transcending those which govern the specialist pursuits. In the absence of a common theoretical orientation or intellectual base, it is difficult to see how criteria could be established for deciding that economics 'needs' sociology at a certain point, or vice versa.

The possibility of a common theoretical base has been considered by some social scientists. Two proposals may be noted by way of illustration. One of these, strongly stated by Homans (1967) asserts that the only strictly scientific, i.e. explanatory, propositions available to social science are those of behavioural psychology. In this view the specialized disciplines have the secondary function of describing the various institutional contexts in which the fundamental laws of human behaviour operate. The second example is that of systems theory, suggested by Lipset (1969) and others as the basis of a unified social science. Both approaches, however, are essentially non-historical and non-dialectical, and fail to provide the means for understanding social

7. In Geertz's metaphor, which scientific quarry are to be pursued across which fenced-off academic fields? The examples given above are chosen to reflect conventional predilections. Capital flows and belief systems of course embody social relationships no less than patterns of land tenure or the sale of labour.

development in either its general or specific dimensions. The models posited aspire to universal validity, disregarding the crucial distinctions between different modes of social organization and the defining characteristics of different historical periods. The first is strictly reductionist, locating explanation at the level of individual behaviour and conditioning and denying any objective autonomy to social forces, while the second employs a model of society conceived as an abstract system with its mechanisms of system adjustment and maintenance. From different starting points, then, these two conceptions ignore both the range of circumstances 'in which men get their living and their material environment' (see below), and the dialectical tension between the inheritance of these circumstances as objective constraints and the possibilities of men acting to change them.[8]

A keen sense of this dialectical tension is a prerequisite for the imaginative comprehension of underdevelopment and development. The latter is no longer conceived as spontaneously generated and in this sense (ultimately) guaranteed, but as a conscious goal pursued today in a distinctive global context. This goes beyond the limited conception of human agency in systems theory and the derived 'policy-science' approach of system manipulation to the relationship between men's actions and qualitative social change. The distinction between underdevelopment and development denotes the transformation of given historical conditions and the question of how this is to be achieved, as well as particular outcomes, will reflect the often conflicting conceptions and interests of different social groups – an intrinsic and crucial consideration with which the assumptions and methods of behavioural psychology and systems theory are ill-equipped to deal.[9]

V

There is little sign that social scientists will ever subscribe to a common stock of ideas about their subject matter in the way Cumper suggests that biochemists and mechanical engineers do

8. Neither can the inadequacies of these two approaches be remedied by the attempt to combine them in a single framework as, for example, by Kunkel, 1970.

9. 'The study of social change through collective action has been one of the great *terra incognita* of sociology'; and 'By viewing social movements and collective action in the context of social change and conflict, we are redressing a balance which, in the past, has minimized the importance that human volition gives to the direction of change in societies' (Gusfield, 1970, pp. 7, 8).

concerning molecular and atomic structure. A single body of theory about development is as unlikely to emerge as it is about any other major social theme engendering political conflict and sharp intellectual divergences. Whether this is a matter for regret is not a question to be pursued here; it does indicate that the major issues dividing social scientists are not necessarily those of disciplinary boundaries which themselves partly reflect (intellectually) irrelevant considerations in the course of academic professionalization. Neither, however, is the issue simply reducible to an ideological dimension.

Historical social science in the sense proposed here provides an alternative basis for interdisciplinary studies in so far as it embodies a certain *type* of theoretical commitment, one which avoids the trap that assigns an idiographic function to the study of history on one hand, and the pursuit of universal, hence non- or extra- historical 'laws' of society and human nature to social science on the other. This commitment derives from a fundamental perception of the historical nature of social reality, in general and in particular, in contrast with the study of history as sequences of unique events or the perspective of formalist social theory. It is in this sense that one might speak of a tradition of historical social science embracing such figures as Marx, Weber, Schumpeter and Polanyi who differ so much in other respects. Unfortunately the further development of this tradition has not been explored by contemporary social scientists with a handful of exceptions.[10]

It is important to consider what historical social science is not, as well as what it is. Clearly its meaning is not covered simply by the use of historical data whether in the manner of a certain kind of history writing[11] or in the common social science practice of

10. This is more applicable to English-language social science than to Europe where historical social science continues to provide a major intellectual perspective. It has been suggested that this reflects the need to confront the political and cultural potency of Marxism, which is much weaker by comparison in Britain and the United States. This is succinctly conveyed in an observation on the foremost theorist of American sociology – 'Parsons took his approach to Marxism from the conclusions but not the experience of Weber, Durkheim, Pareto and Sombart' (Gouldner, 1971, p. 150).

11. It is not my intention to underestimate the value of imaginative historical scholarship. The studies of Hill and Morris from which Readings 5 and 8 are taken demonstrate the function of such scholarship, as one aspect of its contribution to knowledge, in checking the often misconceived and ill-informed generalizations of social scientists.

pouring historical 'examples' into conceptual containers like ill-mixed concrete. A further methodological pit-fall is exemplified by comparative statics of which the literature on development provides many examples. In this context, 'comparative statics' refers generally to the construction of models of development which are applied to situations representing very different historical conditions from those on which the model is based. This is expressed in formulations of the type: 'on the basis of indicators a, b and c underdeveloped country x in the 1970s approximates to the stage of development of developed country y in the 1850s'. Whether put as explicitly as this or employed more as an implicit assumption, this form of historical reductionism is a pervasive one.[12] When events fail to conform to the model there is a temptation to blame the former rather than the latter. This has led to a tendency among some social scientists to view the recent experience of many underdeveloped countries as deviant or pathological rather than regarding their own theories as defective.

Something of the conception of historical social-science pursued here is contained in a characterization of his discipline by an outstanding social historian:

Social history can never be another specialization like economic or other hyphenated histories because its subject matter cannot be isolated. We can define certain human activities as economic, at least for analytical purposes, and then study them historically. Though this may be (except for certain definable purposes) artificial or unrealistic, it is not impracticable. . . . But the social or societal aspects of man's being cannot be separated from the other aspects of his being, except at the cost of tautology or extreme trivialization. They cannot, for more than a moment, be separated from the ways in which men got their living and their material environment (Hobsbawm, 1971, pp. 2–5)

This view stimulates a strict awareness of the limitations of abstracting, say, the economic or the political from the total nexus of social relationships. The economic, the political and paradoxically the sociological also (in a prevalent usage) derive their meaning only from the *prior* totality of the social.

In turn the concrete nature of the social can only be comprehended historically, and this involves the periodization of history

12. Probably its best known expression is in the theory of Rostow, 1960; see the review by Baran and Hobsbawm (1961).

in an analytical as opposed to a merely chronological sense.[13] The first theoretical task is to identify the major types of historical society and their material foundations. These types are situated in an evolutionary schema that constitutes a developmental sequence from the most primitive known societies (usually held to be hunting and gathering bands – Service, 1966; Lenski, 1970, ch. 7), to the advanced capitalist and state socialist societies of today.[14] While the framework of *general* social evolution thus attempts to accommodate the history of human society *as a whole*, the concept of *specific* evolution is addressed to the differentiated experience of *particular* societies in their relation to general evolution. This counteracts those elements of some general evolutionary theories criticized as metaphysical (strict determinism and the assumption of unilinear progression), and ideological (a built-in preference for gradualism).

The necessity for every society to pass through the same stages of development (a deterministic and unilinear progression) has been rightly rejected. The perspective of specific evolution demonstrates that even if certain societies converge in their development, the mechanisms by which this occurs can differ in critical ways. Similarly the opposition of evolution and revolution as exclusive types of change, ceases to be a problem when understood historically.[15] Revolutionary change may be a long-term process, its revolutionary referent being the extent and basic nature of such change rather than its rapidity (e.g. the Industrial Revolution). At the same time revolutions in the more usual and dramatic (political) sense crystallize the social conflicts which accumulate and intensify in any major social change. The outcomes of revolutions in this latter sense (analysis of which must concern what *fails* to happen as well as what does happen) affect the course of future development not only for the society in which revolution occurs, but for other societies as well (Moore, 1969; Dunn, 1972). This perception is especially relevant to the modern

13. Historical chronology acquires its meaning only from the questions we address to it. See, for example, the analysis by Hobsbawm (1954) of the crisis of seventeenth-century Europe in terms of the transition from feudal to capitalist society.

14. For significant examples of theory construction based on evolutionary categories in anthropology, sociology and economic history, see Service (1962), Lenski (1970), Hicks (1969). Also of note is the emergence of a more critical and fruitful discussion of 'pre-capitalist social formations' by Marxists – for example, Meillassoux, 1972.

15. This also helps clarify the question of ideological preferences.

world in which international communication becomes increasingly sensitive and international integration increasingly effective.[16]

Thus, while the emphasis of general social evolution is on the direction of change and the necessarily associated question of what changes, that of specific evolution aims at a more differentiated analysis of the mechanisms, including revolutions, by which a general evolutionary trend is manifested and developed in the experience of particular societies.[17]

An evolutionary *and* historical social science must focus ultimately on the potential for change in particular situations even if its perspective precludes any mechanistic notion of prediction. One of its fundamental insights is that the developed societies cannot offer any final criterion of development (that is to say, historical futures for other societies) any more than the history of their emergence provides 'models' of necessary, possible or desirable change for underdeveloped countries to emulate. History does not stop with the present; as Eric Wolf has remarked – 'every society is a battlefield between its own past and its future' (Wolf, 1959, p. 106), and today the terms of battle, as noted, increasingly reflect forces operating in a supra-national social system.

The implications for the interdisciplinary problem can now be reiterated. Typically, interdisciplinary social science has been discussed in terms of integrating rather than transcending, the different disciplines. As these operate with the assumption that each for its own purposes deals with an effectively autonomous area of social reality,[18] it is difficult to see how a more complete picture can be achieved, in the absence of a common theoretical orientation, merely by pooling a number of fragments or 'factors'. The argument of this essay is that such an orientation is not to be sought as the lowest common denominator (if there is one) of specialized pursuits with their own concerns, methods, and professional rivalries – but in *the effort to comprehend concrete historical forms and processes in their totality*.[19] The usefulness,

16. Integration is not used here in any normative sense.

17. For example, the significant differences in the capitalist development of England, France, the United States, Germany and Japan – see the suggestive comparative study by Moore (1969).

18. 'Unfortunately, many in the social disciplines are trained and rewarded for selecting and interpreting reality only as their respective disciplines see it' (Shorter, 1967, p. 2).

19. For a formulation similar in several important respects, see the Editorial Statement in the new journal, *Economy and Society*, vol. 1, no. 1, February, 1972.

or otherwise, of the concepts and techniques of the occupational specialities of academic life is to be assessed in the framework of this common project which involves, as suggested earlier, a distinct, and distinguishing, type of theoretical commitment. Its application may be illustrated briefly in relation to the conceptualization of contemporary underdevelopment.

VI

In the *International Encyclopedia of the Social Sciences* published in 1968, there is no article on underdevelopment.[20] This is symptomatic of a critical lacuna in the social science literature on the Third World. Underdevelopment is simply defined negatively in relation to development, a form of conceptualization by default expressed in such invidious terms as backwardness, stagnation and tradition (or traditionalism). In conventional usage development means the *process* of developing while underdevelopment is conceived only in a static fashion as a *state* – underdevelop*ing* is not considered as a possibility. This precludes any understanding of underdevelopment as a process, as a phenomenon which has itself emerged historically.[21]

The French anthropologist Balaudier has pointed out that 'Researches devoted to "backward" societies disrupted by the introduction of modern production technology and modern forms of economy (or better, a certain form of capitalism), capture an evolutionary "moment" which differentiates essentially the various types of global societies' (Balaudier, 1965, pp. 386–7).[22] Contemporary underdevelopment assumes a conception of, and an aspiration to development which in turn presupposes

20. The entry on underdevelopment (volume 16) directs the interested reader to articles on 'Economic Growth', 'Modernization', 'Stagnation' and 'Technical Assistance'.

21. Awareness of the 'development of underdevelopment' has been greatly stimulated by the work of Frank (1969a) (See Dos Santos, Reading 3). However, Frank's ideas require considerable qualification and elaboration in more precise theoretical and empirical terms – see, for example, Laclau (1971).

22. In this connection note recent historically informed discussions of peasant society as a generic type (Thorner, 1962; Wolf, 1966), and the associated theme of its disintegration as an element of underdevelopment (Stavenhagen, Reading 4). These statements represent a considerable advance beyond the perspective of the previous generation of writers on peasants such as Redfield.

a world in which the confrontation of different types of society raises new possibilities of social evolution. Myrdal, as noted earlier, and the eminent economic historian Gerschenkron (1952, 1962) have drawn attention to *the relational nature of under-development*. However, neither of these writers investigated the historical content of the relationships between the developed countries and those of the Third World.[23]

The expansion of Western Europe (and the economic, political and cultural changes entailed by this process) was the initial force in the establishment of a global network of relationships. In the early modern period 'the world economy which resulted *was* European in incentive, in organization and in its preoccupations ... (and) has been so centred upon Europe and European needs that political domination has normally ensued as the only sure means of safeguarding those needs.' (Rich, 1967, pp. xiii–xv). The recognition of European domination in these comments stimulates vigilance against the often insidious forms of ethnocentrism already alluded to, such as that comprised by 'comparative statics'. Underdevelopment must be located historically in the penetration of pre-capitalist societies by the expansion of capitalism from its countries of origin (itself a necessary condition of capitalist development; Furtado, Reading 1).

In this perspective the theme is a particular kind of historical development with global ramifications, moreover of a profoundly contradictory nature so that we deplore certain of its effects with the designation of 'underdevelopment'. While the analysis of underdevelopment often refers to traditional social elements, the countries of the Third World cannot be regarded as 'traditional societies'. The analysis of underdevelopment must focus on the *changes* these societies have undergone and particularly the nature of their integration with externally generated social forces. To state the point this baldly is only to announce the initial premises of a manifold programme of theoretical and empirical work. The differential forms of underdevelopment as a continuing process require sensitive analysis which in turn bears on the considera-

23. Myrdal confines himself to noting the factors of economic geography and the maintenance of original competitive advantages by the developed areas – a somewhat underdeveloped characterization in the light of some of the analyses presented in this volume (Readings 3, 6, 16, 18, 20). Gerschenkron's conceptualization of relative backwardness and the ways in which this affects the choices open to development 'latecomers' was formulated in the context of European economies before the First World War.

tion of development possibilities. The interaction between external forces and the internal social dynamics of Third World societies is complex and variable, and clearly is itself subject to historical change. For example, the analysis of Latin American underdevelopment must take account of basic continuities and changes in the periods of Spanish and Portuguese mercantilist colonial domination, British 'imperialism of free trade', and of current technological and financial superiority possessed by international corporations.

All this is to say that the analysis of underdevelopment is inseparable from that of development, and demands the same intensity of theoretical attention which must focus on the nature and types of 'dynamic underdevelopment biases' (Beckford, Reading 6). The historical perspective enhances an indispensable awareness that the forms of development of one period can become those of 'underdevelopment' of another period.

VII

This introduction has drawn on ideas which are sometimes difficult, always controversial. Their presentation has been extremely summary, somewhat heterodox and probably more abstract than is desirable. However, the persistent tendencies in contemporary social science of a piecemeal empiricism on the one hand, and formalist 'model-building' on the other, justify this emphasis on the broad elements of a perspective which does not disassociate 'facts' from theory, *nor* theory from history. In any case it is intended that some of the ramifications of the very general statements advanced can be pursued through a number of the readings that follow. The aim in selecting them has been to provide a useful combination of pieces which discuss general issues and trends in a succinct way with others that exemplify these issues in particular situations. Selection was also governed by the preoccupations which have been discussed. While the volume as a whole represents no single 'line', neither are its contents so random as to preclude the attempt to relate coherently the themes of the different readings to each other, and to those of this introduction. A review of other anthologies on development reveals an alarming tendency to draw time after time on a relatively small number of big names published in a smaller number of big-name journals. Selection therefore has also been related to, perhaps opposed to, what is already easily accessible in other collections, a number of which are given in the section on further reading.

There are things a book of readings cannot do – in this case it can no more 'solve' the interdisciplinary problem than provide even a minimal coverage of the major themes in development studies. The project will be considered worthwhile if it is able to stimulate some critical awareness of the issues and the choices they entail, and to contribute to breaking down the highly artificial barriers between the social sciences.

References

BALANDIER, G. (1965), 'Traditional social structures and economic changes', in P. L. van den Berghe (ed.), *Africa, Social Problems of Change and Conflict*, John Wiley.

BARAN, P., and HOBSBAWM, E. (1961), 'The stages of economic growth', *Kyklos*, vol. 14, pp. 234–42.

BENDIX, R. (1969), *Nation-Building and Citizenship*, Doubleday, New York.

BERNSTEIN, H. (1971), 'Modernization theory and the sociological study of development', *J. of Develop. Studs.*, vol. 7, no. 2.

BERNSTEIN, H. (1972), 'Breakdowns of modernization, a review article', *J. of Develop. Studs.*, vol. 8, no. 2.

CLAIRMONTE, F. (1960), *Economic Liberalism and Underdevelopment*, Asia Publishing House.

CUMPER, G. E. (1968), 'Non-economic factors influencing rural development planning', *Social & Econ. Studs.*, vol. 17, no. 3.

DOWD, D. F. (1967), 'Some issues of economic development and of development economics', *J. of Econ. Issues*, vol. 1, no. 3.

DUNN, J. (1972), *Modern Revolutions*, Cambridge University Press.

FRANK, A. G. (1969a), *Capitalism and Underdevelopment in Latin America*, revised edition, Monthly Review Press.

FRANK, A. G. (1969b), 'Sociology of development and underdevelopment of sociology', in *Latin America: Underdevelopment or Revolution*, Monthly Review Press.

FRANKENBERG, R. (1967), 'Economic anthropology: one anthropologist's view', in R. Firth (ed.), *Themes in Economic Anthropology*, Tavistock.

GEERTZ, C. (1963), *Agricultural Involution*, University of California Press.

GERSCHENKRON, A. (1952), 'Economic backwardness in historical perspective', in B. F. Hoselitz (ed.), *The Progress of Underdeveloped Areas* University of Chicago Press.

GERSCHENKRON, A. (1962), 'Typology of industrial development as a tool of analysis' in *Second International Conference of Economic History*, vol. II, The Hague.

GOULDNER, A. W. (1971), *The Coming Crisis of Western Sociology*, Heinemann.

GUSFIELD, J. R. (ed.) (1970), *Protest, Reform and Revolt*, John Wiley.

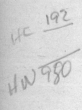

HAHN, F. H., and MATHEWS, R. C. O. (1967), 'The theory of economic growth: a survey', in *Surveys of Economic Theory*, vol. 2, *Growth and Development*, St Martins Press.

HICKS, J. (1969), *A Theory of Economic History*, Oxford University Press.

HOBSBAWM, E. J. (1954), 'The crisis of the seventeenth century', I and II, *Past and Present*, vols. 5 and 6.

HOBSBAWM, E. J. (1971), 'From social history to the history of society', *Daedalus*, Winter.

HOSELITZ, B. F. (1965), 'The use of historical comparisons in the study of economic development', in R. Aron and B. F. Hoselitz, (eds.), *Social Development*, Mouton.

HOMANS, G. C. (1967), *The Nature of Social Science*, Harcourt, Brace & World.

KUNKEL, J. H. (1971), *Society and Economic Growth*, Oxford University Press.

LACLAU, E. (1971), 'Feudalism and capitalism in Latin America', *New Left Review*, no. 67.

LENSKI, G. (1970), *Human Societies*, McGraw-Hill.

LIPSET, S. M. (ed.) (1969), *Politics and the Social Sciences*, Oxford University Press.

MARTIN, K., and KNAPP, J. (eds.) (1967), *The Teaching of Development Economics*, Frank Cass.

MEILLASSOUX, C. (1972), 'From reproduction to production. A Marxist approach to economic anthropology', *Economy and Society*, vol. 1, no. 1.

MOORE, B. JR (1969), *Social Origins of Dictatorship and Democracy*, Penguin.

MORGENSTERN, O. (1963), *On the Accuracy of Economic Observations*, revised edition, Princeton University Press.

MYINT, H. (1967), 'Economic theory and underdeveloped countries', in Martin and Knapp (eds.), *The Teaching of Development Economics*, F. Cass.

MYRDAL, G. (1957), *Economic Theory and Underdeveloped Regions*, Duckworth.

PENROSE, E. (1968), Review of E. Hagen's *The Economics of Development*, in *J. of Develop. Studs.*, vol. 6, pp. 169–70.

RICH, E. E. (1967), 'Introduction', in E. E. Rich and C. H. Wilson (eds.), *The Economy of Expanding Europe in the Sixteenth and Seventeenth Centuries*, vol. 4 of *The Cambridge Economic History of Europe*, Cambridge University Press.

RÖLING, N. G. (1966), 'Towards the interdisciplinary integration of economic theory and rural sociology', *Sociologica Ruralis*, vol. 6.

ROSTOW, W. W. (1960), *The Stages of Economic Growth*, Cambridge University Press.

SEERS, D. (1963), 'The limitations of the special case', *Bull. of the Inst. of Econ. and Stats.*, May, vol. 25, pp. 77–98.

SEERS, D. (1969), 'The meaning of development', *International Develop. Rev.*, vol. 11, pp. 2–6.

SERVICE, E. R. (1962), *Primitive Social Organization*, Random House.

SERVICE, E. R. (1966), *The Hunters*, Prentice–Hall.

SHORTER, F. C. (ed.) (1967), *Four Studies on the Economic Development of Turkey*, Frank Cass.

THORNER, D. (1962), 'Peasant economy as a category in economic history', reprinted in T. Shanin, (ed.) (1971), *Peasants and Peasant Societies*, Penguin.

WILBER, C. K. (1969), *The Soviet Model and Underdeveloped Countries*, University of North Carolina Press.

WOLF, E. R. (1959), *Sons of the Shaking Earth*, University of Chicago Press.

WOLF, E. R. (1966), *Peasants*, Prentice-Hall.

Part One
Underdevelopment in Historical Perspective

Furtado (Reading 1) proposes a framework for the analysis of underdevelopment as a distinctive historical process linked to the expansion of developing capitalism. In analysing 'the underdeveloped structures' he draws on the influential idea of dual economy, that is to say an unbalanced and unintegrated economy characterized by the co-existence of a dynamic 'modern' sector of production, typically export-oriented, and a 'traditional' sector of subsistence agriculture inhibiting the development of an internal market. In his discussion of Java, however, Geertz (Reading 2) points to the kind of integration that was established in dual economy under colonial conditions. The 'traditional' nature of the indigenous sector was maintained and manipulated in order to provide cheap inputs, above all labour, for the modern sector. An instructive contrast is drawn between the historical experience of Japan, the only country of the 'three continents' so far to achieve the status of an advanced industrial society, and that of Java as affected by colonial rule and the legacy it bestowed on modern Indonesia. The more extensive piece by Dos Santos (Reading 3) discusses a number of highly salient issues including the relationship between the conceptualization of development and government policy. This is of great practical importance as many social scientists are involved in the formulation of development strategy. He goes on to propose the basis of a theory of underdevelopment as dependence, a theme which has been debated with increasing urgency in the Latin American crisis of the 1960s.

1 C. Furtado

Elements of a Theory of Underdevelopment –
the Underdeveloped Structures

Excerpt from chapter 4 of C. Furtado, *Development and Underdevelopment*,
University of California Press, 1964, pp. 127–40.

The underdeveloped structures

The advent of an industrial nucleus in eighteenth century Europe
disrupted the world economy of the time and eventually conditioned later economic development in almost every region in the
world. The action of that powerful dynamic nucleus proceeded
to operate in three directions. The first marks the line of development in Western Europe, within the structure of the political
divisions which had crystallized in the preceding mercantile
period. This development, as we have seen, was characterized by
disorganization of the pre-capitalistic artisan economy and progressive absorption at a higher level of productivity of the factors
released. Two phases can be identified in this process: in the first,
the release of labor faster than it was absorbed made the supply
of this factor wholly elastic; in the second, the tendency towards
exhaustion of the labor supply resulting from the disjointing of
the pre-capitalistic economy called for reorientation of technology
in order to maintain the flexibility of the system so that the factors
could be combined in proportions compatible with their respective supplies. Thus the development of technology – the transformations of the capital goods industries – became more and
more conditioned by the relative availability of factors in the
industrial centers.

The second line of development of the European industrial
economy consisted of displacement of frontiers wherever there
was still unoccupied land with characteristics similar to those
in Europe itself. A number of factors were involved in that expansion. In the case of Australia and the American West, gold
played a basic role. The revolution in maritime transportation,
making it possible to bring grain great distances to compete in
the European market, was decisive in other cases. It must be
remembered, however, that this displacement of the frontier
was not basically different from the process of development of

Europe itself, of which it formed a part; the Australian, Canadian and American economies in that phase were mere extensions, so to speak, of the European industrial economy. The populations which emigrated to those areas took with them European techniques and consumption habits, and on encountering a greater abundance of natural resources they rapidly achieved rather high levels of productivity and income. If we consider that these 'colonies' were established only where exceptionally favorable economic potentials existed, we see why their populations achieved right from the start high standards of living relative to those of the European countries.

The third line of expansion of the European industrial economy was towards already inhabited regions, some of which were densely populated, whose old economic systems were of various, but invariably pre-capitalistic, types. The contacts between the vigorous capitalistic economies and these regions of long-standing habitation did not occur in a uniform manner. In some cases interest was limited to the opening up of lines of trade. In others there prevailed right from the start a desire to encourage the production of raw materials for which demand was increasing in the industrial centers. The effect of the impact of capitalist expansion on the archaic structures varied from region to region, being conditioned by local circumstances, the type of capitalistic penetration, and the intensity of the penetration. The result, however, was almost always to create hybrid structures, part tending to behave as a capitalistic system, part perpetuating the features of the previously existing system. The phenomenon of underdevelopment today is precisely a matter of this type of dualistic economy.

Underdevelopment is, then, a discrete historical process through which economies that have already achieved a high level of development have not necessarily passed. To grasp the essence of the problem of contemporary underdeveloped economies this peculiarity must be taken into consideration. Let us, for example, view the typical instance of an economy into which a capitalistic 'wedge' is introduced – let us say productive activities intended for export, a mining undertaking controlled by a capitalistic enterprise which organizes not only production but also marketing of the product. The intensity of the impact of this nucleus on the old structure will depend basically on the relative importance of the income to which it gives rise and which remains available within the community. Thus the impact depends on the volume of labor the enterprise absorbs, the level of the average real wages it offers, and the total amount of taxes it pays. This last item is typically of minor importance during the initial stages of capitalistic expansion, when stimuli of all kinds, including complete tax exemption, are created to attract capital from outside. The level of real wages is determined by living conditions prevailing in the region in which the new enterprises are set up, without any precise connection with the productivity of labor in the new economic activity. Creation of a highly elastic supply of labor requires only that wages in the capitalistic enterprise be somewhat higher than the average for the region. Hence the decisive factor is the volume of labor absorbed by the capitalistic nucleus. But experience shows that this volume of labor did not usually reach large proportions. In the case of the economies specialized in mining, it hardly amounted to 5 per cent of the working age population. Furthermore, the new enterprises tended to encourage and assist local authorities to carry out sanitation and other health measures resulting in a decline in the death rate and a corresponding increase in the rate of growth of the population. After a certain period, the population had increased enough to re-establish the ratio of population to resources prevailing in the stage prior to the penetration of the capitalistic enterprise.

The economic structure of the region into which the capitalistic enterprise has penetrated – as in the example above – does not necessarily become modified as a result of that penetration. Only a small fraction of the available labor is absorbed by the alien enterprise; the wages paid to that labor are not determined by the level of productivity of the enterprise but by the living conditions prevailing in the region. And the increase in the rate of growth of the population is quite significant. But, all in all, as the capitalist enterprise's connection with the region in which it has been established is almost exclusively as a wage-generating agency, the payroll must attain a relatively substantial level before modifications occur in the economic structure. The phenomenon seems to resemble that observed in the first phase of development of a capitalist economy, when the previously existing artisan scheme is destroyed and absorbed. The similarity is only apparent, however; the capitalistic enterprise penetrating into a previously inhabited region with an archaic economic structure does not become dynamically linked with the latter, for the mass of profit it generates does not become integrated into the local economy.

The dynamism of the capitalist economy results, in the ultimate analysis, from the role the entrepreneurial class plays in it, especially in its having to utilize reproductively a substantial part of its constantly accruing income. We have already mentioned that the consumption of the capitalist class is determined by institutional factors and is largely independent of short-term fluctuations in the level of aggregate income. Its consumption is unquestionably the most stable factor in the aggregate expenditure of the community. But consumption by wage earners is determined by the aggregate employment level, a circumstance which tends to minimize the role it plays in the process of development. What ensures the dynamism of the capitalist economy is the manner of utilization of the mass of income that reverts to the entrepreneurs and which they put aside as savings. This portion does not become tied in with the region in which the enterprise is located; its utilization depends almost exclusively on conditions prevailing in the economy to which the owners of the capital belong. Let us consider the case of British capital invested in South East Asia in companies producing tea, rubber, or metals. The income those enterprises generate becomes integrated partly into the local economy and partly into the British economy. The part involved in the local economy probably tends to be the larger. However, it is the portion connected with the British economy that establishes the dynamic characteristics of the capitalist system. As a matter of fact, the mass of savings required by the British economy every year for transformation into productive capacity is derived largely from income of firms located all over the world.

It is because of the circumstances just described that the expansion in international trade in the nineteenth century – an expansion resulting from the industrial development of Europe – did not lead to a spreading of the capitalistic system of production on the same scale. The displacement of the European economic frontier almost always resulted in the formation of hybrid economies in which a capitalistic nucleus, so to speak, existed in a state of 'peaceful coexistence' with an archaic structure; the capitalistic nucleus rarely modified the pre-existing structural conditions but was linked with the local economy merely as a formative element creating a mass of wages. Only when the type of enterprise called for the absorption of a large number of wage earners – as on the tea plantations in Ceylon and the rubber plantations in Burma – did the effect of the capitalistic organization on the local economy become of major importance. If the local labor supply was relatively scarce, as in those two countries, the possibility of an increase in real wages arose early (that tendency could be partially annulled, however – as in the two cases in question – by imports of labor from countries with low living standards). Even so, despite an improvement in living standards, there was no structural modification in the economic system – the basic step required for the creation of a typical capitalistic economy was not taken. When external conditions ceased to permit expansion in the output of tea or rubber in those countries, the situation became one of equilibrium at a level of permanent under-employment of factors, a circumstance inconceivable in a typical capitalistic economy. As wages are determined by the conditions of subsistence – and the profit margin is therefore high – the typical company becomes able to absorb substantial price falls and for that reason the level of employment fluctuates little. Price falls, affecting mainly the profit margin, concentrate their effects on the British income itself, into which the profits of the company are integrated. *Mutatis mutandis*, the recovery in prices and the period of abundance pass almost unnoticed in the country in which the enterprise is located, unless factors of another kind make it advisable to utilize the larger profits for expansion of the business in the region in which they are obtained. The decision in regard to a possible expansion in the business is taken in London; it is made from the British, not the economic, point of view. Thus despite the relative strength of the capitalistic nuclei in economies such as that of Ceylon or the Central American countries, these regions have remained essentially pre-capitalistic structures.

But it would be incorrect to conclude that the hybrid economies we have been discussing have behaved in all circumstances as if they were pre-capitalistic structures. In many cases – Brazil is a good example of this – the mass of wages in the sector connected with the international market has been sufficiently large to give a monetary character to an important sector of the economic system. The growth of the monetary sector has prompted substantial modifications in consumption habits, spurred by and spurring the introduction and spread of innumerable articles manufactured abroad. Diversification in consumption habits has had important consequences on the subsequent development of the economy. We have already seen that the level of employment in an economy of this type tends to be relatively stable, even though the value of exports fluctuates in line with the oscillations in international prices for raw materials. Stability in the internal monetary income, by comparison with the instability of importing capacity, creates strong pressure against the balance of payments in phases of declining international prices, and makes it hard to adopt the rules of the gold standard. To the extent that the relative importance of money income within the Brazilian economy grew because of expansion of the sector connected with the international market, there was a tendency towards increased pressure against the balance of payments during phases of falling international prices. Thus conditions arose favorable to the establishment of activities connected with the domestic market itself, for during phases of strong decline in export prices the profitability of business connected with the domestic market tends to increase in relative terms, inasmuch as the prices of imported commodities rise while the level of money income remains steady.

When exporting activity was partially controlled by national capital – as was the case in Brazil during the period of coffee expansion – the problem presented other important aspects. The mere existence of a large mass of profit formed in activities connected with the external market both opened up new possibilities and created new problems. It must be borne in mind that those profits did not play the same role in the coffee economy that profit plays in an industrial economy. The dynamic factor of the Brazilian coffee economy was external demand, not volume of investment within the coffee sector. If such investments were found to be excessive, the ultimate effect might be a loss of real income through declines in the coffee prices. In the Central American republics two phenomena may be observed side by side, namely: the effect of 'incrustation' of foreign companies, as in the banana plantations; and the effects of an expansion partially controlled by national capital, as in the coffee plantations. The results were not much different, although coffee gave rise to a flow of profit over and above that of wages. The profit flow from coffee was reinvested in the coffee economy itself to the extent that land and labor availabilities permitted. Once possibilities of expansion of the coffee sector had been exhausted, however, the new capital formed therein tended to emigrate rather than look for new fields of application within the system itself.

Brazil's experience, in view of its considerable magnitude, constitutes a special case. Actually, in view of the great abundance of land suitable for coffee planting and the elasticity of labor supply,[1] investments in coffee growing were not limited by factor availability. This explains why ever since the end of the nineteenth century the situation has been one of chronic over-supply while at the same time it was possible to control supply artificially. During phases of prosperity, the profit in the coffee sector tended to concentrate in that same sector without playing any basic role in altering the structure of the system. The only difference from the situation in Central America lay in the fact that, since there was an elastic factor supply, profit was invested in the same sector that generated it. Voluminous investments in the coffee sector – even when their real profitability was relatively low – led to the absorption of the previously existing subsistence economy and financed European immigration, thus promoting expansion of the monetary sector within the economy. As the requirements for manufactured goods within this sector were fairly high, a market for manufactured products arose which was later to justify the creation of an industrial nucleus which eventually induced a structural transformation in the economy.

The dynamic element in the first stage of European industrial development acted, as we have seen, on the side of supply. Entrepreneurial action – through the introduction of new combinations of factors – created its own demand as it became possible to offer a cheaper and more abundant product. In the case of development induced from without – as in Brazil – the first consequence was a demand for manufactured goods. At first this was met by imports; but the dynamic factor began to act internally, here on the side of demand, from the moment demand could not be met by external supply. On the one hand, the stability in the level of money income, and on the other, instability in importing capacity, acted cumulatively to guarantee attractive conditions for investments linked with the domestic market.[2]

1. The first phase of great coffee expansion in Brazil (in the third quarter of the nineteenth century) was based on labor which had remained semi-utilized in the mining region after the gold economy entered into a state of decadence; in the second stage of expansion (last quarter of the past century) the problem of labor was solved by European immigration; the expansion in the 'twenties, 'forties and 'fifties of this century was based on the absorption of excess labor coming from Minas Gerais and the states in the Northeast.
2. The policy of artificial control of the supply of coffee introduced in the first decade of this century gave greater stability to importing capacity and very probably had a negative effect on the development of the industrial

The industrial nucleus based on demand for manufactured goods formerly met out of imports commenced with light industries producing general consumption articles such as textiles and processed foodstuffs. Thus three sectors came to coexist within the economy: one was the 'remnant' economy with a predominance of subsistence activities and a minor money flow; the second comprised activities directly connected with foreign trade; the third consisted of activities connected with the domestic market for general consumption manufactured products. The total constituted an economic structure a good deal more complex than that of mere coexistence of foreign firms along with the vestiges of a pre-capitalistic system.

In the more simple underdeveloped structures, the mass of wages generated in the exporting sector is the only dynamic element; expansion of the exporting sector engenders a greater flow of money income permitting absorption of factors previously engaged in the subsistence sector; if the exporting sector remains stationary, growth in population brings an enforced reduction in the average real wage level and a decline in the income per inhabitant. In the more complex underdeveloped structures, in which there is an industrial nucleus linked with the domestic market, cumulative reactions may arise tending to cause structural transformations in the system. The basic dynamic factor continues to be external demand; but an important difference lies in its impact: its action is multiplied internally. As external induction increases monetary income, the profit of the industrial nucleus linked with the domestic market also grows; increased investment within that nucleus follows, increasing further the level of money income. All in all, the relative importance of the subsistence sector shrinks, even though the expansion of the external sector is accompanied by an improvement in importing capacity and the competitive power of imports in these phases, reducing the real magnitude of the domestic income multiplier.

The greatest difference occurs, however, in the following stage of contraction of importing capacity, with the decline in the prices of exported products. As money income remains at a relatively high level, the decline in importing capacity causes substantial exchange devaluation. The nucleus thus enters into

---

nucleus already in course of formation. Paradoxically, however, even the 'negative' effects of this policy were in at least one situation structurally important: by intensifying and extending the coffee crisis which commenced in 1929 the policy precipitated notable structural transformations.

a boom, precisely during the phase of decline in profitability of the export sector. Although the level of money income declines, exchange devaluation spurs an increase in the demand for domestically produced manufactured goods, and the sector connected with the domestic market shows an improved profit picture. The effective possibilities of growth are partially frustrated, however, by the reduction in importing capacity. High profitability in the industries connected with the domestic market is partly illusory, inasmuch as the cost of replacement of imported equipment increases with exchange devaluation. The existence during a period of relative increase in prices of industrial equipment of a substantial mass of profit due to activities connected with the domestic market gives rise to a tendency to invest capital in activities less dependent on imports, such as the building industry. As these investments do not cause permanent changes in the employment structure of the community, the relative increase tends in the last resort to put a brake on the process of growth itself.

The higher stage in underdevelopment is reached when the industrial nucleus becomes diversified and able to produce part of the equipment needed for expansion of productive capacity. Reaching this stage does not imply that the industrial nucleus connected with the domestic market automatically becomes the main dynamic element. The normal process of development of the industrial nucleus remains a matter mostly of replacement of imports; the dynamic element continues to reside in previously existing demand created mainly by external induction, and not, as in the fully developed industrial economies, in the innovations introduced into the productive processes. But with the system capable of producing a part of the capital goods required for expansion of productive capacity, the process of growth may continue for a far longer time, even if importing capacity is choked off. Under such conditions, development takes place with strong inflationary pressure.

We see, then, that underdevelopment is not a necessary stage in the process of formation of the modern capitalistic economies. It is a special process due to the penetration of modern capitalistic enterprises into archaic structures. The phenomenon of underdevelopment occurs in a number of forms and in various stages. The simplest case is that of coexistence of foreign companies producing export commodities alongside a wide range of subsistence activities. This coexistence may continue in a state of static equilibrium for long periods. The most complex situation, as in the Brazilian economy at the present time, is that in which there are three sectors in the economy: a subsistence structure, a structure oriented mainly towards export, and an industrial nucleus connected with the domestic market and sufficiently diversified to produce a part of the capital goods it needs for its own growth. The industrial nucleus linked with the domestic market develops through a process of displacing importation of manufactured goods, that is, under permanent competitive conditions with external producers. The greatest concern of the local industrialist is therefore to provide an article similar to the one imported and, consequently, to adopt production methods which make it possible to compete with the foreign producer. In other words, the price structure in the industrial sector connected with the domestic market tends to be similar to that prevailing in highly industrialized countries exporting manufactured goods. Thus the technological innovations which appear most advantageous are those making it possible to approach the cost and price structure of the countries exporting manufactured goods, and not those permitting faster transformation in the economic structure through absorption of the subsistence sector. The practical result of this (even if the industrial sector connected with the domestic market grows and increases its participation in the product and even if the per capita income of the population as a whole rises) is that the occupational structure of the country changes only slowly. The part of the population affected by development remains minor, and there is a very slow decline in the relative importance of the sector whose main activity is production for subsistence. This explains why an economy in which industrial production has already achieved a high degree of diversification – with the share of the industrial sector in the product hardly distinguishable from that in more highly developed countries – may present a rather pre-capitalistic occupational structure and have a large portion of its population cut off from the benefits of development.

Again we see that underdevelopment, specific phenomenon that it is, calls for an effort at autonomous theorization. Lack of such an effort has led many economists to explain by analogy with the experience in developed economies problems which can be properly expressed only through full understanding of the phenomenon of underdevelopment. The tendency in countries with an underdeveloped economy, such as Brazil, towards disequilibrium in the balance of payments is one of those which, for lack of a proper theoretical basis, has most commonly been incorrectly presented and misinterpreted.

2 C. Geertz

Java and Japan Compared

Excerpt from final chapter of C. Geertz, *Agricultural Involution: The Process of Ecological Change in Indonesia*, University of California Press, 1963, pp. 130–43.

For Java, the obvious comparative case is Japan. Much differs between them: geography, history, culture, and, of course, per capita income – Japan's being about twice Java's.[1] But much, too, is similar. Both are heavily populated. Both rest agriculturally on a labor-intensive, small-farm, multicrop cultivation regime centering on wet rice. Both have managed to maintain a significant degree of social and cultural traditionalism in the face of profound encounter with the West and extensive domestic change. In fact, in agriculture, the further back one goes toward the mid-nineteenth century the more the two resemble one another. Japanese per hectare rice yields at the beginning of Meiji (1868) were probably about the same as those of Java at the beginning of the Corporate Plantation System (1870); today they are about two and a half times as high (Ohkawa and Rosovsky, 1960; FAO, 1955, pp. 36–7). Between 1878 and 1942 the percentage of the Japanese labor force employed in agriculture dropped from around 80 to around 40; the Javanese figure for the end of the nineteenth century is not known, but in 1930 – and probably still today – it had not fallen below 65 per cent.[2] And, though it is even more a matter of head-long estimate, the percentage of aggregate net income contributed by agricultural production in the Japan of the 1880s was of the same general order as that in the Java of the 1950s, by which time the Japanese percentage was only a third as large.[3] Given, then, all

1. Estimated gross national product per capita (1955) for Japan is about $240, for Indonesia about $127 (Ginsburg, 1961, p. 18). Javanese per capita product is, of course, below that of Indonesia as a whole, though by how much it is impossible to say.

2. Ohkawa and Rosovsky (1960); Statistical Abstract for the Netherlands East Indies, 1935, pp. 143–6.

3. Ohkawa and Rosovsky (1960); Mears (1961). The Javanese figure is again estimated on the basis of the all-Indonesia figure, the percentage of income from agriculture being probably lower in Java than in the Outer Islands.

the admittedly important background differences, one can hardly forbear to ask when one looks at these two societies: 'What has happened in the one which did not happen in the other?'

A satisfactory answer to such a question would involve the whole economic, political and cultural history of the two civilizations; but even if we confine ourselves to predominantly ecological considerations, a number of dramatic differences leap to the eye. The most striking – and the most decisive – is the contrast between the way Japan utilized its rapid population increase and the way Java utilized hers. Between 1870 and 1940 Java absorbed the bulk of her increase in numbers – about thirty million people – into post-traditional village social systems of the sort already described, but

in the first century of modernization, Japan maintained a relatively unchanging population in agriculture while the total population increased two and one-half fold. Practically all the increase in the labor force was absorbed in non-agricultural activities. There was little change in the size of the rural population. Almost all the natural increase of the national population was absorbed in urban areas (Taeuber, 1960).

From 1872 to 1940, the Japanese farm population remained virtually constant around 14 million people (or $5\frac{1}{2}$ million households) at the same time as the total population grew approximately 35 million (Namiki, 1960; Ohkawa and Rosovksy, 1960). Comparable statistics on the farm population of Java are not available, but that it grew at better than an average of 1 per cent a year during this entire period seems a conservative estimate.[4] Japan, in short, did not involute; which should cut the ground out from under any charges of 'paddyfield determinism' which might be brought against our Javanese analysis. But what, then, did it do?

For one thing, it increased agricultural productivity *per worker*, not just *per terrace*. 'Using the latest and best computations', Ohkawa and Rosovsky (1960) estimate that the productivity of agricultural labor (net output/labor force in agriculture)

4. Starting around 1920, Javanese towns seem to have begun, evidently for the first time, to grow more rapidly than the general population, and this trend has accelerated since the revolution (Wertheim, 1956, pp. 185–6; The Siau Giap, 1959). However even today they come nowhere near absorbing the entire increase as the Japanese towns seem to have done since the last quarter of the nineteenth century.

increased 2·6 per cent annually between 1878 and 1917.[5] Thus, as I have attempted (with much less adequate computations) to demonstrate, where Java increased per hectare yields at least to the First World War but not per worker yields, Japan increased both over roughly the same period. The contrast is all the more impressive, because, in Japan as in Java, the basic structure of proprietary control, the general form of the producing unit, and the overall pattern of rural culture seem to have been relatively unaltered:

The increases in output and productivity were based on the traditional patterns of rural organization inherited, in the main, from the Tokugawa period. The small family farm, averaging about one hectare per household, the distribution between peasant proprietors and tenants, high rents in kind – all of these characteristics were maintained during the [1878–1917] period. At the same time, there was no strong trend of land consolidation and this preserved the scattered holdings of tiny plots of ground (Ohkawa and Rosovsky, 1960).[6]

No move to extensify agriculture; no marked trend toward a class polarization of large landlord and rural proletarian; no radical reorganization of the family-based productive unit – characteristics of Java and Japan alike since the turn of the century.[7] But Japan increased productivity per agricultural worker 236 per cent, Java – the estates aside for the moment – hardly increased it at all (Ohkawa and Rosovsky, 1960). For Java, *plus ça change, plus c'est la même chose* may be a fitting epitome. But for Japan it would have to read *plus c'est la même chose, plus ça change.*

The readiest explanation for this difference – and the one most commonly invoked – is the greater technological advance in Japanese agriculture. Irrigation was expanded, land reclaimed, seed selection improved and fertilizer use increased, cooperative activity became more effective and widespread, planting was intensified, weeding and harvesting methods developed, agri-

5. Toward the end of the period this rate tended to slacken, and after the First World War it dropped to about 1 per cent. But by that time Japan's industrial sector had been firmly launched.

6. For a description of the still fairly traditional quality of village life in Japan – in many ways more traditional than in Java – see Beardsley, Hall and Ward (1959).

7. As the fundamental groundwork for the Javanese type of pattern was laid in the Culture System period, so that for the Japanese was laid in the equally decisive Tokugawa (1600–1868), particularly the later phases of it. On this see Smith (1959).

cultural knowledge increased (Ohkawa and Rosovsky, 1960; Dore, 1960)[8]. Though the contrast between the two technologies is often exaggerated, on one level this thesis is beyond question – the sharp rise in productivity per farmer in Japan clearly must rest on 'key improvements in Japanese agricultural practice in keeping with the small unit of production' (Ohkawa and Rosovsky, 1960). Yet it is, nonetheless, unsatisfactory. First, it involves a somewhat uncritical reading of the present into the past. Until about the turn of the century, by which time Japan had irrevocably 'taken off' and Java had definitively involuted, the difference between either the rate or level of technological advance in the two peasant agricultures was not so great as it has been since then.[9] Second, even to the extent the argument is factually valid, it merely restates the question: it is just this difference in technological progress that we wish to explain. There is little in the two technologies around, say, 1870 – the end alike of the Culture System and of the Tokugawa period – which could account for their divergence since that time.

More genuinely determinative of the separation into contrasting courses was the manner in which a traditional labor-intensive, Lilliputian, family-farm, wet-rice-and-second-crop type of ecosystem came to be related to a set of modern economic institutions. Specifically, where Japanese peasant agriculture came to be complementarily related to an expanding manufacturing system in indigenous hands, Javanese peasant agriculture came to be complementarily related to an expanding agro-industrial structure under foreign management. As labor

8. Again, as in Java, these changes began well back in the previous (here the Tokugawa) period. See Smith (1959, pp. 87–107).

9. Rostow (1960, p. 38) tentatively dates Japanese take-off in the 1878–1900 period. A full documentation of the argument that Javanese technological advance in agriculture very nearly kept pace with the Japanese until the beginning of this century or the end of the last would require a thorough review of the two technological histories, which – particularly as the Javanese one has yet to be written – cannot be attempted here. It is worth pointing out, however, that all main improvements listed for pre-twentieth century Japanese agriculture, with the partial exception of artificial fertilization, seem to have been present in Java. Also, it is of note in this connection that in 1910–11, when the first reliable comparative figures appear, Japanese per hectare rice yields are only 80 per cent higher than Javanese, while a decade later they are 300 per cent higher (Wickizer and Bennett, 1941, p. 318), the difference evidently stemming from radically rising inputs of (now mostly commercial) fertilizer, which increased more than 650 per cent between 1898–1902 and 1913–17 (Ohkawa and Rosovsky, 1960).

productivity in the capital-intensive sector in Japan increased, it increased also in the labor-intensive sector; as it increased in the capital-intensive sector in Java it remained approximately constant in the labor-intensive one. In Japan, the peasant sector supported the industrial one during the crucial three decades of the latter's emergence largely by means of extremely heavy land taxation; in Java, the peasant sector supported the industrial one through the provision of underpriced labor and land. In Japan, the industrial sector, once under way, then re-invigorated the peasant sector through the provision of cheap commercial fertilizer, more effective farm tools, support of technical education and extension work and, eventually, after the First World War, simple mechanization, as well as by offering expanded markets for agricultural products of all sorts; in Java most of the invigorating effect of the flourishing agro-industrial sector was exercised upon Holland, and its impact upon the peasant sector was, as we have seen, enervating. The dynamic interaction between the two sectors which kept Japan moving and ultimately pushed her over the hump to sustained growth was absent in Java. Japan had and maintained, but Java had and lost, an integrated economy.

To a great extent, Japan maintained it and Java lost it in the critical four decades of the mid-nineteenth century – 1830–70. At the same time that van den Bosch was superimposing an export-crop economy upon the traditional Javanese *sawah* system, Japan had locked herself away from Western interference and was moving toward a more commercialized, less immobile rural economy on its own (Smith, 1959)[10]. In both societies, peasant agriculture was becoming, within a generally unchanging basi cpattern, steadily more labor-intensive, more skilful and more productive. But in Java the increase in output was soon swamped by the attendant spurt in population; in Japan the

10. This movement went on, to some extent, during the whole Tokugawa period, though it seems to have come to a climax in the last century of it, and was further speeded up after Perry's visit in 1853, at which time the seclusion policy was, at least officially, ended. In any case, steady, if slow and locally uneven improvement in Javanese agriculture might also be traced well back into the seventeenth century were the material available. It is possible that Japan 'started lower' than Java, its natural conditions being less suitable for rice, so that its growth in productivity between the beginning of the seventeenth century and the end of the nineteenth would have had to have been greater in order for it to achieve Javanese levels by the later date. See Rosovsky (1961, p. 81, note 104).

population remained virtually constant.[11] In both societies, the peasant's agricultural productivity increased. But in one it was, so to speak, reserved (largely through the operation of a tributational tax system) for, as it turned out, future investment in an indigenous manufacturing system. In the other, it was immediately expended to subsidize the swelling part-time labor force (i.e. the peasant in his two-fifths corvee role) of a foreign-run plantation system, and its potential for financing a properly Indonesian take-off dissipated.

But to comprehend this tale of two economies fully requires also a comparison of the denouements, which means extending the four-decade critical period to its nine-decade consummation in take-off into sustained growth on the one hand and in involution into static expansion on the other. In outline form, the contrasting patterns of development in the two societies between approximately 1830 and the end of the First World War can be summarized as follows:

	Java	*Japan*
Technique	Gradual improvement through the entire period (and in all likelihood before), but in a wholly labor-intensive manner.	Gradual improvement through the entire period (and, in fact, the whole Tokugawa period). This also took place mainly in a labor-intensive manner until around 1900, after which rapidly increasing capital inputs, mostly in the form of fertilizer, took place.
Population	Rapid growth after 1830, evidently as a result of declining mortality due to improved communications and greater security and of increased fertility due to the labor-tax pressures of	Rapid growth began only after 1870, evidently as a result of a decline in the death-rate attendant on a rising national standard of living and of increasing fertility due (indirectly) to

11. Japanese population seems to have increased more or less steadily from about the end of the twelfth century to the beginning of the eighteenth, at which time it stabilized, evidently because the traditional ecosystem had found its climax equilibrium. Between 1726 and 1852 population was virtually constant. After 1852 and contact with the West it began to rise, but slowly and irregularly. After 1870 rapid rise began, moving from about 35 to 55 million in less than half a century (1873–1918) (Taeuber, 1958, pp. 20–25, 44–5).

	Java	*Japan*
	the Culture System; but not save possibly for a brief initial period, as a result of generally rising Indonesian living standards.	expanding employment opportunities in manufacturing.[12]
Employment	No significant expansion outside of traditional agricultural pursuits but a rapid expansion within them made possible by the perfection of labor-absorbing productive techniques which raised land but not labor productivity. Peasants provided unskilled occasional labor for (first government, then private) plantations, but at a price well below its marginal productivity, the costs of their subsistence being largely borne by the village economy.	Rapid expansion in the industrial sector, absorbing the whole population increase. Agricultural employment virtually constant, both land and labor productivity rising, the latter about 70 per cent more rapidly.[13]
Urbanization	Retarded. Towns and cities grew much less rapidly than total population, and the depressive effect upon fertility rates commonly associated with urban life were largely absent, delaying the usual post-industrial slowing of population growth.[14]	Accelerated, particularly after the Restoration. Towns and cities grew much more rapidly than total population. As rates of natural increase were moderately depressed in the urban areas, this was in the main due to a jump in rural–urban migration.[15]
Per capita income	Probably close to constant over the whole period in the peasant sector; rapidly rising in the plantation sector.	Rising with increasing rapidity in the peasant sector, the rise being used to finance an even more rapid rise in the manufacturing sector after Meiji.[16]

	Java	*Japan*
Economic dualism	Increasingly severe. Increased capital inputs into the plantation sector, increased labor inputs into the peasant. Separation between the two sectors cultural, social and technological at the same time, with little intermediate industrial activity.	Marked, but moderated by close cultural, social and economic connections between the two sectors and by the flowering of small-scale industrial activity.[17]

Whatever value this comparison of Java and Japan may have does not lie in any assumption that had Java been 'left alone' she would have followed the Japanese path, or even that she would now be in an economically more viable state. What would have happened had the Dutch not colonized the Indies is clearly not even an hypothetically answerable question, for it depends upon what historical events would have occurred instead, and their number is infinite. Nor does the value of the comparison rest on the assumption that Java's course now must be to re-enact somehow the Japanese pattern if take-off is to be at length accomplished. The world has moved on, both in and outside Java, and the alternatives which face her today are not those which faced Japan a century ago. Its value lies in providing a

12. The diachronic comparison of the two demographic developments is perhaps most simply expressed in terms of the changing ratio of the Japanese to Javanese population: 1830, 3·8; 1870, 2·1; 1900, 1·6; 1920, 1·6; 1955, 1·6 (calculated from Taeuber, 1958, pp. 22, 46, 70). Thus, the early rise of Japanese population gave it somewhere around $3\frac{1}{2}$ to 4 times the Javanese total by the beginning of the nineteenth century, a gap the Javanese explosion nearly cut in half by 1870, after which time the convergence slowed as the two populations grew after 1900 at about the same annual rate – between 1 and $1\frac{1}{2}$ per cent.

13. Ohkawa and Rosovsky (1960).

14. 'Development in [Southeast] Asia, centered as it was on plantations, mines, oil fields and exports of raw materials, brought more *industrialization* than *urbanization*; the checks on family size brought by the urban industrialization and the New World operated less effectively in the underdeveloped countries. The drops in fertility rates came eventually in most Asian countries too, but too late to prevent serious population pressure from arising before planned economic development began' (Higgins, 1958).

15. Taeuber (1960). Here, it was not so much the fact that urbanization showed an initially higher overall growth, but rather its greater development prevented Japanese transition rates from climbing as high between

contrasting, yet comparable case which can shed light on what happened in Java and therefore on the nature of her present situation. The economic history of Japan is not a norm from which Java has, alas, departed, nor that of Java a pathology from which Japan has, praise God, escaped. Rather, Japanese economic history is Javanese with a few crucial parameters changed (a proposition which could be stated equally well the other way around), and in this consists its comparative significance.

There are two major parameters which are so changed: the existence of colonial government in Java is replaced in Japan by the existence of a powerful indigenous elite; the development of capital-intensive agriculture in Java is replaced in Japan by the development of a capital-intensive manufacturing system. Behind these major parametric differences lie a host of others. The strength of the Japanese elite grew out of the traditional, religiously supported patterns of political loyalty characteristic of the culture generally;[18] Java's colonization was in part a mere reflex of her geographical location at the cross-roads of the Orient, of her neighbors' possession of the right spices at the wrong time, and of the inherent fragility of the classical Indonesian states. The tropical climate and other physical characteristics of Java which, as noted, made export sugar and subsistence rice natural dualistic partners were lacking in Japan, whose more temperate conditions perhaps made a plantation farming pattern less adaptive. Other differences – in the world-views of both masses and elites, in micro-ecological conditions, in pre-seventeenth-century historical

1880 and 1920 or so as Javanese ones seem to have climbed between 1840 and 1880.

16. 'Being fearful of the political consequences of foreign borrowing, the [Meiji] government financed investment almost entirely from domestic sources – mainly agriculture. The land tax accounted for 78 per cent of ordinary revenues (the bulk of total revenues) from 1868 to 1881, and although the figure tended to fall after that it still stood at 50 per cent in 1890. High as the rate of tax on land was, however, it did not represent an increase over the Tokugawa period. Already at the end of that period the take from agriculture by the warrior class was immense, and the Meiji government merely redirected it into new channels. Modernization was achieved, therefore, without reducing rural living standards or even taking the increase in productivity that occurred' (Smith, 1959, p. 211). As this view seems to neglect increased efficiency in tax collection it may be slightly optimistic so far as pressure on the peasants is concerned.

17. On the importance of Japanese small industry, see Ohkawa and Rosovsky (1960).

18. On Japanese concepts of loyalty (or 'obligation') see Benedict (1946); on their religious basis, Bellah (1957).

development, in patterns of social stratification and mobility, in market systems, and so on – could also be cited in the same connection. A full comparative analysis would have to trace them out (or at least the more powerful of them – for the list of parameters whose change might affect the behavior of any given system has no end) and attempt to assess their relative weight.[19] But on the ecological, and to an extent the economic, level their expression was funneled through these two most immediately decisive differences. It is the predicament of all science that it lives by simplification and withers from simplisticism.

The existence of colonial government was decisive because it meant that the growth potential inherent in the traditional Javanese economy – 'the excess labor on the land and the reserves of productivity in the land', to use a phrase which has been applied to the 'slack' in the Japanese traditional economy at the Restoration – was harnessed not to Javanese (or Indonesian) development but to Dutch.[20] This is not a mere matter of monetary returns (though, leaving subsistence farming aside, in 1939 assessed per capita income in the European community in Indonesia was more than a hundred times that in the Indonesian community),[21] for certainly the growth of the plantation industry made possible greatly increased 'native welfare' expenditures – on health, rural credit and so on – in Java. Nor is it a mere matter of immediate benefit or harm, for some accompaniments of its growth certainly redounded, in a residual way, to the short-run advantage of the peasantry – better irrigation, improved communications, increased availability of foreign manufactures, and the like. Fundamentally, it is a matter of the transformative impact upon society implicit in modern industry. The improvement of human capital and the expansion of physical capital; the creation of a modern business class and the crystallization of an efficient market system; the formation of a skilled and

19. For an incisive theoretical discussion of the role of the concept of parameter in systems analysis, see Ashby (1960, esp. pp. 71–9).

20. The quotation is from Ranis (1959), cited in Rosovsky (1961).

21. Calculated from Kahin (1952, p. 36). The figures are income-tax statistics, and as Indonesian wage incomes under 900 guilders were not assessed, they exaggerate the contrast somewhat. On the other hand, they included Outer Island Indonesian 'commercial' incomes, and, as we have seen, these were significantly higher than Javanese. Finally, the 1939 population is estimated, the last colonial census having occurred in 1930. On balance, the times-a-hundred figure is probably conservative. An estimate including Indonesian subsistence production put the 1939 ratio at about 60 to 1 (Polak, 1942, p. 60).

disciplined work force and the raising of labor productivity; the stimulation of higher propensities to save and the construction of workable financial institutions; the inculcation of an entrepreneurial outlook and the development of more effective forms of economic organization – all these to a significant extent endogenously generated cultural, social and psychological resources upon which industrialism feeds were in a sense exported with the commodities the plantations produced. The difference in 'economic mentality' between Dutch and Javanese which Boeke took to be the cause of dualism was in fact in great part its result. The Javanese did not become impoverished because they were 'static'; they became 'static' because they were impoverished.

The fact that the form in which capital-intensive industry came to Java was agricultural simply reinforced this process. Much more than manufacturing, industrial agriculture – and especially sugar cultivation – permits a sharp division of labor between a traditionalized labor force and a modernized managerial elite. The Japanese peasant had to go to town and become a full-time, reasonably disciplined member of a manufacturing system, even if the organization of his factory was modeled along traditional lines and his ties with his village homeland were kept green to ease the transition.[22] The Javanese peasant did not, literally, even have to move from his rice terrace. Plantation agriculture is a much more effective way of marrying a non-industrial labor force to an industrial productive apparatus than is manufacturing, whose functional requirements are inevitably more stringent. No matter how strongly traditional elements are maintained in manufacturing, they inevitably result in some serious dislocations in life-ways and some major reorientations in outlook for those caught up in them at all levels. They are a common school for modernism, as Japanese history since 1920, and especially since 1945, demonstrates. Whether the blunting of such effects is an essential characteristic of plantation industry or a merely accidental one is perhaps debatable, and it is always all too easy to assume that the way things worked out in fact is the way things had to work out in principle. One might at least conceive of an agro-industrial system which is as effective a school for mass economic modernization as manufacturing, and in Hawaii, for example, one might actually find an approximation to one. But it can hardly be gainsaid that such a system has a strong

22. On the persistence of traditional social and cultural forms in modern industrial settings in Japan, see Abegglen (1958).

natural bias toward the production of what Mintz (1956) has called a rural proletariat – a hapless coolie labor force which achieves the agonies attendant upon industrialization without achieving its cultural, social and psychological fruits. The real tragedy of colonial history in Java after 1830 is not that the peasantry suffered. It suffered much worse elsewhere, and, if one surveys the miseries of the submerged classes of the nineteenth century generally, it may even seem to have gotten off relatively lightly. The tragedy is that it suffered for nothing.

References

ABEGGLEN, J. (1958), *The Japanese Factory*, Free Press.

ASHBY, E. (1960), *Design for a Brain*, Wiley, 2nd ed.

BEARDSLEY, R. K., HALL, J. W., and WARD, R. E. (1959), *Village Japan*, University of Chicago Press

BELLAH, R. (1957), *Tokugawa Religion*, Free Press.

BENEDICT, R. (1946), *The Chrysanthemum and the Sword*, Houghton-Mifflin.

DORE, R. P. (1960), 'Agricultural improvement in Japan: 1870–1900', *Economic Development and Cultural Change*, vol. 9, part 2, pp. 69–91.

FAO (1955), *Yearbook of Food and Agricultural Statistics*.

GINSBURG, N. (1961), *Atlas of Economic Development*, University of Chicago Press.

HIGGINS, B. (1958), 'Western enterprise and the economic development of southeast Asia: a review article', *Pacific Affairs*, vol. 31, pp. 74–87.

KAHIN, G. McT. (1952), *Nationalism and Revolution in Indonesia*, Cornell University Press.

MEARS, L. A. (1961), 'Economic development in Indonesia through 1958', *Ekonomi dan Keuangan*, vol. 14, pp. 15–57, Indonesia.

MINTZ, S. (1956), 'Cañamelar: the sub-culture of a rural sugar plantation proletariat', in J. Steward (ed.), *The People of Puerto Rico*, University of Illinois Press.

NAMIKI, M. (1960), 'The farm population in the national economy before and after World War 2', *Economic Development and Cultural Change*, vol. 9, pt. 2, pp. 29–39.

OHKAWA, K., and ROSOVSKY, H. (1960), 'The role of agriculture in modern Japanese economic development', *Economic Development and Cultural Change*, vol. 9, part 2, pp. 43–67.

POLAK, J. J. (1942), *The National Income of the Netherlands Indies*, Institute of Pacific Relations.

RANIS, G. (1959), 'The financing of Japanese economic development' *Economic History Review*, vol. 2, no. 3.

ROSOVSKY, H. (1961), *Capital Formation in Japan*, Free Press.

SMITH, T. (1959), *The Agrarian Origins of Modern Japan*, Stanford University Press.

TAEUBER, I. (1958), *The Population of Japan*, Princeton University Press.

Taeuber, I. (1960), 'Urbanization and population change in the development of modern Japan', *Economic Development and Cultural Change*, vol. 9, part 2, pp. 1–28.

The Siauw Giap (1959), '*Urbanisatie problemen in Indonesie*', *Bijdragen tot de Taal-, Land- en Volkenkunde*, no. 115, pp. 249–76.

Wertheim, W. F. (1956), *Indonesia in Transition*, van Hoeve, Hague.

Wickizer, V. D., and Bennett, M. K. (1941), *The Rice Economy of Monsoon Asia*, Stanford University Press.

3 T. Dos Santos

The Crisis of Development Theory and the Problem of Dependence in Latin America

T. Dos Santos, 'The crisis of development theory and the problem of dependence in Latin America', *Siglo*, 1969, vol. 21; originally titled 'La crisis de la teoría del desarrollo y las relaciones de dependencia en América Latina'; translated by D. Lehmann, edited by D. Lehmann and H. Bernstein.

The crisis of development theory

Latin America is in the throes of a deep and multifaceted crisis. While economic stagnation marks off the decade of the 1960s very clearly from the optimistic years of the 1950s a political instability is manifested in successive *coups d'état* and institutional breakdowns as well as in the growing radicalism of mass movements. As a social crisis it is characterized by a profound awareness of the necessity for structural reforms. Finally, it is an ideological crisis in which arguments between conflicting positions are confronted by the evident perplexity of vast sectors of society.

This is not the place to carry out a thorough analysis of this general situation.[1] The object of this study is, rather, to enquire into the consequences of the present situation for the social sciences.

During the 1950s the social sciences in Latin America demonstrated great optimism, and this optimism grew together with the self-confidence of an intelligentsia in search of a leading ideological role. In this process a critical attitude has arisen toward the scientific output of Europe and the United States, even reaching the extreme romanticism of an attempt to create a 'Latin American social consciousness'.

While the important and positive aspect of this development has been the birth of a specifically Latin American subject matter in the social sciences, this emergence of a critical response to the 'point of view of the colonial centres' has not been followed up by a similar critique of the internal development of the continent and its contradictions.

1. An analysis of the crisis in Brazil can be found in Dos Santos (1966). Empirical references to the crisis only appear in a recent annual survey of the UN Economic Commission for Latin America.

The assumptions of development theory

During the first years of its life as an independent discipline (in Latin America and elsewhere) the theory of development sought to define the obstacles to development raised by anachronistic social structures and the means whereby the aims of development can be achieved. Clearly, such a point of view is based on a number of inexplicit and, in some cases, subconscious assumptions.[2]

The various theories of development evidently differ widely in their approach, and have evolved towards new forms during the 1950s and 1960s. This evolution has itself reflected other changes; in the interests of the various forces seeking to contribute to or retard development, and indeed the very difficulties which have arisen from various attempts to explain underdevelopment and development. My attempt to reduce all these theories to one single schema by extracting only what seem to be their essential elements may give rise to a number of criticisms, but it is a legitimate procedure insofar as it discusses certain epistemological principles underlying positions which when seen from another point of view appear completely divergent. We can sum up these principles as follows:

1. Development means advancement towards certain well-defined general objectives which correspond to the specific condition of man and society to be found in the most advanced societies of the modern world. The model is variously known as modern society, industrial society, mass society and so on.

2. Underdeveloped countries will progress towards this model as soon as they have eliminated certain social, political, cultural and institutional obstacles. These obstacles are represented by 'traditional societies', 'feudal' systems, or 'feudal residues', depending on the particular school of thought.

3. Certain economic, political and psychological processes[3] can be singled out as allowing the most rational mobilization of

2. A more detailed account can be found in Andre Gunder Frank's 'Sociology of underdevelopment and underdevelopment of sociology' in Frank (1969); see also Cardoso (1966) and Lacoste (1965).

3. In many cases a decisive role has been attributed to one or the other of these factors, thus giving rise to sociologistic, psychologistic and other schools of thought.

national resources and these can be categorized for the use of economic planners.

4. To all this is added the need to co-ordinate certain social and political forces in support of a development policy and to devise an ideological basis which organizes the will of various nations in the 'tasks' of development.

Model and formalism

To criticize these assumptions is to criticize in its essence a theory of development which seeks to become a discipline of its own.

In the first place, the model of a developed society which these assumptions use is formal and ahistoric, therefore an ideological abstraction. What is a developed society? The best known models are those of the United States, Europe, Japan and the Soviet Union, and it is thought that the central problem is how to 'arrive' at a stage of development which they represent. It is also claimed that the historic experience of these countries must be repeated or at least that development must lead to a society closely resembling them.[4] It is generally thought that one can reduce development to a formal model whose content would be subject to historical variation. For example, it is supposed that development requires the existence of a particular agent of change which might as well be the entrepreneur (in the case of capitalist countries) or the State (in Socialist countries). The differences between the two social systems are seen as variables which fulfil the same function while assuming a different form. Such assumptions, however, lack scientific validity because of their ahistorical character. Historical time is not uni-linear and future societies will not be able to attain stages reached by other societies at a previous time. All societies move together towards the future and towards new forms of modern society. The historic experience of developed capitalist societies has been completely transcended; their basic source of private capital formation in foreign trade, the incorporation of vast masses of workers in industrial production, their indigenous technological development, constitute options no longer open to underdeveloped countries of today. The history of developed socialist societies is rooted in the experience of 'socialism in one country' or 'socialism in one bloc', of 'primitive socialist accumulation' at the

4. There is quite a wide awareness in the underdeveloped countries of the difficulties of repeating the historical experience of the developed countries.

expense of peasant agriculture, of the autarchic establishment of a heavy industry, and of the closing off of foreign trade and the so-called 'iron curtain'.

The 'models' of development in existence are therefore not to be repeated, nor can 'models' of developed society be taken as a crystallization of aims to be achieved.

Obstacles to development

Another fundamental error of approach lies in the orientation of the study of development towards the resistance which traditional societies may offer to change. Clearly, the social structures created during the period of colonialism and primary exports have a very great capacity for resistance and survival. But this is due fundamentally not to those structures themselves but rather to the characteristics of the very process of development in dependent countries.

To restrict the problem to the economic, social, political and institutional resistance offered by traditional society is to impair irremediably our ability to give an explanation of the Latin American crisis. Analysis should not concentrate on an abstract and formal relationship between two stages of a system (traditional–modern, capitalism–feudalism). Rather it should seek out the concrete relationships prevailing in these societies which are called underdeveloped but which, as we shall show, are better termed dependent societies.

Development cannot therefore be the passage from a state which is relatively unknown towards a state which will never exist. In other words, the theory of development must be concerned with the *laws of development* of those societies which we seek to understand. We must discover to what extent these laws are specific to these societies and to what extent one can also identify them with the laws of development of advanced societies, be they capitalist or socialist.[5]

5. Some theoreticians have clearly been disconcerted by the specificity of the Chinese and Cuban experiences of development, and increasingly so by those of North Korea, North Vietnam, Rumania and Albania, all of which, like Yugoslavia before them, demonstrate the historical specificity of their road to socialism. Although they have commanded less attention, the problems posed by the specific historical experiences of Poland, Czechoslovakia, Hungary and the German Democratic Republic are also very great. The situations of these countries have led to specific forms of socialism – a statement which does not deny the basic unity of the socialist system and of socialist countries – and also to specific policies corresponding to the various

The optimum use of resources

The third assumption, which is intimately linked to the first two, is a theory of development that can codify the optimum use of resources. It arises from the two earlier assumptions that there exist certain definable aims of development, and that the optimum use of resources depends on certain procedures characteristic of modern, rational industrial or mass societies.

The rational use of resources must be understood in the context of particular historical situations. Rationality is defined by men, and men exist in history, in concrete societies and social groups. In other words the rationality of an economic or political measure can only be defined on the basis of an understanding of the social system in which it is taken. Some examples can clarify this proposition. What is rational in a developed capitalist country – such as waste and military industry[6] – is not rational in advanced socialist countries. Whereas in the Soviet Union the use of basic resources to construct heavy industry was rational, this was not the case for other European socialist countries, as was demonstrated by the anti-Stalinist explosion they experienced.

The idea that planning is a generalized characteristic of modern society be it socialist or capitalist deserves special criticism. *Socialist planning* places the blind laws of the market and of competition under the political control of society. *Capitalist programming* seeks to direct these blind forces in such a way as to perpetuate those very institutions which create the fundamentally anarchic character of capitalist society: private property and profit. To confuse these two ways of bringing human control to bear on a social reality is to confuse by formal reasoning superficial similarities with the real relationships existing among men.

Thus we can see the dangers of trying to codify in a 'general' theory the practices to be adopted or created in specific situations.

stages of socialist development. The internal contradictions of the socialist bloc will only be resolved when the straitjacket imposed by an antiquated model of relationships among socialist governments and of proletarian internationalism is broken and a new type of inter-socialist relationship is achieved within which the specific interests of the various countries can be met and in which their general interests can be redefined. It is important to point out, however, that such changes need to be accompanied by deep internal changes in these societies.

6. See Cook (n.d.) and Baran and Sweezy (1966), which describe the need of monopoly capitalism for the military industry, for waste and so on.

Ideology of development

In the same way we would reject the possibility of a general ideology of development. Different ideologies correspond to different social interests and more fundamentally to different social classes. Development cannot resolve contradictions between social classes, as the approach we are criticizing might lead one to suppose. Various social classes have an interest in development and they seek to achieve it by different paths. There are therefore not only different, but also contradictory ways of defining development and the measures necessary for its achievement. The role of social science is to define these paths of development and to study their viability on the basis of an analysis of the global interests of social classes. It will always be an error, however, to refuse, in the name of objectivity, to analyse these opposing interests, for they are the determinants of social processes. The empirical description of superficial facts hides essential aspects of reality, and such a description must therefore be accompanied by a theoretical analysis of society as a whole. To refuse to face up to this problem is to assume an ideological attitude.

Some conclusions about the theory of development

The discussion so far may be summed up as follows:

1. The theory of development must analyse the process of development in its various historical and concrete manifestations.

2. It must extract, through such a historical analysis, the general laws of development of the societies it chooses to investigate.

3. In formulating these laws, development theory must take into account the internal contradictions of the process, abandoning any formalistic attempt to reduce it to a unilineal transition from one type of society to another. Rather the theory would have to show how through these very contradictions society as a whole can reach higher forms of organization. These forces, and the social forms they imply, are better described as social trends than as models of a future situation to which we should aspire.

This theoretical and methodological critique is essential if we are to understand in advance the difficulties of the development model which arose in Latin America during the optimistic period of the 1950s.

We must now go on to define the content of this implicit model of Latin American development which dominated the social sciences during recent years. Our objective – as it was in the analysis of the assumptions of development theory – is to show how these schemata and these concepts can be reduced from positions which are often apparently opposed to one another, to a single model of development for Latin America which from our point of view has underlain, and, to a large extent, still underlies scientific research, government policies and the programmes of parties and political organizations.

The crisis of the model of development in Latin America
The historic conditions of development

The social science which predominates in Latin America defines the continent as a region where underdevelopment has arisen from the survival of a feudal economy and society side by side with an export-based and monoculture economy. In the nineteenth century the region set out upon a course of development 'towards the outside', based on the export of primary products and on the import of manufactured products. The survival of a feudal agrarian economy provoked a situation of social and economic disequilibrium, of misery and low standards of health and nutrition, a situation which is reflected particularly in the unequal distribution of income. On the other hand, development towards the outside contributed to the preservation of industrial, technological and institutional backwardness, and hence to dependence on foreign trade – a situation which deteriorated substantially as a result of the decline in world prices for primary products which followed the end of the Korean War. As these prices declined, so those of manufactured goods tended to rise, thus creating ever more unfavourable terms of trade for the underdeveloped countries.

According to this theory, the only solution lay in industrialization and 'development towards the interior'. In fact, industrialization had already begun after the First World War, and in particular as a result of the Great Crash, and it continued during and after the Second World War, through the mechanism of import substitution. Import substitution has been stimulated whenever there have been difficulties in importing manufactured products from abroad – as, precisely, during the two World Wars and during the crisis of 1929. In order to meet the existing demand for these products the first national industries were created.

Attempts to accelerate this process of import substitution led to a change of emphasis away from the light industries of the early period towards basic industry which called for State-run infrastructure. It was hoped that these factors, with the help of foreign capital, would create a national industry on the basis of an expanding home market.

There is no need to go into the details of these development policies based on export earnings on the stimulation and protection of national industry, and on the planned use of scarce financial resources (above all, foreign exchange), which were accompanied by calls for an international policy to maintain the prices of exported products and channel foreign aid, in order to narrow the gap between developed and underdeveloped countries.

This general theoretical schema was supplemented with some sociological observations about the effects of development on the social structure and on the necessity to adapt a society's superstructure to developmental requirements.

The path of development

It was fundamentally believed that:

1. A change from development towards the 'outside' to development towards the 'interior' would relieve underdeveloped countries of their dependence on foreign trade and give birth to a locally controlled economy. These changes were described as a 'transfer of centres of decision-making towards the interior' of underdeveloped economies, and as replacing a development 'induced' by uncontrollable foreign trade situations by national development as conceived by those in power within the country.

2. As a result of industrialization, the traditional oligarchies devoted to production for foreign trade (land-owners, mine-owners and exporters) would weaken, and a redistribution of power would increase the participation of the middle classes and of the lower classes; in other words, a process of political democratization was expected.

3. This process of democratization was related to a belief, which still exists, that the United States had a relatively more equal distribution of income, or rather that it represented a mass consumption society.[7] In other words, industrialization was to

7. During the 1950s the prosperity of world capitalism generated such optimism that even the validity of theories concerning the cyclical character

integrate the rural masses in the modern capitalistic productive system, both as producers and consumers.

4. As the economy turned 'towards the interior' a national centre of decision-making would emerge. The weakening of the oligarchies, the strengthening of the middle classes and the economic integration of the poorer sectors into a mass consumption society would encourage the establishment of an independent national society, and of an independent State machine which, though interventionist rather than liberal in character, would nevertheless respect private initiative: in short a 'developmentist' state.

5. Finally, at the level of consciousness, it was hoped that industrial development, by creating the bases of an independent society, would allow scientific, technological and cultural backwardness to be overcome. It was hoped that Latin America's so-called 'cultural alienation' would disappear. Cultural alienation had come to signify the process whereby Latin American culture had become a pale imitation of the dominant culture of the colonial centres. Latin American intellectuals, it was claimed, saw their countries from the point of view of these metropolitan centres, and in terms of the interests and values of the metropolis. This alienation was held to be the key to the continuing condition of underdevelopment, and only the creation of a critical consciousness could remove it. Such a consciousness was to manifest itself in an ideology of development uniting national will and national interest in the pursuit of the aims of an independent national society.

---

of the system, which was so clearly confirmed by the crisis of 1929, came to be denied. Even Marxist thought, demoralized by irresponsible predictions of crises which never occurred, was affected by this kind of enthusiasm. Kennedy's advisers also had faith in the theories which pointed towards a qualitative change within the capitalist system which rendered it immune to crises, to under-consumption and so on. The vitality of capitalism has reinforced the optimistic climate of opinion manifested in the work of Galbraith, Rostow, Hoselitz and others .However, the policies arising from these observations review the other aspect of capitalist prosperity. The explosion of the 'Negro problem', the previously forgotten issue of poverty, the continued growth of the militarist state, the foreign policy in which reformism alternated with military coups, revelations about the CIA, the rebellion of North American students all culminate in the world crisis of the dollar and the failure of the Vietnam War. All these problems have been documented in various books, reports and articles and in the face of them the theory about mass society, affluent society, industrial society and so on has tumbled to the ground.

Although dominant, this is obviously not the only model to have been put forward. Within these generalized boundaries one finds divergent positions on the right and on the left. Those on the right, if they can be so called, play down the colonial aspects of the situation and emphasize less structural changes than a greater rationality of behaviour, economic modernization, technological development, the help of foreign investment, the need for a sociology or an economics of development which does not destroy the universality of science, and so on.

To the left – and here again the classification is somewhat arbitrary – one finds a tendency to emphasize the colonial character of the economy, the need for structural changes with only a very restricted role for foreign capital, and the need for a Latin American sociology and economics based on the point of view of the underdeveloped countries.

As I have shown in another work (Dos Santos, 1968), this 'developmentist' and nationalist ideology has acquired a dominant position in Latin America, especially in those countries which have industrialized most rapidly, and I think that this dominance has arisen from the play of class interests which it reflects in its purest form. The industrial bourgeoisie – formed during the 1930s, during a period in which foreign capital in Latin America and in other underdeveloped countries was in a weak position due to the Depression and the Second World War – had by the 1940s already become the ruling class in most of the industrialized countries of Latin America, and became more so in the 1950s and 1960s in the other countries, though under the control of foreign capital. Thus all social classes operate culturally in the framework of the thought of this 'developmentist' and nationalist class. This is true of the middle classes (particularly technicians and intellectuals), the labour movement (Peronist, 'Varguist', certain sectors of the APRA),[8] and even of peasant movements (the Mexican revolution, in particular the Cárdenas period with the nationalization of petrol and the Agrarian Reform, the Bolivian revolution, the Guatemalan revolution).

8. APRA: *Alianza Peruana para la Revolución Americana* – The Peruvian Alliance for the American Revolution – has been Peru's dominant reformist party of the centre, under the leadership of Haya de la Torre, ever since the thirties. 'Varguismo' refers to the Brazilian populist dictator of the 1930's, Vargas. Cárdenas, President of Mexico (1934–40), presided over the most thorough implementation of Mexico's Land Reform and over the nationalization of American-owned petrol plants (Trans.).

The crisis of the development model

Historical developments have given birth to a very serious crisis in the Latin American social sciences. Ten years of optimism were followed by ten years of pessimism, of economic stagnation and of failed development policies.

Arising precisely during a period when Latin American governments were establishing planning machinery and when there was clearly a general acceptance of the principle theses of the dominant development theory, this failure was bound to give rise to a crisis of the entire model of development and of the social science on which it is based.

The crisis becomes even deeper when one examines the principal expectations of the development model.

The transition from 'development towards the outside' to 'development towards the interior' was expected to lead to greater independence in foreign trade, and to transfer the centre of decision-making to the local economy, but reality has, however, proved itself far more complex. As far as foreign trade is concerned, it was hoped that import substitution would give rise to a situation in which the manufacture of the principal products within a country would reduce dependence on manufactured imports and allow developing countries a greater degree of commercial freedom and independence. In fact, however, the combination of import substitution and the deterioration of currencies has provoked greater dependence on foreign trade.[9] There has been a decline in the elasticity of substitution of imports in Latin America. During the colonial exporting phase, imported products were in general luxury goods for the consumption of the ruling classes, and their effects on the economy were therefore quite secondary. During the phase of import substitutions, foreign currency was used to purchase inputs for national industries, for the machines and semi-manufactured primary products which are more and more essential for the very survival of the economy. Since foreign currency is scarce, and since there is a constant threat that it will become scarcer, one can understand the importance of this basic situation. Interdependence among national economies becomes dependence in the case

9. Raul Prebisch places great emphasis on the role of the declining prices of exported products. Other writers insist, rather, on the predominant role of services, freight and insurance charges, technical assistance and prerequisites in balance-of-payments deficits. See Frank (1966) and Dos Santos (1966).

of underdeveloped countries, for they are subordinated to the power of those who control the world market and the most advanced techniques and means of production. The decision whether or not to import these products – some of which are as vital as petrol, chemical products, precision instruments, machines, and so on – is closely tied to balance-of-payments deficits which are caused by declining prices of primary products and rising prices of manufactured products, in particular of freight charges, royalties, technical assistance and capital remittances, as well as increasing debt-servicing burdens which themselves rise as deficits accumulate.

As far as the transfer of centres of decision-making towards the interior of the economy is concerned, hopes have not been fulfilled either. A series of recent publications and data has demonstrated that the industrialization of recent years has been characterized by a growing control of foreign capital over large industries.[10] At the same time the concentration and monopolization of the industrial sector has been consolidated, thereby gradually destroying the possibilities of a national independent development, and subjecting the economy, society, public opinion and the State to the control of foreign capital. Control of the economy as a whole has still continued to pass to foreign hands. Very powerful forces have arisen in underdeveloped countries, linked to the internal market, but they are international and not national forces. Clearly, this increasing control by foreign capital reduces the feasibility of an independent national State. Faced with a reality in which power is in the hands of foreign monopolies formed by international companies with control over technology, capital and administrative techniques, the State is powerless and, in the end, submits to their interests. Although this tendency still sometimes meets resistance, that resistance is doomed to failure by the general evolution of the economy. Resistance is founded in the force of state capitalism in Latin America: state enterprises, although created with the fundamental aim of favouring private initiative and capitalist development, are nevertheless an economic force in themselves on which a civil and military bureaucracy and technocracy rely to impose their own conception of development.

The expectation of democratization has also been belied by events. True, the traditional agrarian, mining and exporting

10. See Dos Santos (1968), Ceceña (1963), Fuchs (1969), Furtado (1967), Cardoso (n.d.), Johnson (1967) and Child (1967).

oligarchies have become weaker in Latin America, and this fact can be measured by the ever-decreasing share of foreign trade in the national income of those countries which have industrialized. However, this economic weakening has not been accompanied by a parallel political weakening nor by a destruction of the old agrarian structure which might have occurred in conjunction with the expansion of urban and industrial life.[11] How has this happened? What aspects of the social and economic structure of Latin America have enabled these elements to survive?

In the first place, the export sector has been the basis of industrial development. Import substitution assumes precisely a compromise between the agrarian exporters and industrialists. Firstly, the industrial sector was concerned fundamentally to satisfy the demand of the oligarchy and of the workers in its factories, and only secondarily with that of the urban middle classes and rural sectors. Secondly the machinery and primary products which enabled industries to be created were bought outside the country with currency earned by the export sector, a process we shall call the extensive accumulation of capital. Thirdly, a large part of the capital invested in industry originated, directly or indirectly, through the banking system above all, in the very high rent earned, but certainly not reinvested, in the agrarian sector. Such was the economic, political and social compromise consolidated in Latin America after the 1930s in which lies the conclusion of the middle class and petty bourgeois revolutionary movements which plagued the 1920s and 1930s.

The old clientele system of the nineteenth century and early twentieth century countryside gradually moved towards the towns and contaminated new forms of political action. Populism reproduces in its own way the old techniques based upon the electoral clientele, compromising between urban mass techniques and traditional personalistic techniques. In spite of the important role played by the masses in national life, there has been no successful construction of bourgeois democracy in the European style. But most dramatic of all in the last few years has been the tendency for military regimes to emerge in some of the most industrialized countries of Latin America. The growing political participation of the masses brought responses in the

11. 'The truth of the matter is that traditional societies have turned out to be fairly flexible, and capable of absorbing highly rational elements, while nevertheless preserving their essential features' (ECLA, 1966).

form of the military *coup* and growing institutional power, especially that of the executive branch.

Contrary to what many expected these military governments have not carried out policies typical of the traditional liberal oligarchy, which may have supported them originally, but has lost influence over them. Paradoxically, the military have taken upon themselves the task of modernization. They raise the level of state investments and declare themselves unconditional allies of the United States, to the point of even defending the doctrine of international 'interdependence' between their countries and that country – as in the case of Brazil. How can this phenomenon be explained? Maybe these governments do not represent so-called traditional interests but rather arise from the needs of monopoly capitalism, an expression of international capital in alliance with the state bureaucracy and managers of large state enterprises, and only in a very secondary fashion with the old oligarchies in a new type of compromise which excludes the popular movements.

The hopes of a mass consumption society were also illusory. True, the great urban centres grew more than the countryside, and within them, the mass consumption sector has become very important. But the marginal population living in shanty-towns and other peripheral areas has grown even faster, and is integrated into the capitalist market only in an episodic fashion. The traditional system cannot be blamed for the formation of this marginal population. It comes in part from natural growth of the urban population whose birth rates are still very high, but also from the large number of immigrants from crisis-ridden rural areas which still expel a large portion of peasant labour to the towns. It is known that in recent years there has been only a small growth of the relative importance of industrial labour as a proportion of the labour force as a whole. The explanation of this fact lies in a development based on monopoly capital which relies on highly advanced capital-intensive technology introduced from the great industrial centres.

One cannot be opposed to technological development as such, but the adoption of this technology, in a capitalist structure which had still not assimilated the migrants who had left the land as a result of the changes of the 1920s and 1930s, has a disastrous effect on the people. The entrepreneurial structure is unable to absorb the labour force freed from the countryside as well as the general increase in population. This type of development has accentuated social and economic marginality – a term which has become a central theme of Latin American social science (see Quijano, 1966).

What then remains of the project of an independent national society based on a strong economy and oriented towards internal markets, of the entrepreneurial class which was to take on the role of a progressive national elite, of the independent national state which was to be the expression of national interest, based on the political democracy and on growing popular participation in the exercise of power and in the fruits of economic development? Finally, what remains of the developmentist ideology which was to co-ordinate and stimulate this process, doing away with an alienated mentality, and bringing the interests of national development to the fore?

The so-called national bourgeoisies who were to have presided over this process have been assimilated by foreign capital, a process which recent research on entrepreneurs has demonstrated with increasing clarity (see Dos Santos, 1968). The managers of multinational corporations are taking up the leading role in economic life and are rapidly reaching into other spheres of social life. Deprived of its social bases the nationalist and developmentist ideology is gradually losing strength and the contradictory interests it conceals are ever more clearly in evidence. However, the various historical stages of this process have not yet played themselves out, and the ideology still emerges in new forms although these are increasingly contradictory and weak. The bourgeoisie is increasingly abandoning it to technicians, bureaucrats and even left-wing politicians and labour leaders who seek in past history a security which will protect them from the rapid changes of today. Thus only the middle class and the petty bourgeoisie still have the vigour to support and defend the project of national and independent development.

Conclusion

This crisis of the model of development (and of the project it implied) which has dominated social science in the continent has thrown that very science into a crisis. The very notion of development and underdevelopment and the explanatory power of these concepts have lost credibility. In this situation the concept of dependence has appeared to offer a possible, if partial, explanation of these paradoxes, seeking to explain why Latin American development has differed from that of today's advanced countries.

The international relationships which condition development can be defined as relationships of dependence whose effect is governed by certain specific laws which allow us to speak of dependent development. Let us, therefore, study the nature of these relationships and the fundamental characteristics of this type of development.

Underdevelopment and dependence
Dependence and internal structure

We have noted that the concept of dependence has emerged in Latin America from discussion of the theme of underdevelopment and development. The concept of dependence allows us to transcend earlier errors, but it has not been sufficiently clarified, even though a series of recent works has definitively conferred a scientific status upon it by placing it at the centre of academic discussions.[12] Whereas this discussion has hitherto concentrated on the methodological mistakes of traditional approaches to dependence, our objective is now to criticize these propositions themselves in order to achieve a clearer understanding of the problem.

Dependence is not the 'external factor' which it is often believed to be. A national situation should be approached – as I have described in an earlier work on Brazil:

by determining its own specific movement. The international situation in which this movement occurs is taken as a general condition but not as a demiurge of the national process because it is the elements within a nation which determine the effect of international situations upon the national reality. It would be too easy to replace internal dynamics by external dynamics. Were it possible, we would be spared the study of the dialectic of each movement of a global process and could instead substitute for the analysis of different concrete situations a generalized and abstract formula (Dos Santos, 1967).

Aníbal Quijano (1967) puts this point more explicitly: '. . . the total problem of the historical development of our societies is radically affected by the phenomenon of dependence, which is not an external point of reference but rather a fundamental element in the interpretation of our history' (p. 5).

This insight is also found in the work of Fernando H.

12. See Cardoso and Faletto (1969), Sunkel (1967), Paz (1967), Quijano (1967), Vasconi (n.d.), Maurini (1966), Dos Santos (1968), Frank (1967), Weffort (1968) and Espartaco (1966).

Cardoso and Enzo Faletto, and of Weffort, and provides the key to a development of the concept of dependence as an explanatory scientific category.

To understand dependence as a conditioning context of certain kinds of internal structure is to understand development as a world-wide historical phenomenon, as a consequence of the formation, expansion and consolidation of the capitalist system. This approach implies the need to integrate into one single historical account the capitalist expansion of the developed countries and the consequences of that expansion in the countries which are today adversely affected by it. These consequences are not 'effects' of capitalist development in a simplistic sense, but rather they are integral and determinant parts thereof. This theoretical step enables us to see quite clearly the historical specificity of the development of advanced capitalist countries and, *ipso facto*, of underdeveloped countries. Just as the study of capitalist development in the hegemonic centres gave rise to the theory of colonialism and imperialism, so the study of development in the underdeveloped countries of today must give rise to a theory of dependence. It follows that the approaches of the authors of the theory of imperialism suffer from inherent limitations. Neither Lenin (1917), nor Bukharin (1966) and Rosa Luxembourg (1964) – the most prominent Marxist to develop the theory of imperialism – nor the few non-Marxist writers like Hobson[13] (1965) who concerned themselves with it, approached the question of imperialism from the point of view of the dependent countries. Although dependence has its place in the general framework of a theory of imperialism, it also possesses a force of its own which entitles it to a specific place in the general process which is itself influenced by it. By understanding dependence and conceptualizing and studying its mechanisms and its historical force one both expands and re-formulates the theory of imperialism. Let us take, for example, the case of certain confusions in Lenin's rather superficial interpretation of some of the tendencies of his time. Lenin expected that imperialism would result in a state of parasitism and stagnation in the central economy and that the capital invested abroad by imperialist powers would stimulate economic growth in backward countries.[14] If this was a logical conclusion to

13. See also Schumpeter (1951) and Strachey (1959).

14. 'The export of capital speeds up enormously the development of capitalism in the countries which receive it' (Lenin, 1917).

draw from the observation of trends existing at that time, then we must find out why it turned out to be mistaken.

In the first place, Lenin passed over the effects of capital exports upon the economies of the backward countries themselves. Had he not done so he would have seen that by investing in the modernization of the old colonial exporting structure capitalists allied themselves with those very forces which preserved their backwardness. More than straightforward capital investments, this was imperialist investment in a dependent country, and it strengthened the commercial and exporting oligarchy even though it did also pave the way to a new stage in the dependency of those countries.

This example demonstrates the need to bring a broader approach to bear upon the theme of dependence. A unilateral outlook which only analyses the problem from the point of view of the hegemonic centre must be transcended and the peripheral areas must be integrated into the analysis as part of a world-wide system of social and economic relationships. Thus the analysis of dependence and its dynamics can acquire its full theoretical and scientific value.

The concept of dependence, then, does not allow for an analysis of underdevelopment simply in terms of certain isolated pre-capitalist structures. Rather, it allows us to transcend such a vision of history from the outset for, as has been said, underdevelopment arises from a world-wide situation which is to be explained in the light of the expansion of capitalism. If this is the case, as dependence theory leads us to think, then to what extent can the countries which grow up in a dependent situation and hence within the process of capitalist expansion, be considered to be capitalist?

In a series of very important works André Gunder Frank (1965, 1966, 1967, 1969) has insisted that Latin American economy and society have been capitalist ever since 'the cradle', a thesis previously advanced by Sergio Bagú (1949) and Luis Vitale (1966). Frank's arguments are as follows: Latin America was colonized by Europe in a period of mercantile capitalist expansion and the economy thus formed is complementary to the world economy. The Continent produces mostly for export, its product is therefore mercantile, and therefore we cannot call the economy a feudal one. The most underdeveloped areas of Latin America are precisely those which went through a period of flourishing export activity and hence of flourishing mercantilism;

again it is absurd to link their underdevelopment with feudalism. The capitalist system arises like a central star which exploits an entire system of satellites and sub-satellites which in their turn exploit those lower down in the system. Within underdeveloped countries, therefore, we find a system of internal exploitation linked to the international system.

Frank's critique is correct in so far as one cannot speak of feudalism in the context of economies and societies whose organization is almost entirely a response to the obligation to export primary products. However, one consequence of this was that an internal market was not created. Manufactured goods were imported rather than locally produced, and as a result of these features a colonial export economy was created rather than a manufacturing mercantile capitalist economy such as arose in certain parts of Europe at the time. This system contributed to the existence of a natural or self consumption economy side by side with it and did not provoke important secondary effects, in particular in the manufacturing sector; it neither permitted nor stimulated the full development of capitalist relations of production but rather based itself upon servile forms of work or slavery. How can one characterize such a system of production? Is it a particular case of capitalism, a completely different mode of production, or a system in transition towards capitalism which happened to take on the form of a colonial exporting economy just as Europe at that time was passing through a transition towards capitalism known as the mercantile manufacturing period?

This last description seems to approximate most closely to the phenomenon of dependence. The industrial revolution in England at the end of the eighteenth century created the conditions for an expansion of the capitalist mode of production in Europe, transforming it into the dominant system of production, precisely because the mercantile manufacturing period had paved the way for a division between the ownership of the means of production on the one hand, and a free labour force on the other. That period had also created conditions favourable to intensive primitive capital accumulation on the basis of a monopoly of international trade, of concentrated and flexible financial activity, and of the destruction of the small peasant economy. Finally, the division of labour was stimulated in those manufacturing sectors which faced constantly growing internal and external markets.

The situation of Latin America, as a producer of metals and tropical products and as an important market for European rather than its own products, obliged to pay vast sums to the Spanish Crown and to merchants, was quite different, and once the restrictions of the colonial period had been lifted, the continent found itself in a situation of dependent, export-based capitalism. The parameters of the newly 'independent' continent are given by the imprint of the colonial exporting system. This is the case not only because of the drainage of a large portion of the surplus, as Frank thinks, but more fundamentally, because the anti-colonial revolutions, dominated as they were by the Creole oligarchy, were unable to alter the dependent character of the social and economic structure.

Thus, underdevelopment, far from constituting a state of backwardness prior to capitalism, is rather a consequence and a particular form of capitalist development known as dependent capitalism. The process under consideration, rather than being one of satellization as Frank believes, is a case of the formation of a certain type of internal structure conditioned by international relationships of dependence.

What is dependence?

We can now define more clearly what is meant by dependence. In the first place, dependence is a *conditioning situation* in which the economies of one group of countries are conditioned by the development and expansion of others. A relationship of interdependence between two or more economies or between such economies and the world trading system becomes a dependent relationship when some countries can expand through self-impulsion while others, being in a dependent position, can only expand as a reflection of the expansion of the dominant countries, which may have positive or negative effects on their immediate development. In either case, the basic situation of dependence causes these countries to be both backward and exploited. Dominant countries are endowed with technological, commercial, capital and socio-political predominance over dependent countries – the form of this predominance varying according to the particular historical moment – and can therefore exploit them, and extract part of the locally produced surplus. Dependence, then, is based upon an international division of labour which allows industrial development to take place in some countries while restricting it in others, whose growth is conditioned by and subjected to the power centres of the world.

The international division of labour between producers of primary and agricultural products and producers of manufactured products is a typical consequence of capitalist development, which necessarily assumes the form of combined inequality among countries. This inequality arises from the characteristics of that capital accumulation in which economic growth is based upon the exploitation of the many by the few, and upon concentration of ownership of the resources needed for social and economic development. The concentration of the ownership of capital, dominance in the world market, and the monopoly of the savings and investment opportunities in the hands of small national groups are complementary elements in the establishment of a combined and unequal international system. The interdependent character of this system at the international level gradually increases as the commercial and industrial revolutions bring about the application of new technologies in production and communication. These revolutions allow previously isolated economies to develop a complementary role. But this complementarity or interdependence arises in the framework not of collaboration among men, but rather of competition among private owners. In this struggle, 'man is wolf to man' and monopoly is the basis of victory.

The great centres of capital arose in Italy, Portugal, Spain, Holland, France and finally in England and by their side the expanding centres of production grew up on which the new regime of capitalist production was to be based. The centres of capital were not in Latin America nor were the centres of production established there either. For this eventually to occur, the centres of domination had first to spread violently and dramatically through the world, in order partially to incorporate the continent. Only when Latin America can create a self-sustaining and independent economy will she cease to be simply a necessary complement of an international system over which she has no control.

Let us now pass to the meaning of the term *conditioning situation*. A conditioning situation determines the limits and possibilities of action and behaviour of men. Faced by it, they may either choose among the various alternatives internal to that situation or they may seek to change the conditioning situation itself. The first choice is never completely free for a concrete situation includes further factors placing added limits on action and choice. The second choice opens the way to new possibilities, seeking to bring about a qualitative change which itself must be considered in terms of its concrete possibilities.

If dependence is a conditioning situation, then it establishes the possible limits of development and of its forms in dependent countries. However, such a description is incomplete for two reasons: firstly, concrete development situations arise as much from the specific characteristics of the conditioned situation which re-define and specify the general conditioning situation, as from the general conditioning factors of dependence themselves. Secondly, the very situation of dependence can be and is susceptible to change as the hegemonic structures and the dependent structures themselves change. Such changes need not cut off the relationship of dependence but may simply re-direct it by, for example, a transition from mercantile to industrial and financial dependence. But one can also break off the relationship and seek to consolidate an independent economy, as in socialist countries of the Third World such as China, North Korea, North Vietnam and Cuba, despite the problems which they still face because of the heritage of past situations and structures.[15]

The concept of dependence itself cannot be understood without reference to the articulation of dominant interests in the hegemonic centres and in the dependent societies. 'External' domination, in a pure sense, is in principle impracticable. Domination is practicable only when it finds support among those local groups which profit by it. Thus we see the irrelevance of the concept of alienation which claims that our elites are alienated because they look upon themselves with alien eyes.

According to this thesis, which the reader will recall, our élites

15. A difference must be drawn between China, with its nationally integrated economy, and Cuba, which still relies on sugar exports for a large part of its income. Socialist countries do not base their society and their power on the expansion of consumption, as is the case under capitalism where production constitutes a value in itself. For this reason, socialist countries can face external economic pressures more easily. This is the secret of the political independence of countries which are economically dependent on foreign trade, such as Cuba, and this is why we cannot include this species of dependence under the heading of dependence as we have been discussing it. The situation is specific and follows different laws, so it must be studied with specific concepts. The problem of East European countries, too, must be studied in the light of their own specificity, on account of their higher level of industrial development, their proximity to the USSR, and the Stalinist experience.

look upon their countries from the colonialist's point of view – an alienation which supposedly reveals the under-developed and dependent nature of our culture. Yet if we demonstrate that there is a necessary coincidence between dominant local and foreign interests, if we demonstrate that the specificity of the ruling classes in dependent countries lies in their condition as 'dominated dominators' even allowing for internal conflicts among these dominant interests, the concept of alienation is seen to give a distorted picture; the concept must therefore, be replaced by a concept of 'compromise' among the various international and national elements which make up the dependent situation. This concept of compromise or collusion of the various interests involved is an essential element in the elaboration of a theory of dependence.

Thus we arrive at a theoretical conclusion which is immediately related to the practical problems of development and to the daily political, social, economic and cultural life of our peoples. For if dependence defines the internal situation and is structurally linked to it, a country cannot break out of it simply by isolating herself from external influences; such action would simply provoke chaos in a society which is of its essence dependent. The only solution therefore would be to change its internal structure – a course which necessarily leads to confrontation with the existing international structure.

References

BAGU, S., (1949), *Economía de la Sociedad Colonial*, Buenos Aires.
BARAN, P., and SWEEZY, P. (1966), *Monopoly Capital*, Monthly Review Press, Penguin edition, 1962
BULCHARIN, N. (1966), *World Economy and Imperialism*, H. Fertig, NY.
CARDOSO, F. H. (1966), 'Análisis sociológico del desarrollo económico', *Revista Latinoamericana de Sociología*, vol. 1, no. 2, July.
CARDOSO, F. H. (n.d.), 'Empresarios industriales y desarrollo nacional en Brasil', CESO, mimeo.
CARDOSO, F. H., and FALETTO, E. (1969), *Dependencia y Desarrollo en América Latina*, Mexico.
CECENA, J. L. (1963), *El Capital Monopolista y la Economía de México*, Cuadernos Americanos.
CHARÁMONTE, J. C. (1964), *Problemas del Europeismo en Argentina*, Universidad Nacional del Literal, Paraná.
CHILD, J. (1967), 'Subdesarrollo y ganancias monopolistas', *Pensamiento Critico*, nos. 2–3, March–April, Havana.
COOK, F. (n.d.), *The Military State*,
DOS SANTOS, T. (1966), 'Subdesarrollo y ciencia social', *Hermes*, no. 3.

DOS SANTOS, T. (1967), 'Crisis económica y crisis política en Brasil', CESO, mimeo.

DOS SANTOS, T. (1968), 'El nuevo carácter de la dependencia', *Cuadernos del Centro de Socio-Económicos*, no. 10, Santiago.

ECLA (1966), *El Desarrollo Social de América Latina en la Postguerra*, Montevideo.

ESPARTACO, . (1966), 'La crisis latinoamericano y su marco externo', *Desarrollo Económico*, July-December, Buenos Aires.

FRANK, A. G. (1965), 'El confusionismo del precapitalismo dual en América Latina', *Economía*, no. 4, May–June, Mexico.

FRANK, A. G. (1966), 'Servicios extranjeros o desarrollo nacional', *Comercio Exterior*, vol. 16, no. 2, February.

FRANK, A. G. (1967), *Capitalism and Underdevelopment in Latin America*, Monthly Review Press.

FRANK, A. G. (1969), *Latin America. Underdevelopment or Revolution*, Monthly Review Press.

FUCHS, J. (1969), *La Penetración de los Trusts Yanquis en la Economía Argentina*, Buenos Aires.

FURTADO, C. (1967), 'La concentración del poder económico en los Estados Unidos y sus proyecciones en América Latina', *Estudios Internacionales*, vol. 1, nos. 2–4; see also the March 1968 issue.

HOBSON, J. A. (1965), *Imperialism*, Univ. of Michigan Press.

JOHNSON, D. (1967), 'The national and progressive bourgeoisie of Chile', *Studies in Comparative International Development*, vol. 3, no. 7.

LACOSTE, Y. (1965), *Géographie du Sousdeveloppement*, Paris.

LENIN, V. I. (1917), *Imperialism. The Highest Stage of Capitalism* (many editions).

LUXEMBURG, R. (1964), *The Accumulation of Capital*, Monthly Review Press.

MAURINI, R. M. (1966), 'La interdependencia brasileña y la intergración imperialista', *Monthly Review – Selecciones en Castellano*, no. 21, April.

PAZ, P. (1967), 'Dependencia externa y desnacionalización de la industria interna', ECLA, mimeo

PREBISCH, R. (1963), *Hacia una dinámica del desarrollo latino americano*, Mexico City and Buenos Aires.

QUIJANO, A. (1967), *Dependencia Cambio Social y Urbanizacion en Latinoamerica*, ECLA, mineo.

QUIJANO, A. (n.d.), 'Notas sobre el concepto de marginalidad', ECLA, mimeo.

SCHUMPETER, J. (1951), *Imperialism and Social Classes*, Augustus Kelly, N.Y.

STRACHEY, J. (1959), *The End of Empire*, Gollancz.

SUNKEL, O. (1967), 'Política nacional de desarrollo y dependencia externa', *Estudios Internacionales*, vol. 1, no. 1, May, Santiago.

VASCONI, T. (n.d.), 'Cultura, ideología, dependencia y alienación: notas para discusión de una problemática', manuscript.

VITALE, L. (1966), 'América Latina: feudal o capitalisto?', *Estrategía*, no. 3, Santiago.

WEFFORT, F. (1968), 'Clases populares e desenvolvimento social', *Latin American Institute for Economic and Social Planning*, ILPES, mimeo.

Part Two
Agriculture: Resources, Power and Change

Most underdeveloped countries have an urgent agrarian problem. The forms of agricultural production and rural social organization are often catalogued as 'obstacles' to development at the same time as they define some of the major conditions in which industrialization is to be successfully created, or perhaps imposed. The readings in this section contribute to breaking down some of the misleading conclusions associated with such a perspective. Stavenhagen (Reading 4) presents a general framework for analysing change in agrarian communities in the light of underdevelopment and understood as a (variable) historical process. The pioneering studies of Hill (Reading 5) have disturbed simplistic notions of 'traditional behaviour' by investigating in a painstaking and detailed way the development of the cocoa industry in Ghana by African farmers, and showing how in certain conditions existing forms of social organization could be utilized as the basis for new and productive economic enterprises. The intricacies of analysing particular rural structures without losing sight of the broader issues are also exemplified by Keddie (Reading 7) in a discussion of attempted land reform in Iran. Beckford (Reading 6) in the context of Caribbean plantation agriculture, undermines the widely held assumption of a single economic rationality raising in an effective manner the question of who benefits, a question that development studies cannot afford to ignore and which cannot be confined within local or national boundaries.

4 R. Stavenhagen

Changing Functions of the Community in Underdeveloped
Countries

R. Stavenhagen, 'Changing functions of the community in
underdeveloped countries', *Sociologica Ruralis*, vol. 4, 1964, pp. 315–31.

A paper on the changing rural community in the underdeveloped
countries faces the problem that these nations, generally grouped
together for descriptive purposes, are frequently as different from
each other as they are from any one developed country. If we are to
speak of them in a group, therefore, it will be necessary to abstract
from their diversity and to concentrate our attention on those
aspects which they do, indeed, have in common.

Several points must be clarified at the outset. The concept community is by no means used in a clear and unequivocal fashion in
sociological literature. As Kötter (1956) has remarked, it is both a
methodological tool for research and the object of investigation.
In fact, the most common type of research in the sociology of rural
life in the underdeveloped countries, particularly in Latin
America, is community research.

Another point which deserves attention is the fashion in which
change is envisaged in particular studies. Whereas some scholars
approach it from the historical angle, as Berque (1957) tried to do
in lower Egypt, or as Lefebvre (1963) has done in Campan, in the
Pyrenees (also an underdeveloped area), others, such as Redfield
(1941) in Mexico, or Fei and Chang (1948) in pre-revolutionary
China, have preferred the approach that has been called 'comparative statics', that is, the comparative study of a number of
communities which presumably occupy different levels of development. The latter approach, with variations, has become very
common lately, particularly when the effects of certain particular
changes in rural life are analysed, such as the impact of technological innovations. It is noteworthy that the former approach
usually leads to a greater emphasis on internal change in the community, while the latter orientation tends to emphasize external
factors in change.

A third point which must be mentioned refers to the nature of
the so-called underdeveloped societies. Some observers simply

identify the whole of society in the underdeveloped nations with the small, isolated, homogeneous rural community, that is, the folk society. Thus, in a recent paper, Hoselitz (1964) considers the folk society as being 'among the most important aspects influencing, and in fact determining stratification patterns in little industrialized countries'. And Hertzler (1956) goes so far as to say that up to two-thirds of the world's population lives in static, archaic, change-resistant folk societies. In fact, however, as has been pointed out repeatedly, the folk society, if it exists at all in the fashion in which Robert Redfield conceived of it, is strictly limited to a few areas of the underdeveloped world, and there is certainly no country in the world whose social structure can be described in terms of the folk society. It seems perhaps more adequate to say, with Lambert (1960), that the underdeveloped countries are above all unequally developed societies and that their underdevelopment is in great measure a result of their unequal development. Thus it would seem that the dual society, and not the folk society, is the essential ingredient in underdevelopment. However, even on this point, there are certain ambiguities. The traditional or backward sector of this dual society (which includes, of course, most of the rural communities) is often considered as being quite independent of the other, modern or advanced sector. Indeed, it is argued that all change is diffused outward from the so-called pockets of modernism into the rural hinterland. Rural communities are considered as being passive recipients of all change coming from the urban areas. If they are attributed any dynamic role at all, it is mostly in terms of their selection of the cultural elements which they accept or refuse, or else of the possible reinterpretation of such elements.

This point is closely linked to the final introductory remark that I wish to make. Many students of social change in underdeveloped areas not only suffer from an ethnocentric fallacy but also from a time-centric illusion. In fact, it is frequently thought that change is a recent phenomenon, perhaps dating from the end of the Second World War, that the so-called traditional communities are only just now, as Hoselitz (1964) puts it, 'being drawn into a social framework with much more complex and more highly stratified structures'. It is believed, or at least implied, that before the present-day processes of 'modernization', rural society was essentially static, and the term 'traditional' is used to refer to some sort of eternal or perhaps slowly drifting type of social organization which is only now awakening under the impact of external innovations.

Underdevelopment – like development – is, however, a total process. Countries that for several centuries have been objects of European colonial expansion have long ago changed considerably, even in the most backward of their rural areas. The African slave trade, the forced labour of Indians in Latin America, the required cultivation by peasants of cotton in India or of spices and sugar in Java, has effected lasting and still-continuing changes in the countries involved. These changes are from one hundred and fifty to four hundred years old. The rural communities that are considered 'traditional' today more often than not became so as a result of mercantilist and colonial policy (Wolf, 1957). Under-development – not as a state-of-being but as a process – evolved hand in hand with development in these areas. It is, as Myrdal (1955) has shown, a cumulative process, and most rural communities in the agrarian societies find themselves, in fact, in the 'back-wash' of regionally localized development, and they tend towards increased underdevelopment rather than the other way around.

Peasant societies, as anthropologists are wont to state, are part-societies. This means that they are linked through communications, markets, power structure and so forth to the wider society: to regional and national complexes, from which they are differentiated by economic, political and cultural variables. Except for an extremely small number of primitive and more or less isolated tribal groups, most of the world's rural people have been living in some sort of systematic interaction not only with local urban centers but also with larger complex societies for many centuries. In considering recent transformations in rural society in underdeveloped countries, it will be well to consider also some of the older transformations which are, in fact, greatly responsible for the present state of rural society in the underdeveloped nations, and many of which are processes still at work in different areas.

Changes in economic and social relationships attendant upon changes in agriculture

Small, completely self-sufficient, agricultural communities have probably always been a rarity since neolithic times. A certain amount of surplus food has at all times and everywhere been available for trading purposes, no matter how isolated or traditional a society might be. Nevertheless, we speak of subsistence agriculture when the greater part of agricultural produce is consumed within the producer's community. This was certainly the case in most of the world's areas before European expansion and is still the case in many agricultural communities all over the world. Just how many, it is difficult to determine, because they usually do not show in census data. A recent survey in tropical Africa estimates at 60 per cent the proportion of the labor force engaged in subsistence agriculture (BIT, 1958). In India, one author estimates that about 80 per cent of the smallholders are subsistence farmers (consuming more than 75 per cent of what they produce) (Rangnakar, 1958). In most Latin American countries, only some of the surviving Indian communities engage primarily in subsistence agriculture. Though in all of these countries most of the rural population has an extremely low standard of living and hardly any buying power, it would be a mistake to confuse them simply, as some authors do, with subsistence farmers in a closed economy. They are, on the contrary, incorporated in a market economy and respond to its pressures. Even where agricultural production for direct consumption is widely prevalent, the communities thus engaged are by no means self-sufficient units. Some agricultural produce is always exchanged for manufactured articles, and it is not always the surplus that finds its way into the money economy: not infrequently, the poor peasant sells foodstuffs he is in need of in order to satisfy some other immediate necessity, and then buys back the food, at a considerably higher price, later in the season. Usually these communities are equally suppliers of wage labor on a temporary basis, during slack periods in agriculture. Thus, they are linked to the national economy through wage labor precisely because of their subsistence agriculture, that is, because subsistence agriculture does not offer full-time employment and because it does not produce the monetary income that the community needs. In fact, the maintenance of an agricultural subsistence base in the areas that supply wage labor to South African mines and industry has been a declared policy objective of British colonial and South African administration in some cases in order to depress wages and keep industrial costs low (Hailey, 1956). Similarly, in north-eastern Brazil, a belt of subsistence farms grew up around the original sugar-cane plantation areas as increasing concentration and monopolization of land forced the independent peasant producer into less fertile and more isolated areas.

In general, however, the process has been the other way around. European colonial expansion tended to destroy subsistence agriculture in the colonial areas and to substitute cash crops for the European market. Nowhere in the underdeveloped world has a generalized system of rational and well-balanced mixed-farming oriented towards supplying the internal market developed. This is one of the characteristics of agriculture in underdeveloped areas; perhaps it is one of the causes of underdevelopment itself. Subsistence agriculture is partially responsible for the low nutritional level and the general poverty characteristic of backward rural areas; but on the other hand, its substitution by monoculture for export has in many places made matters worse and the people poorer (Cépède & Lengellé, 1953).

Among the general characteristics of traditional subsistence agriculture in underdeveloped areas, observers have usually noted the low productivity per food producer and per unit of land. In the tropical areas, shifting slash-and-burn cultivation has long been a factor in unstable village life, subsistence level of living and low demographic growth (Gourou, 1948). Typical colonial agriculture is also not based on modern technology, but on the exploitation of cheap labor and the availability of land. In many parts, sophisticated techniques of irrigation and erosion control (as in pre-hispanic America) fell into disuse in colonial times. Brazilian sugar-cane cultivation underwent major technological changes only after the abolition of slavery, and in Cuba not until after the Revolution have attempts been made to rationalize and mechanize the production of this crop. Despite the appeal of technification of agriculture, in many cases modern technology, erroneously used, has greatly speeded up deforestation, erosion and soil exhaustion and results frequently anti-economical and in increasing rural unemployment (Dumont, 1961 and 1962). And FAO statistics have shown a decrease in per capita food production in underdeveloped areas in recent years (FAO, 1962).

Subsistence agriculture is based on family work. In many of the underdeveloped world's rural areas clans, lineages and extended families have been traditionally the economic units in agricultural production. In recent years wage labor in agriculture has become widespread. Not only do landless peasants in Asia and Latin

America work for wages on plantations and *haciendas*, but also in low-density Africa agricultural laborers are increasing in numbers. In many parts of the world cultivators leave their plots during part of the year to work for wages in the cities and in industry (sometimes in other countries), and come back to take care of their crops only at certain times. Moreover, in many places, such as in Africa, while the man is away working for a wage, the womenfolk have taken over agricultural tasks which have traditionally been the special domain of the men. In Northern Rhodesia, for example, this has been one of the factors contributing to a decrease in agricultural production among the Bemba (Kay, 1962). In Latin America, where peonage is still widespread, a marked tendency towards a decrease in share-cropping and increase in purely monetary relationships between landowner and worker is occurring; the same process occurs in India. Wage labor, of course, was originally introduced among colonial peoples where forced labor was no longer available. It has not always contributed to the economic development of rural areas. To get a peasant to work for a wage (be it in agriculture or in industry) is still one of the main headaches of capitalist enterprise in the underdeveloped world (Moore and Feldman, 1960), and to achieve this end his land is encroached upon or taken from him, his taxes are raised and new needs are stimulated which can only be satisfied with money. But once established, the process sustains itself: wage labor becomes an integral part of the peasant's life. This has several consequences for family and community. It tends to break up corporate lineages, it has contributed to the disappearance of various forms of cooperative labor; to the greater economic independence and responsibility of women (particularly when the menfolk have to migrate); to increased mobility of the rural population and in some cases to its greater concentration. In Latin America, displaced share-croppers on isolated plots move into nucleated villages or towns, from which they follow the agricultural labor market. Wage labor has also stimulated the development of rural labor unions and increased political consciousness and participation of the rural population. It is the basis of a new social class in underdeveloped nations: the rural proletariat which in at least one case (Cuba) has actively contributed to a radical transformation of traditional social and economic structure.

The money economy – through cash crops and wage labor – has affected the traditional home-consumption patterns all over the underdeveloped world. Thousands of industrial products are to be found in the most remote villages. To draw backward rural people into the money economy has been the declared policy objective both of national and colonial governments in under-developed areas. For many observers, the principal consequence of this is to open a vast, untapped consumer market for industrial products and, at the same time, to raise living standards in those areas. This conclusion, however, is not always warranted. Though the buying power of the rural population may increase, the standard of living does not necessarily rise along with it. Pro-duction of foodstuffs frequently drops with a change to the money economy. Much of the money earned is often spent on inessentials (the burgeoning beer market in Africa and the stark increase in alcoholism with all its negative consequences is a case in point). Also, the money economy creates an enormous sector of small and big merchants, middlemen and money-lenders, who usually absorb the greater part of the regional income. In Mexico, for example, in some areas agricultural produce goes through fifteen different hands till it finally reaches the urban consumer; while manufactured articles of low quality are usually sold at prices several times higher in the rural areas than in the cities. Where large-scale and cheap credit is not widely available, as in most agrarian societies, local money-lenders and merchants play a growing role in the community. West African cocoa and coffee farmers fall increasingly into debt, and the role of the money-lender in the Far East is too well known to need repetition here. The high ideals of the Mexican agrarian reform have to a great extent been frustrated by the monopolistic structure of credit and commercialization of crops in the rural community. Crops as well as property become mortgaged and new links of economic and political dependence tie the cultivator to forces outside the community which neither he, individually, nor the traditional communal means of social control, can cope with. Thus the benefits of a money economy (increased monetary income and buying power) are usually not equally distributed among the members of a community.

The money economy is generally hailed because it fosters entrepreneurship which, it is argued, will produce development. These entrepreneurs, possessing the capitalist spirit, or the need for achievement, or a creative personality, or some other such presumably essential quality, are thought to maximize their economic efforts, and this, supposedly, redounds to the benefit of all. As a group, moreover, these entrepreneurs will displace, it is said, the old 'traditional' conservative élite which is opposed to economic progress. This is not the place to go into a detailed critique of such arguments. It is true that entrepreneurship creates a new elite; indeed, that is about all it does. Rural communities that have been drawn into the money economy have generally, on the whole, lost more than they have gained: in India they lost their capacity to feed and clothe themselves; in Africa they lost their manpower; in Latin America their land and liberty (we may recall that 'land and liberty' was the rallying cry of the Mexican agrarian revolution). The money economy *per se* is no boon to agrarian communities. Most of the money earned through cash crops or wage labor is drained into pockets other than those of the worker or producer.

Both cash crops and wage labor contribute to the rise of new social classes and strata in the rural community. In Africa, where the process is most recent, the new social categories are not yet clearly defined and show many transitional characteristics. There is no doubt that in some places the money economy has weakened the power of the traditional ruling groups in rural communities (though in others, as in Java, it has occasionally strengthened them). In other places, as in India (Mukherjee, 1957), it has helped create a new dominating class based on the ownership and control of land. In some parts of Latin America it is even today tending to break up the egalitarian organization, the result of Spanish colonial policy, of some Indian communities, at the same time that it increases the economic subordination of these groups to the dominating non-Indian populations in the rural areas. Wage labor and cash crops have here created clear-cut class relationships where only ethnic relations (of the colonial type) were dominant before (Stavenhagen, 1963). In Africa, on the contrary, the money economy has added ethnic conflicts to class relations, e.g. in West Africa (Dupire, 1960), or has contributed to a modification of traditional ethnic-economic relations of a feudal type (e.g. Ruanda).

Whereas cash crops have tended to make rural populations more sedentary, they have also contributed to increase the number of individual farms and to the dispersion of formerly concentrated villages. However, there can be no general tendency discerned here, because these factors are obviously dependent upon many local conditions. Wage labor, on the contrary, contributes to a concentration of the population in certain types of localities (workers' camps, nucleated villages in market areas, plantations, etc.), while it also stimulates seasonal and large-scale migrations.

Perhaps the most important transformation in social and economic relationships that has taken place in agrarian societies has been the introduction and extension of private property in land. Though individual holdings and transfer of land were not unknown in underdeveloped areas in pre-colonial times, private property never developed to any extent. Land was nowhere considered a merchandise. Individuals were depositaries of land, but the actual possession of land was the prerogative of the lineage, the community, the tribe, the king, the ancestors. In Latin America, as a result of conquest, the Spanish and Portuguese conquerors were rewarded by their kings with great tracts of land from which the Indians were either expelled or to which they were tied as serfs. In some areas, communal holdings survived till the end of the colonial period, but were later destroyed by the liberal reforms of the nineteenth century. Private ownership of land has become the general pattern in Latin America. Communal Indian property only survives in some isolated areas. In Mexico an attempt at a reconstruction of communal ownership was made with the *ejido* system. In Cuba, collective ownership was established by the socialist government. In Africa the private property of land was at first established for the benefit of the European settlers by the colonial governments, through treaties imposed on African chiefs or by way of downright expropriation. It has been established more recently among African cultivators by decree and legislation. In Indonesia, the Dutch created private property of land by declaring the feudal lords as owners of the lands they received tribute from, or by attributing property rights to the traditional village chiefs. In India, the British did likewise through the Permanent Settlement Act creating the Zamindary landowners and by establishing the *ryot* peasant freehold.

Private ownership of land has been the necessary concomitant of cash-crop agriculture and the money economy; it has greatly modified community relationships. No doubt private property has given the agriculturist a greater stake in increased productivity of his land; it has favored greater capital investments and perhaps increased rationalization in agriculture. Yet it has also led to widespread loss of land and to the growth of landless peasants everywhere. Private landholdings have not been the universal solution to the peasant's problems, as has been suggested (Bauer and Yamey, 1957). Conflicts and litigation over land boundaries have become a permanent aspect of community life. Property as such, when not accompanied by adequate credit systems, technical aid and general economic development has effected few positive changes in agriculture. On the contrary, private property in land has stimulated the appearance of increasing inequalities among the rural population. It has led everywhere to concentration of land on the one hand, and to dispersion of holdings and microfundism on the other. Latin America and the Middle East are perhaps the extreme examples of inequality in land holdings; but everywhere the same process has occurred. Even in West Africa, where an 'indigenous peasantry' was created through colonial policy, the process of land concentration and dispersion is already under way. As agrarian unrest in Latin America and South East Asia has shown, inequality in land distribution – when combined, as it usually is, with oppressive systems of tenure and work – may lead to grave economic and political problems. Despite a number of attempts carried out by the most diverse governments at different periods of their history, nowhere in the underdeveloped areas has there arisen a workable system of medium-sized family farms devoted to a rational diversified agriculture supplying the internal market. Foreign colonization in Brazil during the nineteenth century, for example, did not produce such a result; neither have any number of development schemes in Africa (e.g. the Niger project, the Gezira scheme), whatever else their merits may have been. Recent timid attempts at agrarian reform in those Latin American countries that have not already carried it out by revolutionary means (Mexico, Bolivia and Cuba) are promoting such a model peasantry. What their eventual results will be, in the face of a rapidly increasing population and of the highly speculative nature of traditional colonial agriculture in those countries remains to be seen.

The demographic consequences of the problems that have been mentioned are important. The rural populations in underdeveloped areas are more and more becoming migrant populations. Rural exodus and urban hypertrophy are prevalent everywhere; but intra-rural migrations also play an important part in the process. Some of these migrations are permanent, others are partial and temporary. An important aspect of this is labor migration on a seasonal basis. Thus, many rural communities in underdeveloped countries are regular suppliers of seasonal labor and find themselves without able-bodied men (and often without young women, who seek domestic or factory employment) during a part of the year. Other local communities (principally small towns on roads and railways) become necessary points of passage of migrants and contain a constant floating population. Mostly, new ties are wrought between the community and the city, through the community's members who have gone there. In the face of insecurity and anomie in the city (always a danger, but not necessarily always present) the local community that supplies migrants plays an important role in social cohesion (Lewis, 1952; Van Velsen, 1960).

The efforts at community development

The impoverishment of the rural population in the underdeveloped areas and the tensions and maladjustments created everywhere by the processes of change that have been mentioned, have produced world-wide efforts at community development. Community development, it might be argued, is a *prise de conscience*, a reaction to the increasing underdevelopment of the rural community in agrarian societies. Though the notion has not been clearly defined and includes everything from primary school education to agricultural extension and medical care, the underlying assumption is that many of the problems besetting the rural populations in underdeveloped countries can be solved at the community level, with community resources and with outside intervention limited to education and technical aid. The movement for community development has been greatly stimulated by international organizations such as UNESCO, and by special funds channeled into these activities by technical aid programs of the developed countries. Many governments (India, Ghana, Mexico, for example) have established community development programs on a nation-wide level and have devoted important resources to these activities.

The results of these programs, after several years, are meager. It is becoming clearer that community self-help which contributes effectively to economic and social development can only prosper if accompanied by profound transformations in the social and economic structures of the countries involved, by regional and national planning and by large-scale investments in the backward areas. Community development is no substitute for agrarian reform, for effective political organization and for centralized economic planning for overall national development. Moreover, if carried out within the existing social and economic framework in rural communities, community development programs tend to favor the strata or classes that already occupy a dominant position in the rural community, and thus, in fact, tend to aggravate problems instead of solving them.[1]

Conclusions

The rural community in underdeveloped areas has been characterized in different ways. It is generally considered that the more backward a community, technically speaking, the more corporate its social structure. These corporate communities may be based on kinship, as in Africa, or on territoriality and cultural identity, as in Indian America, or on caste, as in India. They may be egalitarian, as in some parts of Africa, Latin America or Java, or highly stratified, as in the African feudal societies, the Indian *jajmani* system, or the Arab village. These traditional communities have been changing for some generations now. The Latin American corporate community is in itself a result of Spanish colonial policy. In Java, as well as in India and some parts of Africa, the feudal lords have become the landowners and in some parts the entrepreneurs. In other places, the traditional chiefs have been displaced by new elements, usually officials tied to the colonial or the national administration. The traditional tenant, as in India, sharecropper, as in North Africa, or peon, as in Latin America, is increasingly becoming the migrant laborer, the wage worker, the rural proletarian, and, in some cases, due to incomplete agrarian reform, the microfundist, returning – as owner this time – to a subsistence economy.

The rural community in underdeveloped countries has long ago ceased to be a closed world. It takes part in the market system. It supplies labor to the 'poles of growth' in the developing economies, it becomes, often, the unit of certain new types of social and economic organization (the *ejido* in Mexico, the commune in China, the 'granja del pueblo' in Cuba).

Perhaps the most striking feature in changing rural communi-

1. For India, see Berreman (1963), Retzlaff (1962) and Desai (1958), quoted in Kaufman (1962). In Pakistan, the nation-wide program 'Village-Aid', financed by the US, has been abandoned.

ties in the underdeveloped countries is the emergence of new class relations which are closely linked to the class and power structures at the national level. These new relations between social groups often upset longstanding hierarchies and enter into conflict with traditional community power and stratification patterns. The rural community becomes at times the locus of grassroot political movements which are tied to the great social issues of our time, e.g. the Mexican and Cuban revolutions, the Algerian and Angolan wars of independence, the civil war in South Vietnam). Thus, the rural community is not always the most appropriate focus of analysis of social and economic changes in the underdeveloped areas today. The great social changes, such as agrarian reform, regional development projects, resettlement of populations, or, indeed, the necessary political solutions to at times violent conflict in the rural areas, such as in Columbia or Cameroon, require a frame of reference much broader than the limited optic of the community.

References

BAUER, P. T., and YAMEY, B. S. (1957), *The Economics of Underdeveloped Countries*, Cambridge University Press.

BERQUE, J. (1957), *Histoire sociale d'un village egyptien au xxème siècle*, Mouton, Paris.

BERREMAN, G. D. (1963), 'Caste and community development', *Human Organization*, vol. 22, no. 5.

BIT (1958), *Les problèmes du travail en Afrique*, Bureau International de Travail, Geneva.

CÉPÈDE, M., and LENGELLÉ, M. (1953), *Économie alimentaire du globe. essai d'interpretation*, Librairie de Médicis, Paris.

DESAI, A. R. (1958), Community development project – a sociological analysis, *Sociological Bulletin*, no. 8, p. 2.

DUMONT, R. (1961), *Terres vivantes*, Plon, Paris.

DUMONT, R. (1962), *L'Afrique noire est mal partie*, Seuil, Paris.

DUPIRE, M. (1960), Planteurs autochtones et étrangers en Basse Côte d'Ivoire', *Études Eburnéennes*, vol. 8, Abidjan.

FAO (1962), *La situation mondiale de l'alimenation et de l'agriculture*, FAO, Rome.

FEI, HSIAO TUNG and CHIH-I CHANG (1948), *Earthbound China: a study of rural economy in Yunnan*, Routledge & Kegan Paul.

GOUROU, P. (1948), *Les pays tropicaux*, PUF, Paris.

HAILEY, L. (1956), *An african survey revised*, London.

HERTZLER, J. O. (1956), *The crisis in world population. A sociological examination with special reference to the underdeveloped areas*, University of Nebraska Press.

HOSELITZ, B. (1964), 'Social stratification and economic development', *J. International Social Science* vol. 16, no. 2, UNESCO.

KAUFMAN, H. F. (1962), 'Rural community development in India', *International Review of Community Development*, no. 9.

KAY, G. (1962), 'Agricultural change in the Lutikila Basin development area. Human problems in British Central Africa, *Rhodes Livingstone J.*, no. 31, June.

KÖTTER, H. (1956), 'Die Gemeinde in der ländlichen Soziologie', *Kölner zeitschrift für soziologie und sozialpsychologie*, Sonderheft 1.

LAMBERT, J. (1960), 'Les obstacles au développement provenant de la formation d'une société dualiste', in: *Resistências à Mudança. Fatôres que impedem ou difficultam o desenvolvimento*, Latin American Center for Research in the Social Sciences, Rio de Janeiro.

LEFEBVRE, H. (1963), *La vallée de Campan, étude de sociologie rurale*, PUF,

LEWIS, O. (1952), 'Urbanization without breakdown; a case study', *Scientific Monthly*, vol. 75.

MOORE, W., and FELDMAN, A. (1960), *Labor Commitment and Social Change in Developing Areas*, Social Science Research Council.

MUKHERJEE, R. (1957), *The dynamics of a Rural Society. A Study of Economic Structure in Bengal Villages*, Akademie Verlag, Berlin.

MYRDAL, G. (1955), *Economic Theory and Underdeveloped Regions*, Duckworth.

RANGNAKAR, D. K. (1958), *Poverty and Capital Development in India*, Oxford University Press.

REDFIELD, R. (1941), *The Folk Culture of Yucatán*, University of Chicago Press.

RETZLAFF, R. H. (1962), *Village Government in India*, Asia Publishing House, Bombay.

STAVENHAGEN, R. (1963), 'Clases, colonialismo y aculturación. Ensayo sobre un sistema de relaciones interétnicas en Mesoamérica', *America Latina*, vol. 6, no. 4.

VELSEN, J. VAN (1960), 'Labor migration as a positive factor in the continuity of Tonga tribal society, *Economic Development and Cultural Change*, vol. 8, no. 3.

WOLF, E. (1957), 'Closed corporate peasant communities in Meso-America and Central Java', *Southwestern J. of Anthropol.*, vol. 13, no. 1.

5 P. Hill

Cocoa-Farming and the Migratory Process in Ghana, 1894–1930[1]

Excerpt from P. Hill, *Migrant Cocoa-Farmers of Southern Ghana: A Study in Rural Capitalism*, Cambridge University Press, 1963, chapter 7, pp. 178–92.

'We travel to go and buy.'

Although the underlying purpose of this whole inquiry was that of obtaining some understanding of *present-day* economic processes and motives, the journey itself proved so interesting that the destination was almost overlooked. Nor, for the time being, can this aberration be remedied with the help of others, for it seems that what actually happened in Ghana was so much at variance with conventional notions of what 'ought' to have happened, that few of the many general works on 'problems of economic underdevelopment' which have been published during the last fifteen years have much practical, as distinct from theoretical, relevance to the present analytical purpose.[2] Economists (other than agricultural economists) *working in the field* in Africa, and there have been few of them so far, have usually regarded trade or distribution (including transport), not production, as their proper concern and few of them have paid more than cursory attention to the rural areas; no such subjects as 'the organization of production of export crops' is presumed by them to exist – it is

1. The steadily expansionary period ended in about 1930, being succeeded firstly by a period of consolidation (in the thirties) and secondly by a vicious circle of contraction resulting from swollen shoot. This chapter in general relates to the expansionary period.

2. In the theoretical field it may be that the ideas of Professor Gunnar Myrdal, especially as expounded in his *Economic Theory and Under-Developed Regions*, could be fruitfully applied, particularly the notion of 'circular cumulative causation'. As noted in Benjamin Higgins (1959) (p. 410), the 'chief problem in attempting a synthesis of theories of under-development is still empirical' – 'we do not need elaborate econometric models before we can explain the behaviour of underdeveloped economies or prescribe policies. But we do need to know what the strategic functional relations are and we need to know their general shapes'. As for the interest of anthropologists in economic aspects of West African society, they, as remarked by Sir Keith Hancock (1942, p. 271), 'have been preoccupied with other matters'.

only *after* the goods have been produced that economic organization is supposed to become interesting.

Why should this be? The twin assumptions that production is usually small-scale[3] and organizationally simple are partly responsible for this neglect. But there has, also, always been a tendency for economists to exaggerate the importance of the role of the expatriate trading firm – and this in a part of the world where trade was already well developed when Europeans first arrived there in the fifteenth century! It has been unconsciously, or implicitly, assumed that it was the expatriate traders who 'taught the natives', if only by example, the elements of the facts of economic life – that the whole nature of the economic response of the indigene was determined by his contact with these 'agents' of colonialism. But present inquiries have shown, on the contrary, that the influence of the trader in the vital first fifteen years, or so, of commercial cocoa-growing was minimal – that he merely sat at (or near) the port receiving the produce and had no more knowledge than any other outsider as to how production was organized. Nor was the Department of Agriculture (in the old days) in much better case.[4]

So as things have turned out, the initial contention that problems of internal collection of export crops are of negligible interest and importance compared with problems of production (for export)[5] has been shown to be even better justified than had been expected. And it is hoped that readers of this chapter will at least agree[6] that such problems of production are as

3. It is, of course, the contention in this book that the statistical picture as a whole is too complex and heterogeneous to be summed up as either small or large scale. As for the migrant farmers, they are apt to stand in varying relations to their various farms and lands, so that the notion of scale of production is fraught with special difficulty.

4. Because the farmers have always been supposed, in a sense, to have been guided by 'instructions' issued to them by others, so they have always been blamed for not following these instructions sufficiently closely. The official literature emanating from the Department of Agriculture during the first quarter of a century was one long wail of complaint about the farmers' inefficiency – partly justified, no doubt, by the very poor quality of the crop.

5. On the other hand, problems of distribution of food for local consumption may, in some areas, be more interesting and important than problems of food production; the organization of the long-distance trade in yams, plantain, *gari* (cassava meal), shallots, kola, salt, etc., is usually far more complex than the arrangements required for the relatively simple operation of collecting export produce for transport to the ports.

6. Despite the tentative nature of the approach adopted in this chapter – which has, accordingly, been arranged as notes classified under headings.

much the province of the economist as they are of the sociologist, the anthropologist or the agronomist.

The essential nature of the migratory process

The essential nature of the migratory process is that it is forward-looking, prospective, provident, prudential – the opposite of hand-to-mouth. Had the farmers, like so many retail traders, simply been concerned to 'get rich quick' and then to go out of business, they would, to use their own terminology, have 'eaten'[7] the proceeds from their early cocoa-farms, rather than re-investing them in other lands. Almost from the beginning, the farmers regarded themselves as involved in an expansionary process from which they had no intention of withdrawing. Almost from the beginning, cocoa-farms established on purchased land were regarded as investments – i.e. property which existed for the purpose of giving rise to further property. The farmers found no difficulty in handling the practical notion of putting money to work – of loosing it out to multiply itself. It is quite erroneous to suppose, as some have done, that the process is merely a sophisticated variant of shifting cultivation; had this been so, the farmers would have tended to lose interest in their earlier-acquired lands – whereas there is plenty of evidence that they often remained more attached to their earlier than to their later acquisitions. Nor has there ever been any tendency for farmers to complete the planting of one land before proceeding to the cultivation of another. The pace of land acquisition was so rapid in the early days that it is perhaps reasonable to assume that, at that time, the farmers allowed themselves little scope for investment other than in land. They regarded their initial capital as a fund to be employed within the business only – this being a familiar notion to women traders and others. The Twi noun *dwetiri* is defined, by Christaller (1933), as 'a capital or stock of money to begin trade with; a fund employed in business or any undertaking; principal'.[8]

Why so expansionary?

It is hard to disentangle the various motives. Certainly the expansionary process soon became desirable for its own sake – it was creative, adventurous and all-absorbing. It has been noted that many Akwapim men had highly expansible sets of wants

7. One of the manifold meanings of the Twi verb *di* is 'eat'.
8. *Dwetiwani* is carefully, and interestingly, defined as: 'a possessor of some little property, not exactly rich, but on the way to become so'.

when the process first began, being aware, through education, trade, the exercise of craftsmanship in distant places and work as labourers, of conditions elsewhere in the world. The need to secure the future was involved with the idea, so reasonable in Africa, that there is no resting-place between stagnation and growth: a business cannot be healthy unless it is expanding. On the one hand there is a desire, which took particularly strong expression with the matrilineal Aburi, to create lineage (or family) lands for the support of the lineage in general; on the other hand, much of the farmers' restlessness is to be explained as a resistance to the drift towards family property – as a desire to exert personal control over a new land.[9] Although the form of organization adopted by the patrilineal farmers was streamlined compared with the amorphous family lands of the Aburi and Akropong farmers, the results were not so different, in terms of numbers of lands acquired and so on, as might have been expected, and in this general discussion there is no need to distinguish the two types of organization.

Cocoa takes a long time, fifteen years or more, to come into full bearing and the farmers have never had any difficulty in taking an appropriately long view. The Akwapim were not as preoccupied as the Akim or the Ashanti with the glories of their past, and were thus, perhaps, more inclined to build for the future. It is because the farmers were prepared to take their time (and held as rigid a view as many old-fashioned capitalists or communists as to the wastefulness of consumption expenditure) that the pace of the expansion during the first few decades was so fast and regular. The Akwapim surveys show that the process seldom petered out, except in a few towns such as Tutu,[10] and that most farmers (or their forebears) had purchased more than two lands. As most farmers seem to have dispensed with working capital, there was little danger (certainly insufficient to match the uniformed apprehensions of successive governments of the Gold Coast, especially around 1914 when the migration was in full flood) of the farmers finding themselves unable to maintain their older farms (their past investments) as the pace of expansion increased. These past investments were financially self-sustaining provided (as was nearly always the case except in time of war)

9. '. . . the wish to possess some object over which they might enjoy an individual and undisputed control . . .' (Rattray, 1929, vol. 3, p. 33).

10. A town which became financially exhausted by litigation.

the price received by the farmer for his cocoa exceeded costs of transport to the buying agents by a small margin.[11]

A migration which involved everybody

The expansionary process was much encouraged by the fact that, after a short initial hesitation in the 1890s, it tended to involve all the inhabitants of the main Akwapim towns. Not that it was centrally organized; it was rather a contagious enthusiasm for private enterprise. As it was everyone's aspiration to participate, so there was no question of men being motivated by a desire to free themselves from their rapacious kin[12] – in practical (not legal) terms the new lands were considered as an extension of the homeland, and there was no idea of leaving home for good. Those, like chiefs and other office-holders, who were obliged to remain at home most of the time, participated with the help of their relatives and there was never any risk of the home towns becoming totally depopulated, though they must have lost a good deal of their vitality, if not their viability, especially in the earliest days when it was not so much the practice as it is today to send the children home to school. In a town like Larteh-Ahenease it would be difficult today to find anyone (other than a stranger) whose forebears failed to participate in the migration half a century or more ago. This universal participation reflects a sort of classlessness: there are rich people and there are poor people, but none who suffer from a social inferiority preventing them from migrating. Although rich and poor alike joined companies, they were primarily devices for assisting small men to migrate – farmers who could subscribe at most £5 or £10 towards the purchase of a piece of land. The fact that in the early days the richer inhabitants were often prepared to help their poorer kinsmen and neighbours to buy land through companies, by lending them money, sometimes on the security of pawns, is another aspect of the willingness to wait for a return on money – though it was even truer then than it is today that a condition of indebtedness was apt to reflect a pre-existing personal relationship between the two parties, there

11. Labourers, like farmers, are capable of waiting and of taking a long view. If as a result of a fall in the price of cocoa their remuneration per load was much reduced, they would neither run away nor stop plucking. Their interest in future cocoa-farming prospects, their work in establishing new farms and their own food-farming activities, tended to stabilize them.

12. This common quasi-myth is better expressed the other way round: that those who migrate and make money are partly motivated by their wish to help their less enterprising or indigent kin, who therefore urge them on.

being no concept of large-scale philanthropy in the Akwapim towns. Then there were the rich men, like Akogyram of Mamfe, who were guided by commercial (or speculative) considerations – but who yet resold land (sometimes on 'hire-purchase terms') to their fellow-townsmen only. Soon after 1900 it had become shameful, in some of the larger Akwapim towns, not to have bought a land: 'people were laughing because we were so late', said a Mampong farmer, in 1960, who had failed to buy land before about 1902. If a man 'ordered' a piece of land through a company and later found that he lacked the cash to pay for it, the company would be able to dispose of his portion to someone else – and for this and other reasons the company leader could regard his members as a group of shareholders, among whom the risks could be spread.

The land-seller's willingness to take payment in instalments

If the capitalistic process is to develop satisfactorily, each of the various parties involved must be prepared to wait. The farmers were prepared to wait for a return on the sums they invested in land-purchase and the process of reinvestment in another land was dependent on their willingness to go on waiting. But given the farmer's poverty, this would not have been sufficient to ensure the establishment of a rapid process of expansion, involving everybody in the home towns, had it not been that the land-sellers, also, were prepared to exercise patience, so that land could, in part, be paid for from its own proceeds. Historically regarded, it is rather misleading to express the matter thus. Originally the Akim land-sellers were not so much tolerant of the fact that the eagerness of the Akwapim farmers outdid their financial capacities as they were themselves eager to collect such windfalls as occurred, whatever the accompanying conditions. There was no competitive market for land and indeed from the land-sellers' point of view there was something to be said for a system which assured them a future income (rather than 100 per cent down-payment) – provided, of course, they could depend on the farmers to pay up. The strength of the land-sellers' position, in the early stages, was dependent on the fact that there were so few of them: the farmers were concerned to remain in friendly commercial relationship with them, against the day that they might be returning to ask for some more land. The introduction of the company system coincided with the creation of a market in land in the areas concerned, and there may have been a time, between about 1906 and 1918, when the interval between purchase and full payment was much reduced. Later on, as the farmers came to own more and more unplanted lands, as everyone tended to migrate by company and as (owing to improved transport facilities) the number of land-sellers greatly increased, the interval between purchase and payment tended to lengthen again – so that the willingness of the land-sellers to wait for payment was again an institutional factor of the greatest significance.

Land as a savings bank

'Our money doesn't stay: we buy different lands with it.'

Land has two main aspects: it is both a necessary factor of production and a savings bank. That it is a savings bank in a literal sense is suggested by figures which show that the greater prosperity of the farmers consequent upon a higher cocoa-price was *instantly reflected in increased purchases of land*. The sensitive growing-point of the economy is here displayed. It could not be supposed, given the amount of unplanted land the farmers already possessed, that they had any intention of planting these newly-acquired lands in the immediately foreseeable future. But the money was not necessarily locked up in the savings bank, for fortunately there existed (see below) a class of financier- or creditor-farmer who specialized in buying second-hand lands, or farms, from farmers who chose, or were obliged, to resell. In a part of the world where for climatic reasons most non-precious material objects developed since the stone axehead are apt to 'spoil',[13] the great merit of land is that, as farmers put it, it 'lies down' – sleeping peacefully, not wasting away.

It is true that land is often lost or mislaid (it is sometimes spoken of as 'going astray'), if it happens that the leader dies and none of his surviving associates is known to the land-vendor – or if the survivors simply do not know where the land is situated. Then there are all the well-known risks of litigation. But that the farmers' reliance on the 'keeping qualities' of land is, on the whole, well founded is shown by the frequency with which it happens that land is first cultivated a quarter of a century or more after its first acquisition. Farmers who hold long strings of

13. The fatalistic connotation of this much-used, poignant word has to do with man's inability to withstand or understand the inevitable process of destruction and decay – especially, nowadays, in relation to complex objects like lorries. The nearest Twi equivalents are *see* and *hwere*, each of which also means 'spend'.

never-planted lands are seldom wistful about the waste of money involved, though there may be an element of injured pride which they do not care to reveal. Of course they are apt to go on hoping beyond hope that one day their financial and family circumstances will permit them to plant the forest lands; and then, sometimes, they are able to obtain some return by selling timber or other produce from land which is useless for cocoa.

Paradoxically, land-purchase is a form of 'conspicuous expenditure', as well as a form of investment, for although the land may be situated in a distant place and may never have been seen by the purchaser, nonetheless his fellow-townsmen, the people whose esteem matters most to him, will have been his associates and will be familiar with his land-purchasing activities. And if the notion of the land itself as a savings bank seems strained, then the reader may prefer to regard the company as a form of savings club – a club which invests its resources in land.

The farmers' attitude to land as a safe depository is, of course, bound up with their attitude to money.[14] While farmers are very frank about most of their farming affairs, and have no objection whatever to talking about land-purchase, their reticence over money, as such, is profound, as all social investigators in West Africa are aware. It is not sufficient to note, in this connection, that in western society it is very improper to ask people about their monetary affairs, for in West African rural society fears on this subject run deeper, making it almost impossible to discuss such practical questions as where farmers in general, not the informant in particular, keep their money, whether in tin trunk, under mattress, in bank, etc. However questions may be phrased, they always seem to have some kind of personal connotation, usually affecting third parties; and so great is the reluctance to contemplate money, as such, that questions about where it is deposited are invariably answered in terms of the use to which it is put.[15] Much of this reticence is, presumably, bound up with fear of theft – and fear drives the farmers to invest in land. If a

14. And with the rigid distinction they make between 'capital' and 'spending money', the former being invested in land. In *Ashanti Law and Constitution* Rattray (1929) describes the public accounting system of former times and mentions (p. 117,) a large chest in which no sum less than a *pereguan* (about £8) was deposited, lesser sums being accumulated in another box: he actually refers to the large chest as a kind of 'capital account'.

15. Cocoa-farmers are, of course, obliged to hold cash to finance their day-to-day purchases during the off-season.

man has a bank account or owns a safe, he may say so (he may even untruthfully boast about the former); but most other depositories are very unsafe – farmers are much given to padlocking the doors of their rooms, forgetting that their windows may be flimsy, their roofs vulnerable.

There are many reasons, apart from the virtual lack of banks in rural areas until quite recently, why many of the migrant farmers have an aversion to banking money. Basically, perhaps, these can be summed up by saying that they feel that there is an equivalence between banking money and handing it over to 'the government' – so generalized a concept that the type of government needs no specification. In more practical terms, farmers may be embarrassed by the need to trust mediators, or clerks, with whom they are unfamiliar. Then, there is a belief that those who bank money are automatically obliged to pay income tax.[16] And finally, of course, the rate of interest offered on deposit accounts seems paltry.

Apart from the matter of safe custody, there are other objections to holding cash as such, one of which relates to the farmer's fear of what might happen after his death. There is the risk that some unauthorized member of the family might lay hands on the money, and the difficulty of expressing intentions clearly, when dealing in terms of a medium so slippery and elusive as notes and coin, is obvious enough. A man may say: 'half of this land is intended for the use of my sons and half for the members of my *abusua*' – and his wishes are much more likely to be put into effect than if money for the purchase of the land were found in a tin trunk after his death.

Farmers also buy land for persuasive reasons – as an encouragement to their sons and nephews to go and work there. Lacking the vigour of the younger generation, they are anxious that their money should work harder, multiply itself more rapidly, than if it remained with them. Sometimes a trustworthy son is given money to buy land for himself – 'My father gave me money to come and buy.' More often the father himself buys land on behalf of his son. As a Mampong farmer put it in 1960: 'It is

16. The question of the farmers' liability to income tax has never been properly examined – in recent years they have been taxed so heavily through the export duty that they have been implicitly (though no explicitly) regarded as not liable to pay income tax, unless they also derive income from other sources. The problem of determining net cocoa-income, after deduction of labour and other expenses, would present almost insuperable difficulties at present.

usual when a farmer buys a piece of land somewhere and starts to till it, he thinks of his children in the future and so with the proceeds he purchases other lands. And usually he divides the unplanted land between his children while he is alive and encourages them to work there.'

Finally, there are traditional values, apart from 'rational considerations', which require emphasis. Land is to the agrarian Akan what cattle are to East African pastoralists.

The managerial function

The analogy with industrial capitalism proceeds farther. Not only is the cocoa-farm a long-term investment and the business inherently expansionary, but the farmer is a manager, one of whose functions is to oversee the work on all his various plantations, to some extent co-ordinating the activities on them. Although farmers with long 'land-sequences' spend much of their time travelling between their lands, there is no real problem of absenteeism, for whether or not labourers are employed (see below) it is usual for a relative or wife to be left in charge at each place. That the managerial work is full-time and specialized is shown by the fact that it cannot usually be satisfactorily combined with another time-absorbing occupation; the many teachers who, around 1900, abandoned their ill-paid profession for cocoa-farming did not later return to teaching; ministers of the church were pioneer farmers, but they put their profession first and seldom bought long sequences of land; many well-to-do Aburi families include one brother who is a farm-manager and another who is a produce-buyer, and if it turns out that the latter is their uncle's successor the former will continue in effective charge of the farms.

The large Akwapim creditor-farmer

Most creditor-farmers in Ghana are 'average' farmers[17] and it happens that most debtor-farmers are in like position. But some of the most famous of Ghana's migrant farmers have been large

17. See (Hill, 1956, chapters 5 to 7), for a general discussion of the pledging of cocoa-farms. In general, creditor-farmers are not a class apart – and there are nearly as many creditor-farmers as debtor-farmers (farmers who have pledged their farms). Nor are debtor-farmers a special class either, for, contrary to general belief, it is not so much the most poverty-stricken farmers who pledge their farms, as those whose security is reasonably good – farmers who will continue to live on their unpledged farms and thus not embarrass their creditors.

Akwapim (or Ga) creditor-farmers (or farmer-financiers), who have assisted a great many other farmers by buying, or otherwise acquiring, rights over their land or farms. Such financiers sometimes spend much of their time at home, conducting their operations from, as it were, the City of London – the Akwapim ridge; more often they play the mixed role of farm-manager and financier. As farmers they are peculiar: it is not only that they acquire many second-hand lands, but that they have a real aversion to joining companies which are too staid, cumbersome and slow-moving for their purposes. Like financiers the world over, they are volatile and ruthless and can be very helpful on occasions. They acquire their second-hand properties in a variety of ways, by private purchase, at auctions and by pledge – they take advantage of the fact that (unknown to their families) debtors often have no intention of redeeming their pledged farms. They are even more given than other farmers to the *instantaneous* investment of cash-in-hand in farm or land. During their lifetimes they sometimes appear to behave as though they had largely freed themselves from the 'family system', and this individualism, when combined with the fact that they are no more inclined than other farmers to draw up written wills, sometimes brings about financial chaos following their deaths, especially as (the social attitude to them being highly ambivalent) their debtors are apt to seize the opportunity of reclaiming their unredeemed farms, leaving the bereft female relatives in the home town to bewail their fate.[18] But if a large farmer-creditor has been sufficiently willing to delegate responsibility to his relatives on his various lands, then on his death it may turn out that he has been the founder of a great inheritance.

The employment of labourers[19]

Labour employment is *not* the crux of the matter: many capitalist farmers who, over the generations, have been accustomed to invest their surpluses in the expansion of their businesses, have never employed labourers. Many Krobo, Shai and Ga farmers,[20] in particular, continue to this day to pride themselves on their

18. They are often miserably embarrassed by their inability to maintain their large house – their situation has greatly worsened as a result of swollen shoot.

19. See the chapters on cocoa-labourers in Hill (1956).

20. Dr J. M. Hunter points out that these are the traditional hoe-farmers – in comparison to whom the cutlass-wielding Akwapim (and Akim) seem like mere amateurs.

reliance on help given by their wives and kin. (Nor is the distinction between relatives and labourers necessarily hard and fast, as sons and other relatives are sometimes, for instance, employed on an *abusa* basis to pluck cocoa.) But although nearly all Akwapim farmers who own large farms, of, say, twenty acres or more, employ labourers (sometimes a great many of them) and although many quite small farmers do likewise (an element of prestige being involved), it is important to note that systematic large-scale employment of farm labourers marked the second, not the first, stage of the developing capitalistic process. Certainly the pace of expansion would have been much slower had the Akwapim not been determined to employ many labourers during this second stage, which may be regarded as starting around 1900, and had a plentiful supply of non-Akwapim labourers not been forthcoming; certainly, also, cocoa-carriers, as distinct from farm labourers, had been essential from the earliest times – they were relatives as well as non-relatives, women as well as men. But the point under emphasis is that the launching of the migration depended mainly on the farmers' personal efforts and was not associated with the development of new, or large-scale, systems of farm-labour employment.

It is a general rule, to which there are exceptions, that migrant farmers are reluctant to 'waste their savings' on the employment of labour. This important point of principle is unrelated to the fact that in the early days the ordinary Akwapim farmer spent all that he had on the purchase of land and on unavoidable items such as seed-pods. During the first stage of the migration the farmer depended on family labour and his cash outlay on day-to-day operations was possibly negligible. Food- and cocoa-farming have always been intimately related activities. Newly planted land might first be planted with food crops and then, a little later, with cocoa. The cover crops, plantain and cocoyam, provided basic carbohydrates for the farmer and his dependants and sometimes, also, a saleable surplus. As for protein, the forests were then much better stocked with game and edible snails than they are today – and, presumably, the streams with fish. The earliest-acquired lands were not far away from the homeland – where food was grown on much the same scale as formerly, the women continuing to be responsible for most of the work. Nor is there any evidence that sales of palm produce were reduced. So while waiting for their first cocoa-plantings to come into bearing, the farmer and his family were presented with no unusual maintenance problems.

The second stage in the developing capitalistic process was reached when the farmer had successfully established a sufficient area of bearing cocoa *to support a labourer from its proceeds*. On his first employment the labourer might be entitled to 'use' all the cocoa he plucked from the young farm on condition that he assisted the farmer in establishing new cocoa-farms – which, later on, he would have a right to harvest. As the yield of this original farm increased, the proportion of the crop to which he was entitled fell to one-third – the traditional *abusa* share. Later on still, perhaps seven to ten years after his first employment, he might (especially if he had not been concerned with the original establishment of the farm in question) be transferred to an *nkotokuano* basis, receiving a certain sum of money for each load of cocoa he plucked, a sum always less than one third of the value of the cocoa. The labourer who harvested the cocoa was always paid, on a piece-work basis, *from the proceeds of the farm at the time of the sale of the produce* – the farmer thus avoiding the use of working capital. Although a farmer who employed labourers was free, as a consequence, to devote more time to 'management' and could more quickly develop his newly acquired lands farther west, he would not himself stop working on the land, though certain tasks, such as plucking and weeding, tended to devolve more and more on labourers as time went by.

While an active farmer with many willing relatives and enough land might have been able to pass from the first to the second stages in no more than five to seven years (for Amelonado cocoa yielded rapidly on the rich virgin soils of the old days), many farmers advanced more slowly, perhaps not attaining the second stage until a quarter of a century after they had first started buying land.

As time went by and the labour force became more settled and permanent, especially on the larger lands, a new form of family labour largely superseded the old one, this consisting of the wives and children of the labourers. With the aid of a large family a single labourer might handle up to a hundred loads of cocoa in a season. But as it cost the farmer no more to employ additional 'plucking labourers', and as supplies of labour were always plentiful, there was a tendency for more labour to be employed than was strictly necessary – except perhaps during the weeding season.

So much for these 'plucking labourers'. Annual labourers, who were never traditionally employed on plucking, but rather on work on new farms, are a different case. Unlike the *abusa* or *nkotokuano* men (who are in some ways best thought of as pseudo-farmers), they are employees proper, on the western model, whose remuneration depends on time (not effort), who work regular hours, who never bring their dependants with them, and who generally undertake all the tasks allotted to them by their master. As such labourers have to be fully maintained during their period of employment and provided with working clothes, tools and all their requirements, including money for meat and fish if meals are not prepared for them, they are not only very costly compared with other types of labourer, but are liable to involve the farmer in making cash outlays at times other than the main-crop season. It is the mark of an efficient farmer to aspire to employ such labourers, for only those with an unusual degree of progressiveness in their outlook can overcome the conventional reluctance to employ working capital in this way. But perhaps, though there is no evidence of this, the timing of the engagement of these labourers (who are sometimes employed for six months, rather than a year – but never for more than a year) is sometimes planned so that their wage (which is payable at the end of their period of employment) falls due during the main-crop season, when the farmer has cash on hand.

As for the other two types of farm labourer, the contract labourer (who is paid an agreed sum for clearing, weeding, etc., a certain area) and the daily labourer (who is paid for a day's work), it is seldom necessary for farmers to draw on their savings for their remuneration, though, again, unusually progressive farmers may overstep their reluctance and employ gangs of daily labourers when they want to get a job done quickly. The contract labourer is free to take his time over his task and the farmer, likewise, feels free to pay for the job when it suits his convenience.

In the earliest days, up to about 1910, the ranks of labourer included many aspirant farmers – Shai, Anum/Boso, and others who lacked the finance to buy land. They were enthusiastic and their ambition to save enough money to buy a land of their own was early fulfilled. Thereafter the southern labourers were drawn from farther afield – they were mainly Ewe, not northerners. Few of these labourers have evolved into farmers (though there are some interesting exceptions) – a fact which provides yet another reason, if such be needed, for viewing the migratory process historically.

Other permitted (or enjoined) forms of investment

Apart from land, what other forms of investment have the farmers customarily permitted themselves? The present concern is with tangible forms of investment only: the chief intangible forms include expenditure on funerals and celebrations generally, on sickness and death and on other 'family calamity'.[21] The tangible forms of investment include: house-building in the home town; educational expenditure; the building of houses for letting in Accra, Koforidua, etc.; cocoa- and other produce-buying – no longer of much importance; lorry ownership and operation. The last two of these, produce-buying and transport, were the only common forms of *economic enterprise* which sprang directly from cocoa-farming: especially in the early days, trading profits were an important source of capital for cocoa-farming, but never *vice-versa*.[22]

The houses in the home town are self-made memorials, expressions of civic pride,[23] useful residences (for schoolchildren, indigent relatives, retirement, visits, etc.). Normally they are non income-yielding and unsaleable assets. Usually, though not always, they are built 'in instalments', as the money for the building materials becomes available, and many of them, especially in Larteh, are never completed, a state of affairs only partially

21. Traditional-style celebratory expenditure is regarded with such condescension by outsiders that the fact that it is sufficiently long-term in intention to qualify as 'investment' is overlooked. See *The Gold Coast Cocoa Farmer*, p. 78, for mention of some of the forms of family calamity (including 'inherited indebted uncle') which can only be made good by substantial outlay, analogous (if not equivalent) to investment.

22. This observation is confirmed by Mr P. Garlick's work in other parts of Ghana. Trading is commonly regarded as a form of 'gambling' – understandably, for trading businesses are not assets like cocoa-farms, and 'goodwill' is not saleable. The Kwahu are among the best-known Ghana traders, but even with them a business seldom outlives its founder, it being each young man's ambition to set up his own concern; there is thus no counterpart to the family land. The term 'trading' in this context refers to men traders in non-foodstuffs, most of which goods are in fact imported. There is no close financial link between migrant cocoa-farming and food wholesaling as those of the food wholesalers who are not women are nearly all northerners or non-Ghanaians.

23. 'It is the houses which show strangers a town' – a reflection of an old Akwapim resident, reported by Mr D. Brokensha.

explainable in terms of swollen shoot.[24] They are memorials not only to the farmer who built (i.e. paid for) them, but also to the far-away cocoa-land which provided their economic foundation. But as such they have drawbacks. They lack that especial quality which so commends land to the farmers as a form of investment – the quality of 'lying down' and waiting: these houses require far too much maintenance, especially in times of swollen shoot.

The prestige which an Akwapim man derives from massive, sometimes ostentatious, educational expenditure is analogous to that obtained from building a colossal house. The results have been very impressive. Just as remarkable are the modest efforts of impecunious farmers to provide their sons and daughters with a good start in life. Like expatriates in West Africa, they prefer to send their children (other than the smallest) 'home' to school. A recent count made in Larteh, by Mr D. Brokensha, showed that 1100 (out of 1917) schoolchildren came from 'abroad' and were boarding with relatives or at school – and the number would have been much higher had it not been for the poverty resulting from swollen shoot.

Such are the rents commanded by decent residential accommodation in the main commercial centres, especially Accra, that the farmers have naturally been eager to invest their swollen-shoot 'compensation' in houses for letting. This is something 'separate' from cocoa-farming. As of old, the farmers are replanting their devastated farms with their own labour and are not looking for 'outside' funds for this purpose.

The nature of the financial interplay between migrant cocoa-farming, produce-buying and lorry ownership has not, as yet, been investigated. Profits from cocoa-farming were invested in the equipment required for these enterprises, in sheds, tarpaulins, scales, lorries – as well as in the mortgage deeds (or cash) required as security by the expatriate buying firms. But whether the profits

24. The never-to-be-completed house is a distressing and common feature of the West African urban scene – one which has never been examined in economic terms. Among its 'causes' are: over-impetuous investment in building materials as the cash becomes available (this corresponding with over-impetuous land-purchase by some farmers); theft and decay of these materials on the site; the death of the owner and lack of interest or poverty of his successors; unforeseen calamity; the failure to keep pace with dilapidation; migration; the belief that it will never be too late; dishonest contractors; superstitions about death following completion. It may be, also, that goodwill can be engendered by the very act of 'trying' to build a house.

from produce-buying and transport were often put back into land is not clear. In the 1930s nearly all the produce-buyers were effectively employees of the expatriate buying firms[25] (the slump of 1920 and the great depression having dealt mortal blows to most indigenous businesses); it yet remains to record, before it is too late, the history of cocoa-buying associations such as the Eastern Planters' Association (said to have been founded in 1907 by Akwapim, Krobo and Shai farmers) and the Larteh Planters' Union (founded about 1908), as well as of countless cocoa-buying firms set up by individual farmers such as Elisha Tette of Larteh and John Ayew of Mampong.

That the migration remains a migration after three generations – that the farmers are migrants not emigrants – is best illustrated by the contrast between the houses in the home towns and the farming areas. The scale of house-building in the home town – the number of separate residences, their size, quality and ornateness – is a faithful reflection of the former wealth of the farmer who built them. In the farming areas (though this is not altogether true of a town like Suhum) everyone lives in the same simple style: there is no visible means of distinguishing rich and poor – by residence, or by dress. Certainly most of the houses have galvanized iron roofs, wooden window frames[26] and sturdy (padlocked) doors and many of the compounds are, or were, cemented. They are reasonably weatherproof dwellings – which is the main intention, for no one goes indoors unless it is raining or bed-time. Certainly, also, some of the houses have many rooms: near Asikasu there is a barrack-like Krobo compound of over forty rooms, which is always called 'Police Station'. But the number of rooms merely reflects the number of people who are apt to be resident there, and this bears little relationship to the farmer's wealth. Possessions, also, apart from clothing, tin trunks and cooking pots, are cut down to an absolute minimum. And although, nowadays, the farmer may aspire to own a bed and mosquito net, the atmosphere of the camp continues to prevail.

25. See The Nowell Report, cmd 5845, 1938.
26. The present writer had the pleasure of conducting Professor I. I. Potekhin, of the Moscow Academy of Sciences, to the Nankese area in 1957 and of witnessing his delighted surprise over the high standard of housing enjoyed by certain Shai farmers there. He had not expected peasant farmers to have window frames – but then, as he later agreed, they are not peasants.

References

CHRISTALLER, J. G. (1933), *A Dictionary of the Asante and Fante Language called Tshi (Twi)*, Basel Evangelical Missionary Society, 1st edn. 1881.

GARLICK, P. C. (1959), *African Traders in Kumasi*, University of Ghana (cyclostyled).

HANCOCK, W. K. (1942), *Survey of British Commonwealth Affairs*, vol. 2, part 2, Oxford University Press.

HIGGINS, B. (1959), *Economic Development*, Constable.

HILL, P. (1956), *The Gold Coast Cocoa Farmers*,

NOWELL REPORT (1938), *Report of the Commission on the Marketing of West African Cocoa*, cmnd 5845, HMSO.

RATTRAY, R. S. (1929), *Ashanti Law and Constitution*, Oxford University Press.

6 G. L. Beckford

The Economics of Agricultural Resource Use and Development in Plantation Economies[1]

G. L. Beckford, 'The economics of agricultural resource use and development in plantation economies', *Social and Economic Studies*, Jamaica, 1969, vol. 18, pp. 321–47.

Plantation agriculture has been generally ignored in the rapidly expanding literature on underdeveloped agriculture.[2] To a large extent this reflects a view that plantation agriculture is 'efficient' and 'modern'; that it is particularly suited to certain tropical crops; that the plantation system has served to bring previously isolated areas into the modern world economy; and that large-scale plantation units make possible 'economies of operation by the use of labour-saving machinery'.[3]

More recently, a few development economists have drawn attention to the fact that differences in factor combinations, production technology, etc., among export industries lead to differences in patterns of growth among export economies. And in this connection, the plantation system of resource organization has received some attention.[4]

So far the most important contributions to the study of plantations have come from the sociologists and social anthropologists. The study of Puerto Rico by Steward *et al.* (1956) is an out-

1. This is a revised version of a paper presented in April 1969 to a staff–student seminar at Cornell University. It is a preliminary statement from a larger on-going study of the economics of plantation agriculture. The ideas presented here have been developed as part of teaching material on the economics of underdeveloped agriculture over several years and I have benefited from comments by numerous students during that period. The present version of the paper has had the advantage of comments from several colleagues at the UWI, who were kind enough to read the earlier draft. Havelock Brewster, Wendell McLean, Lloyd Best, A. W. Singham, B. Persaud and David Edwards were particularly helpful. Mrs. Ruth Rawlins of the Central Statistical Office, Trinidad, also provided very useful comments and information. I have chosen to reserve some of the points made by colleagues for incorporation in the larger study and must assume full responsibility for doing so and for any errors that appear in this presentation.

2. The overwhelming concern has been with 'peasant' or 'traditional' or 'subsistence' agriculture.

3. See, for example, Wickizer (1958a).

4. See, for example, Baldwin (1956 and 1963).

standing example of this pioneering work and a number of subsequent symposia on the Caribbean have focused on 'plantation society as a sociohistorical determinant of contemporary subcultures'.[5] These studies have provided very useful insights for understanding the internal dynamics of plantation societies. But they emphasize the need for similar work on the economic relations, organization and institutions that characterize the plantation system.[6]

This paper is an initial attempt to fill the existing gap. But the gap is so wide that it would be impossible to bridge it fully in an article. Consequently, attention is directed to one type of plantation – the modern multi-national corporate enterprise. This is perhaps the most important type in present-day underdeveloped countries and the economics of this type of farm-firm has hardly been explored. As the title states, the concern is with economic aspects, though it is obvious that sociological and political variables would need to be considered in a fuller treatment.

The discussion begins with an examination of the characteristics of plantation agriculture: how it developed, where it exists, and what factors distinguish it from other types of agriculture. Detailed consideration of the internal organization of modern plantation enterprises provides the background for subsequent analysis of the economics of production and resource use. This represents a re-examination of the view that plantation agriculture is 'efficient'. The concern in this paper is not with efficiency of the firm but with efficiency of resource use in the agricultural sectors of countries in which these enterprises operate.

The final part of the exercise is to assess the development potential of plantation agriculture. It is not sufficient merely to state that the plantation system brought backward and isolated areas into the modern world economy. The important question is whether the system makes it possible for these economies to achieve structural transformation and a self-sustaining pattern of growth and development.

Characteristics of plantation agriculture

The word 'plantation' has fallen into such common use that it denotes different things to different people. Generally speaking,

5. See Pan American Union (1959) and Rubin (1957).
6. For an interesting and pioneering effort in examining the social organization of the plantation, see Wolf and Mintz (1957).

it is considered to refer to a large farming unit. However, as the discussion below indicates, this is an inadequate description.

Plantation production

According to Jones (1968),

a plantation is an economic unit producing agricultural commodities (field crops or horticultural products, but not livestock) for sale and employing a relatively large number of unskilled labourers whose activities are closely supervised. Plantations usually employ a year-round labour crew of some size, and they usually specialize in the production of only one or two marketable products. *They differ from other kinds of farms in the way in which the factors of production, primarily management and labour, are combined* (p. 154).[7]

Production on plantations is undertaken not just 'for sale', as indicated above, but specifically for sale in overseas markets (export sale).[8] The special factor combination that distinguishes plantation production from other kinds of farms is the bringing together of as many unskilled farm labourers as possible with each of the few highly skilled supervisor-managers who direct production. As Jones puts it, 'the plantation substitutes supervision – supervisory and administrative skills – for skilled, adaptive labour, combining the supervision with labour whose principal skill is to follow orders' (p. 156).

Two other aspects of plantation production deserve mention here although they are considered in more detail below. They are (a) foreign ownership, usually by a corporate enterprise; and (b) a 'relatively high degree of vertical integration, even of self-sufficiency' – i.e. the plantation enterprise supplies inputs for its agricultural operations and processing and marketing facilities for its agricultural output.

Plantations are mainly involved in the production of certain tropical crops – mainly tree crops and other perennials. Sugar, bananas, tea, rubber and coffee are the main commodities involved. It has frequently been suggested that the 'complementarity between agricultural processing plants and farm-producing units has been one consideration in the establishment of plantations. Many of the major tropical export crops must undergo

7. My emphasis.
8. Wolf and Mintz (1957), for example, emphasize this point as one of the characteristics that differentiate the plantation from the hacienda as systems of agricultural organization.

preliminary processing shortly after harvesting...' (Jones, 1968, p. 156). [9]

However, the association of plantation production with certain tropical crops cannot be explained in such narrow technical terms. It must be seen in the larger context of the way in which these commodities were introduced into the international economy.

The plantation system

Plantation agriculture is the outgrowth of the political colonization of tropical areas by the metropolitan countries of Europe. Temperate areas which had been colonized by Europe – e.g. the United States, Canada, Australia, New Zealand, Argentina, Chile, etc. – involved the movement of people. Those areas developed as 'colonies of settlement' and the pattern of agriculture that emerged was significantly different from that in the tropical colonies where mainly capital and enterprise were involved in the movement from the metropole to produce 'colonies of exploitation'.

As Greaves (1959) has pointed out, 'one of the outstanding characteristics of the plantation is that it has brought together enterprise, capital and labour from different parts of the world in an area which offered opportunity for new and increased production' (p. 13). Enterprise and capital came from the metropole which was usually, though not always, the centre of direct political control. Labour was brought mainly from other tropical areas. With the possible exception of Java, plantations were originally established in sparsely populated areas. And because of the shortage of labour in these areas, the plantation system depended on large-scale (involuntary and voluntary) movement of labour from other tropical areas. Slavery and then indenture provided labour supplies for the establishment and development of plantations in the New World. Chinese, Japanese and Filipino labourers were brought to develop Hawaii's sugar plantations; the rubber plantations of Malaya and Sumatra drew most of their workers from China, Java and India; and so on. In the New World, even after slavery and indenture, 'new' plantation economies drew labour supplies from 'mature' plantation economies. [10]; 'Thus the plantation came to be asso-

9. See also Wickizer (1960 and 1958b).

10. For an interesting historical analysis of the development of New World plantation economies, see Best (1968).

ciated not only with a resident labour force, but more often than not with one of alien origin' (Greaves, 1959, p. 15).

Perhaps the most important consideration for present purposes is the international dimension of the plantation system. As Greaves puts it:

Historically and economically the plantation system is fundamentally international in character. Wherever it is found it derives from external stimulus and enterprise; it has always depended on external markets; and it is still largely involved in external finance. Because of this character the plantation has been associated with most political and international developments of modern times; mercantilism and free trade; slavery and independence; capitalism and imperialism ... (p. 14).

Further, we are warned that 'although we are apt to speak of a "plantation economy" as though it were in itself a complete and separate economy, *plantations are in practice only a special part of a much wider economic system with a financial and industrial centre usually in a region remote from the plantations.* The extent to which this part of the system is dependent upon the center is determined by how far the latter controls it; control can take two forms, property ownership, and political connections which affect such matters as prices, tariffs and loan funds' (p. 15).[11] Thus, for example, nineteenth century British economists rightly described the West Indies as 'a place "where England finds it convenient to carry on the production of sugar, coffee, and a few other tropical commodities", and the trade between them was similar to the town and country trade at home' (p. 16).[12]

These characteristics apply as much today as in earlier historical periods. Even where *direct* metropolitan political control is absent, property ownership and indirect political connections still control the pattern of resource allocation and production in countries where plantations are located today. Indeed, even in the absence of property ownership, control from the centre (metropolis) may result from economic connections; for example, financial control through the banking system or the specificity of the raw material export to metropolitan refining capacity.[13] These characteristics of metropolitan control are evident in the case of the politically independent banana republics of Central

11. My emphasis.
12. The reference in this quotation from Greaves is to John Stuart Mill.
13. The latter example is given further consideration in a subsequent section of this paper. On the former, see Thomas (1965).

America which are in fact extensions of the United States economic system, as well as in the constitutionally independent sugar dominions of the West Indies which still remain extensions of the British and American economic systems.

Plantation economies

Taking note of the fact that plantations form only a part of a wider economic system, the term 'plantation economy' can be used cautiously to describe situations where the *dominant* pattern of agricultural resource organization is the plantation system. It is not necessary that the agricultural sector of countries involved should consist only of plantation units. No such countries in fact exist. Dominant is used in the sense that the bulk of the country's agricultural resources are owned by plantations, and/or plantation production provides the main dynamic for development. The latter condition requires some elaboration. It is used here in the broadest sense to encompass sociological, political and economic dynamics. Thus, for example, there are situations – as in the West Indies – where peasant producers are more numerous than plantation enterprises but where, because the peasantry is a creation of the plantations their behaviour reflects the plantation influence. In the political sphere, political decision-makers are imbued with a psychological dependence on an established plantation sector and agricultural development policy tends to reflect this attitude.[14]

On the basis of this definition, plantation economies are to be found mainly in tropical America and tropical Asia. Although plantations exist in tropical Africa, e.g. oil palm plantations of the Congo, they do not dominate the scene as in the other regions mentioned.

In Asia, countries like Ceylon, Malaya, Indonesia and the Philippines would classify as plantation economies. So would Mauritius and Reunion in the Indian Ocean; and Hawaii and Fiji in the Pacific. The crops involved in these cases are tea, rubber, sugar and to some extent coconuts.

In America, the *locus* of the plantation system is the Caribbean. Indeed, this region is generally regarded as *the* classic plantation area. So much so that social anthropologists have described the region as a culture sphere, labelled 'Plantation-America'. According to Wagley (1957):

14. For further discussion of some of these considerations, see Braithwaite (1968).

Briefly, this culture sphere extends spatially from about midway up the coast of Brazil into the Guianas, along the Caribbean coast, throughout the Caribbean itself, and into the United States. It is characteristically coastal; not until the nineteenth century did the way of life of the Plantation-culture sphere penetrate far into the mainland interior, and then only in Brazil and the United States. This area has an environment which is characteristically tropical (except the Southern United States) and lowland (p. 5).

Wagley goes on to describe some of the basic common features in this culture sphere. Among these are:

monocrop cultivation under the plantation system, rigid class lines, multi-racial societies, weak community cohesion, small peasant proprietors involved in subsistence and cash-crop production, and a matrifocal type family form. In addition there are a series of cultural characteristics common to Plantation-America which derive often from similarities in environment, often from the common historical background, and often from the presence of such a large population of African origin (p. 9).

Common cultural characteristics are said to be reflected in the similarities of peasant crops, production techniques, and marketing arrangements: cuisine, music and folklore with common African influences; and similar traditions or values affecting social life.

The boundaries of Wagley's Plantation-America extend beyond what is normally regarded as the Caribbean. It includes sub-regions of larger continental economies – the North-east of Brazil and the South in the United States. It is of some interest to note at this stage that each of these sub-regions is the most backward of the national economies of which they are an integral part. Thus it may be useful for us to speak of plantation economies not only in terms of nation states but also in looking at sub-regions of individual nation states. In this connection we may wish to extend further the spatial boundaries indicated by Wagley to include the lowlands of Central America where plantation banana production is the main type of economic activity.

The main plantation crop of the Caribbean is sugar cane. But in the wider area described above as Plantation-America bananas must be added for the Central American lowlands and cotton for the United States South. For present purposes, it may be necessary to exclude some of the Caribbean islands from the class of plantation economies. In Cuba, the plantation system that existed prior to 1959 has since been transformed into a state-controlled system of agricultural resource organization. Even though sugar is still the main crop and even if many of the cultural traits of plantation societies still remain, the absence of foreign ownership and changes in the social and class structure are enough to set Cuba apart. Also several of the smaller islands may have no significant agriculture or may not have plantations in the sense that we have here defined.[15]

Analysis of the development experience in particular plantation regions is outside the scope of the present paper.[16] However, insofar as the discussion requires empirical foundation at various points, the Caribbean is the basic reference area.

Plantation enterprises

The analysis of resource use and production and of the development problem in plantation economies requires prior examination of the characteristics of the major decision-making units – the plantation enterprises. This has largely been ignored in previous contributions; and the result has been a superficial view of the role of plantation agriculture in promoting agricultural development and change in such societies.

Plantation agriculture in the modern world economy is dominated by large scale multi-national corporate enterprises. The United Fruit Company, the Standard Fruit and Shipping Co., and Unilever are the best known. Several others, less well known, are of particular importance in certain areas. For example, sugar production in the West Indies[17] is dominated by two such companies – Tate and Lyle Ltd, a British sugar-refining firm with

15. It should be noted, however, that even in such situations past plantation experiences may have left a cultural legacy which could lead to patterns of resource allocation and development similar to that which one finds in plantation economies. I am grateful to Lloyd Best for bringing this to my attention.

16. For a collection of papers which examine the Caribbean experience against the background of plantation agriculture see Beckford (ed.) (1968). It will be interesting at a later stage to see how the pattern developed from the Caribbean experience fits other plantation regions such as those in Asia and the Pacific.

17. In this paper, the term 'West Indies' is used to refer to the Commonwealth Caribbean which includes all the former British islands and the mainland territories of Guyana and British Honduras. When the term Caribbean is used without qualification, reference is to the wider region which includes non-English speaking islands such as Cuba, Hispaniola, Puerto Rico, the French and Dutch West Indies.

wholly-owned raw sugar-producing subsidiaries in the region; and Booker Brothers, McConnell and Co. Ltd of London (Bookers).

In addition to the metropolitan basis of ownership, three important characteristics of these enterprises which directly affect resource use in countries where they operate plantations are: (a) a high degree of vertical integration; (b) a lateral spread in their agricultural operations among a number of countries; and (c) each firm accounts for a significant share (often the bulk) of the export output of particular commodities from individual countries.

Three examples from Plantation-America

The features mentioned above are brought out by the following examination of the structure and organization of British-owned Bookers, and Tate and Lyle[18] – the main sugar plantation enterprises in the West Indies – both operating out of London; and the American-owned United Fruit Company (UFCo.) – the main banana plantation enterprise in Central America – operating out of Boston.

Figure 1 is a reproduction of a diagram showing the organizational structure of Bookers. The chart relates only to the firm's operations in Guyana (where most of its agricultural activities are concentrated)[19] and related activities. The company is also engaged in sugar-cane production and raw-sugar manufacture along with rum distillation in Jamaica (two establishments) and Nigeria. The vertically-integrated structure of this company can be traced through the following stages: manufacture of sugar machinery, merchants for agricultural equipment, sugar-cane production, raw-sugar manufacture, distillation of rum, other spirits and alcohol, bulk storage of raw sugar, wharf owners, shipping agents and insurance, and finally ocean transport of raw sugar. At the end of 1968 the fixed assets of the company were distributed as follows: land and buildings £17·7 million,

18. The treatment of Tate and Lyle is limited to its Western Indian operations and related activity. This firm is more international in scope than Bookers which has a greater concentration of its resources in the Caribbean (Guyana in particular).

19. In 1967, two thirds of the company's overseas, i.e. outside of Britain, investment was in the Caribbean – mainly Guyana. Other overseas territories in which this firm operates include Zambia, Canada, Nigeria, Jamaica, Trinidad, Malawi, India, Barbados, and St Lucia; but in most of these places the interest is in non-agricultural activities.

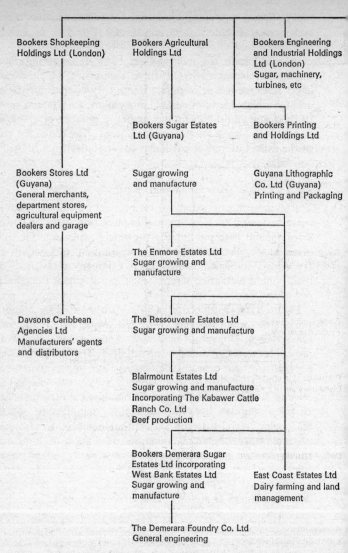

Figure 1 Booker Brothers, McConnell and Co. Ltd (London) — firm structure. Adapted from the Report of a Commission of Enquiry into the Sugar Industry in Guyana (Government Printer) Georgetown, September 1968

plant and machinery, ships and equipment £10·6 million, making a total of £28·3 million. It would have been desirable to look at the asset structure according to the share of assets in agriculture as distinct from associated activities such as sugar manufacture and shipping, but the data are not available in such form.

Bookers is of strategic importance to the economy of Guyana. So far as sugar is concerned, the company has produced well over 80 per cent of the country's output in recent years. In addition the company owns all the bulk storage capacity and sugar-shipping facilities and provides ocean transport for most of Guyana's sugar exports. When it is recognized that sugar is Guyana's largest agricultural export and the biggest single employer of labour, it seems reasonable to conclude that Bookers dominates the agricultural economy of that country.

The detailed information provided in Figure 1 could hardly be shown in diagrammatic form for Tate and Lyle and United Fruit which are much larger and more complex company systems. For these, some relevant descriptive information is given in the following paragraphs and simplified diagrams summarizing these organizational complexes are provided in Figure 2.

The West Indian subsidiaries of Tate and Lyle must be viewed in the context of the wider firm structure of the parent company. Although these subsidiaries produce raw sugar which is eventually refined by the parent company, it is important to note here that the latter depends only to a limited extent on its own West Indian raw sugar for inputs at the refining stage.

Tate and Lyle operates in three West Indian sugar-producing countries through almost wholly-owned subsidiaries – the West Indies Sugar Company (WISCo.) in Jamaica, Caroni Ltd in Trinidad, and Belize Sugar Industries Ltd in British Honduras.[20] In addition, the company engages in sugar refining mainly in the United Kingdom, Canada, Zambia and Rhodesia, sugar storage and distribution, molasses production and trading in the West Indies, Africa, Europe, Asia and North America, manufacture of syrup and liquid sugar, distillation of alcohol, manufacture of machinery and world-wide shipping (including insurance). For the last-named activity, the company owns a

20. The company also has raw sugar-producing subsidiaries in Zambia, Nigeria and Rhodesia but its influence on the agricultural economies of those countries is minimal.

fleet of eleven tankers for bulk shipment of sugar.[21] As a sugar-refining enterprise, Tate and Lyle accounts for a substantial share of refining activity in two metropolitan markets. In the United Kingdom the company handles about 65 per cent of total supply (for example, in 1967 Tate and Lyle refined 2,052,000 long tons of the total of 3,162,000 tons of raw sugar refined in the UK). Tate and Lyle's Canadian subsidiary, Canada and Dominion Sugar Company Ltd, refines about 30 per cent of all sugar refined in Canada in a normal year.

In Jamaica,[22] the resident arm of this multi-national enterprise – WISCo. – primarily engages in sugar-cane growing, raw sugar production, sugar refining (for the domestic market), rum and alcohol distillation and molasses trading. Through its subsidiaries, WISCo. Wharves, Sugar Shipping Ltd, and Computer Service and Printery Ltd, the company also engages in sugar storage, stevedoring and computer and printing services. To Tate and Lyle, the central importance of WISCo. is its sugar-producing activities. According to recent company reports, Tate and Lyle is beneficially involved with 90·63 per cent of the issued share capital of WISCo. At the end of 1968, the fixed assets of WISCo. stood at just over £7 million (this figure includes the assets of the subsidiary companies of WISCo. listed above).

Both the issued share capital and the value of fixed assets of WISCo. represent about 35 per cent of those of the entire Jamaican sugar industry. And the combined output of raw sugar from the two WISCo. factories has been, over the years, in the region of 35 per cent of total sugar output in Jamaica. Through its subsidiary wharf and shipping companies, WISCo. undertakes storage and loading at two ports and thus handles about 56 per cent of total sugar exports from Jamaica. Furthermore, all raw sugar from Jamaica bound for the United Kingdom and Canada (normally over 70 per cent of total sugar exports) is shipped in vessels owned by Sugar Line Ltd, the Tate and Lyle shipping subsidiary. And WISCo., through a London director, markets the entire export sales of sugar from Jamaica. WISCo. is also the leading force in the Jamaica Sugar Manufacturers' Association,

21. The company also owns building supplies and building service industries in Canada and the United Kingdom.

22. The information on Jamaica was provided by Mr S. A. Osborne in a student class essay prepared for the author. We are grateful to the Managing Director of WISCo., Mr P. Bovell, who read Mr Osborne's essay and made a number of important corrections and comments.

a powerful lobbying group that promotes the interests of sugar at all levels[23]

In Trinidad,[24] the Tate and Lyle subsidiary – Caroni Ltd – owns and operates four of the country's six sugar factories. This represents 80 per cent of total factory capacity. In sugar-cane production, Caroni Ltd accounted for 60 per cent of the total produced in 1967. In addition, Caroni Ltd accounts for all of the bulk storage and shipping facilities for sugar in Trinidad. The following tabulation shows the structure of fixed assets of Caroni Ltd in 1967. The high percentage of fixed capital represented by plant and machinery (mainly factory capacity) is worthy of note, as subsequent discussion will show.

	£ (000s)	%
Land	1907	24·8
Buildings	1758	22·8
Plant and machinery	3727	48·6
Other	291	3·8
Total	7683	100·0

Finally, Tate and Lyle has a complete monopoly of raw-sugar production in British Honduras. There its resident subsidiary, Belize Sugar Industries Ltd, owns and operates the two sugar factories in that country as well as all the available storage and shipping facilities. The company's sugar-cane production on its own estates represents some 80 per cent of total sugar-cane production in that country. The importance of sugar to the economy of British Honduras is reflected by the fact that sugar represents 54 per cent of agricultural export sales and about 30 per cent of total exports.

The United Fruit Co. is a giant enterprise, both in respect of banana production in Central America as well as banana imports into the United States. For example, in 1966 UFCo. accounted for 55 per cent of total US banana imports. In the same year, the company controlled 100 per cent of export banana acreage in Guatemala, 70 per cent of that in both Costa

23. Official government delegations to various international sugar conferences and councils usually consist of representatives of the SMA. And the chief officers in the SMA are usually Tate and Lyle personnel.

24. The information on Trinidad was derived from recent annual reports of Caroni, Ltd.

Rica and Panama and 56 per cent of that in Honduras (Arthur, Houck and Beckford, 1968, pp. 33–53). According to the company's annual report, about 53 per cent of all the fruit sold by it was purchased in recent years, i.e. only 47 per cent of the bananas handled by the company was derived from its own plantations. As part of its tropical American operations, the company operates its own corrugating and box-making plants, producing box 'flats' only for bananas, in Panama, Costa Rica and Honduras.

In addition to these operations, the company is involved in the purchasing and shipping of bananas from Ecuador and Colombia in South America. And, through various subsidiaries, it is involved in the marketing (and some production) of bananas from other tropical-producing areas as well as shipping, importation, ripening and distribution in other metropolitan areas – chiefly the United Kingdom and Western Europe.

Again, available data on the asset structure of this company are not presented in the form that is required for present purposes. However, some rough idea can be obtained from the following tabulation which shows investment in fixed assets of 1966. (United Fruit Company, 1966, p. 20).

	$ (US 000s)
Lands	10,374
Houses and buildings	59,536
Cultivations	62,839
Equipment	92,216
Railways, tramways and rolling stock	38,440
Wharves, boats, etc.	6755
Sugar mills and refineries	17,804
Steamships	117,071
Total	405,035

It is not possible to assess from this the actual share of agricultural operations in the company's total fixed capital stock. 'Lands' and 'cultivations' can be attributed to this but a share of the amounts listed under 'houses and buildings', 'equipment' (and possibly 'railways etc.') needs to be allocated to agriculture as well. At a guess, fixed capital on the agricultural side is probably 50 per cent or less of total fixed capital.

Some significant characteristics

In terms of the scope of their activities, the three firms considered above are, to a large extent, representative of foreign-owned plantation enterprises operating in tropical America. Indeed, together they account for a significant share of plantation output in this region. A factor which is worthy of note is that each firm is large as compared with the agricultural sectors of individual countries in which they operate. For example, the total value of agricultural output in Guyana was estimated to have been in the region of £17 million in 1966 while the 'turnover' (mainly sales) for the entire Bookers organization in that year was of the order of £78 million. Even the sales from Bookers 'tropical agriculture operations' and 'rum and other spirits' alone (£18·7 million) exceeded the total value of agricultural output in Guyana.[25] Another significant feature is that each of the three firms accounts for the major share (in several cases, 100 per cent) of the total output of the particular crop in individual countries where they operate. This means that decisions relating to the adjustment of output for particular commodities in individual countries are made by a central authority located within the structure of a single firm.

A high degree of vertical integration is characteristic of these firms. This vertical integration extends far beyond the stage of the 'factory-farm combines' repeatedly discussed in the established literature on plantation agriculture. In addition to processing of the agricultural raw material, these enterprises are substantially engaged in supplying their own agricultural inputs and, more importantly, in the shipping and marketing of the products at higher stages of production.

Vertical integration has indeed been carried to a stage where the actual plantation operations of the enterprises may no longer represent the bulk of firm investments. What is more, operations at higher stages of production are only partly based on the firm's own supplies from lower stages of the production process. Consequently, the firm is in a position to hedge possible losses on its farming operations against consequent gains further up the scale.

25. The figure for Guyana was derived by adding the GDP attributed to sugar cane, padi, other, livestock, sugar processing and rice processing in the *Economic Survey of Guyana 1966*, p. 89. Figures for Bookers were taken from *The Booker Group Report and Accounts 1967*, p. 8. The *total* GDP of Guyana in that year (about £75 million) was less than Bookers total 'turnover' (£78 million).

Metropolitan ownership and control is another factor which has much significance. For one thing, it means that the *locus* of decision-making is outside of the countries in which plantation production activities are carried out. This is bound to affect the pattern of production, resource use and development in the countries with which we are here concerned. For example, it is generally recognized that 'foreign investors prefer investments which are directly linked with the foreign exchange-earning ability of the economy' in which they invest (Baldwin, 1956). Surpluses for re-investment therefore tend to flow back into established export activities in which these investors have developed an infrastructure of expertise and organization – thus creating rigidities in the overall adjustment process in the agricultural sectors of the countries involved.

The typical geographic spread of plantation operations of individual firms is also significant. The production adjustment process in this event must be considered, not in terms of individual countries but from the point of view of the firm. Decisions relating to expansion or contraction of output in a particular country are made within the context of the firm's overall supply drawn from several countries. The relevant unit for analysis is therefore the plantation enterprise and not the nation state in which only a part of the firm's operations is located.

Yet another feature worthy of note is that the capital investments of these enterprises are highly specific to the production and marketing (including processing) of a particular commodity. In addition to specific capital investment on the agricultural side, complementary investments at other levels tend to be specific to the plantation commodity; for example, bulk terminals, special bulk-sugar vessels and refining equipment in the case of sugar; and specially designed banana boats in the case of United Fruit.[26] As we shall see below, this high degree of specificity influences the pattern of resource use and the adjustment process.

Agricultural production and resource use in plantation-type economies

The concern here is with production and resource use in the agricultural sectors of what we have described as plantation

26. In 1966, the forty-one vessels owned by the company accounted for as much as 28 per cent of total investment (see the company's *Annual Report 1966*, pp. 19–20).

economies; in other words, with the way in which plantation operations influence resource use and overall production in the countries where these enterprises are engaged in agriculture. In this connection, efficiency considerations relate to the agricultural sectors of the plantation economies and not to the firm. The two are not the same. What is good for the firm is not necessarily good for the country where it produces. Indeed, the general thesis of this paper is that in plantation-type economies efficient resource allocation in individual production units tends to co-exist with inefficient resource allocation for the agricultural sector as a whole.

The efficiency conditions for the agricultural sector can be briefly set out in the conventional way to provide a general background. Resources are allocated most efficiently when the following conditions hold: (a) resources are allocated within each farm in a manner that equates the marginal value productivities of the resource services, i.e. a unit of labour or capital should not be used to grow sugar if it can produce a greater value product in livestock; (b) resources are distributed between farms and farming areas so that marginal value productivities are equal; (c) resources are distributed between farming and other producing areas to equalize value productivities; and (d) resources are allocated over time such that their discounted value products are equal.[27]

The rest of this section considers some of the aspects of the operations of plantation enterprises. Inferences regarding allocative efficiency in the context outlined above are made at various points in the discussion.

Production objectives

The plantation production unit is a corporate enterprise which is chiefly concerned with making profit for its shareholders. Profit maximization is, therefore, one of the primary objectives of plantation enterprises. However, because the plantation itself is part of a wider organizational complex, profit maximization may not be a guiding principle at the level of its agricultural operations. Insofar as the firm draws heavily on raw material supplies other than its own at the higher levels of production (and marketing), lower profits on the agricultural side may result in

27. For elaboration on these conditions see, for example, Heady (1952, ch. 24).

higher overall profits. Furthermore, profit maximization at the farm level is constrained by the firm's specific capital commitments.[28]

The way in which farming profits relate to total profit of the enterprise as a whole requires an examination of the structure of costs and profits. An example of this is provided by the following schematic representation of the Tate and Lyle sugar situation.[29]

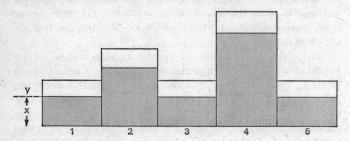

1 Sugar cane growing
2 Raw sugar production
3 Shipping
4 Refining
5 Distribution

Figure 3

Each block represents a different level of operation in the integrated enterprise. Costs (x) are indicated by shaded, and profits (y) by unshaded areas. Blocks (1), (2) and (4) are directly related. (1) shows costs and profits of the firm's subsidiaries on farming (growing of sugar-cane) in the West Indies. The firm also produces raw sugar in the West Indies at stage (2) from its own supplies of cane plus that purchased from independent cane farmers. The imputed price of its own cane output is therefore equal to the price at which it buys from cane farmers $(x + y)_1$. This, plus a margin for factory costs, set the cost level at stage 2, i.e. $(x)_2$. At stage 4, the firm refines its own, plus purchased supplies of raw sugar, at going prices.[30] So that its costs at this

28. This aspect is considered in more detail later in this section under 'capital specificity'.

29. Figure 3 has been simplified by omitting certain by-product operations like rum, molasses and alcohol production.

30. In actual practice, the Commonwealth preferential system for West Indian sugar places the firm in a unique position. The raw-sugar output from its West Indian factories is sold together with other sugar produced

level are $(x + y)_2$, plus shipping, plus refining costs, leaving a refining profit of y_4.

In so far as changes in output prices at various levels affect levels of profit, the firm is in a position to hedge losses at one stage against gains at higher stages of production so long as the final disposal (consumer) price does not change proportionately with changes in the prices of primary and intermediate outputs. For example, the lower the price of raw sugar purchased for refining (stage 4), the lower will be profits on the West Indian operations (stages 1 and 2) but the higher will be profit on refining since the value of x_4 has been reduced.

One characteristic of the plantation which has been noted by Jones (1968) is 'the ability to exploit market imperfections or to manipulate them to its advantage' (p. 155). This applies not only to the factor market but to the product market as well. The firm is therefore usually in a position to control final disposal prices, perhaps more so than prices of primary and intermediate outputs.

The upshot of the foregoing discussion is that the maximization of total profit for the firm as a whole is not dependent on profit maximizations for its agricultural activities. The importance of agriculture in this connection depends partly on the share of agriculture in the firm's total investments. The smaller this share, the less will be the need for using the profit maximization principle on its agricultural operations.

Since the agricultural operations of plantation enterprises are located in the tropical economies with which we are here concerned, this observation has implications for agricultural resource use in these economies. Changes in the structure of output prices (for the whole range of agricultural products which can be grown in these countries) which offer more profitable opportunities than the particular plantation crop do not induce a shift of resources from production of the latter because the profit horizon of the plantation enterprise (which controls these resources) extends beyond these purely agricultural opportunities. Even in the long run, the *adjustment process tends to be limited to output adjustments for the particular crop* rather than to

in the West Indies to the British Sugar Board at a special negotiated price which is usually in excess of the world market price. The Sugar Board is however obliged to sell to British refiners at the world market price. So that normally this firm sells its raw sugar at one price and buys back the same sugar at a lower price for refining it.

a more flexible deployment of resources over the range of production possibilities in line with differential marginal value productivities.

Capital specificity

It will be recalled from the preceding section that one of the characteristics of plantation enterprises is that the capital stock of these firms is highly specific to the production and processing (including marketing) of particular crops. This produces further inflexibility in the pattern of agricultural resource use. The more integrated is the firm structure the more important is this limitation. For this means that the firm also has investments outside of agriculture which are geared to the particular crop.

The degree of specificity tends to be least at the actual farming level. Equipment used in cultivation, field labour, land, etc., can be used for the production of any number of crops. But the capital required for the processing (in the farm-factory and elsewhere) and shipping is quite specific. For example, sugar mills cannot be adapted to processing vegetables and banana boats are specially designed to their task. In the vertically integrated structure of the firm it is these specific non-farm investments that help to create rigidities in resource use on the plantation. For capital specificity in related non-farm operations of the firm makes it less profitable to undertake crop switching or diversification at the farm level.[31]

Once ancillary investment commitments have been made, the firm is constrained to a short-run production possibilities curve with a limited scope for the switching of resources to alternative products.[32] This is illustrated below. Figure 4 shows the long-run

31. Certain factors at the farm level tend as well to be highly specific; for example, laboratories and managerial functions. It has been suggested, for example, that these rigidities may derive as much from the circumscribed entrepreneurial horizons of firm managers as from the existence of capital specificity in a physical or engineering sense. Firm managers who have established themselves as 'sugar men' or 'banana men' are unlikely to contemplate crop changes which would erode their established authority. Although this is a factor which is of relevance, it does not really set plantation operators apart from other types of agricultural producers. This same kind of 'psychological attachment' to crops can be found among peasant farmers. It seems therefore that the degree of capital specificity is the more important consideration.

32. The set of production possibilities at the farm level are not influenced by ancillary non-farm investments in a technical sense, but are affected indirectly by the resultant relative profitability of alternatives once specific commitments have been made.

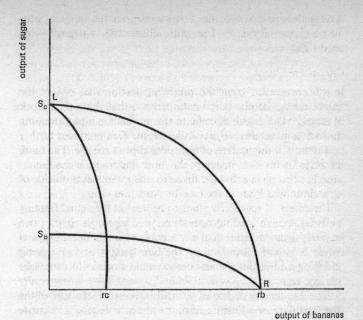

Figure 4

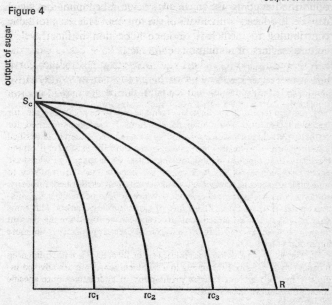

Figure 5

production possibilities for combinations of two crops, sugar and bananas, with a given set of resources. This is denoted by the curve LR. Once the firm commits itself to specific investments relating to one or the other crop, the long-run production possibilities (opportunity) curve is no longer relevant. If the investments are specific to sugar production, the operative opportunity curve then becomes $s_c\ r_c$ while if they are specific to bananas it is $s_b r_b$.[33] The degree of flexibility for product–product combinations is reduced as a result of the specific commitments.

Figure 5 shows different degrees of capital specificity for a set of firms involved in sugar production. The more resources the firm has tied up in activities linked to sugar, the greater the degree of inflexibility. Thus in the case of West Indian sugar producers, for example, if rc_1 represents the position of Tate and Lyle subsidiaries, Bookers would operate on a curve to the right of this, say rc_2, since the latter does not have sugar refining investments, while a simple farm-factory combine (sugar estate) without shipping and refining investments would operate further right, on say, rc_3.

The greater the degree of vertical integration, the less will be the flexibility of adjusting resource use of changing production opportunities across the range of agricultural commodities which can be produced with available resources. This is one factor contributing to inefficient resource allocation within the agricultural sectors of plantation economies.

33. In a comment on the earlier draft, Havelock Brewster raises the question as to whether specificity 'is not shown by a lack of, or only partial, continuity in the production function rather than, as you show it, an alteration in the convexity'. In that event the illustration would be as follows,

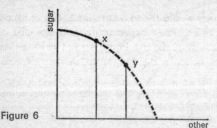

Figure 6

showing that in the sugar case 'the curve is continuous up to x in the short run and/or with a certain degree of inflexibility (i.e. vertical integration). It would be continuous up to y in a longer period and/or with a greater degree of flexibility'. It seems to me that either interpretation will lead to the same conclusion.

Land use

The farm-factory operations of plantation enterprises are located in the tropical plantation economies. Here the factory for processing plantation output represents a substantial capital investment. The firm is therefore concerned that adequate supplies of raw material will be available for utilizing factory capacity in a reasonably efficient way. Sufficient land must be acquired to produce the desired flow of raw material.[34] Even where raw material supplies are available for purchase from independent farmers, the firm would be in too vulnerable a position if it relied exclusively on such supplies.

This means that the plantation enterprise will try to secure sufficient land to produce some, or all, of its raw material requirements and to allow for some degree of flexibility of output adjustment over time in response to changing market opportunities.

The land area required by a plantation will be influenced by several factors: the price of land, the size of factory investment, the ratio of factory investment to total farm-factory investment, the availability of raw material supplies from other sources (preferably contract suppliers), and expectations concerning future market possibilities which influence desired flexibility of output adjustment. The actual land area acquired by plantations will depend on the resources of the firm, the cost of land and the scale economies of processing particular crops. Given a scale of plant, then the minimum area required would be determined by the level of output required to cover fixed costs in processing where non-plantation supplies are available. Where these are not available a larger area will be necessary to make processing profitable.[35]

Normally, plantations would try to secure land well in excess of the technical minimum. Price expectations and the cost of land would mainly determine the maximum area. The lower the cost of land and the brighter the long-term market expecta-

34. The argument applies as well to enterprises which have shipping capacity, such as in the banana case where no elaborate processing is done but where shipping is an important part of the firm's operation. By producing its own bananas, U F Co. has greater control over utilization of its shipping capacity.

35. The same applies to shipping. For example, for bananas 'there is a certain minimum area required to justify the specialized shipping facilities that the trade demands. United Fruit Company usually specifies that at least 5000 acres of first class land . . . be available in one block before a farm can be established' (Arthur, Houck and Beckford, 1968, p. 48).

tions, the greater would be the area secured for plantation production. Because the establishment of plantations has historically been associated with the opening up of new territory, low-cost land was usually available and this led to the alienation of vast areas even beyond expected requirements at the time of establishment.

The land area actually in use at any particular point in time is a function of the price of output, the cost of production, the technical requirements of plant scale and the price at which the firm can obtain other supplies of the raw material. High rates of profit are characteristic of the early stages of development of plantations as a result of the natural fertility of virgin land. But over time profits get squeezed as diminishing returns and rising costs set in.[36] This stimulates technological improvements to raise the productivity of land, e.g. new improved varieties, irrigation, fertilizers. As technology changes, some lands previously in production may become marginal but the plantation will keep these in reserve since future favourable changes in output prices may justify their use at a later date. (In Central America, for example, United Fruit maintained possession of thousands of acres which had been abandoned in the wake of Panama disease for several years and was able to bring these areas back into production quickly during the 1960s with the advent of the disease-resistant 'Valery' variety and favourable market prospects.)

There is therefore a tendency toward under-utilization of land in plantation agriculture. The extent of under-utilization, i.e. size of acreage reserve, will depend on the cost of securing land and of holding it. So we would expect smaller acreage reserves in countries which are short of land than in land-abundant plantation economies.[37] Under-utilization of land is one means of providing for flexibility of output adjustments over time. Though this may represent an efficient pattern of resource

36. See Best (1968) for a discussion of the historical sequence of transition from what he describes as the 'golden age' to the stage of 'gall and worm-wood'.

37. In Central America, for example, UFCo. normally has only one-third of its total owned acreage in bananas while the share of estate land in sugar-cane in the West Indies is generally about 80 per cent. However, population density may work in the opposite direction. Strong competition for land will lead to a secular rise in land prices which would encourage the holding of idle land for speculative purposes. David Edwards informs me that there is evidence that this has been the case for certain sugar estates in Trinidad and Antigua.

use for the firm, it creates inefficiencies in allocation within the agricultural sector. This is most acute in situations where land is generally in short supply.

Risk and uncertainty considerations

The heavy capitalization and the crop specificity of investments expose plantation enterprises to an inherently high degree of risk and uncertainty – particularly in respect of crop losses from natural or other, e.g. political, causes and of price fluctuations. This induces at least two counter-measures which affect resource allocation within the plantation economies.

The first is the exploitation of market imperfections. On the product side this is expressed in enterprise control over disposal prices. United Fruit Company achieved this so effectively in the United States banana market that it had to face a Consent Decree of the Department of Justice to divest itself of part of its capital for the formation of another smaller company. In any event, UFCo. will still be able to maintain its position of price leader in the trade. Tate and Lyle subsidiaries on the other hand achieve this through industry collusion in the West Indies, i.e. Sugar Manufacturers' Associations, and political lobbying in the UK for preferential pricing arrangements. In matters relating to overseas sugar markets it is normal practice in the West Indies for industry leaders to 'speak for the Governments'. The consequences of this counter-measure is artificially to distort the structure of output prices for the range of farm products that can be produced in the plantation economies; and thereby to bias resource use in favour of the plantation crop. On the factor side, market imperfections arise from control over supplies of inputs produced within the vertically-integrated structure of the firm and from the normally monopsonistic position of the plantation in the labour market. The latter derives from the fact that the land area covered by the plantation enterprise is so vast that it is usually the only source of employment within fairly wide areas.

The second counter measure is the geographic dispersal of the firm's plantation operations. This minimizes the risk of crop losses. In addition to losses from weather and disease, this measure is a hedge against unfavourable changes in the political and economic situation in individual countries and it increases the flexibility of output expansion for the firm itself. But it also leads to perverse supply responses for individual countries. For although the firm may increase overall acreage and output in response to an increase in the relative price of its output, it may, in the process, contract acreage and output in a particular individual country.[38] The firm is concerned with efficient resource allocation between its different areas of agricultural operations. And this often results in inefficient resource allocation within a particular plantation economy. Because of the multi-national character of plantation enterprises, efficiency conditions tend to be met on the overall operation, i.e. between plantation sectors of nation states but not within the agricultural sectors of individual nation states.

Development problems in plantation-type economies

The discussion in this section falls into three main parts: first, a brief consideration of the general conditions of agricultural development provides the background for an assessment; next, of factors which limit development with plantation agriculture; and finally, of the factors which seem to favour development.

Conditions of agricultural development

A great deal has been written about the role (or contribution) of agriculture in overall economic development. The main considerations here are, first, that agriculture must provide the food supplies required to meet an expanding demand resulting from population growth and rising incomes. When this expansion of food supply is not forthcoming, food prices increase and/or supplies must be imported. In either event, development is constrained.

Agriculture must provide not just an increasing supply but one in which the pattern of supply needs to be adjusted to satisfy changing patterns of food consumption that are associated with rising incomes. That is, the supply of high income elasticity foodstuffs must increase at a faster rate than that of low income elasticity products. This demands a certain degree of flexibility of resource use and adjustment within agriculture.

Secondly, the agricultural sector acts as a source of factor supplies for expansion of other sectors of the economy. In this

38. In a recent study of banana supply functions for each of four Central American countries, the author could find no correlation between changes in planned output (using acreage as an index) and changes in relative prices for bananas. But some significant correlations were derived when acreage data for each of two companies (United Fruit and Standard Fruit Co.) were aggregated for all four countries and plotted against relative price over a number of years.

connection particular emphasis has been given to labour and capital transfers. Thirdly, agriculture is the basis of important market relationships which create spread-effects for development. All primary output requires processing of some form and this provides forward linkage effects. Similarly, commercial agriculture relies increasingly on purchased off-farm inputs which provide opportunities for income and employment creation in sectors producing these inputs, the backward linkage effects. The sum of forward and backward linkage effects from agriculture can be quite substantial, given the right conditions.

Fourthly, the agricultural sector is an important earner of foreign exchange in many countries. And foreign exchange is usually required to secure certain critical capital inputs for development. Given the present structure of the world economy, the export trade of underdeveloped countries is dominated by primary products – mainly of agriculture and mining.

Agricultural development *per se* involves several necessary conditions; for a start, adequate supplies of resources, especially land and capital. Complementary human resources – with skills in management and adaptable labour services – are essential as well. A developed infrastructure – roads, water supplies, electricity, etc. – provides a foundation for development. Appropriate institutional arrangements, e.g. affecting incentive for effort, land tenure, marketing, credit and adequate scope for the organization of 'large-scale units of collective action' (progress-oriented values, attitudes, social structure, etc.) are pre-conditions for development.

The *dynamics* of agricultural development, however, involve much more. Technological change is crucial. The development process involves an expansion of agricultural output at the same time that labour is moving out of agriculture. The productivity of labour remaining in agriculture must therefore expand substantially. For this, research can play an important part since it serves to increase knowledge of new inputs and of possibilities for raising the productivity of old inputs. Capital accumulation is also essential to the process. And, finally, enough flexibility to facilitate resource adjustments to changing income opportunities is necessary.

Underdevelopment biases in plantation agriculture

The characteristics of plantation agriculture are such that this type of agriculture tends not to fulfil the basic conditions set out above in the brief discussion of the role of agriculture in economic development. First, this type of agriculture is not geared to supplying food demand within the plantation economy. Instead, it is geared to metropolitan consumption requirements. As such it fulfils another condition by earning foreign exchange. The question that arises is whether over time the foreign exchange-earning ability will be more than enough to provide for imported food supplies so as to leave a residual of earnings for importation of 'critical capital inputs'.

Plantation export output consists of primary products with relatively low income-elasticities of demand. On the other hand, the food import requirements of plantation economies normally consist of high income-elasticity products.[39] Therefore for any given increase in consumer incomes in both the metropolis and the plantation economy, the required increase in plantation output will be less than the required increase in food imports. In order to compensate, the export price for plantation output must rise relative to food import prices. In other words, over time the terms of trade must move consistently in favour of plantation export output. But in point of fact the historical pattern has generally been the reverse; so that the export earnings of plantation economies tend toward failing to meet food import requirements unless the rate of income growth in the plantation economy falls consistently behind that in the metropolis.[40] It is of considerable interest to note here that despite the deteriorating terms of trade more export agricultural output continues to be produced in the plantation economies. The reason for this is that to the private foreign-plantation owners the commodity terms of trade has no economic significance. The terms of trade is really a social concept which does not have much significance in the private accounting of the plantation. To put it another way, the terms of trade of the *firm* may be altogether different from the terms of trade of the *society*.

In addition, it must be noted that the foreign exchange-earning capacity of plantation agriculture is limited by the normally high import content of plantation production and consumption. On the production side, this results partly from the fact that metro-

39. Basic starchy staples (the low income-elasticity products in the consumer food basket) are usually supplied from within plantation economies.

40. This condition itself implies limited economic progress in the plantation economy where incomes are already at much lower levels than in the metropolis.

politan capital brings with it its own technology, which usually requires inputs not available in the plantation economy; and partly from the vertically-integrated structure of plantation enterprises. On the consumption side, because plantation labour has been mobilized for export production there is relatively little production for the home market leading to a characteristic heavy reliance on imports of food and other consumer goods. The actual available foreign exchange is therefore what is left after deducting the value of imported inputs used in plantation production, factor incomes going to the metropole and the consumer expenditure on imports in the second round.[41] On the whole, then, the foreign exchange-earning capacity of plantation agriculture seems to be less than is normally assumed.

Another effect of the primary export orientation of plantation agriculture is that the benefits of productivity improvements tend to accrue mostly to metropolitan consumers. This is so primarily in those countries where plantations exist along with farmers producing for their own consumption. In looking at the Jamaican experience, for example, Arthur Lewis (1961) observed that although productivity in export agriculture increased by 27 per cent between 1890 and 1930, consumption per head increased only by 13 per cent in the same period because the terms of trade moved adversely from 137 in 1890 to 84 in 1930. Lewis explains this general pattern among tropical exporting countries as follows: '. . . so long as productivity is constant in subsistence production, practically all the benefit of increases in productivity in the commercial crops accrues to the consumer and not to the producer . . . Greater productivity is offset by adverse terms of trade' (pp. xviii-xix).

The same author had outlined the position at greater length in his *Theory of Economic Growth* as follows:

If nothing is done to raise the productivity of peasants in producing food, they constitute a reservoir of cheap labour available for work in mines or plantations or other export enterprises . . . So long as the peasant farmers have low productivity, the temperate world can get the services of tropical labour for a very low price. Moreover when productivity rises in the crops produced for export there is no need to share the increase with labour, and practically the whole benefit goes in

41. There is also the question of the valuation of exports where the product leaves the plantation economy as an intra-company transfer and not through sales. For a discussion of this problem in relation to Central American banana exports and the United Fruit Company, see La Barge (1961).

'reducing the price to industrial consumers. Sugar is an excellent case in point. Cane sugar production is an industry in which productivity is extremely high by any biological standard. It is also an industry in which output per acre has about trebled over the past seventy years, a rate of growth unparalleled by any other major agricultural industry in the world – certainly not by the wheat industry. Nevertheless, workers in the cane sugar industry continue to walk barefooted and to live in shacks, while workers in wheat enjoy among the highest living standards in the world. However vastly productive the sugar industry may become, the benefit accrues chiefly to consumers. This is one of the disadvantages to tropical countries (advantages to industrial countries) of the fact that their economic development has concentrated upon the export sector of the economy, and that foreign entrepreneurs and foreign capital have been devoted in the first place primarily to expanding exports . . (Lewis, 1955, p. 281).

Lewis has been quoted at length here because he is describing a phenomenon that is characteristic not so much of all export agriculture but of plantation agriculture in particular. For this is perhaps the only type of agriculture that by definition always satisfies the two basic conditions that erode retention of the benefits of productivity improvements: export production and a continuous supply of cheap labour.[42]

It should be pointed out, however, that in recent times productivity improvements have brought more benefit to the plantation economies than in the past. This has resulted mainly from increasing trade-union activity which has managed to cream off some of the benefits of improved productivity in the form of higher wages for plantation labour. But against this must be balanced the consideration that improvements in productivity on plantations have invariably involved the oft-neglected cost of increased unemployment.[43]

Plantation agriculture also has a limited capacity for the two other functions mentioned in the earlier discussion of 'conditions of agricultural development'. As concerns transfers of factor supplies, there are two important limitations. Firstly, because of foreign ownership capital transfers are to the metropolis and not to the non-agricultural sectors of the plantation economy.

42. Other types of agriculture may satisfy one or the other conditions but seldom both. For example, the commercial farm-firms producing wheat in Canada and the peasants producing cocoa in West Africa are export producers without the cheap labour condition while the *haciendas* of Latin America base production on cheap labour but are not export-oriented.
43. I am grateful to Havelock Brewster for reminding me of this.

And, secondly, because the skill content of plantation labour is low (by the specification of the production function), the adaptability of plantation labour to the requirements of other sectors is extremely slow.

So far as market relationships are concerned, the vertical integration of plantation enterprises stretches across national boundaries. Linkages are established within the structure of the *firm* and not within individual plantation economies. For the latter, then, potential linkage effects are dissipated and this minimizes inter-industry transactions with their potential development-spread effects.

Some other factors which further restrict development possibilities in plantation economies and which deserve elaboration are the inherent rigidities in resource adjustment, the element of foreign ownership, the unequal pattern of income distribution and the characteristic rigid social structure.

In our examination of the economics of resource use, it was observed that the high degree of specificity of plantation enterprise investment and the distorted structure of agricultural output prices create a built-in rigidity in the pattern of resource use in plantation agriculture. Because of this heavy commitment to the production of a particular export crop and because foreign investors have little or no interest in production for the domestic market, opportunities for agricultural development deriving from changing patterns of consumer food expenditure tend not to be taken up. The normal development pattern, implicit in a model based on more perfectly competitive conditions, does not emerge.

Foreign ownership of plantations limits development in two additional ways not previously considered. Firstly, there is the leakage of income in the form of dividends which reduces the investment capacity of the economy. Secondly, when reinvestment out of the surplus occurs, there is no assurance that the economy in which the surplus was produced will benefit. This follows from the spatial distribution of the firm's operations among a number of countries. Surpluses produced in one country can be re-invested in any other country where the firm owns plantations or at home-base in the metropolis.

The low wages of plantation labourers stand in dramatic contrast to the earnings of the skilled supervisory and management staffs which operate the plantations. This sets the stage for a generally unequal pattern of income distribution among all households in plantation economies. The adverse development consequences of this are two-fold. Aggregate effective demand is low; this limits the size of the market and rules out the establishment of consumer goods industries with significant scale economies. In addition, the low incomes of the bulk of the population restrict household savings and the scope for domestic investment, while the high-income classes engage in conspicuous consumption of luxury imports and invest heavily in non-productive assets.

Finally, the rigid class lines and weak community cohesion of plantation societies serve to restrict social mobility and to impede the development of large-scale units of collective action. Restricted social mobility adversely affects individual incentive for economic advancement and affects labour adaptability as well.

Contributions of plantation agriculture to development

Two factors which are repeatedly mentioned in the literature on plantation agriculture deserve consideration here so as to round off the discussion. The first is that plantation agriculture has served in the past to open up previously inaccessible areas. In so doing, it has developed an infrastructure of roads, ports, water supplies, electricity, etc., in underdeveloped countries much more rapidly than would otherwise have occurred. This is undoubtedly an important contribution to these economies. But the benefits of this must be weighed against the dynamic underdevelopment biases considered above. What is more, it should be noted that, like everything else, the infrastructure is geared to the specific needs of the plantations and does not necessarily benefit other producers to any significant degree. Thus, for example, we normally find villages and farming areas just outside the boundaries of plantations without water and electricity though the plantation itself is well supplied with these.

The second consideration is that unlike other types of agriculture in underdeveloped countries, plantation agriculture is 'scientific'. Plantations invest in research which produces a high rate of technological change. Furthermore, the implementation of research findings is quick and easy because of the centralized authority structure of plantations. This can be contrasted with the slow rate of adoption of new techniques by peasant farmers and the overwhelming problem of extension in peasant farming areas.

This point is also well taken but requires qualification. Again, the research input of plantations is specific to particular crops and may not apply across the range of technical production possibilities. For example, United Fruit undertakes an elaborate programme of research on bananas, and West Indian sugar plantations maintain their own research stations for studying the problems of sugar. Neither of these invests very much in research on other crops and/or livestock which may offer better economic prospects *to the countries* involved than the particular plantation crop. This raises the problem of the allocative efficiency of research resources. But, in addition, it underscores the existing dynamic bias against high-income production opportunities in the domestic market; for in the absence of technical knowledge such opportunities cannot be readily seized.

Summary and implications

This paper represents a first attempt to examine the economics of resource use and development in economies based on plantation agriculture. The analysis suggests that the particular character of plantation enterprises of a certain type (multi-national corporate enterprises) and the dependent nature of the economies dominated by these enterprises create certain inefficiencies in resource allocation *within these economies* and, in addition, limit the potential for development.

Allocative inefficiencies arise from the structural characteristics of the plantation enterprises considered here – in particular vertical and horizontal integration across national frontiers, and the high degree of capital specificity that characterizes the production process. The inefficiencies within the agricultural sectors of plantation economies co-exist with efficient resource use for the firm itself, reminding us of the maxim that what is good for the firm is not necessarily good for the country.

Similarly, biases toward underdevelopment in plantation economies derive from certain structural factors – foreign ownership and export orientation, the inherent rigidities in resource adjustment, the low skill content of plantation labour, unequal distribution of incomes, and rigid social structure – that inhere in this type of agriculture.

By and large, the analysis has been exploratory. It now requires further refinement and expansion to provide a framework for constructing a model of development which is appropriate to this type of agriculture. Subsequently, the model would require testing by setting it against the historical experiences of selected plantation economies. Hopefully this will lead to a better understanding of the process of change and the possibilities for transformation in economies of this type.

References

ARTHUR, H. B., HOUCK, J. P., and BECKFORD, G. L. (1968), *Tropical Agribusiness Structures and Adjustments: Bananas*, Division of Research, Harvard Business School.

BALDWIN, R. E. (1956), 'Patterns of development in newly settled regions', *Manchester School of Economic and Social Studies*, May.

BALDWIN, R. E. (1963), 'Export technology and development from subsistence level', *Economic Journal*, March.

BECKFORD, G. L. (ed.) (1968), *Agricultural Development and Planning in the Caribbean*, Social and Economic Studies special number, September.

BEST, L. (1968), 'Outlines of a model of pure plantation economy', *Social and Economic Studies*, September.

BRAITHWAITE, L. (1968), 'Social and political aspects of rural development in the West Indies', *Social and Economic Studies*, September.

GREAVES, I. (1959), 'Plantations in world economy', in *Plantation Systems of the New World*, Pan American Union.

HEADY, E. O. (1952), *Economics of Agricultural Production and Resource Use*, Prentice Hall.

JONES, W. O. (1968), 'Plantations', in D. L. Sills (ed.), *International Encyclopedia of the Social Sciences*, vol. 12, UNESCO.

LA BARGE, R. A. (1961), 'The imputation of values to intra-company exports: the case of bananas', *Social and Economic Studies*, June.

LEWIS, A. (1955), *The Theory of Economic Growth*, Allen & Unwin.

LEWIS, A. (1961), 'Foreword' in G. Eisner, *Jamaica 1830–1930: A Study in Economic Growth*, Manchester University Press.

PAN AMERICAN UNION (1959), *Plantation Systems of the New World*, Pan American Union.

RUBIN, V. (ed.) (1957), *Caribbean Studies: A Symposium*, University of the West Indies.

STEWARD, J. H., *et al.* (1956), *The People of Puerto Rico*, University of Illinois Press.

THOMAS, C. Y. (1965), *Monetary and Financial Arrangements in a Dependent Monetary Economy*, University of the West Indies.

UNITED FRUIT COMPANY (1966), *Annual Report*.

WAGLEY, C. (1957), 'Plantation America: a culture sphere', in V. Rubin (ed.), *Caribbean Studies: A Symposium*, University of the West Indies.

WICKIZER, V. D. (1958a), 'The plantation system in the development of tropical economies', *Journal of Farm Economics*, February.

WICKIZER, V. D. (1958b), 'Plantation crops in tropical agriculture', *Tropical Agriculture*, July.

WICKIZER, V. D. (1960), 'The smallholder in tropical export-crop production', *Food Research Institute Studies*, February.

WOLF, E. R., and MINTZ, S. W. (1957), 'Haciendas and plantations in middle-America and the Antilles', *Social and Economic Studies*, September.

7 N. R. Keddie

The Iranian Village Before and After Land Reform

N. R. Keddie, 'The Iranian village before and after land reform',
Journal of Contemporary History, 1968, vol. 3, no. 3, pp. 69–91.

Agriculture in Iran, as in most of the Middle East, has traditionally produced a surplus that has gone to support city dwellers
with only the barest minimum of investment returned to the
countryside. The 'city feudalism' of the Middle East and much of
Asia, where the major landlords dwelt in, and often dominated,
the cities, has been seen as one of the reasons why modern
capitalism did not develop indigenously in these areas. In the
discussion of this question, stress has usually been put on the lack
of independent municipal communes in Asia and on the stifling
economic effects of landlord domination of the cities. Whatever
the merits of this argument, recent research would indicate that
the agricultural part of the pattern was perhaps even more
important. The manorial system of western Europe and Japan,
and the increasing productivity of agriculture in these areas of
heavy soils and rainfall, seem to have produced an expanding
agricultural surplus. In both Europe and Japan men with
agricultural origins played a key role in the development of
modern capitalism. In the arid Middle East, however, agricultural
production seems to have shown a general decline over many
centuries, due in part to deforestation, soil erosion and the
salinization of irrigated lands. There appear to have been no
major agricultural improvements in the area for many centuries
before the recent imports from the West. Perhaps improvement
was more difficult in the Middle East than in the West – such an
important European innovation as the heavy wheeled plough is
useless on most of the soils of the Middle East. One may also
suspect that the residence of landlords in the cities and the vul-
nerability of the villages to nomadic and other pillaging were
positive obstacles to the building up of a surplus or of heavy
investment in the countryside. Investment was confined to such
things as the traditional irrigation networks, which were essential
to maintaining a minimum productive level, and the countryside

remained an area that provided a surplus for the cities but received almost nothing in return. With neither the capital nor the incentive to raise production, the peasantry remained a bastion of conservative ways, generating neither an innovating gentry nor a bourgeoisie.[1]

In the nineteenth and twentieth centuries Iranian agriculture became increasingly oriented to national and international markets, and this changed the crop patterns and methods of exploitation in many areas. A comparison of eyewitness reports from different periods indicates that changes in agriculture and the rise in government taxes actually worsened the position of the peasantry from the early nineteenth century to after the Second World War.[2] Contributing to the worsening of peasant conditions were the creation of absolute property rights in land, including foreclosure of delinquent mortgages, the registration of tribal land in the name of chiefs, the continued fall in agricultural prices relative to prices of manufactures, the desire of old and new landlords to extract more for new markets, and the rise in taxes on land and on articles of mass consumption to finance modernization.

Since then, however, it has become increasingly clear that there is a limit to the economic progress that can be achieved on an agrarian base that discourages investment, gives the cultivator no incentive to make improvements, and leaves the great majority of the population without significant purchasing power. Since the war there have thus been various attempts at reform, including notably the Shah's sale of (disputed) crown lands to some of the peasants working them, and the law under Mosaddeq raising the peasant's share of the crop. The most important reforms were those begun in January 1962, which required landlords to sell land above 'one village'[3] to the government, who in turn would sell it to certain categories among the cultivators.

1. Three books touching on the consequences of the urban draining off of the agricultural surplus in the Middle East may be especially recommended: Adams (1965), English (1966) and Weulersse (1946).

2. See Keddie (1960), Lambton (1953, pp. 143–5); and the extensive studies by Professor M. Atai, showing a decline in real peasant income in most areas between the late 1920s and the early 1960s being published over several issues of the Tehran English language journal, *Tahqiqat é eqtesadi.*

3. The law gave the landlord the option of choosing (the best) fractions from several villages, and exempted certain types of land, including that under mechanized cultivation.

The magnitude of the problem to be faced by any land reform, and some of the specific problems of the approach used in the reforms begun in 1962, are indicated by the results of two pre-reform multi-village sample surveys whose results are available. The first of these, whose results were not published, was done in 1954 by a three-man team (two Americans and one Iranian) under the auspices of the Iranian Ministry of Agriculture and the Ford Foundation. Since the reasons for its non-publication no longer exist, it seems useful to publish the results, tabulated from its data sheets.[4]

The survey's purpose is indicated by its title: 'A Reconnaissance Survey to Determine the Possibilities of a More Equitable Distribution of Farming Population on the Arable Lands of Iran'. It was hoped that some parts of Iran would turn out to be relatively underpopulated, and hence suitable for resettlement from over-populated areas. However, it turned out that none of the villages surveyed, which were scattered throughout Iran, was underpopulated in terms of resources then in use, or that could be brought into use without considerable capital outlay. On the contrary, nearly every village was relatively overpopulated; there was general disguised unemployment; and many redundant labourers eked out the barest existence on land where their labour was needed only at the peak agricultural seasons.

Like other studies, the 1954 survey documented the extremely low living levels, poor resource use, lack of landlord investment and low yields of Iranian agriculture. More important, because of their novelty and relevance to land reform, were its conclusions regarding regional variations of income, class stratification within each village, and the conservative function of the village hierarchical structure below the landlord level. To speak of regional variations first, there were villages in the south-east where the poorest peasants made eight, ten or fourteen dollars a year, and even the richer cultivators made only five or six times that much per family; at the other extreme, in one atypical village in Mazanderan, a prosperous province below the Caspian Sea, the peasant families averaged $1037 per year. Average family income, computed from all cases in the thirty-seven villages where the number of families getting a given income was noted, was $516

---

4. Two of the participants, Howard Bertsch and H. L. Naylor, wrote up the survey results. Additional tabulation from the survey's data was done by myself and W. H. Keddie in 1960 and by my research assistant, Gene Garthwaite, in 1968.

(38,610 r.) in the prosperous northern provinces of Gilan, Mazanderan and Azerbaijan (lower if the atypical village were eliminated), but only $47 (3500 r.) for the rest of the country.[5] The difference between *area* averages, ignoring the differences within a village, was thus of the order of *1 to 11*. Even assuming that this figure is skewed because there was no practical way of ensuring a random sample, the differences are large enough to be significant.

The median income for all peasant families in this survey, excluding casual agricultural labourers whose incomes were not given, but were included in the incomes of the peasants who paid them, thus making the median *too high*, was $112 (8425 r.).

This survey was taken following a period of political instability and financial crisis resulting from the international oil companies' boycott of Iran's nationalized oil industry, so that these figures may have been unusually low. Instability plus the vague threat of land reform may have influenced the disinvestment by landlords noted in the survey in village after village. Underground irrigation channels and other water supplies had been allowed to fall into disrepair, and nothing was being done to keep up, let alone improve, the investment level. It would thus be unfair to take these figures as firm averages, or to use them as a base from which the progress of land reform a decade later could be judged.[6] It seems likely, however, that the regional and class variations the survey revealed are more persistent phenomena.

The most significant finding, and one which retains its full relevance in the era of land reform, was the existence and social importance of a pattern of class division or stratification among

5. In the survey Mr Garthwaite found a conversion ratio of 80 rials to 1 dollar. Our tabulations here are at the official 75 to 1 rate.

6. This is shown by a resurvey of the same areas conducted by Iranian specialists in 1964 and gradually being published, along with the 1954 survey, in *Tahqiqat é eqtesadi* ('Rural economic problems of Khuzistan', August 1965, and 'A study of rural economic problems of Gilan and Mazanderan', January 1967). From these it is clear that peasant prosperity increased in the decade 1954–64 quite apart from land reform, except for day labourers, who often got the same wage as in 1954 despite the rise in living costs. This contrasts with the apparent *fall* in real peasant income from the late 1920s to the 1960s noted above. What is suggested by these incomplete figures is thus a notable fall in peasant income between the 1920s and 1954, and a partial recovery since then. Unfortunately, the published data on the 1954–64 study do not cover the same areas as the 1920s–1960s study, and one wishes that both studies would now be published *in toto* instead of piecemeal.

the peasants in virtually every village surveyed. This pattern existed even in that majority of villages surveyed where the peasants were all landless; meaning that any analysis of peasant stratification based purely on amounts of land owned is inadequate. The stratification pattern among landless sharecroppers usually worked as follows: peasants worked a certain area of land (which might be periodically redistributed) in organized work-teams, headed by an oxen-owner. Theoretically, every owner of two oxen should head such a work-team, but in many villages there was not enough land to make this possible, while in other villages there were not enough owners of two oxen, so that a team might be headed by a man with only one ox. In any case, the crucial 'top-class' sharecropping position went to a man with one or two oxen, who received extra income both for supplying one of the factors of production and for heading the work-team; anyone owning oxen was assured of a position on the work-team and of a higher income than was received by the peasants without oxen. These latter, who often made up the majority within a village, had the lowest incomes and were in the most precarious position. Because of relative overpopulation, they had to vie for favour with the landlord-appointed headman, who usually assigned the positions on the work-team, and with the work-team heads themselves. If they got a position on a work-team they were assured of a regular, although very small, share of the crop (or, in some cases, a fixed cash income). If they did not get such a position they became casual labourers, getting a daily wage only at peak agricultural seasons, and often forced to migrate. Some owners of oxen or other factors of production (tools, water) chose to rent these out without working.

From this survey plus other recent studies of rural Iran one may construct a chart showing the important agricultural strata. On the chart below Persian terms are excluded, since it was found that such common terms as *govband*, *khoshneshin* and *khordeh malik* are used in different senses by different authorities – reflecting regional variations and possibly misunderstandings. The chart also excludes mechanized areas and persons not in direct relationship to the land, even though these make up part of the rural stratification picture (moneylenders, peddlers, shopkeepers, artisans, teachers, *mullas*, shepherds, etc.). For a complete picture of village stratification one would have to include the moneylending classes, as recent surveys have demonstrated that the majority of peasants are in debt and that by far the greatest part is owed to sources other than the government or landlords. Interest rates of 50 per cent and more help to make the shop-keepers, townsmen, peddlers, and others who indulge in rural moneylending one of the most powerful rural classes.[7]

Strata of adult male agriculturalists widely found in Iranian villages

Almost every village has several of these strata with some peas-ants in more than one of them. In generally declining economic and prestige order:

A Non-cultivators

1 Absentee landlord, including the state, crown, and *vaqf* trustees.
2 Large-scale renter from above, often absentee.
3 Village officials: headman, landlord's agent, water official, field-watcher, etc.
4 Non-cultivating small owner.
5 Non-cultivating small renters from strata 1 or 2 (one village or less).
6 Non-cultivating leaser of productive instruments, usually cattle, sometimes water.
7 Non-cultivating head of work team, providing at least one instrument of production.

B Cultivators

8 Cultivating small owners.
9 Cultivator paying a fixed cash rental.
10 Cultivating head of work team.
11 Sharecropper with some productive instruments, usually oxen, not head of a work team.
12 Sharecropper with only his labour to sell, but with a regular position on a work team or on land.
13 Labourer with regular wage, in cash or kind.
14 Casual labourer, without a place on work team or land, often hired by the day only at peak seasons.

Extreme regional variations, especially in irrigation needs and in the degree of orientation of agriculture towards distant markets,

7. The two articles listed in footnote 6 above give details of peasant debt and its sources.

make it impossible for the chart to be fully comprehensive, either for all existing strata or for their relative prosperity.[8] Even this simplified chart, however, should give some idea of the complexity and importance of stratification in the village.

One may note here that only part of strata 1 and 2 were eliminated in that minority of villages distributed in the recent reforms. Below that stratification remained, and in some cases became more marked. The 1962 land reform law gives priority in receiving land to those who own some instrument of production; it calls them cultivators, but does not ensure that they actually work the land themselves either before or after reform. In practice this has meant that non-cultivating classes 5, 6 and 7 got land, while cultivating classes 12, 13 and 14, who probably account for 40 to 50 per cent of the villagers, did not.

Among the poorest peasants the 1954 survey found appalling conditions; locusts and clover as the main food supply in a few areas; a majority seriously diseased; interest rates of 240–800 per cent per annum, etc. Later surveys show that, apart from landlord advances, annual rural interest rates rarely fall below 50 per cent, and it is common for a peasant to mortgage his future crop for half the amount he will pay to buy the same amount of grain.[9] With the end of advances from large landlords, the need for credit to fill the gap and to increase investment is immense. Unless it is met, the poorer will lose out to the richer, whatever the legal provisions discouraging sale of distributed lands. Almost nowhere did the 1954 survey find minimally decent conditions, and it found only one village where the landlord was making the investments necessary to improve production and village life.

Most significant are the 1954 team's conclusions on the part played by stratification and by overpopulation in maintaining conservative social control in the villages. Of one case where the

8. Thus, cultivators paying cash rentals are concentrated in prosperous and market-oriented areas like Gilan, and are often much wealthier than small owner-cultivators, who before reform were found mainly in areas with little surplus to tempt a landlord. In areas where irrigation water is crucial, ownership or even leasing and sub-letting of water may give more income and power than landownership. This has created problems for a reform based on landownership, and it is too soon to say how the recently announced nationalization of water resources will affect the situation.

9. In addition to the sources in footnote 6, see especially the excellent and comprehensive paper delivered at Harvard in 1965 by Hossein Mahdavy, who participated in the 1964 survey, 'Iran's agrarian problems', only part of which has been published.

competition for a place on the work team was intense they quote the *kadkhoda* (headman) as saying:

Every year we must go to the landlord at harvest time and give him gifts for the opportunity of cultivating his land for the next year. Those outside the *govband* (here meaning work team) compete by saving what they can from their earnings during the year to buy presents for the landlord in hopes they can replace some *govband* member. For example, a man works the harvest in Gorgan. His family stays alive by gleaning the fields of the *govbands* here. Then this family spends most of their earnings for presents for the landlord to get a place in a *govband* . . . owners throw out *govband* members at their slightest whim. If one of us would forget to say 'Good morning' to the landlord be would throw us off the land (Survey village no. 20).

Discussing a village where a few families headed two work teams each, and could gross about $435 a year, while a labouring family might average only $27, the survey goes on:

This fact indicates an insight into the part played by the *govband* in the land tenure pattern of Iran. It may be observed here and in all other villages visited in Iran by this team that the *govband* system, which provides a vested interest group in a village, provides stability for the landlord or his representative to maintain control. This system is also partly responsible for overloading the land with underemployed people because there is a tendency for the *govband* owner to withdraw from actual work and to perform merely a management function while hiring cheap farm labour for only part of the agricultural season (Survey village no. 26).

As noted below, in villages where the top landlord stratum has been removed, the persistence of the rest of the stratification pattern, including competition for scarce work, has maintained social control by the top classes, to whom some of the power formerly held by the landlord has been transferred.

The survey team also had some general remarks about settled tribesmen which may be relevant to the continuing governmental efforts to settle the tribes:

No groups of people in Iran are more poverty stricken, more miserable, more exploited, than the sedentary tribal peoples – the Baluch, the Arab tribes, the peoples of Sistan, and the Kurds, to name only a few. They are ground down by their own khans or Sardars or Shaikhs under the guise that the government is the culprit, while the government answers any signs of unrest by stationing large bodies of troops in the areas with no apparent attempt to solve one of the basic difficulties of an archaic and vicious land tenure system (Survey village no. 33).

The team also commented significantly on a village in Sistan, where land had been distributed with none of the accompanying investment and services that could have made the distribution programme a real success. Although the farmers were earning only $32.50 per family and were all in debt, the team noted:

Despite the contention that the Sistan land distribution is a failure, the individual farmer on the Zabul plains cultivating land only one-third as productive as that in Jiroft is making a net cash return three times that of the Jiroft *khoshneshin* (farmer in a *govband* without oxen) [who net $10.25]. Despite their abject poverty, when the freeholders of these villages were asked if they were better off under their former landlords than now, they defended to a man their present independence on their own tracts of land (Survey village no. 7).

The general conclusions of the team (given at the end of the survey), several of which are relevant to land reform, were as follows:

1. More people are trying to make a living on the land than it can presently support.

2. There is considerable evidence to suggest to us that the government institutions in the rural areas of Iran are derived from, and give support to, the present land tenure system; that the social and economic institutions are conditioned by the same pattern of land ownership.

3. It follows (from 2 above) that the political and economic structures in the provinces are maintained to a large extent by the land tenure system. Under the present government, the power is divided between the land-holding power groups in the provinces and the army.

4. There is conclusive evidence that benefits from public works in the provinces – dams, factories, etc. – are enjoyed in the main by special interests, i.e. those power groups that also benefited by the present land tenure system.

5. Our data would suggest that lands operated by government agencies . . . are merely an adaptation of the local land tenure, crop-division system, that the farmers on these lands are not materially better off than the private landlord's tenants.

6. In certain areas where it is possible to supplement the normal one cereal crop per year by supplementary summer crops or dates, it was noted that if the increased level of a few persons in the villages rose above that of the average, such farmers tended to stop work and hire labour which actually reduced their cash incomes. We believe this phenomenon to be due to (a) the cultivation pattern in which the land-lord design is the preferred living pattern, (b) the pressure of unemployed

population in every village which puts social pressure and moral obligation on the better-than-average-to-do villager to provide employment for unemployed persons, (c) on the observational level it would appear that the lack of *alternative investment opportunities* supports the relative preference for leisure attitudes.

7. It was observed and our data supports the conclusion that there is a tendency for landlords to maintain a vested interest group within each village as evidenced by the *govband* system in which a preferred economic group helps maintain stability and preserves the land tenure *status quo*.

8. There has been a retrogression of agriculture in Iran during the last three years due to lack of capital reinvestment on the land (principally *ganat* repair and maintenance) due perhaps to a period of general political instability.

9. There is no evidence in our sample (which covered every province of Iran, even to the remotest agricultural areas) that there is any cessation whatsoever on the part of the farmers to pay the landlord's share. By virtue of the *govband* vested interest system and the forces of social control such as the gendarmerie, the Ministry of Interior officials down through the *kadkhoda*, and the legal processes, the farmer cannot escape payment.

Similar conclusions arise from a more extensive Agricultural Sample Survey undertaken in 1960 by the Iranian authorities and the FAO, whose results have been published (in Persian) in fifteen volumes. This survey was made in a period of greater prosperity than the 1954 survey, but the general features it reveals are the same. The rural population of Iran is given as 15·4 million, and the cultivated area as 11·4 million hectares, of which 39·9 per cent was annually left fallow; 1·9 million rural families had regular positions on holdings averaging about six hectares (including fallow), enough for subsistence in Iranian conditions, but another 1·3 million rural families had no such regular positions and most had to live off the same holdings.[10] Half the total farm units had under 2·9 hectares, including fallow. In addition to the widely varying size of holdings, even within the same area, the survey found overall that 14·4 per cent of the

10. In Mahdavy and other writers using the 1960 survey, there is a confusing usage of 'peasant holdings' and 'peasant holders', which in this survey refer not to peasant ownership but only to peasants having a regular position on plots of varying sizes. I have seen no indication of ownership statistics in this 1960 survey. The statistics here are cited in Mahdavy (1965, pp. 13–19).

employed rural population were wage labourers, and 33·1 per cent were 'family workers' (corresponding to the non-oxen owning members of the work team in the original survey).

This 47·5 per cent of the employed rural population with nothing to offer but their labour generally received no land in either phase of the land reform. They remain dependent on the farmers or on the new landowning peasants for their employment, or else they must continue to migrate to the cities, where unemployment and underemployment are still prevalent.

As Hossein Mahdavy, an Iranian economist who participated in studies of the early effects of land reform, has noted:

About ten million out of the 15·4 million rural population of Iran belongs to the poorer classes who have either no land at their disposal or have less than 4 hectares to cultivate. This is at the root of Iran's 'Agrarian Problem', irrespective of the ownership of land which undoubtedly aggravates the situation. The land reform programme, as will be explained below, left the existing land allotments untouched. In the villages affected by the land reform, only the title deeds of the lands previously farmed by the peasants were passed on to them. No redistribution or levelling of the existing disparities between different classes of peasants took place.

The distinction between different classes within the village community is seldom appreciated by those who have not had loose ties with rural Iran. The peasants have their own *bourgeoisie*. These richer men of the village usually control the better lands, operate the village mills, own the village shops and act as general moneylenders and traders and can afford to acquire more land and livestock and even aspire to become some sort of a government appointed or landlord appointed functionary in the village.

. . . any land reform which, even when fully implemented, fails to touch the basic problem of two-thirds of Iran's rural population clearly misses the greater part of the target.

Mahdavy goes on to note the communal pattern of agriculture in Iran, with open fields for grazing, and frequent redistribution of farms by landlords. A modernization pattern based on individual farms would result (and in fact has begun to result) in enclosing the common lands to the detriment of the poorer peasants, as happened in much of modern Europe. Writing early in 1965, Mahdavy adds:

The communal open-field system of agriculture, prevalent in Iran, is by nature more amenable to a co-operative form of production than to a system of production based on individual enterprise. In a co-operative system, the over-fragmentation of lands and the grazing problems can be overcome by introducing production plans for the entire village. The need for enclosures on tiny plots of land will thus not arise.

The incompatibility of the communal form of production organization with a land system based on individual initiative and enterprise is not yet fully appreciated or perceived in Iran for an obvious reason: there has been little time for any intended change to encounter difficulties. But this difficulty will increase proportionally with the attempts on the part of the village *bourgeoisie* to break away from the communal and traditional patterns and to undertake more profitable farming in cash crops, fruits and vegetables (pp. 15, 17).

The government hoped that the extension of the cultivated area through new irrigation schemes and rising crop yields on cultivated land through improvements in productive technique might meet the problem of agricultural unemployment and under-employment. Since some improvements actually reduce the number of men who can be employed, as does mechanized farming, which has been expanding for years, especially in dry farming areas near some cities, it seems doubtful that agricultural improvement will mean significantly more agricultural employment. Within the existing limitations the government might have opted either for a cooperative farming solution that would have given all villagers a similar stake in agricultural improvement and modernization, or for an individualist solution that counted on the initiative of farmers and of capitalist landholders. Not surprisingly, in view of Iran's general political and economic orientation, the government chose the second option. A bourgeois land reform that lessens the control of parasitic and non-productive absentee landlords is a significant reform whose positive effects on production and modernization are apparently already being felt; it is, however, a reform that contains within it profoundly contradictory features that promise continuing problems.

The crucial land reform measures in Iran were adopted in 1962–3 at a time when the landlord-controlled parliament had been dismissed and a reformist government dominated by Premier Ali Amini and Minister of Agriculture Hasan Arsanjani was in power. The Shah had already indicated his interest in land reform, and a rather mild reform bill had been introduced in parliament late in 1959, to be so emasculated in 1960 as to make parliament seem a hopeless instrument for this reform.

In addition to urgent political reasons for land reform,[11] one reason for its adoption was that some change was imperative if the country was to become stronger and more modernized. The impetus to Iranian modernization had been given under Reza Shah in the 1920s and had continued in the post-war period with some notable growth, but there had been a constant and increasingly grave lag in agriculture, which meant both inadequate agricultural production and the lack of a rural market that could encourage the further growth of Iranian industry. The traditional pattern of draining the entire agricultural surplus to the cities and leaving only the barest minimum for agricultural investment was one result of absentee-landlord dominance that could not be overcome by the various foreign-sponsored technical aid programmes that were so abundant in the post-war years. The middle classes and the technically educated were increasing in number and more and more of them were entering government agencies. Like the Shah, many of them saw that the large absentee landlords were prejudicing Iran's chances for further economic development.

The early 1960s was a period of severe economic recession and stagnation after a boom in the late 1950s. If growth was to be encouraged, on a less speculative and more productive basis than before, the expansion of agricultural production and of a peasant market was essential. Although the Shah's rule had been said, with some justice, to rest in large part on landlord support, there were some fundamental differences in interest between the Shah and the absentee landlords. The Shah was interested in modernizing and strengthening Iran, and hence in increasing production, as quickly as was compatible with the safety of his own rule, while the landlords as a class were not. The Shah seems to have been willing to take the small risk of alienating the absentee landlords in order to do what was necessary to put Iran's economy on a sounder basis; particularly since he could hope to replace landlord support with that of some of the middle class and peasant elements.

In January 1962, the Shah and Arsanjani announced a new decree-law among whose main features were the following: (a) nobody was allowed to own more than one village (or selected fractions totalling one village). Excluded were orchards, tea

11. On the politics of land reform, see, in addition to Mahdavy, Op't Land (1966) and Scarcia (1962), which gives an Italian translation of the January 1962 decree-law.

plantations, groves, homesteads and mechanized areas worked by wage labourers; (b) the government was to indemnify landlords in ten years (later changed to fifteen on the basis of the taxes they had been paying; this sum plus 10 per cent administrative costs was to be paid over fifteen years by the purchasing peasants; (c) only persons who were members of a village co-operative were eligible for land, and the deeds would remain with the Agricultural Bank as security until all instalments had been paid. According to one source, the purchase price was later revised upward, after landlords unashamedly protested that the taxes they had been paying were based on ridiculously low valuations of their land (Op't Land, 1966, p. 109). A further major feature of the reform was that peasants should be allotted the land they were actually farming, and those providing more than labour got first priority. In practice this seems to have meant that the heads of work-teams got land, while the approximately 47·5 per cent whom the 1960 survey counted as labourers selling nothing but their labour did not.

The landlords, having had fair warning at least since the 1959–60 bill that a division of their land based on maximum holdings might be enacted, had had two years to transfer ownership of their villages to their wives, children and relatives, and this land was allowed to remain where it was.[12]

The actual area distributed under this first phase of reform is a matter of some dispute. The official government figures are between 13,000 and 14,000 villages (out of a total of 49,000 villages in Iran). According to Mahdavy (1965), however, who helped to survey the effect of reform:

The information released by the government in Tehran is invariably found to be inconsistent with data provided by the authorities in the field . . . Even if one-hundredth of a village were to be sold to the government, in most statistics issued by the government that village

12. That such transfers were widespread is indicated by the great discrepancy between scholarly and official estimates that the majority of Iran's villages were owned by large landlords, and the official decision that 13,904 villages out of Iran's 49,000 were eligible for distribution. As noted below, this figure includes villages of which only a part was to be distributed, so that the number of eligible villages probably equalled fewer than 9000 complete villages. By contrast, as noted in the excellent section on agriculture in the US Army *Area Handbook for Iran* (Washington, 1963), in 1962 the Minister of Agriculture estimated that about 15,000 villages belonged to landlords with *more than five villages,* and the government stated that 400 to 450 large landlords owned *57 per cent* of all Iranian villages(p. 443).

would be classified as 'reformed'. More accurate statistics can be obtained from provincial offices of the Land Reform Agency . . . From time to time the government issues information concerning the number of households affected by land reform. The figures are not reliable as they include many-fold counting . . . If only a fraction of a village is sold by one landlord, the entire households of the village are claimed to have benefitted from the reform. If a second landlord sells another fraction, the entire village household is counted again as having benefitted from land reform (pp. 22–3).

Extrapolating from the areas he has studied, Mahdavy judges that the equivalent of about 5000 complete villages, or a bit over 10 per cent of all Iranian villages, had been distributed by mid-1964, at which time the first phase had been declared completed, although further distributions have occurred. Another analysis of official figures casts similar doubt on them.[13]

An assessment of the first and later phases of land reform awaits an independent scholarly survey. A detailed published study of one reformed village reveals trends that accord so well with what might be expected from previous knowledge of peasant stratification that they may be of general validity. This study provides another cautionary note about official statistics: the land reform law said that only peasants who joined cooperatives would get land; it seems likely that this condition accounts for the over-enumeration of cooperatives in official statistics. In the village studied and other villages in the area, cooperatives were officially in existence, but did not actually exist in any form; a condition that helped to intensify the dependence of the poorer peasants on loans from richer ones.[14]

13. 'A review of the statistics of the first stage of land reform', *Tahqiqat é eqtesadi*, March 1964. The authors state that of the 13,904 villages said to be eligible for distribution, 3788 were fully eligible and 10,116 only partly eligible. In the absence of data as to what proportion of the latter were eligible, the authors guess that it averaged half of each village, thus reducing the eligible figure to 8836 whole villages, or 18 per cent of the Iranian total (p. 140). According to the *Iran Almanac* (Tehran, 1966), 12,875 villages of the 13,904 had been bought and distributed by February 1965. With so many gaps and inaccuracies in official figures, it seems impossible to estimate the proportion of full villages distributed beyond saying that it should lie between 10 and 18 per cent, and one may guess at 14–15 per cent.

14. Miller (1964): 'In the Khamseh only land distribution has taken place. Cooperatives have been formed in theory; they have not yet been brought into effective use in any of the villages observed. Money has been collected from the peasants for the cooperatives, but after a year the government

To quote the most relevant portions of this study of a relatively prosperous region south of Zanjan that had recently been distributed:

Under the old landlord system, lots were drawn every three or four years by the farmers for the lands to be farmed. In this way, a poor farmer might draw the best land, and with hard work and good harvests could improve his position. The land distribution law has done away with this possibility. Under present circumstances, except for a few fortunate smallholders who are on exceptionally fertile land, the larger peasant landowners have already begun to grow richer in comparison with their fellow villagers who own less land. In Hosseinabad, several families out of the 52 peasant landowners own half the village. A tendency has already begun to emerge: the larger farmers, two and a half *joft* or more, lend their surplus capital at a high rate of interest to their less prosperous fellow villagers and as a result are gradually replacing the land capitalism of the former landlord with the oxen and cash capitalism of the new system. . . . The removal of the landlord from the power structure has put control of village government firmly in the hands of the wealthier landholders. It was in the landlord's interest to balance power between the wealthier farmers, the small farmers and the *khoshneshin* [labourers]. The removal of the landlord has broken the balance and the *rish sefid* [council of elders] as a consequence primarily press for the interests of the larger and wealthier landholders with little regard for less privileged groups.

. . . a feeling of discontent is growing among the *khoshneshin* [40 per cent of this village] even though they still harbour some hopes that the government will give them some land as well. The development of new lands through large-scale irrigation projects could absorb some of the *khoshneshin* but the limited land available for new farmers and the introduction of labour saving techniques will make the problem of providing work for the *khoshneshin* a major national problem (pp. 487, 489, 594).

The writer expresses the hope that the introduction of election of the village council by secret ballot and of effective cooperatives will overcome the problems of exacerbated class division that he observed. The experience of a country like India, with a longer experience of cooperatives and of village self-government, justifies a certain scepticism. Although it is true that effective cooperatives can meet the immediate problem of low-interest loans, it seems

---

has done nothing about contributing its share of funds or allowing these funds to be used in the village' (p. 496). Similar conclusions are found in other recent studies.

probable that the cooperatives and village council, even if secretly elected, will continue to be dominated by, and to favour, the wealthiest elements in the village.[15]

This is not to say that the land distribution programme is a meaningless fraud, as some of the Shah's more strident critics would have it. The reduction in the sums transferred to absentee owners, and the consequent increase in locally available funds to be used for both investment and consumption, has evidently given an impetus to both production and living standards in the villages, to judge by recent informal reports. Similarly, one class of peasants can for the first time be sure that the benefits of capital investment and time spent on their land will accrue to them, and this has apparently resulted in some enclosure of farms, a rise in the use of chemical fertilizers, and new receptivity to the suggestions of the government's growing extension services. What have not been met, even in the distributed areas, are the needs of the poorest stratum, variously estimated as including 40–50 per cent of the population. Their situation may even be worsening, whatever temporary relief they receive in a good harvest year. The land reform, even if the cooperatives spread more effectively than they have until now, remains an essentially bourgeois reform, favouring both the large owners who farm reform-exempt plantations and fields with hired labour, and the more prosperous villagers who can now profit from more rational investment and agricultural techniques. The large labouring class, however, is given no protection – no minimum wage, no unemployment relief, no gleaning rights on the now-private fields, and no land.

The second phase of land reform, covering most of that large majority of villages untouched by the first phase, is of a much more conservative nature than that put through by Arsanjani. Landlords are allowed to retain a maximum of thirty to 150 hectares of non-mechanized land, depending on the region, and must dispose of the rest in one of several ways chosen by themselves. The landlord may:

15. 'A survey of rural cooperatives up to Mehr 1342 (September 1963)', *Tahqiqat é eqtesadi*, March 1964, notes (p. 160) for example, that cooperative regulations allow much larger loans to those who contribute larger shares to the cooperative, thus increasing the land reform's bias in favour of the more prosperous peasants. However, Professor Lambton wrote me, after this article was finished, that on the whole her impression of the land reform, and in particular of the cooperatives, was favourable. She observed that many of the cooperatives worked very well.

1. Rent the land to the peasants on the basis of the average net income of the past three years; the lease to be for thirty years and subject to five-year revisions.

2. Sell the land to the peasants at a mutually agreed price.

3. Divide the land with the peasant, retaining a section equal to the share of the crop he formerly received.

4. By mutual agreement set up a joint stock company with the peasants, with the landlord share in the company to be equal to his former share of the crop.

5. Sell his share to the government to be resold to the peasants on terms equal to those of the first phase.

This may represent more a *regularization* of the existing situation than any profound reform. Particularly where leases revisable every five years are chosen, the landlord loses nothing and gains a government-enforced lease, while in the other alternatives (except no. 5) the peasant may lose as much as he gains. The percentage of self-sufficient farmers, even among those who buy or receive land, will be smaller among those affected by the second than among those affected by the first phase, since the former group of new owners may have to meet a price set by the landlord, or if they get a plot of land based on the crop division, it will in most cases be too small to provide subsistence and will rarely provide a surplus for improvements.

The second phase was declared completed in January 1967. According to official figures, which may be biased and which are in any case incomplete, of the over one million tenants affected, only 46,000 were able to purchase land from their landlords; 17,000 landlords chose to distribute their land on the basis of the former crop division to their 153,000 tenants, and 6392 landlords bought out their tenants (the several hundred thousand tenants unaccounted for may have entered into the leasing or joint-stock arrangements).[16] Official figures thus show 199,000 ex-tenants getting *some* land in the second phase, although over three-quarters of these got significantly less than they formerly

16. Economist Intelligence Unit, *Quarterly Economic Review: Iran.* March 1967, p. 11. More recent, although still defective, statistics from the Bank Markazi Iran *Bulletin*, July–August 1967, p. 194, are more dramatic in showing the small proportion of landlords who chose to sell land under the second phase. The official figure for such sellers of land is 3238, as compared with 203,049 small landlords who chose to lease their lands.

farmed, while the rest of the more than two million peasants (with families totalling 11·4 million) who are said to have benefited from this phase got no land. The procedures and figures of the second phase must be kept in mind when grandiose claims about the Iranian reforms are made.[17] If about 14–16 per cent of Iran's villages and villagers were affected by the first phase, and if 40–50 per cent of these got no land, it can be seen that about 8 per cent of Iran's peasants got land in the first phase. In the second phase, relying on official figures we can say that, at most, less than 10 per cent of the villagers affected got any land, and that the villagers affected accounted for 60–70 per cent of the total, so that another 6–7 per cent of the total peasant population received some land; making a grand total of perhaps 14–15 per cent of Iran's peasants as new landholders. *This is not an insignificant figure*, for all its divergence from more extravagant propaganda claims.

The United Nation's publication, *Progress in Land Reform*, summarized the situation in 1966:

These land reform measures have, however, by no means solved the problems of Iranian agriculture. In the first place, it is not clear that they have solved the social and political problem of landlord dominance. There was nothing to prevent landlords from reordering the cultivation pattern in their villages before the land reform reached them in such a way as to ensure that the best land – or indeed any land at all – went only to their friends, relatives, and loyal dependants. Again, landlords who exercised their option to retain a collection of parts of villages might contrive to retain the best parts of each and even, perhaps, those parts which dominate the water supply for the rest of the village. It also remains to be seen whether the second-stage reforms will, in fact, end traditional forms of tenancy. Without adequate enforcement measures, traditional relations could still be continued under the cloak of a thirty-year cash-rent lease. And it will be remembered that the tenants of landlords who owned only parts of villages (the owners who were left largely undisturbed) were often worse off than others.

. . . Again, in those districts where there was a tenancy hierarchy, the land has sometimes gone to the entrepreneurial *govband* who did not cultivate directly, rather than to the crop-sharing labourers who have

17. Aside from statistical inflation, confusion is sown by the practice of referring to land leased to peasants on terms revisable every five years (including the 99 year leases for *vaqf* property stipulated by the reform) as having been *distributed* or *given* to them. Under such semantic rules the vast majority of Iran's peasants may be claimed as beneficiaries or even as new 'owners'.

derived no benefits from the reform. Thus a new class of landlords may have been created. It is, indeed, the explicit intention of the reform not to establish equality, but to create an extended tenure ladder. As the Shah said in one of his speeches, 'our aims are not to destroy small landlords. What we are doing is a means of making it possible to become small landlords. Those who become owners of land today, we hope, will become small landlords in the future'.[18] The shift in power from the feudal magnates to the new larger class of small landlords could still represent a significant political change, however, and it may be that these new landlords, being closer to the productive process, are in fact more concerned with raising productivity than were the original absentee landlords, though there may be compensating disadvantages in an increase of social tension. . . .

. . . A second problem concerns the cost of the land to the beneficiaries. . . . Many will find this too large a sum to pay off over fifteen years. Similarly, it is doubtful how secure the new leasing system will actually be even if it can be enforced, since rents have not been reduced; they are to be fixed in cash at pre-reform levels (thus exposing the tenant to the vagaries of market fluctuations) and the landlord may evict if the rent is not paid within three months of the due date.

. . . The third immense problem is to find some rapid substitute for the organizational and physical services formerly provided by the landlords and their agents. It is not clear how effective the new co-operatives will be in this respect, in view of the fact that Iranian farmers have very little experience of egalitarian co-operation. . . . By December 1963, nearly 2000 co-operative associations had been formed, but it is certain that many of these were co-operatives in name only, their sole function being to enable the tenant recipients of redistributed land formally to conform with the requirements of the law. . . .

. . . The potentialities of these [village] councils are great. At the same time, in those villages where the land reform has left a stratified population with a few of the large landholders being the only obvious candidates for office, there are equally clear dangers – the possibility of an oligarchic system of exploitation of the poor by the rich, for instance, or, alternatively, of debilitating factional struggles between rival leaders

18. The quotation is from *Facts about Iran*, 20 November 1962 (Iran, General Department of Publications and Broadcasting). A related view is expressed by the Shah in *Mission for my country* (New York, 1961), p. 200: 'Much of the worst-managed land in Iran is in the hands of the biggest landlords . . . as a class the big private landlords are parasites . . . Quite different are many of the smaller landlords, who may own one or a few villages and not infrequently live in close association with their tenants. While some of them are selfish and self-centred, many take a lively interest in the welfare of the families who live on their land. Often they freely give land for schools, clinics, or mosques, and many of the best-managed villages in Iran are run by them.' It is unclear to what degree this distinction is supported by scholarly studies.

and their dependent followers of the kind which has plagued the Indian *panchayat* (pp. 24–5).

Given the partial and contradictory nature of the reforms, it seems too early to predict the degree to which they will even succeed in introducing more productive capitalist relations into the countryside. Although the bias in favour of cash rents and large farmers, and the exemption from redistribution of mechanized farms using hired labour, work in a capitalist direction, in the majority of villages not covered by the first phase old patterns may continue under new forms. It seems clear that the *trend* is towards capitalism and increased investment and productivity in agriculture, but it is not clear when and whether this trend will come to dominate the traditional patterns of Iranian agriculture. The experience with similar reforms in other countries with impoverished land-hungry peasants does not inspire easy confidence.[19] Among the many remaining problems is that the success of cooperatives and of the necessary extension and educational services depends on having numerous dedicated government representatives in the villages, whereas the government and its agents have in the past acted more as additional exploiters than productive aides. This pattern is changing, but how much it is too soon to say.

Recent figures and reports indicate that agricultural production and village consumption are rising, and although it will take several years to show whether this is a steady trend, and not the result of a few good harvests, there seems no reason to doubt that the reform will have a favourable effect on the average production and consumption of villagers.[20] There is still a great need for increased government services and more effective cooperatives if the reforms are to result in more than temporary improvements.

Central to the above discussion is the socio-political effect of the reforms. As already indicated, they have a bourgeois-capitalist bias, and in this they fit in well with the other changes now occurring in Iran, which is undergoing a boom in productive investment, helped both by the foreign exchange reserves provided by oil and by very favourable low interest loans and barter

19. See especially reports on the failure of reforms favouring the wealthier peasants even to spread capitalism significantly, such as Thorner and Thorner (1962), ch. 1; and Mosse (1965).

20. Issawi (1967, p. 455), notes the primacy of weather conditions as a factor in three successive good harvests. On other points this author seems too ready to accept inflated official statistics.

agreements with east European countries. It is something of an irony that Iranian capitalism, because of oil and the country's strategic location, has been able to profit from the rivalries of two groups not intrinsically friendly to the successful independent capitalists of new nations – the old capitalist powers and the new communist bloc. Benefiting from the rivalry of these two groups, Iran may be on the way to setting up a largely self-sufficient capitalist economy: as planless, wasteful, and indifferent to the human cost as that of the United States, but with the magic GNP curve moving upward.

In this process land reform is playing a role. Those who rightly note the inadequate and contradictory nature of this reform sometimes conclude that the majority of the peasants excluded from its benefits will become for the first time a revolutionary class.[21] I have usually found historical trends too complex and contradictory to make any such predictions, and two results of the reforms that will operate against rural revolt should be noted (quite apart from 'peasant fatalism' and the difficulties of rural revolt in the widely scattered villages of Iran and the Middle East; it is surely no accident that the Left in Asia has successfully organized peasant revolts only in the more densely populated areas). Firstly, if increases in agricultural output should continue, the labourers may be better off even though they are getting the same or, even a lower share of the crop than they used to. Secondly, and more important, if it is true that a dissatisfied class with new aspirations has come into being, it is also true that a relatively satisfied class with a greater stake than ever before in existing relations has also been created. For the moment it seems clear that the power and resources of this new landed class enable them to keep effective control over the landless. No matter what the institutional formalities, the richer and more powerful villagers will continue to dominate village government and institutions, and to hire workers from a pool that exceeds the demand. How long the stabilizing effect of the new owners and the old hierarchies will continue to outweigh the dissatisfactions of the excluded labourers is not a matter for confident prediction.

21. See Mahdavy (1965a), 'The Coming Crisis in Iran'. Several other sources note the early active discontent of excluded peasants and villagers, including Lambton (1963). I have seen no reports indicating whether this discontent has come more or less active in the past few years.

References

ADAMS, R. M. (1965), *Land Behind Baghdad*, Chicago University Press.

ENGLISH, P. W. (1966), *City and Village in Iran*, Wisconsin University Press.

ISSAWI, C. (1967), 'Iran's economic upsurge', *Middle East Journal*, Autumn.

KEDDIE, N. R. (1960), *Historical Obstacles to Agrarian Change in Iran*.

LAMBTON, A. K. S. (1953), *Landlord and Peasant in Persia*.

LAMBTON, A. K. S. (1963), 'Rural development and land reform in Iran', in CENTO, *Symposium on Rural Development*, September, Teheran.

MAHDAVY, H. (1965), 'Iran's agrarian problems'.

MAHDAVY, H. (1965a), 'The coming crisis in Iran', *Foreign Affairs*, October.

MILLER, W. G. (1964), 'Hosseinabad: a Persian village', *Middle East Journal*, Autumn.

MOSSE, W. E. (1965), 'Stolypin's villages', *Slavonic and East European Review*, June.

OP'T LAND, C. (1966), 'Land reform in Iran', *Persica*, vol. 2.

SCARCIA, G. (1962), 'Governo, riforma agragia e opposizione in Persia', *Oriente Moderno*, October–November.

THORNER, D., and THORNER, A. (1962), *Land and Labour in India*, Asia Publishing House.

UNITED NATIONS (1966), *Progress in Land Reform*, 4th Report, Dept. of Economic and Social Affairs, New York.

WEULERSSE, J. (1946), *Paysans de Syrie et du Proche-Orient*, Paris.

Part Three
Industrialization: The Human Material

The large literature on industrialization includes a number of
crucial themes some of which are touched on in other sections of
this reader (Readings 11, 18, 20 and more broadly, 3). Here
selection is confined to a question with which both economists
and sociologists have been much concerned, namely the 'human
material' of industrialization and problems of the quality of
industrial labour and leadership. The historical approach of the
two readings illuminates the dangers of generalizing certain
abstract behavioural models as prescriptions for development, in
this context theories of labour committment and
entrepreneurship. Morris's (Reading 8) analysis of the formation
of a work force in the Bombay cotton industry is informed by the
perspective of comparative economic history. His scholarly study
showed that the behaviour of workers in the industry has been
consistently misinterpreted (as traditionalistic or 'uncommitted'),
and is explicable in terms of the system of production which
developed, including the labour policies of its organizers. By
implication this advises an emphasis on the relationship between
underdevelopment and industry itself rather than on supposed
inadequacies of labour quality and supply. Cardoso (Reading 9)
on the other hand, demonstrates that appropriate criteria for
analysing the record of national capitalism in underdeveloped
countries are to be sought in its historical situation and
relationships, rather than derived from ideal – typical
formulations of entrepreneurship.

8 M. D. Morris

The Emergence of an Industrial Labour Force in India

Excerpt from M. D. Morris, *The Emergence of an Industrial Labor Force in India: A Study of the Bombay Cotton Mills, 1854–1947,* University of California Press, 1965, chapter 11, pp. 198–210.

Modern factory industry requires methods of organizing productive activity that are significantly different from those employed in pre-industrial societies. If the shift from traditional modes of production to industrial technology is to be successful, it is necessary to mobilize a labor force which will serve the necessities of this novel situation. Labor must somehow be drawn out of the old and transferred into the new environment. It must be given new tasks and sufficient training to perform them; it must be taught to work to a different pattern of rules and relationships.

Scholars have tended to stress the radical character of this transformation and the difficulties of its achievement. For example, it has been the claim of students of the subject that during the past century Indian industrialization was inhibited in many ways by the tenacious persistence of commitments to the traditional social order in the countryside. Apart from its other purported consequences, it is argued that the institutions of the older social order seriously inhibited the creation of an industrial labor force. Claims of kinship, caste and village supposedly served as bonds keeping people on the land or operated as powerful forces to bring them back. Thus any movement to the city was a temporary one. In this view, the expansion of the Bombay cotton textile industry, particularly before 1920, was inhibited by the limited supply of raw labor available to it and by the consequent effects of this shortage on work-force stability and discipline. Moreover, this shortage of labor, so it is said, forced employers to depend on the foreman-jobber for hiring and disciplining the workers, a dependence which added to the difficulties of properly organizing the labor force. And even after the First World War, when all observers agree that labor was not in short supply, it is claimed that the persistence with which mill hands retained their rural connections made for a labor force only 'partially committed' to factory employment, one character-ized by indiscipline and rates of absenteeism 'much higher than in more advanced industrial countries' (Myers, 1958, pp. 43–54). Actually, however, very little systematic historical evidence has been adduced in defense of these notions. When the career of the Bombay industry is analysed, quite a different interpretation emerges.

Not only did the industry steadily expand the size of its labor force, but the evidence suggests that during the critical period, the half century before 1920, mills were able to obtain new recruits without any significant upward pressure on the wage rates at which novice mill hands were employed. If labor short-ages had persisted for long periods of time – i.e. if market conditions had favored a more rapid expansion of output than actually occurred – we would expect to find evidence of a steady upward trend of hiring-in wage rates, particularly when labor costs were a relatively small proportion of total costs and profit expectations were quite high. Moreover, we would have expected evidence of a shift in the industry's technology increasingly in the direction of more capital-intensive methods of production. Neither of these two tendencies can be found in the period before 1920.

Nor can it be argued that wage rates, for cultural reasons specific to India, were unresponsive to a labor shortage when it appeared. The general behavior of wages during the plague-induced labor shortage of 1897 as well as the changing occupa-tional wage rate structure over time prove that we are dealing with a situation responsive to market forces. The relative stability of hiring-in rates is clear evidence that the industry never was faced by a problem of labor shortage. It generally could recruit all the new raw labor it required to meet its needs for expansion.

The overwhelming proportion of mill hands came from dis-tricts in the Bombay Presidency, but within the recruitment pattern there were certain specific features. The main body of workers did not come from the hinterland immediately surround-ing Bombay but from more distant sources, from places at least 101 to 200 miles from the city. Initially, mill hands seem to have come from a limited number of districts, but as the years passed the operatives tended to be drawn from a greater number of localities and from increasingly distant regions. I have not been able to explain why these specific tendencies existed and were modified over time. To find an answer will require studies of the changing economic situations in the rural areas and changing employment opportunities in Bombay City itself. However, my data should at least put an end to the notion that the structure of Indian society and the character of the traditional ideology impeded the movement of people over long distances to places where economic opportunity existed.

The place-of-origin data I have been able to compile suggest an additional feature about the labor force, one running counter to the widely accepted view that the industry depended almost entirely on workers who migrated only temporarily from the countryside and returned to the countryside at the end of their period of service. My evidence, limited though it is, suggests that over time an increasing proportion of the work force was recruited from people born or permanently resident in Bombay. The fact is significant because it casts very serious doubt on the propositions which attribute labor force instability to the persistence of a rural nexus.

The instability theme itself seems to have been exaggerated, although it is difficult to be precise about the degree to which this has been so. My evidence suggests that a not insignificant and growing proportion of the work force exhibited considerable attachment to the industry, if not to an individual mill. The fragmentary length-of-service information suggests a steady rise in the proportion of the workers with records of long service in the industry. As would be expected, length of service in a single mill was shorter although even here there was a significant tendency toward increasing stability. There is no way, quantitatively, to determine the extent to which labor turnover in the individual mills was associated with transfers to other mills rather than with a return to the countryside. It is clear, however, that a great deal of the labor turnover in the mills was in fact a response to changing employment and income possibilities in the industry and in Bombay generally rather than to the lure of the countryside.

Just as the analysis supports the view that a growing proportion of the labor force was permanently tied to the industry for its livelihood, a reassessment of the materials on absenteeism suggests that these rates have been grossly overstated. It is likely that willful absenteeism by mill hands was typically less than 10 per cent, and much of this could be attributed to illness. Moreover, statistical evidence does not support the claim of an enormous seasonal swing in absenteeism associated with agricultural requirements of the rural sector.

Just as other traditional institutions did not seem seriously to inhibit either the movement of people to Bombay or their recruitment into the mills, so traditional village caste (*jati*) divisions apparently did not have overwhelming effect on the mobilization of a factory labor force. I have cautioned that the information on caste is particularly treacherous to deal with, and one must proceed with caution. Nevertheless, it seems safe to say that though there certainly were caste clusterings in Bombay mills, they were not exclusive and did not prevent members of different *jatis* from working side by side with one another.

The traditional subcaste distinctions of the countryside did not affect the employer's ability to recruit as much labor as he needed of the type that he wanted. This does not mean that certain caste attitudes did not persist in the mills, but they do not seem to have affected the employer's ability to utilize labor or to operate his enterprise profitably. At no place in the vast mass of material bearing on the industry's history have I been able to find a complaint by an employer that caste divisions made the working of a mill financially less rewarding. Moreover, whatever distinctions did persist survived only because they were irrelevant to mill operations. Whenever and wherever industrial functioning required the disruption of traditional distinctions, they were apparently swept away with ease.

There was only one significant exception to the general proposition that caste was unimportant in the industry. Hindu untouchable caste members seem to have been systematically excluded from weaving departments. This has been explained as a refusal of non-untouchable weavers, Muslim as well as Hindu, to work with them because of the fear of a specific type of ritual defilement. Though the logic is ideologically impeccable, there is no strong evidence one way or another on this point. There is some indication that the fear of pollution was only one, and perhaps a minor, aspect of the situation. The weaving department was historically the highest paid section in the industry. Untouchable groups seem to have come into the mills relatively late and moved into the lower-paid jobs. The exclusion of untouchables from weaving jobs may well have operated as a device to preserve the monopoly of particularly well-paying jobs for all Muslims and clean-caste Hindus against all untouchables more than it constituted a carryover of traditional ritual barriers into the factories. This interpretation is supported by rather scanty evidence that untouchables were also excluded from other well-paid occupations in the industry, jobs in which the specific threat of ritual pollution did not exist.

The slow appearance of untouchables and their limited employment in cotton mills throws doubt on much that has been written about the sources of labor for modern Indian industry. The labor force did not, as Weber (1958, p. 105) suggested, come mainly from the 'declassed and pariah castes' of the countryside. Why this was so is not clear. It is possible that the traditional values held by the employers of labor may have had something to do with this. But once untouchables began to be employed in large numbers, they tended to seep into most occupations. Their exclusion from weaving may have been an apparent qualification to the tendency of industrial employment to act as a subverter of traditional social norms. But even this situation had no adverse effect on the adequacy of labor supply.

One final point should be made about the persistence of traditional attitudes in the mills. If comments of virtually all observers can be accepted, the group divisions which were created in the mills were of a substantially different type in fact than those which existed in the countryside. Where employers found it necessary to grapple with work-force distinctions, language, region and religion were the operationally relevant ones. To the extent that caste appeared as a category, it was not the *jati* concept so familiar in the villages. In the transition from village to factory the institution seems to have undergone a major transformation which lumped all clean-caste Hindus together and pitted them against all untouchable-caste groups. Nor did even these divisions persist with the sharpness that one might have expected. As strikes became increasingly frequent and as union organization began to emerge, these activities exhibited very few of the divisive features of the traditional rural inheritance.

Since there was no difficulty in obtaining recruits for the expanding industry and those who did enter were more firmly attached to it than most observers assumed, it seems safe to conclude that the labor problems with which the industry had to contend did not flow primarily from the psychology of the work force or from the rigid traditions and structure of the rural social order. Such instability and indiscipline as did exist stemmed from the character of employer policies which were determined by the economic and technical characteristics of the enterprises and the competitive nature of the markets in which they operated. In these terms it is probably safe to say that at least until the 1920s the industry got precisely the kind of labor force and the kind of labor discipline that it wanted and needed. And after 1920, when circumstances dictated the development of a different system of labor utilization and administration, the difficulty of modifying disciplinary patterns arose out of the industry's own past organization and institutional arrangements.

The early mills laid down very stringent work rules, and these set the model for all subsequent enterprises. Though penalties for infringement were harsh, unlike the situation in many of the early British cotton factories, the work-discipline actually demanded was quite lax. Perhaps the most notable features of labor utilization in the Bombay mills were the large amounts of labor employed and the looseness of the regulations imposed at the work place. All observers were struck by the fact that, compared with the situation in Lancashire, there was always a very large number of millhands away from the machines.

Given the supply of labor available to them, there is no question that early employers were free to choose virtually any pattern of work organization they desired. Moreover, they were in a position to model their labor deployment schedules on British experience. But the industry very quickly adjusted its forms of operation and its labor routines to the specific conditions it confronted – to the relative costs of capital and labor in Bombay and to the markets in which it had the greatest comparative advantage. Mills were established with the knowledge that capital costs were relatively high, unskilled labor was relatively cheap, and the industry's competitive advantage lay in the production of coarse yarns and cloth from cheap, short-staple local cottons.

The adjustment of the industry to its specific relative factor costs and market requirements clearly determined the forms of labor utilization. The object was to run the expensive equipment as continuously each day and every day as circumstances permitted and at the highest achievable speeds. These practices made it possible to use very large amounts of absolutely minimally trained labor, precisely the sort that was easy and cheap to obtain in Bombay. But the work schedule also made it necessary to employ enough labor to permit workers to take breaks while the machines were running, to develop what in effect amounted to an informal shift system.

Not only did the output on which the Bombay mills concentrated not require a highly trained labor force in any of the numerically significant occupations, but production did not depend on an elaborate system of expensive supervision. A manager and a few skilled masters, supported by a small cadre of fairly well-trained artisans, sufficed to determine operational requirements and guarantee the continued working of the machines. There was no need to lay down a rigorous set of regulations which defined with precision the relation of each worker to his task. Recruitment and supervision could be left to the jobbers because the quality of output and the stability of individual millhands were not critical to the success of an enterprise.

There is no question that employers could have initiated a tighter and more precise system of labor utilization and discipline had they so wished. But such an approach would have required more expensive supervision than could be obtained from the jobbers without producing any obvious immediate benefits to the enterprises. Given the particular competitive advantages which the Bombay mills possessed, it is unlikely that a more elaborate and exact system of labor recruitment and supervision would have contributed to the enhancement of profits. The added costs may in fact only have reduced them. In other words, thoroughly rational economic calculation encouraged what seemed to so many outsiders to be a thoroughly ramshackle system of labor use and discipline. But this casual organization of the mill labor force, early introduced and long preserved, created a tradition of work that was to be difficult to change.

In this respect, a good deal has been said on the effects of *dasturi*, the payments jobbers exacted from workers as the price of getting and holding jobs. Most of what has been written on this subject has been concerned only with the immorality of the exploitation of helpless workers. Doubtless the phenomenon encouraged a much higher labor turnover rate than might otherwise have existed. But apart from the minimal effects of labor instability on mill profitability, a fact which explains the employers' lack of concern with the situation, it seems unlikely that *dasturi* could have been eliminated by a reduction in the power of the jobber. The pervasiveness and persistence of *dasturi* was an expression of the desperate eagerness with which people sought employment. Lacking any device to stem the flow of job seekers, no system of labor recruitment and administration could have remained uncorrupted by the opportunities for making money out of the pressing demand for jobs at going wage rates.

In addition to factors within individual mills which made for labor instability, there were inter-mill forces also at work. The industry was very competitive, not only in the product market but in the labor market as well. During the first six decades, when new mills were being opened rapidly, experienced workers were lured from factory to factory by the promise of higher wages. It was this phenomenon about which already established mills complained most bitterly and which led them, unsuccessfully, to propose wage-standardization schemes at a fairly early date.

Furthermore, the product mix in each mill tended to vary with changing market demand, and wage rates seem to have fluctuated accordingly. Workers tended to move from mill to mill in search of the most advantageous rates. The absence of clear lines of promotion within an individual mill also encouraged workers to seek improvement by moving to another factory.

There is no question that the lack of any necessity for stable work relations within the individual mill and the specific forces which encouraged mobility among mills created what to all intents was a casual labor force in the industry. There were no rewards for constancy and many encouragements to instability. Skills were easily learned, and there were no incentives which encouraged workers to stick with their jobs. When to all this were added the effects of arbitrary discharges and not infrequent cutbacks of work by individual mills to meet market fluctuations, it is easy to understand why those workers who could refused to sacrifice their connections with the countryside. The village link, frail bulwark though it was, offered the only protection against the uncertainties of employment in the cotton mills.

This situation existed without substantial challenge until the 1920s. But with the collapse of the post-First World War boom the industry found itself confronted by a major crisis caused by increasingly vigorous competition from up-country and Japanese mills. The first attempt to deal with the problem, an all-industry assault on the wage level, produced a dramatic reaction in the general strikes of 1924 and 1925. An alternative solution, supported by the Indian Tariff Board's 1927 report, involved a shift toward finer count output combined with a rationalization of production which would lower labor costs. This development, involving more costly raw materials and a higher value of product, necessitated the transformation of traditional methods of labor utilization and discipline. But attempts to carry through these reforms provoked the great strikes of 1928 and 1929.

The four general strikes in six years made it clear that the older methods of administering the work force could not easily be modified. All efforts at change provoked the hostility of an aroused and suspicious labor force, particularly in the context of declining employment opportunities. Radical changes of work and discipline in the mills could be obtained either over the violent protests of millhands who had become self-consciously militant or with their cooperation. The employers were no longer free to manipulate the situation without regard to millhand sensibilities. In this sense, the unilateral attempt by millowners to transform the methods of labor utilization, to intensify discipline, had come too late.

In another sense the great crisis in the industry came too early. It occurred just as the millhands were generating a strong sense of militancy but before trade unions were strong enough to channel that combative spirit toward the achievement of orderly objectives. The unilateral efforts of the millowners to solve their problems had generated a tumultuous and suspicion-ridden atmosphere in the mills. The moderate and the Communist union leaderships struggled for the operatives' loyalty, a loyalty denied to the employers who were now beginning to pay the price for the loosely organized system of labor administration which had existed for three-quarters of a century. The bitter conflicts and all-round mistrust made efforts at compromise unavailing. The 1929 strike collapsed and the infant unions vanished from the industry.

The great strikes from 1924 to 1929 suggest a point which has been ignored or misinterpreted. Strikes were evidence of work force attachment to the industry, of acceptance of a web of working rules and customs. Had workers been only casually attached to factory employment, they would not have struck when confronted with unsatisfactory conditions. They would have voted with their feet, quietly returning to their villages. The willingness to strike and to resist – often for unbelievably long periods – any undesirable changes in work circumstances suggests a profound involvement in the industrial situation.

Nor does it seem reasonable to argue that the occurrence of industry-wide strikes only after the First World War indicates some change in work-force attitudes after that date. Certainly there was no dramatic change in rural social structure which would account for the difference. Moreover, we have to recognize the existence of serious, if less extensive, strikes before the First World War. The explanation of increased militancy lies rather in the conjunction of three factors at work in Bombay itself.

Firstly, the changes which a number of mills began to undertake after 1924 were far more profound than any which had previously occurred. Earlier adjustments to changed competitive circumstances had typically been achieved within a general environment of expansion and usually involved the addition of new mill functions and new workers. The rationalization which began in the 1920s, on the other hand, required a thorough-going revision of tasks and a reduction of employment. Secondly, the end of labor-force growth meant that the existing labor force was no longer diluted by masses of raw recruits from the countryside who did not possess the experience of the industry's long-standing traditions of work. And finally, the sharp increase of Nationalist activity and the appearance of the Communist Party produced elite groups anxious to provide leadership for existing discontent. These are the elements which explain the generalized character of the outbursts after the First World War.

The collapse of the unions in 1929 did not end the tendencies toward modification of work organization. The worsening economic crisis, causing mill after mill to close, forced the survivors to push ahead. For example, between 1930 and 1933 the Bombay mills reduced their labor requirements in the weaving sheds from ninety-four to sixty-one men per 100 looms. This process of reorganization was not carried out in an orderly fashion or with cooperation of the unions which the Fawcett Committee had envisaged in its 1929 report. The changes, typically accompanied by drastic wage reductions and pushed through over enfeebled protests from the exhausted work force, were achieved by the mills on an individualistic and piecemeal basis. Pressed by urgent financial difficulties, not comprehending the scope and complexities of the total task, reluctant to undertake changes along lines unfamiliar to them, virtually all employers attempted to make only the obviously necessary modifications while preserving most of the old order of things. They intensified the work load without redefining specific work responsibilities and without accompanying adjustments in the quality of materials and in the supervisory set-up.

In immediate terms, the cotton mills of Bombay which survived seem to have worked their way out of the worst of the crisis by 1937, but, as the general strike of 1934 indicated, the long-run consequences, both economic and political, were ominous. The frantic individualistic and typically inchoate efforts of the employers to grapple with the desperate financial situation, though capable of yielding some of the productive adjustments needed, accomplished these only by exacerbating work-force fears and hostilities. And no technical transformation could be economically viable in the long run if the industry was to be wracked by continuing industrial tension and disrupted by periodic general strikes.

The unrest of the work-force was being caused not only by ruthless wage reductions but also by the fact that the work rules remained ambiguous and extremely cavalier in application. Whatever else it had achieved, the industry had failed to produce any orderly system of labor administration which would provide stable expectations for the operatives. The millhands were not themselves capable of imposing a more rational system upon their employers. In this state, their sullen frustration could only express itself in seething discontent and a susceptibility to strike at the slightest provocation. Whenever articulate leadership appeared to kindle the spark, protest could burst out in an industry-wide conflagration. The 1934 general strike merely confirmed what had been discovered in 1928 and 1929, not only that voluntary groups within the industry were incapable of grappling cooperatively with the task of reforming labor discipline but also that the demoralized work force could, in this condition, easily come under the control of the Communists.

The cotton mill operatives, large in numbers and concentrated at one of the key urban centers of the country, constituted a potential revolutionary force of disturbing dimensions. In a situation where the employers were unable to solve the problem autonomously, where moderate unions powerful enough to force solutions upon the industry had failed to appear, the State, fearful of a contingency that threatened to undermine the established social order, was forced to intervene.

The initial objective of the State in the Trade Disputes Conciliation Act of 1934 was a very limited one, to induce employers systematically to apply their own work rules. However, the initial intervention revealed how difficult it was to obtain an orderly response when the work regulations within individual mills were themselves so vague. In an effort to achieve greater precision of administration than employers were willing to develop voluntarily, the State was forced step by step to undertake after 1934 its own definition of the terms of employment, discipline and wage payment. In the process, much of the authority of the individual mills to determine the framework of their own labor discipline was eliminated. Not only did the State establish new and more systematic forms of labor administration consistent with the new requirements, but its intervention gradually established, by the end of my period, a high degree of industry-wide conformity to the solutions. Moreover, at the very end of the period, when trade unions once again began to make their appearance in a substantial way, the State, through these same statutory devices, had created the legal apparatus by which the role of unions could be subjected to the sharp constraints of public policy. The effects of these developments on the subsequent career of the industry's labor force were to manifest themselves in the period after 1947, years that are beyond the scope of this study. But by 1947, the year of Independence, the main lines of the new direction had been laid down.[1]

The history of the Bombay cotton mills suggests that it was not difficult to create an industrial labor force in India. The acceptability of my analysis as a general interpretation, however, waits on comparative evidence from other industrial situations. As I pointed out in Chapter 1, there have been very few intensive studies of this problem in any society and there is none that explores the experience of other Indian industries in detail. However, there is a very brief discussion of the development of an industrial labor force at the Tata Iron and Steel Company (TISCO) plant at Jamshedpur in Bihar which does support my analysis of Bombay developments.[2]

The Jamshedpur enterprise, established in a very lightly populated district in 1908, built up a labor force which by 1957 amounted to 40,000 workers. The entirely new city which grew up around the steel plant claimed a population of nearly a quarter of a million in 1951. As in the Bombay situation, the evidence suggests that at no time during the first half-century did TISCO

1. For some discussion of the post-1947 consequences, see James (1957) and Morris (1955).
2. What follows is based on Morris (1960a). For some tentative international comparisons, see Morris (1960b).

suffer from an inadequate supply of raw labor which it could train to its needs.

As I have suggested, it has not been possible to eliminate ambiguities in the Bombay evidence regarding stability and instability of the labor force. Given the very large number of cotton mills as well as the alternative employment opportunities in the city, it has been impossible to prove conclusively that a very large part if not most of the labor turnover involved a movement of workers between mills rather than from mill to countryside. However, in Jamshedpur, where there was only one important employer, the situation is much clearer. Within a decade of the production of the first iron ingots there is evidence of substantial stability in the labor force. In fact, by the 1950s the firm found itself actually embarrassed by the lack of labor turnover.

The relative work-force stability in Jamshedpur as compared with Bombay certainly did not arise from any fundamental differences in the cultural characteristics of the workers recruited. What are involved are dissimilarities in the technical necessities of the two industries and the consequent variations in policies demanded of the employers.

For the bulk of its career the Bombay textile industry required workers who needed only very casual training and the most limited sort of supervision. The stability of individual workers was of no fundamental concern to employers; recruitment and administration of labor therefore could be turned over to jobbers. By contrast, the steel operation required a much broader range of skills and more elaborate investment in training. On the whole, TISCO could not tolerate a free-floating, near-casual work force if efficient and profitable operation was to be maintained. As a consequence, recruitment and administration of the labor force was always a matter of strong concern to the Company. Although the labor recruited was certainly as cosmopolitan and the cultural and linguistic distinctions as complex as in Bombay, the management never found itself forced to give to its low-level jobber equivalents the basic responsibilities for the administration of its work force. The ramshackle discipline appropriate in Bombay mills until the 1920s was never feasible in Jamshedpur, and it never appeared.

The evidence from Bombay and Jamshedpur suggests that the creation of a disciplined industrial labor force in a newly developing society is not particularly difficult. A comparison of the cotton textile and the steel industries makes it clear that the difference in worker stability cannot be accounted for by any substantial difference in the psychology of the raw labor recruited. Nor can it be attributed to dissimilarities in the traditional environment from which the workers came. If there were differences in work-force behavior, these flowed from employer policy. The necessities imposed by industrial technology and markets required employers to select different systems of discipline, and these determined the way labor would work.

References

JAMES, R. C. (1957), 'Labor and technical change', unpublished Ph.D. dissertation.

MEHTA, S. D. (1954), *The Cotton Mills of India, 1854–1954*, The Textile Association, India.

MORRIS, M. D. (1955), 'Labor discipline, trade unions and the State in India', *J. of Pol. Econ.*, vol. 63, No. 4 August, pp. 293–308.

MORRIS, M. D. (1960a), 'The labor market in India', in W. Moore and A. Feldman (eds.), *Labor Commitment and Social Change in Developing Areas*, Social Science Research Council.

MORRIS, M. D. (1960b), 'The recruitment of an industrial labor force in India, with British and American comparisons', *Comparative Studies in Society and History*, vol. 2, No. 3, April, pp. 305–28.

MYERS, C. A. (1958), *Labor Problems in the Industrialization of India*, Harvard University Press.

WEBER, M. (1958), *The Religion of India*, Free Press.

9 F. H. Cardoso

The Industrial Elite in Latin America

Excerpt from F. H. Cardoso, 'The industrial elite', in S. M. Lipset and
A. Solari (eds.), *Elites in Latin America*, Oxford University Press, 1967,
pp. 94–114.

The problem of the industrial elite in Latin America is presented
in specialized literature as an aspect of development. In a few
works that have been published on this topic, all the basic hypotheses stress that in order to have development the thinking of
entrepreneurs must be brought up to date. There is also an
attempt to describe the entrepreneur's role in the light of the
forms of behaviour manifested in industry as a whole, as a closed
social system.

These studies have an implicit reference to what might be
called a 'general theory of the industrial elite'. This is simply the
theory derived from an analysis of how entrepreneur groups are
formed in Europe and the United States, where 'original development' occurred.

Industrialization in Latin America needs both a change of the
individual entrepreneur's behaviour in the individual industry
as well as more dynamic action in the national economic system.
But to put the problem in this way tends to produce a mere
analogy of form, or else an expression in tautological terms. In
the former case, the interpretations fail to account for the structural and historical differences that entrepreneurial activity has
taken in Latin America; nor do they explain the limitations of
that sector as a pressure group and a political force.

The first aim of the present study will be to set forth briefly the
fundamental differences of historical structure which determine the
possibilities of action and the mode of existence of the Latin
American industrial elite, as compared with those of Europe and
the United States. The distinction thus drawn will be illustrated
by behavior of Latin American entrepreneurs. I shall then
indicate what conditions appear to govern the different forms of
action which have taken place in Latin American countries
where sample surveys have been conducted among leading

industrial figures.[1] In conclusion I shall discuss certain results of research conducted in Latin America and attempt a few hypotheses to explain the different patterns of behavior and social mobility in Latin America as opposed to Europe and the United States.

In the nineteenth century, industrial firms were managed and controlled by private individuals. It is true that the state played a comparatively important role during the initial period, when capital was being assembled and the world market organized; but the fact remains that the private firm was the characteristic unit of the economy. In this sense, the traditional middle class not only became the 'conquering bourgeoisie' in the sphere of foreign affairs, but also provided the impetus for domestic development. Furthermore, the national states which came into being under capitalism were not confronted with the problem of the existence of states capable of opposing them, so that private industry was not hampered by strong pressure from outside.

The historical, social and economic conditions which determine the possibilities of action of private industry in the present-day underdeveloped countries are very different. Economically, the basic features of production and marketing appear to be laid down *a priori* by the already developed economies (technology, trading methods, type of enterprise, etc.). Socially, the entrepreneurs find themselves confronted by other component groups of the industrial community who bring pressure to bear to restrict industry's freedom of action, whether directly or through the state. Politically, the expansion of the market and the adoption of a policy of industrial development have ceased being the nation's main goal. Instead the central government is concerned with ending the domination of the large landowners and in securing international agreements to advance the industrialization of the country – something which usually encounters the opposition of the big international combines and of the nations which dominate the world stage.

1. This study was originally sponsored by the Centro de Sociologia Industrial y del Trabajo of the University of São Paulo, for the study of industrial managers in Brazil. Subsequently, thanks to financial assistance from the Latin American Social Science Research Center at Rio, it was expanded to include interviews with industrial managers at Buenos Aires, Santiago and Mexico City. The investigation of the subject is now being continued under the auspices of the Latin American Institute of Economic and Social Planning, not as a survey, but through the analysis of systematically chosen samples of entrepreneur groups.

Within this framework, the problem of the entrepreneur as 'demiurge' becomes meaningless if considered in isolation. For economic creativity no longer finds expression in terms of the 'enterprise' – as in the economic system based on private enterprise – but moves to a larger scale, becoming a matter of formulating and implementing a 'development policy'.

The typical entrepreneur in underdeveloped countries is no longer merely an industrialist striving to introduce new manufacturing or marketing methods so as to increase profits (a process which has its limits, owing to the state of technological subordination in which the entrepreneurs in the underdeveloped countries are placed), but a man with the ability to steer his activity in such a way that he can benefit from the social and economic changes. Therefore, industrial activity is taking on political implications.

Hence any study of the entrepreneur system, while it must take into consideration the typical 'characteristics' of the entrepreneurs themselves and the social conditions governing the emergence of the industrial middle class, must not ignore the practical circumstances of the entire community in each of the countries where an entrepreneur group exists.

The theory usually advanced to account for the emergence of entrepreneurs in the countries now industrializing assumes the slow but steady development of the traditional system of craftsmen and artisans, which played a decisive part in countries whose foreign market conditions were propitious. The slow speed of the process of change is declared to be the fundamental variable which accounts for the *backward* responses of the entrepreneurs as a group when confronted with the exigencies of the situation: their assimilation of new patterns of behavior is not immediately apparent, and even if it were, it would not be vigorous enough to modify their attitude toward society as a whole.

This theory, however, does not pay sufficient attention to situations in which the entrepreneurs' behaviour is more advanced than that of the workers or of the productive system, e.g. Colombia. It is also unable to take account of the possible coexistence of different types of entrepreneurs *from the beginning* of the process of industrialization. In Argentina from the late nineteenth century, for instance, the type of employer who was a convinced supporter of rational, but not progressive, business values seems to have existed in the food-processing sectors, while industrial growth was fostered by dissatisfied and dynamic groups belonging to the agricultural and ranching sectors.

Our first task, therefore, will be to examine the basic features from which to derive a classification of the two fundamental types of business action. The essential thing is to arrive at an understanding of the problems of development as produced by the structural adjustments of relations among the workers, the entrepreneurs, and the state; thus, our main criterion for distinguishing between the different types of entrepreneur must be the contrast between the collective (or public) interest and private interests. The collective view will be the necessary condition for *development*, while the individual enterprise will be the unit yielding prosperity as such, given the conditions required for industrialization and modernization; these conditions include leadership among workers (with a maximum of vertical mobility and assimilation, which we shall symbolize as $M+$; $A+$), as well as initiative among the entrepreneurs for both prosperity and national planning. This is the ideal situation in which the state committed to development derives legal authority and maximum consensus from the social forces which support it.

We can formulate a typology of entrepreneurs based upon their differential orientation to the society as a whole and their individual enterprise (S = society; E = the enterprise). (1) $S-$, $E-$: This is the extreme case of the speculating entrepreneur, whose prosperity is based on bold strokes, the manipulation of stocks, opposition to the tendency for wages to rise (recourse to casual labor), etc.; (2) $S-$, $E+$: Here we have the 'puritan' entrepreneur whose inclination may lead him to introduce more rational methods within the individual enterprise; this category includes the 'captain of industry', who usually began as an old style master-craftsman; (3) $S+$, $E-$: This is the progressive but speculating entrepreneur; he manipulates the system of taxation and the machinery of trade at state level and accumulates capital by more or less fraudulent manoeuvres, but has no interest in planning technical improvements in industry, or in manipulating wages in the factory; his chief efforts are directed toward winning a place for himself in a kind of independent system of economic development which will work to his own advantage; (4) $S+$, $E+$: This is the modern entrepreneur, interested in planning at the level of the community and in rationalization and the introduction of bureaucratic methods at the level of the enterprise.

By regrouping the above types, we see that the entrepreneurs may follow either of two tendencies in their form of action at the level of the community or of the enterprise. At the community level: (a) 'economists': puritan entrepreneurs (S−, E+) and modern entrepreneurs (S+, E+); (b) the 'politicians': progressive but speculating entrepreneurs (S+, E−). At the level of the enterprise: (a) the 'founders of enterprises': the puritan entrepreneurs (S−, E+) and speculators (S−, E−); (b) the 'organizers of enterprises': the progressive speculators (S+, E−) and the modern entrepreneurs (S+, E+).

This second grouping, at the level of the enterprise, suggests an observation which is important to the study of the industrialization process. It will be noted that both groups fit into the historic sequence in which the 'founders of enterprises' precede the 'organizers of enterprises'. However, as I pointed out at the beginning, we must be on our guard against unilateral interpretations, based on the course of development in the 'central' countries. The likelihood of this sequence is mitigated by at least two factors:

1. The presence of foreign capital, which may be employed from the very outset among the general group of 'organizers of enterprises'.
2. The creation of industrial complexes based on initial technical requirements of extreme rationality and bureaucratic structure. The indivisibility of investment in the capital goods sectors is quite a distinct problem from that of industrial development in the 'central' countries and it calls for special attention, because even where ample protection *vis-à-vis* foreign capital has been provided, the type of business activity thus introduced may create serious difficulties, which only the state can solve.

In accordance with our initial hypotheses, a particular *phase* in the practical development of a country cannot be inferred simply from the types of entrepreneurs then in action, but from the interaction of the different sectors in the industrial system. It seems advisable also to try to draw up a 'panel' by which to detect which categories have been dominant at different times. To give a further illustration of this procedure, it may be maintained that in Argentina, before the time of Perón, business activity was carried on mostly by 'creators of enterprises', with a relative preponderance of the 'puritan entrepreneur' – chiefly because the absence of standards for industry at the level of the community tended to encourage an 'economic' withdrawal into the enterprise rather than the expression of its interests in terms of 'political action'.

The war and state-support rapidly changed this picture by facilitating the second stage, a notable increase in the 'speculator-entrepreneur' (as evidenced in the spectacular development of the textile industry, for example), coinciding with the lack of commitment to economic development which has already been mentioned with reference to the state. The third stage, shaped by the crisis with which the 1950s opened, further demonstrated this maladjustment between the official efforts to promote development and the prevalent type of industrial action, which operated to the principal advantage of the 'progressive speculator'.

In the method I propose to follow, the analysis of these different types of entrepreneurs is not in itself significant. In other words, the predominance of one particular type of entrepreneur, such as the 'speculator', in a particular country does not decisively affect that country's prospects of development and modernization, since the other social forces and the particular historical circumstances also have to be taken into account. These other factors have to be considered, firstly because the transfer from one type of entrepreneur to another may well result from economic and social changes which are often brought about by the actions of entrepreneurs of the 'traditional' type who find themselves obliged to change their attitude or to break new economic ground,[2] and secondly because in Latin America the market situation and the process of development are not solely or directly governed by business conduct. We shall not deal with the first point in the present study, but it is obvious that it must produce certain effects upon the process of industrialization and modernization of the community; in other words, the action of what might be called traditional entrepreneurs, in the light of the general theory of industrial activity, may produce changes favorable to development.

The second point deserves fuller consideration, owing to its bearing upon the theory of industrial activity in the underdeveloped countries. The basic criterion for defining such activity is that of the entrepreneur's attitude toward the market and toward the state. Any consideration of the circumstances in

2. See Cardoso (1963).

which markets and nations came into existence in Latin America makes it evident that the countries were brought into the world market in one of three basic ways:

1. Through the introduction of foreign economic elements, as illustrated by the Central American plantations, the mines of Bolivia and Chile, or the oil wells of Venezuela.

2. Through an economic system based on the exploitation of resources by local producers, as in the coffee plantations of Brazil and Colombia and the stock-breeding economies of the South.

3. Through the enforced substitution of imported goods: this resulted in an expansion of the domestic market initially created by economic development following the second type of integration into the foreign market.

In the first two of these types of development there is a very clear connection between a dominant local class ('political' in the first case, 'landowning' in the second) and the representatives of the central economies. These political classes, or oligarchies, seem to have been both a means and a condition of emergence as a nation. The connection between the market (which was *foreign*, and which had existed, as we have seen, from the very earliest days of Latin American history) and the local interests was mediated through the state, which was itself controlled either by the non-productive local oligarchy or by the landowning producers, to the exclusion of the other classes and social groups. Reference to the nation (the whole body of society) was in the nature of a recourse to outside pressure, for the purpose of bargaining with foreign groups in the case of situation (1), or to provide the agricultural classes, in the case of situation (2), with the political instruments they required, in an international trial of strength, to bargain over quotas and export prices.

Therefore, only the third case of the integration of the Latin American countries in the world market situation (3) appears to provide conditions in which the industrial entrepreneurs and merchants could emerge as the protagonists of national development. According to the previously mentioned theory, prevalent in Latin America, which draws an analogy between the course of development in Europe and the United States and that in the developing countries, the groups of entrepreneurs, as representatives of the urban and industrial economic classes, should have lent impetus to industrialization and national development and turned into the avant-garde groups in Latin America. This interpretation assumes a dual analogy with the original circumstances of development – it assumes the modernization originated among 'puritan entrepreneurs' (in the style of Weber) and that the autonomy of the entrepreneur class conformed to the political behavior patterns of the European bourgeoisie during their rise to power. The significance of the first assumption is diminished by the importance of the other types of entrepreneurs in Latin America, who were in no way characterized by economic asceticism. As for the second assumption, it has not been confirmed by research.[3]

On the contrary, the first two types of Latin American integration in the world market, though led by the traditional and landowning classes and by the state which had been created to to serve those very classes, demonstrated the possibilities available to the urban industrial elite which was bound up with industrial development. The plan of development[4] observable in the most industrialized countries of the region was decisively marked by the following successive circumstances and social pressures.

1. Intensive urbanization, preceding industrialization, as a consequence of the favorable economic results produced during the period of development.

2. Formation, as the result of (1), of lower-class groups who pressed for access to the market and a place in political life, through the actions of popular movements (led by Vargas, Perón, Gaetano, etc.).

3. Formation of urban middle-class groups (civil servants, professional men, military men, civil engineers, etc.) who gained some control of the political machinery, because of the imbalance created in the traditional power structure by the *presence* of the masses, even when they were not active, during export crises. The middle classes obtained this partial control of the machinery of government whether through movements of their own (radicalism

3. See Cardoso (1964).
4. This is not the place to refer to the economic explanations of Latin American development, which are well known, chiefly from the writings of Raul Prebisch and Celso Furtado. It is obvious that the initial factors in industrial development are related to the depression of the 1930s and to the World War. The disruption of the world trading system, later aggravated by the scarcity of hard currency, facilitated and stimulated the market (independently of any economic policy) and was favourable to industrialization.

in Argentina and Chile, *Battlismo* in Uruguay, etc.) or through 'anti-oligarchic' movements which, however, had the support of certain sectors of the oligarchy (*Tenentismo* in Brazil). The first type of movement appears to have been linked to a new middle class, of immigrant origin, while the second was allied to pressure groups in the traditional middle classes.

4. Within this politico-social framework, where the export oligarchies were beginning to lose their absolute dominance, the groups created by industrialization (to meet the expansion of the domestic market which had resulted from the success of textile and foodstuff exports) *began to have marginal participation in the national political system*. In fact, when the entrepreneur groups came to the fore there was already an active state organization and an established market, and the other social forces – the urban masses and middle-class groups, the oligarchies and exporters – were competing for control of the state machinery, and thus for the possibility of influencing decisions relating to investment and consumption.

5. The 'technological' sectors of the middle classes (economists, army men, engineers, etc.) appear to have been concerned about the 'unbalance of power' resulting from pressure by the masses and the danger implicit in it. Once they were to some extent participating politically in the state machinery, they began to favor an industrial policy based on public investment and aimed at achieving national independence and at creating a sufficient demand for labor to offset the disruptive effects latent in mass pressure.

6. Not until somewhat later did the entrepreneur groups take over responsibility for industrial development. Even then, they did so under the protection of the state, and therefore with the benefit of the expansion resulting from government investment (in energy, oil, iron, and steel), which opened up new sources of profit for private investment as a substitute for imports.

This picture, applicable to the principal industrialized countries in the region (Brazil, Chile, Mexico, and with less consistency, Argentina), indicates the content and values of entrepreneur action in Latin America. In this instance, the existence of markets did not involve such values as free competition, productivity, etc., because the market was 'protected' by state measures which benefited the industrialists. Similarly, our reference to society does not imply, in the conditions prevailing in Latin America, that a deliberate scheme existed for controlling the politico-social situation; much less does it imply commitment to the construction of a democratic community for the masses, on the terms usually attributed to industrial societies. In point of fact the entrepreneur groups werè emerging from a comparatively marginal politico-social situation at a time when other social forces, including the traditional exporting class, the middle groups, and the masses themselves, occupied key positions already in the political game. Moreover, these entrepreneur groups found their options restricted by the ambiguity of the situation: either they joined forces with the masses to bring pressure on the state in opposition to the exporting groups, or else their chances of political and social authority might be disturbed by mass action. In some circumstances they supported the state in its development efforts; in others, they competed with the state in the attempt to wrest certain fields of investment from it, or joined with foreign capitalists because of the technological dependence characteristic of underdeveloped countries. On occasion they sponsored measures for the extension of political rights; on other occasions they allied themselves to the oligarchy and its narrow interests because, as a propertied class, they were afraid the control of the community might pass to the masses. It is essential to analyse the responses of entrepreneurs in the dependent economic systems in terms of the problems which arose, limiting their options especially because of the existence of *underdeveloped* masses of population in the countries concerned. We shall examine later the problems in this. All that can be done for the moment is to point to their existence, in the absence of any consistent empirical analysis.[5]

Three basic problems appear to be involved. In what economic and social conditions, and under the thrust of what social movements, did the modernizing entrepreneur groups emerge and take action? What tendencies and characteristics of economic action put new dynamism into the Latin American businesses? What type of structure framed the basic choices these groups adopted with regard to social change, and to what extent did their desire to gain power dispose them to accept popular pressure on the one hand, or to placate the traditional governing classes on the other hand?

5. The questions mentioned here are taken from a study programme on the subject which the author submitted to the Latin American Institute of Economic and Social Planning.

To answer these questions would require an elaborate historical and social analysis of industrialization in Latin America. On the basis of existing work, one can say that once launched, industrial growth followed a twofold pattern in almost all the countries of that region. Firstly, there was a slow growth of the handicrafts and manufacturing system, usually reinforced by the expansion of the domestic market (related, of course, to the increased exports of raw materials and the growth of towns, the latter accelerated by immigration resulting from the expansion of the export trade). Secondly, there was the rapid and increasingly dynamic process which set in whenever market conditions were favorable (war, devaluation for the protection of exports, etc.). Sustaining these stimuli depends to a great extent upon the ability of the leading groups to frame an adequate policy of investment in the basic sectors, to accept the views of the technical sectors which lay down investment policy. From the sociological standpoint the chief problem is to discover how well the social forces have taken advantage of the influences favorable to the automatic growth of the market (either in the slow, traditional manner, or with the speed produced by exceptional circumstances) to transform that process into a development policy, and the conditions in which this occurred. Did the industrial entrepreneurs create and exploit the opportunities offered by a development policy? Did it prove possible to harmonize the interests of the various dominant groups, and how great are the divergencies between the different classes participating in the development process? What form was taken by, and what solution found for, the divergencies between the groups concerned in the export sector and those concerned with production for the domestic market? What opposition was there between foreign economic interests and the national groups, and how was it overcome?

Here again, the answer must depend on a concrete analysis of typical social situations: the initial impulse was sometimes provided by general, widespread and violent pressure exercised by the urban populace against the established forms of domination (Mexico). There was sometimes an alliance between the popular movements, the traditional interests and the entrepreneur groups (Brazil under Vargas). Elsewhere, conditions approximated a phase of vigorous entrepreneur action at the economic level, including action by the exporter groups, together with comparative isolation and political antagonism of those groups in the face of mass pressure (as in Argentina under Perón). There were situations where the entrepreneurs' pressure in favor of development met with indifference from the other social groups (as in Colombia). What were the effects of these different circumstances upon opportunities for development? In what conditions did the entrepreneur classes manage to steer toward development the impulses for social transformation of other groups or classes whose objectives were different?

It is true that an analysis of these questions naturally involves summing up, referring to, the structural, economic, and social characteristics mentioned. However, we still need to restate, in terms of the Latin American situation, the classical problem of entrepreneur mentality and action. How did modernizing groups come into existence, always at the level of the enterprise? What types of entrepreneurs, recruited from what social groups, guided by what values, and stimulated by what social and economic pressures, had an important influence on development?

A study of this last group of problems should undoubtedly concentrate chiefly on patterns of investment and the mechanism of action by the entrepreneur sector. In the type of industrial growth which exists in Latin America, the composition and functioning of the economic classes are largely determined by use of the managerial capacities of immigrants who are active in smaller industries, or by manipulation of favorable market conditions by entrepreneurs whose original activity was linked to the agricultural-export sector – both groups representing small firms of the 'family' type. Among these, the need to obtain quick financial results restricts the possibility of large investment in basic enterprises, and impedes the creation of modern economic organizations. The latter can dispense with quick profits owing to their rational methods; and their efficiency is measured by their ability to guarantee long-term advantages based on increasing differentiation of production, technical expertise, and the economies resulting from mass production. How is it possible to advance, at the level of the individual firm, from the old pattern of managerial activity to a new and more dynamic one? What role does the 'foreign firm' play in this process? By what values are the former heads of enterprises impelled as they turn into captains of industry or modern industrial managers? To what extent has this process resulted from internal developments in the employer classes as they modernized themselves, and to what extent was it accelerated by pressure from outside the entrepreneur sector? What restrictions does the state of 'dependency' place upon the process of industrial modernization?

Starting with the assumption that development is an inclusive process which derives its impetus from sources outside industrial economy and depends on the formulation of a policy for society as a whole, we will discuss the general problem of the tendencies displayed by the entrepreneur groups in their dealings with the state and with the community. Here we should concentrate our attention on the possibilities and obstacles confronting the entrepreneur class in Latin America for taking action outside the business sector in order to promote the necessary 'conditions of development' and to transform itself into a dominant middle class (bourgeoisie), and the obstacles to such action. From this angle there are two problems which take precedence: the extent to which the entrepreneurs come to terms with policies deriving from the 'traditional situation' (with the corollaries of abstention from political activity, restriction of state action, opposition to trade union interference in public life, the search for foreign capital, etc.); and the extent to which the entrepreneur groups show themselves able to formulate a 'social scheme', recognizing the right of other progressive groups to share in framing development policy. That is to say, to what extent are the entrepreneur groups willing to let rivalry for the future of investment be carried from the business to the national level? And to what other groups are the entrepreneurs prepared, for structural reasons, to allow a share in defining national policy? In what conditions can a 'nationalist policy' have meaning? What are the prospects that popular pressure for development will coincide with an investment policy controlled by the entrepreneur groups, and within what limits can this happen? The general theory underlying these questions is that the traditional dominant classes can be permeated by the effect of social change. It would be an oversimplification to suppose that the entrepreneur groups represent 'modernity' and that their alliance with the lower-class pressure groups is therefore natural, and sufficient in itself to alter the traditional balance. On the contrary, the history of Latin America demonstrates the flexibility of 'traditional society'. Consequently, the theme of the 'traditional classes' has to be considered in any analysis of development which does not start from the preconception that the progressive industrial groups can alone, or in alliance with popular pressure, break up the traditional framework of society and redirect development in such a way as to secure a better distribution of income, greater economic dynamism, and a fuller participation of the masses in the national political and economic decisions.

References

CARDOSO, F. H. (1963), 'Tradition et innovation: la mentalité des entrepreneurs de São Paulo', *Sociologie du Travail*, No. 5, July–September, pp. 209–24.
CARDOSO, F. H. (1964), *Empresário Industrial e Desenvolvimento Economico no Brasil*, Difusão Européia do Livro, São Paulo.

Part Four
Development Strategies: Policy, Practice and Possibility

Today development is virtually inseparable from planning. The problems of formulating and implementing efficient plans are formidable, and their technical aspects cannot be isolated from the total social context in which planning is pursued. Lange (Reading 10) provides a broad overview of basic aims and issues of planning, while Griffin and Enos (Reading 11) review important questions arising from experience with industrialization policies. The wide ramifications of choices involved in planning are summarized by Petras and La Porte (Reading 12) in relation to the highly charged question of agrarian reform in Latin America. Lipton (Reading 13) discusses the record and prospects of rural planning in India, and illustrates the social density of the planning process which involves interaction between a number of different and unequally placed groups. He shows that the values of planners and the political weight of urban-oriented economic interests can be as problematic for effective agrarian development as any intransigence which may be encountered in villages. This is followed by a piece on the other great 'agrarian giant', China, in which Gray (Reading 14) uncovers issues of development strategy often neglected in discussions of the vicissitudes of Chinese political life. In his analysis the broadest meaning of development clearly emerges as that interaction between philosophy, politics and economic practice which points to social transformation and the effort to direct the course of future social advance.

10 O. Lange

Planning Economic Development

Excerpt from O. Lange, *Essays on Economic Planning*, Asia Publishing House/Statistical Publishing Society, 1960, pp. 11–20.

What is the essential of planning economic development? I would say that the essential consists in assuring an amount of productive investment which is sufficient to provide for a rise of national income substantially in excess of the rise in population, so that per capita national income increases. The strategic factor is investment, or more precisely productive investment. Consequently the problem of development planning is one of assuring that there be sufficient productive investment, and then of directing that productive investment into such channels as will provide for the most rapid growth of the productive power of national economy.

These are the essential tasks of development planning. The problems which planning faces can be divided into two categories. One is the mobilization of resources for purposes of productive investment; the other is the direction of the investment into proper channels. These are the essential problems implied in planning.

The first problem is that of mobilizing resources for investment. Taking the experience of the socialist countries and of the countries following a national revolutionary pattern, a certain picture of methods employed for the mobilization of resources can be drawn. These methods consist in the following: one is – and this is the method which was paramountly applied in the socialist countries – nationalization of industries, finance, trade and the use of the profits thus derived for purposes of investment. The other method, which particularly plays a role in the countries following the national revolutionary pattern, is nationalization of foreign-owned natural resources and the use of the profits from these resources for investment purposes.

A further method is the contribution of the peasants in countries where agrarian reforms are carried out. The peasants are required, in return, to make some contribution to the state finances, which are used for purposes of investment. This frequently does not suffice and an appeal is made to resources derived from general taxation, public loans and, in certain cases, also to deficit financing.

These methods of raising resources for investment are applied both in socialist and national revolutionary countries in various proportions. There is, also, a method which plays a particularly important role in the national revolutionary countries, and which in certain socialist countries during a transition period played a role too. This is the inducement of private savers to undertake productive investment. This implies inducing private industrialists, traders, landowners and financial groups to invest a considerable part of their income in the direction which is conducive to assuring the country's rapid economic development, that means essentially investment in production. This can be achieved in various ways such as, for instance, taxation of unproductive uses of wealth, compulsory saving, restrictions of distribution of profits and of such uses of profits as do not consist of productive investment, compulsory loans and all kinds of other measures. Finally, import of foreign capital may be also a source of financing productive investments. I shall deal with the latter source in greater detail later on.

Thus there is a whole catalogue of means applied in various proportions in different countries which provide the resources necessary for substantial productive investment. By substantial productive investment I mean investment which is large enough to achieve a break-through, or as some economists call it – to produce the 'take-off', the passage from stagnation to intensive development. This obviously cannot be done by small amounts of investment which are likely to peter out in a great number of minor projects. Sufficient investment is required to produce a real number of minor projects. Sufficient investment is required to produce a real, a qualitative change in the structure of national economy. This is one problem of developmental planning, namely to secure these resources for productive investment.

The second problem is the direction of investment and here I shall distinguish three sub-problems. The first is how to allocate investment so as to assure the most rapid growth of production; the second is how to secure balanced development of the economy, balance between the different branches of national economy; the third is how to assure efficiency of the use of resources in economic development, how to avoid waste of resources. These are three sub-problems of the general problem of directing investment so as to assure economic development.

The first sub-problem is the most important one. It is concerned with choosing such types of investment as will most rapidly increase the productive power of the economy. This implies a concentration of investment in fields which increase the capacity of further production; that means building up the industries which produce means of production. It is only through development of the industries which produce means of production that the production capacity of the economy can be raised.

This can be done, however, either directly or indirectly. It is done directly through investing in the construction of, say, power plants, steel plants, machine industries, raw material production and so on. It is done indirectly through foreign trade: instead of investing directly in the production, say, of certain machines it may be possible to get these machines from abroad by investing in the production of such commodities which can be sold abroad in order to import the machines required. Thus the productive power of the economy can be increased either directly through investing in the production of means of production, or indirectly through developing export industries which make it possible to import in the future the needed means of production. Which of these two methods is used depends on all kinds of circumstances, of existing facilities for developing either directly the output of means of production, or for producing commodities for export. However if investment in exportable commodities is undertaken then obviously it must be associated with importation in exchange for these exports of machinery, steel and other means of production to increase the country's productive power.

However, investment in the production of means of production is not the only type of investment needed. There are two complementary types of investment which are necessary. One is investment in agriculture to increase food production. The experience of economic planning, particularly in the socialist countries, has shown that with the growth of industrialization, with an increasing part of the population being employed in industries or transport services and so on, a considerable surplus of agricultural products is needed to feed the non-agricultural population. Consequently, complementary to the investment in the development of the output of means of production must be investment in agriculture to increase agricultural output. Also, a certain amount of investment in industries producing consumer goods for the population is required, for the standard of living rises with the expansion of industrial employment and output. These are then the chief directions of developmental investments. The first one is the strategic one, the one which brings about economic development, and the other two are of a complementary nature necessary in order that economic development can proceed smoothly.

Finally, there is one important field of developmental investment, namely investment in the general economic infrastructure of the country, such as transport facilities, roads and also social services. These, too, are complementary investments needed to assure smooth economic development. However, they by themselves are not a factor bringing about development. One of the problems in many, if not most, underdeveloped countries was – and this was a part of the colonial or imperialist system – that there took place a large construction of this economic infrastructure purely for the needs of colonial exploitation, and not for development of the productive power of the country.

In choosing various allocations of investment, or rather the right proportions between various allocations of investment, the problem of the choice of technology arises, the question whether to use labour- or capital-intensive methods of production. Very frequently it is being argued that since in underdeveloped countries there exists a large supply of unemployed or underemployed labour power, the most labour-intensive methods should be chosen so as to secure a rapid increase of employment.

Usually the situation is such that there is a distinction between the methods of production which employ much labour and those which are more productive in the sense of contributing to the increase of net output of the economy, i.e. of national income. Thus there emerges a dilemma in underdeveloped countries whether to use methods which are less labour-intensive, provide less employment, but rapidly increase output and national income, or whether to choose methods which are labour-intensive but which lead to a slower rate of increase of output and national income. The decision to be made depends on the period for which you plan. If planning is made only for a short period, then one might argue that the most labour-intensive method is the best because it leads most rapidly to the absorption of unemployment or underemployment.

However, if you take a longer view of development then you find the following: by investing in methods, as well as in industries which yield a rapid increase of output, you get a more rapid increase in national income. If a certain proportion of national income, for instance 20 per cent, is invested it turns out that by choosing the method and allocation of investment which more rapidly increases national income, even if less labour-intensive, after a number of years national income will have grown to such an extent that the total amount of investment will become so great that it will provide more employment. Instead, a more labour-intensive method would have led to a slower growth of national income, and consequently also to a slower increase in the absolute amount of investment. Thus after a certain period it always pays – also from the point of view of employment – to use that method and that allocation of investment which contributes most to the increase in national income, i.e. the net product of society.

This is the basic principle to be observed in a plan which aims at a rapid increase in the productive power of the eoconomy. It may be that a certain amount of unemployed labour can be 'on the side' employed in ways which use very little capital resources, and thus also be called to make some contribution to the increase in production and consequently to national income. This is being done very successfully in China. But still this is, so to speak, a secondary line of activity. The strategic activity in securing rapid development must consist of such methods of production and such allocation of investments which most rapidly contribute to an increase in net output. In the long run this proves the way which provides more employment than the alternative method of starting with labour-intensive, but less productive investments simply in order to diminish underemployment.

In planning economic development, usually the problem of foreign trade turns up as a major difficulty. The development of industry requires in any less developed country, in the initial stage, a considerable increase in imports of machinery, steel and other means of production. For at the very first stage of economic development these cannot be produced at home; this immediately puts a burden on the balance of payments. In the second stage, when the basic industries which create the country's productive potential are already constructed and start producing, there arises a requirement for increased imports of various raw materials and also of further imports of machinery to continue the process of industrialization. The process of industrialization requires increased imports.

There are certain countries which are in a particularly fortunate position, which have large exportable resources providing considerable revenues in foreign exchange. Before embarking on planned development, these revenues usually were not used, or only to a small extent were used for productive investment. Now they can be used for that purpose. To cite examples: in Iraq export of oil provides such a resource, in Ceylon the export of rubber and tea. There are such resources in the United Arab Republic such as cotton; I would also classify as such an exportable resource the Suez Canal. Countries which are in such a fortunate position have immediately available a certain amount of foreign exchange, to import machines and other commodities necessary for industrial development.

Countries where such exportable resources do not exist or exist in small quantities have to go through a period of austerity in imports, cutting down imports of consumer goods, particularly luxury goods, in order to free the exchange necessary to import producer goods and raw materials. Very frequently, it is exactly this necessity, to impose a high degree of austerity on the consumption of imported goods, which limits the possibility of rapid economic development. Here, of course, the situation can be aided by foreign capital, foreign loans, but this I will deal with a little later. These are roughly the directions of investment required to assure economic development. These investments, however, must be co-ordinated; balancing investment and production in the different branches of national economy is another important aspect of planning.

There are two kinds of balances which must be secured: one is the physical balance and the other is the financial or monetary balance. The physical balance consists in a proper evaluation of the relations between investment and output. In the countries which already have experience in economic planning investment coefficients are computed. These coefficients indicate the amount of investment and also the composition of that investment in terms of various kinds of goods needed in order to obtain an increase in output of a product by a given amount. For example, how much iron, how much coal, how much electric power is needed in order to produce an additional ton of steel. On this basis the planned increase in output of various products is balanced with the amounts and types of investment. It is also necessary to balance the outputs of the various sections of the economy because, as we know, the output of one branch of the economy serves as input for producing the output of another branch. For instance, the output of iron ore serves as an input in the steel industry. In the last-mentioned field a special technique, that of input–output analysis, has been developed.

The physical balancing mentioned is necessary in order that the outputs of the different branches of the economy proceed smoothly. This is a condition of the internal consistency of the plan. If this condition is not observed bottlenecks appear. The plan cannot be carried out because of physical obstacles, such as lack of raw materials, of manpower, etc.

The second kind of balancing is monetary balancing, assuring monetary equilibrium in the economy. This consists in establishing an equilibrium between the incomes of the population – wages, incomes of peasants and others – and the amount of consumer goods which will be available to the population. If the amount of incomes, or more precisely that part of the incomes which is spent for purposes of consumption, should turn out greater than the amount of available consumer goods, inflationary processes develop. Thus the financial or monetary balance must establish an equilibrium between the part of incomes devoted to consumption and the output of consumer goods. Further, it must establish equilibrium between the part of incomes of the population which will be used for private investment and the amount of investment goods made available to private investors. Finally, in the public sector a balance must be established between the financial funds made available for investment purposes and the amount of investment goods which will be produced or imported. In addition to those balances it is necessary to establish the balance of foreign payments and receipts. The financial balances are an important part of planning. Just as the lack of physical balance leads to physical obstacles to the smooth process of production, so the lack of financial balance leads to disturbances in the supply and demand for physical commodities, and finally also to physical disturbances in the process of production.

Looking back upon the experience of the countries which applied planning as a tool of economic development, I must say that it usually turned out to be difficult to maintain the proper financial balance. Few of these countries escaped inflationary processes during certain periods. These processes were due to the wage bill rising more rapidly than the output of consumer goods. However, in theory and with the experience which has been gained in earlier years it is today quite possible to plan the financial equilibrium of economic development in a way which avoids inflationary processes.

A last point – to be only mentioned briefly – is that of securing efficiency in the use of resources in the process of economic development. This is connected with the use of the price system. The function of the price system in economic planning is twofold. Prices serve as a means of accounting, namely as a means of evaluating cost of production, value of output, and comparing the two. For this purpose it is necessary to have a proper price system which reflects the social cost (and in the short run – the scarcity) of the various means of production and the social importance of the various products. Without such a price system, cost accounting would not have any objective economic significance. This is one role of the price system; the other role is that of an incentive.

The plan of economic development has two aspects: in the public sector it is a directive to various public agencies and enterprises to do certain things, e.g. to invest that much in such a way, to produce in such a way at such a cost. With regard to the private sector, the plan has not the power of a directive, but is a desire expressed which must be followed by creating such incentives as will induce private producers to do exactly the things which are required from them in the plan. It is quite clear and does not require further explanation that with regard to the private sector, the price system, including interest rates, is an important incentive serving to induce the private sector to do things required from it in the plan. But also in the public sector the need for incentive exists. It is not sufficient just to address administrative directives to public agencies and public enterprises. In addition to that it is necessary to create such economic incentives that the public agencies, enterprises, etc., find it in the interest of their management and their employees to do the things which are required from them in the plan. This again requires a proper price system.

Thus the price system plays in planning a role both as a basis of accounting and as an incentive inducing the people to do the things required from them in the plan. A certain general observation may be made here. It seems rather general historical experience that in the first phase of economic development, particularly of industrialization, the problem of a proper price system is not the most important one. In both the socialist and the national revolutionary types of economic development we find that in the first period the main problem is not that of the details of accounting or incentives. The main problem is assuring rapid growth of productive capacity. The question of rapidity of growth overshadows the more subtle questions of high grade efficiency. It is more important, for instance, to develop at all the machine industry than to do it in the most efficient manner. Too much preoccupation with the subtleties of economic accounting may hold up action and slow down progress. It is only at a higher stage of economic development, when the national economy has become more complex and diversified, that the problem of efficiency and incentives becomes increasingly important. It is then that the subtleties of assuring the highest efficiency of economy through proper cost accounting, through properly established incentives, etc., come into play.

Thus – not wanting to minimize the importance of the problem – I do believe that it is not the most important problem in the first stage of economic development. In this first stage, the take-off stage, the real issue is to mobilize the necessary resources for productive investment, to allocate them to the branches of the economy which most rapidly increase the productive potential of the country, and to do so by the most productive technological methods. At a later stage more subtle aspects of planning come into play. Thus a certain crudeness of planning in the early stages of economic development is, I believe, quite justified.

11 K. B. Griffin and J. L. Enos

Policies for Industrialization

Excerpt from K. B. Griffin and J. L. Enos, *Planning Development*, Addison-Wesley, 1970, chapter 9, pp. 141–53.

One of the most notable features of the underdeveloped countries as a group is the low proportion of total output produced in the industrial sector. In most underdeveloped countries manufacturing output accounts for less than 20 per cent of GDP (see Table 1). Indeed, for many years the poor countries of the world were frequently called the 'non-industrialized nations'. Implicit in this description was the assumption that the way to develop was to concentrate effort and resources on expanding employment and output in the manufacturing sector. In most of the theoretical literature on the so-called 'dual economy' this assumption was made explicit. For example, in a recent article Professor Jorgenson (1967) says, 'The process of economic development may be studied as an increase in income per head or as an increase in the role of industrial activity to that in agriculture' (p. 288).

This statement may be misleading for several reasons. Firstly, it associates development with a single goal, namely increasing per capita income, and ignores all other possible objectives, e.g. improving the distribution of income. Secondly, it poses the problem of growth in terms of a crude agriculture-versus-industry model. The most difficult problem confronting planners, however, is not how to choose one sector over another, but how to select the best combination of projects from the various sectors so that, given the resources, information and institutions of a society, the plan's targets can be achieved. Finally, Jorgenson begs the vital question whether in practice industrialization has accelerated development. It is on this final point that we wish to concentrate in the present chapter, the first two points having been discussed earlier.

It is true, of course, that rich countries tend to be industrialized and poor countries not. Colin Clark (1951) called our attention to this phenomenon some time ago, and further evidence has been

supplied by Simon Kuznets (1957). In a later article, Hollis
Chenery (1960) applied multiple regression techniques to cross-
section data from over fifty countries to produce what he calls
'normal growth functions'. These 'normal growth functions' are
intended to indicate the changes in the composition of national

Table 1 **Manufacturing output as a percentage of GDP,** *circa* 1965

Argentina	35	Malaysia	11
Bolivia	12	Mexico	25
Brazil	22	Morocco	12
Burma	15	Nicaragua	13
Ceylon *	8	Nigeria	6
Chile	19	Pakistan *	13
Colombia	19	Panama	16
Costa Rica	15	Paraguay	16
Cyprus *	21	Peru	20
Dominican Republic	16	Philippines	18
Ecuador	17	Rhodesia	19
El Salvador	17	Sierra Leone	7
Ethiopia	7	South Korea	18
Guatemala	15	Sudan	6
Honduras	14	Taiwan	20
India †	21	Tanganyika	4
Iran *	29	Thailand	12
Iraq *	47	Togo	4
Jordan *	12	Tunisia	14
Kenya	11	Uganda	7
Liberia	5	Uruguay	23
Libya	3	Venezuela	15
Malawi	4	Zambia	8

* Manufacturing, mining and utilities.
† Manufacturing, mining, utilities and construction.
Source: Agency for International Development.

output that are likely to occur as growth proceeds. Chenery's
findings suggest that the share of industry in national income, i.e.
manufacturing plus construction, rises from 17 per cent at a per
capita income level of $100 to 38 per cent at a level of $1000, while
the share of manufacturing alone rises from 12 to 33 per cent over
the same range of income. At the same time, the share of primary
production, i.e. agriculture plus mining, declines from 45 per
cent to 15 per cent (p. 635).

Having indicated the broad trends in the pattern of output,
Chenery then goes on to examine changes that occur within the

manufacturing sector as per capita income increases. Given a population of 10 million and a per capita income of $100 the 'normal' composition of manufacturing output would be as follows: 12 per cent would be investment goods (machinery, metals, etc.), 20 per cent intermediate goods (chemicals, rubber, etc.), and 68 per cent consumer goods. As per capita income rises to $600 the composition of manufacturing output would change: 35 per cent would now be investment goods, 23 per cent intermediate goods and only 43 per cent consumption goods (p. 638, Table 5). In other words, over this range of incomes the share of investment goods in total manufacturing production would rise by 192 per cent while the share of consumer goods would fall by almost 37 per cent.

This analysis of patterns of industrialization was continued in a recent article by Chenery and Taylor (1968). Fifty-four developed and underdeveloped countries were classified into three groups: (a) large countries, i.e. those with a population greater than 15 million; (b) small countries whose trade is heavily oriented towards exports of manufactured goods; (c) small countries whose trade is heavily oriented towards the export of primary (agricultural or mineral) commodities.

In the large countries the share of industry rises swiftly from 16 per cent of GNP at a per capita income of $100 to 32 per cent at $400. 'Thereafter the increase is much slower and a peak share of 37 per cent is reached at $1200' (p. 399). The share of primary production falls steadily from about 45 per cent at $100 to 12 per cent at $1200. The behavior of the small, industry-oriented countries is similar to that of the large countries. Small, primary-oriented countries, however, behave somewhat differently. The share of primary production in GNP tends to decline much more slowly and agriculture plus mining remains more important than industry up to a per capita income level of nearly $800 (p. 400). The share of primary production falls from about 50 per cent to 30 per cent as per capita income rises from $100 to $500; on the other hand, the share of industry, over the same income range, rises from roughly 17 per cent to 19 per cent.

Of the 57 countries in the sample, 39 are obviously underdeveloped, i.e. have a per capita income of less than $600. Fourteen of these nations are small, primary commodity-oriented countries, and for them promotion of industry is likely to remain less important than the further exploitation of their rich natural resources. The remaining 25 underdeveloped countries can hope to benefit considerably from industrialization, either because they are large nations and can take advantage of their large domestic markets and economies of scale or, if small, because their comparative cost position suggests that specialization in industry would be more rewarding. Thus, in principle, the majority of underdeveloped countries can gain by encouraging industry. Whether in practice they have done so is a subject to which we now turn.

Import substitution

Industrialization, as Professor Hirschman (1968) has emphasized, may be initiated for many reasons (pp. 4–6). A country's supply of imports may suddenly be cut off because of war, and the government may respond by promoting domestic import-replacing industries. Or industrialization may occur 'naturally' as incomes rise in response, say, to growth of exports. Alternatively, industry may develop as part of a planning strategy. Finally, manufacturing may be encouraged in an attempt to economize on scarce foreign exchange.

Of the four impulses favouring industrialization – wars, expansion of demand, planning and balance-of-payments difficulties – the last, in fact, has been most important in many underdeveloped countries. A vast array of policies has been concocted, usually on an *ad hoc* basis, in an effort to reduce the expenditure of foreign currencies. Tariffs have been erected to exclude the importation of 'inessential' goods; licences, quotas, import deposits and other trade restrictions have been used for the same purpose. As a consequence, incentives are created to channel domestic savings towards investment in 'inessential' production rather than in 'essential' goods. At the same time, exchange rates have frequently been over-valued so that the cost of importing the inputs necessary to produce domestically the 'inessential' goods is low. This accentuates the tendency to concentrate on producing the less essential commodities and, further, introduces a bias in favour of adopting techniques of production which are intensive in imported inputs. Thus policies designed to economize on foreign exchange have affected both what goods are produced and how they are produced. These side-effects of commercial policy probably are harmful to development and often are unanticipated by the authorities who formulate them.

Even the primary object of these policies, reducing the import bill, seems to have been frustrated. Firstly, the substitution of imported finished goods by domestically produced goods may require the importation of a considerable volume of raw materials and intermediate products, particularly (as we shall see) when domestic industries are relatively inefficient, i.e. when they need more inputs to produce a given output than foreign industries. Net import substitution, or domestic value added, is often a very low proportion of the value of the final product. Secondly, the establishment of an import-substituting industry requires large investments. Unless the country possesses a domestic capital goods industry, which is rather unlikely, the additional investment will generate a demand for imported capital goods. Thus, especially in the short run, the direct savings of foreign exchange from a strategy of import-substituting industrialization may be less than the indirect expenditure of foreign exchange arising from the need to import investment goods and inputs. In other words, if a country wishes to import less, it may first have to import more.

This can be illustrated very simply. Imagine that a country wishes to replace £100 of imported goods. Let us assume that (a) there are no lags, (b) the incremental capital–output ratio is 3:1, (c) two thirds of all investment goods are imported, and (d) 50 per cent of the gross value of output is absorbed by imported inputs. In the first year the direct saving of imports will be £100, but the indirect costs will be £250, i.e. £200 of imported investment goods and £50 of imported inputs. Thus, in the initial year, there will be a net loss of foreign exchange of £150. In each subsequent year there will be a net gain of £50. Not until the end of the fourth year, however, will the cumulative direct savings of foreign exchange be as great as the cumulative indirect costs of foreign exchange.[1]

Even if import-substitution does not save very much foreign exchange and even if it is less successful in resolving a balance of payments problem than a policy of export promotion, import-substitution might still be defended as a device for achieving a high rate of domestic savings and investment. Tariffs, quotas, licences and other such restrictive instruments shelter domestic manufacturers from the chilling winds of international competition, enabling them to raise the prices and lower the quality of their products and thereby obtain high profits. These profits may be saved and the resulting reinvestment may accelerate the

1. For a more complex and comprehensive model, see Diaz-Alejandro (1965).

pace of development. That is, it is sometimes argued that a policy of protection, by turning the internal terms of trade against the non-protected sectors, will alter the distribution of income in such a way that savings, investment and growth are promoted.

Against this view John Power (1967) argued that import substitution of *finished consumer goods* is likely to lead in the long run to lower rather than higher savings. A bias towards the *production* of consumer goods – rather than towards the production of either exports or investment goods – is likely to be reflected in a rise in the *consumption* of consumer goods. If imports of consumer goods fail to fall, absolute savings will remain constant but the proportion of national income devoted to savings will gradually decline, as will the rates of investment and growth. The implication of this is that, if industrialization is intended to accelerate the rate of growth of national product, investment should be channelled to the capital goods and exports sectors rather than into the sector producing final consumer goods for the domestic market.

In the early stages of import-substitution of consumer goods this implication may not appear to be correct because the rise in the production of consumer goods may be fully offset by a fall in imports of consumer goods, thus permitting savings to increase, both absolutely and as a proportion of total income. As the process continues, however, 'a kind of automatic decontrol of consumption takes place' (Power, 1967). One reason for this is that the proportion of total consumption constrained by import restrictions falls and goods become more readily available. Another reason is that this strategy tends to lead to a change in the distribution of income away from government customs revenues and public savings towards the income recipients in the new industries (who may have a lower marginal propensity to save than the government). Thus one of the important tasks of planners is to determine at what point an additional increase in the production of consumer goods will lead not to a fall in imports but to a fall in the savings ratio. If the planners fail to determine this point correctly they may find that further industrialization via import-substitution of consumer goods neither saves foreign exchange nor causes more rapid development.

Expansion of manufacturing output and employment

Industrialization may not have economized on foreign exchange as much as was once hoped, nor has it led to a noticeable increase in the rate of savings, but the evidence from the national income accounts suggests that the rate of growth of manufacturing output can be rapid. The annual rate of growth of manufacturing output for seventeen countries from roughly 1960 to 1967 is presented in the first column of Table 2.

The experience of these countries varies considerably: manufacturing output in Senegal and Rhodesia has grown slowly, namely, about 2 per cent a year, whereas that in Taiwan has grown 16 per cent a year. The average for the seventeen countries, however, is over 8 per cent. *Prima facie* this appears to be a commendable record although, as we shall see in a moment, on closer inspection the growth record does not appear to be so bright. Indeed, for some countries, the industrial output figures published in the national accounts can be seriously misleading.

Reliable data on the growth of employment in manufacturing activities are difficult to obtain. The evidence that we were able to collect from eighteen underdeveloped countries is included in the second column of Table 2. The reader should note that in some cases the statistic refers to non-agricultural employment while in others it refers to employment in manufacturing. The two concepts obviously are not identical. Moreover, the period covered is not the same for each country. Thus one must be careful in attempting to generalize from this information.

Nevertheless, certain things seem reasonably clear. Firstly, for the nine countries with entries in both columns, the growth of employment in manufacturing is not in the least comparable to the growth in output. In fact, employment seldom increases unless manufacturing output is growing by about 4 per cent a year. Secondly, although the data are not reproduced, it is clear that in almost all of the countries included in Table 2 industrial employment is growing considerably less rapidly than the population. Only El Salvador and Ghana have managed substantially to increase the proportion of the labour force engaged in industry. In most of the other countries the proportion of the total labour force employed in large-scale manufacturing is probably falling. Finally, in several African countries the absolute number employed in non-agricultural activities has declined since 1955.

Thus once again we see that the belief that industrialization is the key to the solution of all development problems is unjustified. The problem of unemployment and low productivity employment is, as all would agree, one of the major difficulties confronting most underdeveloped countries. Yet employment in manu-

Table 2 **Rates of growth of output and employment in manufacturing** (average annual rate of growth per cent)

Country	Output	Employment
Argentina	3·6	n.a.
Cameroons	n.a.	−1·0
Chile	5·6	1·1
Colombia	n.a.	0·7
Ecuador	n.a.	2·6
El Salvador	14·2	5·5
Ghana	8·6	6·3
Greece	7·8	2·2
Guatemala	4·3	0·0
India	5·8	n.a.
Iran	11·1	n.a.
Kenya	n.a.	−0·5
Malawi	n.a.	−0·7
Mexico	8·5	n.a.
Nigeria	n.a.	0·1
Pakistan	12·1	n.a.
Philippines	6·1	1·5
Rhodesia	1·9	0·2
Senegal	2·0	n.a.
South Korea	14·2	n.a.
Sierra Leone	n.a.	3·0
Tanzania	n.a.	−0·4
Taiwan	16·0	n.a.
Uganda	n.a.	−0·1
Venezuela	7·4	3·1
Zambia	14·1	−0·9

Notes: Output: average rates of growth over period 1960–67, except Ghana (1962–67) and Zambia (1961–67). Employment: average rates of growth of employment in manufacturing over period 1960–67 (Chile, Colombia, Guatemala and Philippines), 1960–66 (Ecuador) and 1961–67 (El Salvador, Greece and Venezuela). Average rates of growth of non-agricultural employment 1955–64 (Cameroons, Kenya, Rhodesia, Sierra Leone, Tanzania, Uganda and Zambia), 1955–63 (Ghana and Malawi) and 1956–63 (Nigeria).

Sources: UN, *Monthly Bulletin of Statistics*, November 1968, Frank (1968).

facturing activities frequently has not even grown as rapidly as the labour force. Industrialization, in practice, has not alleviated the problem of unemployment.

Industrial efficiency

We have talked about the growth of industrial output without considering efficiency. It is well known, of course, that manufacturing establishments in underdeveloped countries tend to be inefficient. Indeed, the infant industry argument for protection virtually takes inefficiency and non-competitiveness for granted, but assumes that unit cost will gradually fall with the passage of time and the accumulation of experience. Just how great is inefficiency, and how long it can persist, is only now becoming apparent, however. In Ghana in 1964, for example, twenty-two out of thirty-one state industries failed to make a profit despite the considerable protection provided by the government. In fact the overall net loss of the state industries in that year was £15 million on a capital investment of £30 million!

State enterprises are not unique in being inefficient; private firms are equally as bad. Leland Johnson (1967), for instance, has shown that the Chilean automobile industry is extremely wasteful in its use of resources. The industry was first established when the government prohibited imports of finished automobiles. The intention was to force assembly operations to take place in Chile so that domestic value added would rise. In order to provide employment in an impoverished region, however, the government insisted that the assembly plants be located in Arica, a small town 1000 miles north of Santiago, the main market and source of supply of domestic components. This location decision greatly reduced efficiency because it increased transport costs of both the inputs and the finished output. Finally, the government compelled the companies to use an increasingly large proportion of Chilean made components. (The proportion was planned to rise from 27 per cent in 1964 to 45 per cent in 1966.)

About twenty auto assembly firms were established in Arica, with a total production in 1963 and 1964 of less than 8000 vehicles, i.e. a production run of roughly 400 cars per plant per year. Obviously this production run was insufficient to enable the firms to take full advantage of economies of scale. Indeed, it is commonly assumed that economies of scale are important in auto assembly operations up to a production level of roughly 200,000 vehicles per year. But economies of scale are not confined to assembly operations; they can also be important in the production of components. Chilean suppliers were unable to mass produce components of a standard specification, however, because of the large variety of autos assembled. If only one make of automobile had been offered instead of twenty-seven the cost of domestic components would probably have been much lower. Given the organization of the assembly process, it was bound to be inefficient, and this inefficiency in a consumer goods industry worked its way back to the intermediate and producer goods industries as well.[2]

The final feature of the automobile industry in Chile that should be noted is the seasonal nature of its activity. Because the industry's quota of foreign exchange must be spent within the year it was allocated, and also because firms are anxious to complete automobiles by the end of December before the required minimum proportion of nationally produced components rises, output and employment are heavily concentrated in the second half of the year. Demand, of course, does not have this seasonal pattern. As a result, the assembly plants tend to accumulate large inventories of components and finished cars. In real terms this is an expensive policy. First of all, in countries where the opportunity cost of capital is high, the cost of holding inventories is high. Secondly, in the harsh desert climate of Arica the stocks of finished automobiles deteriorate badly during the lengthy storage period and must be repaired and re-finished before they can be sold. This is financially possible because the prohibition against importing automobiles gives the assembly companies a protected market and enables them to impose a high markup over their costs.

Unfortunately, Ghana and Chile are not special cases. Inefficiency in both private and state manufacturing enterprises is widespread throughout the underdeveloped countries. In fact it is now believed that government policies and planning in many countries have been so poor that the contribution of industry to national income, when measured at the appropriate prices, has been negative. That is, the value of material inputs into the manufacturing sector often exceeds the value of the final output, so that value added in some industries is negative.

A technique for assessing the real contribution of an industry to national product has recently been developed. This technique has evolved out of the literature on effective protection[3]

2. Economies of scale are of great importance in underdeveloped countries. Professor Chenery (1960, p. 646) estimates that at a per capita income level of $300 they are probably significant up to a population of 100 million or more.

3. See, for example, Johnson (1964).

and represents a marriage of tariff theory and input-output models.[4] The method is quite simple and does not require an excessive amount of data; thus it should be quite useful to planners in underdeveloped countries.

Value added in an industry may be expressed as follows:

$$V_i = X_i - \sum_{j=1}^{n} X_{ji},$$

where

$V_i =$ value-added in industry i,

$X_i =$ gross value of output for industry i, and

$\sum_{j=1}^{n} X_{ji} =$ total deliveries of industry j to industry i,

all measured at domestic prices.

Similarly, value added at world prices may be expressed as

$$V^*_i = X^*_i - \sum_{j=1}^{n} X^*_{ji},$$

where the starred symbols indicate that quantities are being valued at world prices. In other words, V^*_i indicates the amount domestic factors of production (capital and labour) *could* receive if outputs and inputs were sold and bought at world prices. A discrepancy would arise between V_i and V^*_i whenever tariffs or other taxes on trade were imposed. In our analysis below we shall assume, for convenience, that tariffs are the only cause of the discrepancy.

A tariff is a subsidy to an industry. It raises value added in domestic prices (V_i) above what it otherwise would have been. The proportionate subsidy provided by tariff protection (U_i) can be represented as

$$U_i \equiv \frac{V_i - V^*_i}{V_i} = 1 - \frac{V^*_i}{V_i}.$$

This enables one to measure the percentage of actual value added that is 'due to' protection.[5]

4. The model we are about to present, like most input-output models, is based on the assumption of fixed technical coefficients and constant returns to scale.

5. U_i is related to the effective rate of protection, i.e. the protection given to value added in industry (Z_i). Since,

$$V_i = (1+Z_i)\, V^*_i, \quad \text{then} \quad Z_i = \frac{V_i}{V^*_i} - 1 = \frac{U_i}{1-U_i}.$$

To calculate U_i one must know V^*_i. In practice, however, world prices may not be known, and hence it may not be possible to calculate V^*_i directly from the formula used above. But if it is assumed that the exchange rate reflects the opportunity cost of foreign currencies and that the domestic price of a commodity is equal to the world price plus the tariff, V^*_i can be estimated from the following simple equation:

$$V^*_i = \frac{X_i}{(1+t_i)} - \sum_{j=1}^{n} \frac{X_{ji}}{(1+t_j)},$$

where t_i and t_j are the tariff rates on commodities i and j.

To summarize so far, the percentage rate of subsidy granted to an industry by a tariff can be estimated, provided we have information on domestic prices, nominal tariffs, the gross output of an industry and its purchases of inputs from other industries. All this information, with the possible exception of the X_{ji}'s, usually can be obtained quite readily, particularly for the most important activities.

How are the U_i's to be interpreted? Since value added at domestic prices (V_i) is not likely to be negative, U_i will rise as protection is increased. If $V^*_i > V_i$, U_i will be negative, i.e. effective protection will be negative and the tariff structure will have acted as a tax on the output of the industry. For $0 \leqslant U_i \leqslant 1$ the industry will be effectively protected and value added measured at world prices will be positive. A curious and important case arises when U_i exceeds unity. If $U_i > 1$, *value added measured in world prices must be negative* ($V^*_i < 0$), since otherwise ($V_i - V^*_i$) could not exceed V_i.

From our last equation above it is clear that when V^*_i is negative,

$$\sum_{j=1}^{n} \frac{X_{ji}}{(1+t_j)} \text{ must be greater than } \frac{X_i}{(1+t_i)},$$

that is, the value of inter-industry inputs measured at world prices must be greater than the total value of output measured at the same prices. This is most likely to occur in industries in which material inputs comprise a high proportion of the value of gross output, transport costs are high, e.g. because of poor plant location, and inputs are used wastefully, e.g. due to factory breakdowns, damage to final products, the necessity for frequent repairs and lost components. Inefficient assembly industries can satisfy these conditions quite easily, as we saw in our examination of the Chilean automobile industry. The tendency for the value of the X_{ji}'s to exceed that of the X_i's may be further strengthened if the tariff structure provides heavy protection for processing and little or no protection to intermediate and producer goods industries, i.e. if t_i is substantially larger than t_j.[6] This too is common in many underdeveloped countries.

In a pioneering study of Pakistan's industry, Soligo and Stern (1965) used the above model to estimate U_i for forty-eight manufacturing activities. In three industries – grain-milling, rice-milling, printing and publishing – U_i was negative. That is, the tariff structure acted as a tax on output. In twenty-three industries – nearly half of the total! – U_i was greater than unity, implying that value added measured at world prices was negative. Fourteen of these were in the consumer goods sector, although the most inefficient industry of all was classified as an investment good: motor vehicles with an U_i of 3·96. The general pattern of industrial efficiency is indicated in the table below.

Other studies have confirmed Soligo and Stern's conclusion that Pakistan's industry is remarkably inefficient. Research by Richard Mallon (1967), for example, suggests that the jute and

Table 3 **Industrial efficiency in Pakistan** (number of industries)

	Consumer goods industries	Investment goods industries	Total number of industries
$U_i < 0$	3	0	3
$0 \leqslant U_i \leqslant 1$	8	14	22
$U_i > 1$	14	9	23
Total	25	23	48

Source: Soligo and Stern (1965).

cotton textile industries are responsible for a net loss of foreign exchange despite the fact that they are major exporting industries. Nurul Islam (1967) has shown that the costs of domestically manufactured goods are nearly 100 per cent higher than the c.i.f. price of similar foreign goods. Recently Maurice Scott has re-calculated value added in over two dozen Pakistani industries in order to estimate the 'real' contribution of manufacturing to national income. Value added in fifteen consumer goods indus-

6. Ellsworth (1966, p. 400).

tries in 1963–4 was Rs 1185 millions as conventionally measured, and Rs – 354 million when corrected. Similarly, value added in ten intermediate goods industries fell from Rs 545 million to Rs 291 million, and value added in six capital goods industries declined from Rs 563 million to Rs 194 million. Considering his entire sample, value added fell sharply from Rs 2293 million to Rs 131 million (Scott, 1969, Table 2). In other words, the conventional national accounting methods over-estimated the real value added in these thirty-one manufacturing industries by about 1650 per cent! Evidently, any downward reassessment of industrial value added will affect one's calculation of the aggregate growth rate. Mr Scott believes that the conventional estimate of 5·1 per cent per annum as the rate of growth of GDP over the period 1957–59 to 1964–66 is incorrect; he suggests that the correct figure may be between 4·5 and 4·8 per cent (Scott, 1969, p. 23n).

In our opinion these results are broadly correct. None the less, there are certain limitations to this approach. Firstly, the conclusions are based on a comparative static method: dynamic effects are ignored, the infant industry argument for protection is implicitly rejected, external economies are neglected. Secondly, the conclusions are based on the assumption that industry is operating at full capacity. Yet there may be excess capacity in the early stages of industrialization and this will lead to high unit costs and low value added in terms of world prices. As industrialization proceeds, however, excess capacity may decline and efficiency may increase. Thirdly, in using world prices as a reflection of opportunity costs one is implicitly assuming (a) that the country concerned is 'small' and is unable to influence world prices by its actions and (b) that the world distribution of income and the world market structure which underlie international prices either are satisfactory or are incapable of being altered. In some cases these assumptions may not be valid; in other cases they may do no harm. For example, there may be instances in which the static disadvantages of a policy or project are outweighed by the dynamic benefits. The evidence we have presented, however, does not suggest that industrialization policies *as pursued by most underdeveloped countries* can be defended on these grounds.

Thus, in conclusion, it seems that the benefits of industrialization have not been as great in practice as is often claimed and hoped. The strategy for industrialization most commonly adopted, namely, concentration on import substitution of consumer goods, has frequently neither saved foreign exchange nor contributed to real output. Errors in policy have been enormous and widespread, yet planners have at their disposal a simple method for detecting industries in which value added is negative. What little evidence we have suggests that the consumer goods industries are prone to be inefficient. Intermediate and producer goods industries, on the other hand, appear less frequently to have negative value added. It may be that the process of industrialization would be more satisfactory if planners would devote more attention to encouraging exports of manufactured goods and establishing an investment goods sector. Be that as it may, the analysis in this chapter implies that in the future planners should be much more selective in encouraging manufacturing activities. It does not follow from this that investment in other sectors, notably agriculture, would be more efficient or generate more employment. But there is *prima facie* a strong case in favour of considering whether investments in other sectors would yield higher social returns.

References

CHENERY, H. B. (1960), 'Patterns of industrial growth', *Amer. Econ. Rev.*, September.

CHENERY, H. B., and TAYLOR, L. (1968), 'Development patterns: among countries and over time', *Rev. of Econ. and Stats.*, November.

CLARK, C. (1951), *The Conditions of Economic Progress*, Macmillan.

DIAZ-ALEJANDRO, C. F. (1965), 'On the import intensity of import substitution', *Kyklos*.

ELLSWORTH, P. T. (1966), 'Import substitution in Pakistan: some comments', *Pakistan Devel. Rev.*, Autumn.

FRANK, C. R. (1968), 'Urban unemployment and economic growth in Africa', *Oxford Econ. Paps.*, July.

HIRSCHMAN, A. O. (1968), 'The political economy of import-substituting industrialization in Latin America', *Q. J. of Econ.*, February.

ISLAM, N. (1967), 'Tariff protection, comparative costs and industrialization in Pakistan', *Pakistan Inst. of Devel. Econ.*, Research Report No. 57.

JOHNSON, H. G. (1964), 'Tariffs and economic development', *J. of Devel. Studs.*, October.

JOHNSON, L. L. (1967), 'Problems of import-substitution: the Chilean automobile industry', *Econ. Devel. and Cultural Change*, January.

JORGENSON, D. W. (1967), 'Surplus agricultural labour and the development of a dual economy', *Oxford Econ. Paps.*, November.

KUZNETS, S. (1957), 'Quantitative aspects of the economic growth of nations: 2. Industrial distribution of national product and labor force', *Econ. Devel. and Cultural Change*, July supplement.

MALLON, R. D. (1967), 'Export policy in Pakistan', *Pakistan Devel. Rev.*, Summer.

POWER, J. (1967), 'Import substitution as an industrialization strategy', *Philippine Econ. J.*, Spring.

SCOTT, M. F. G. (1969), 'Effective protection and the measurement of output', Nuffield College, Oxford, mimeo.

SOLIGO, R., and STERN, J. J. (1965), 'Tariff protection, import substitution and investment efficiency', *Pakistan Devel. Rev.*, Summer.

12 J. Petras and R. La Porte Jr

Two Approaches to Agrarian Reform in Latin America –
Redistribution *v.* Incremental Change

Excerpt from J. Petras and R. La Porte Jr, 'Modernization from above
versus reform from below: US policy toward Latin American
agricultural development', in J. Petras, *Politics and Social Structure
in Latin America*, Monthly Review Press, 1970, pp. 250–53.

In the societies of Latin America, agrarian reform has been very
widely considered an important component of any policy of
structural change. Agrarian reform, however, has been con-
strued in sharply varying ways. To some it entails the distribution of large landholdings among the landless and small
farmers. To others it means better utilization of existing tenure
patterns to increase the products available for consumption and
export. Still another view interprets agrarian reform as primarily
involving improvement of transportation, communication and
storage facilities to expedite the flow of farm products to marketing outlets.

Even those who agree in favoring the redistributive approach
may differ on whether agrarian reform policy calls for distribution of public or unused lands, or division of large private
estates, or consolidation of small farms; and on whether the
land is to be obtained through expropriation, taxation, confiscation or a combination of these measures. Accompanying
programs may or may not include technical modernization, increased educational facilities, diversification of products and
development of communications (Alba, 1965, p. 194).

In our use of the term, agrarian reform involves both a redistribution of political and social power and a fundamental
reordering of the economic structure of the agricultural sector,
since land ownership in Latin America involves social and political power in addition to the control of economic resources.
Landholding and the style of life which accompanies it not only
confer social status and prestige, but, through traditional pater-
nalistic social relations and physical coercion, confer the power
to control the political behavior of the peasants, who are thus
little more than pawns in the hands of the large landholders.
Possessing wealth, status and the captive votes of the rural areas,
the landowners are able to influence executives, legislatures,

bureaucracies and judiciaries. Through their control over political institutions they influence taxation, government expenditures and the use of the police and army, all toward the end of perpetuating their own privileged position (US Congress, 1962, p. 12).

Because changes in land tenure can have multiple effects on the distribution of political, economic and social power, it is scarcely surprising that there is disagreement among scholars and political men over the employment of a comprehensive approach to agrarian reform. Some writers see Latin America's agricultural problems largely in terms of a more efficient use of the land and increasing technical capacity – in essence, as merely a matter of technology. The ends of such a policy would be to expand production and to secure a larger share of the export market. 'Development' and reform would refer to the building of farm-to-market access roads, better marketing facilities, production of cheap fertilizers, importation of farm machinery, rationalization of credit, diversification of output to provide a better balance between supply and demand in the country and, perhaps, a broadening of the export base. Largely premised on the maintenance of existing land-tenure patterns, the only type of land distribution consistent with this policy would be the development of previously uncultivated areas. The underlying assumption is that the overall growth of the agricultural sector will indirectly cause the income of small farmers and peasants to rise, along with educational and health levels. This strategy of modernization-from-above (the gradualist approach) argues that development can best occur through increased production *without* land redistribution. Those not receiving land in the countryside would migrate to the city as literate workers, thus supplying a labor market for industrial development.

Unfortunately, while intense exploitation of the peasantry and rural labor force has been commonplace throughout Latin America during the better part of four centuries, the landowners have not utilized the economic surplus to industrialize society. While in Europe, the Soviet Union, Japan and even the United States, coercion of the agricultural population to extract the economic surplus was accompanied by rapid industrialization, this has not been the case in Latin America. 'Foreign investors and Latin American elites have exported their earnings to the industrial capitalist world, invested in land, commerce and real estate, and engaged in speculative activity. Historically the Latin American landowners have not matched Barrington Moor's description of the modernizers-from-above: they have exploited and coerced but they have hardly 'developed' (Moore, 1967).

Obviously, some elements or techniques of the two approaches are not mutually exclusive and could be integrated into a single program for agricultural development. The fact that the 'client' group emphasized is different in each case, however, presents an insurmountable obstacle to such integration. The redistribution-ists, concerned with bettering the conditions of the majority of agrarian population as rapidly as possible, stress land reform as a necessary precondition for agricultural development. For the pro-ductionists, on the other hand, the immediate needs of the rural populace are not primary; at best they may assume that these needs will ultimately be met by the increased production achieved through technical innovation. But the social forces that would be called on to implement the productionist approach suggest such a result is unlikely, for whereas the redistribution strategy de-pends on mobilization of heretofore ignored segments of the population, the productionists work through existing channels and institutions. Thus, while modernization-from-above may bring greater technical efficiency and raise production, it will not alter, but probably enhance, the economic, political and social resources of the few who own land at the expense of the many who work it.[1] The modernization-from-below strategy of the redis-tributionists sees agrarian reform as an aspect of social change that will eradicate inequality in rights and income, thereby minimizing inequalities of access to the political system.

1. Increased emchanization of agriculture eliminates the need for manual labor and, consequently, decreases jobs in the rural sector, resulting in the redundancy of the rural laborer. Given the very limited absorption quality of the industrialization process, the rural unemployed usually become the penny vendors and slum dwellers who increasingly are found in and around all the major metropolitan areas of Latin America.

References

ALBA, V. (1965), *Alliance Without Allies*, Praeger.
US CONGRESS (1962), *Hearings on Economic Development in South America*, Joint Economic Committee, 87th Congress, 1st Session.
MOORE, B. Jr (1967), *Social Origins of Dictatorship and Democracy: Lord and Peasant in the Making of the Modern World*, Beacon.

13 M. Lipton

Urban Bias and Rural Planning in India

Excerpt from M. Lipton, 'Strategy for agriculture: urban bias and rural planning in India', in P. Streeten and M. Lipton (eds.), *The Crisis in Indian Planning*, Oxford University Press, 1968, pp. 130–47.

We have not yet resolved the paradox of Indian agriculture: necessarily ambitious production targets, low and sometimes unproductive public outlays, low incentives to private outlays, yet a high rate of return to *potential* extra spending. The explanation lies neither in the composition and location of plan outlays within agriculture, nor in a direct linkage of ancillary spending to investment in production. Nor is there any conscious failure by the planners to appreciate the abstract need for 'top priority in agriculture'. Two successive plans have aimed at self-sufficiency in foodgrains. To ram home the lesson, the adverse conjunction of population growth, poor harvests and scarce foreign exchange in 1965–7 showed how an underdeveloped agriculture can stultify industrial development by diverting foreign exchange from industrial raw materials to food imports. Economics is reinforced by psychology. Only 3 per cent of Indian workers are employed in modern industry.[1] India's planners have lived through the colonial atmosphere of enclave development; they understand the futility of trying to promote attitudes favourable to economic growth (or political stability) by development allocations that widen the huge gulf between this 3 per cent and the rest. Yet this understanding remains somehow abstract, and so does 'top priority for agriculture'.

We have seen that neither allocations of public money, nor incentives to the movement of persons and other resources, have favoured agricultural development; that 70 per cent of the workers get less than 35 per cent of investment finance and a far smaller share of human skills. Several types of pressures on opinion and policy have combined to bias the allocation of cash, effort, personnel and research away from rural needs. First, skilled, literate and articulate persons congregate in cities. There, they

1. Dhar and Lydall (1961). 'Modern' means 'using electric power' *or* 'in plants with more than fifty persons'.

have access to senior political and administrative officers. However conscientious these officers may be, the balance of pressures on them is overwhelmingly urban. A BDO (Block Development Officer) spends most of his life in the biggest town in his Block; so does his agricultural assistant. A CEO (Chief Executive Officer) spends most of his life in the district capital. Tours of duty take them to villages, and by and large they welcome such visits; but 'visits' they remain. A BDO covers thirty to fifty villages, and does well to visit each village twice a year. The influences, pressures and conversation of the market town outweigh the contradictory, unorganized complaints of numerous villages, each fleetingly experienced. For the CEO the balance is even more urban. And in centres of State Government, where business, trade union and mass pressures are constantly heard and felt, the pressure of the remote village is very faint. Riots for lower foodgrain prices (and strikes and *gheraos* for higher wages, i.e. for dearer manufactured goods for farmers) are an immediate threat; famine, caused by failure to use price incentives to persuade farmers to grow enough food, seems a distant cloud. The high and rising representation of villagers in State Parliaments (Rosen, 1966, pp. 72–3) is hardly relevant as a counterpoise; these MLAs (Member of the Legislative Assembly) are usually big landlords and their interests are those of the urban élite, not of the often more efficient mass of small farmers.

The second aspect of urban bias concerns the relative pay and status of urban and rural personnel. It means that the best doctors, lawyers, businessmen and administrators gravitate to cities and influence policy there. This impedes the development of worm-free farmers, litigation-proof consolidation schemes, private agricultural investment and the efficient organization of rural life.

Townsmen naturally prefer those villagers who speak and write their language, sell them food and invest in urban industry. Insofar as a direct rural presence is felt in the towns, it is unrepresentative. It is the big landlords and moneylenders that can afford city houses, and sometimes control rural votes. Laws to reform tenure and credit therefore have built-in loopholes. As for the permanent migrants from villages to towns – if employed, they identify themselves with the urban élite they have joined; if unemployed, they have little influence on policy. Full-time small farmers have practically no direct impact in State capitals.

Hence, as we have seen, agricultural development is geared to bigger farmers, with irrigated land and a marketable surplus, in ways that often increase risk and reduce incentives for other farmers.

Another aspect of urban bias is an intellectual successor to Brahmanism. Gandhi was Banya by caste; but growing population gives urgency to his advocacy of manual work, and outside South India it is hard to find a Brahman who religiously refuses to touch the plough. It is, however, very common to find smooth-handed Agricultural Development Committees at all levels from Zilla Parishad (district) upwards. I asked the headmaster of a boys' high school in Maharashtra how many of his candidates for the Senior School Certificate (taken at age eighteen) returned to agriculture. Ah, he sympathized, a tragic problem; some of these intelligent young men actually did have to go back to the villages. In Delhi, research village studies are sometimes dismissed as 'cow-dung economics'.

The planners' emphasis on industry is not due only to the fact that industrialists are more powerful, articulate and accessible than farmers. Output is more easily measured, and relevant inputs more easily specified, in industry than in agriculture. This has long been a partial explanation of their respective plan allocations; tangible yields, traceable to specific inputs, are attractive because they can be put into a growth model (or a Plan Frame) and checked afterwards. However, since 1958, the Agro-Economic Research Centres have been producing quantitative studies of villages at five-yearly intervals, designed to illuminate the processes of agricultural change; studies which, for all their deficiencies, are the raw material for similarly precise planning in agriculture. Yet they are not used for policy-making at any level. The IAAP (Intensive Agricultural Areas Programme) has been submitted to closer analysis than the earlier arrays of agricultural schemes, and the projections for 1970–71 divide farm output into more components than was the case in previous plan periods. But research into the relations between inputs and outputs still concentrates on industrial sectors. We do not know, even roughly, whether IAAP yields more than an equal outlay on, say, improving traditional implements and practices; or whether an extra hundred rupees yields more rice in Kerala or West Bengal, in dysentery relief or in fertilizer subsidy.

It is quite mistaken to suggest that Indian agricultural planning has achieved nothing. 'The growth rate [since Independence is] a marked improvement over . . . preceding decades, when agricultural output grew by less than 1 per cent per annum' (p. 172). Indeed, urban bias in agricultural planning has great rural achievements to its credit, especially in schemes that can be organized centrally without treading on powerful urban toes. 'The village, unchanged for 2000 years' is romantic (or Cassandra-like) rubbish. The village, since Independence, has seen a social revolution, raising the level of living in ways that seldom express themselves as rises in estimated income per head. Malaria affected 108 per 1000 in 1953–4, and 5 per 1000 in 1965 (1968, p. 340). Since Independence, primary-school enrolment has almost trebled (1968, p. 328). Most villagers can get some sort of medical help, and can educate their children. A much higher proportion than ever before can get conveniently to the nearest town by road, at least in the dry season; possess a hurricane lamp and see to it that the village street is lit at night; have access to a communal radio – and so on, over a wide range of social and private durable consumer goods. What, then, is wrong with urban bias in agricultural planning?

Anyone who has observed a particular village must admire the achievements of planning in village India, but he will be saddened by the small extent to which social advance has led to increased agricultural efficiency. Social change *has* been induced. Caste restrictions on well-use, commensality and joint farmwork are weakening, both because population growth has loosened job rigidity and because of direct Government pressure. Economic change, however, has been small. The proportion of Indians dependent on agriculture was much the same at the 1951 and 1961 censuses; yet food production per head of population in 1964–5 was barely 1 per cent higher than in 1953–4, and agricultural output per person 2 per cent higher (FAO, 1966, p. 198). In view of the increases and improvements in non-human inputs over the period this is disappointing progress. Most Indian farmers plough too seldom, sow their seed rows too close, make inefficient manure heaps instead of compost pits and waste their crops through poor protective measures, both in the field and in storage. In every case the expected value of extra output exceeds the extra labour cost.

The small farmer's reluctant economic response to social improvement and technical change is not born of stupidity. Farmers first seek to insure themselves against disaster, not to incur *certain* efforts and costs with new techniques for a merely *probable* return; secondly, they seek to maintain their family's status by means including expensive weddings in the ploughing season, division of holdings among the sons to avoid landlessness, and cow-worship – all this, if necessary, at the expense of investment and output. Such behaviour is fully compatible with the farmer's known readiness to change his cropping pattern if incentives are right. The farmer's behaviour is not irrational, but its rationale is not simply the maximization of expected profit. Effective agricultural planning must recognise and bridge the gap between the peasant's varying mixture of goals (status, income, security) and the planning maximand (value added in agriculture) (Bailey, 1966).

The most serious aspect of urban bias is the city dweller's inability to appreciate the peasant's thought processes. This is less marked in the Draft Fourth Outline than in earlier planning documents, as is clear from its more realistic discussion of land reform. A sense of unreality nevertheless permeates the agricultural sections of the Draft Outline (see the quote below). The effect of this remoteness from rural realities on agricultural planning has been discussed at several points. The suggestion that crop-share rents *increase* the tenant's insecurity is an extreme example. The origin of the remoteness lies in the almost exclusive exposure of planners and politicians to the thought, pressure and company of the tiny sections of India's population involved in modern urban politics, trade unionism, industry, universities and administration. Planners and Ministers show a deep, sincere concern for the welfare of farmers, and (foreigners often assume) understand rural India because they are Indians. However, concern and goodwill are not substitutes for direct, prolonged contact with particular villages, and study of micro-level data collected from many more.

Planning under urban bias is well able to treat rural backwardness, provided the treatment satisfies three conditions: amenability to large-scale central organization, absence of affront to powerful interests in the villages and lack of conflict with rural values and attitudes. Thus Indian planning can eradicate malaria, build big dams, provide big areas with electricity. But if there is an intra-rural power struggle, as with land reform; or a complex situation requiring detailed case studies, as with diffusion of innovation; or a need to transform attitudes, as with castration of stud bulls – then planning under urban bias is unlikely to succeed. The townsman is a contractualist and thus disguises his failure from himself by paper legislation[2] – ceilings on holdings evaded by *mala fide* transfers to relatives, laws against dowries and untouchability, limitation of rents and interest rates to unenforceably low levels. The townsman's life is compartmentalized, and he can learn to improve some aspects of it without much effect on others; so he also honestly believes in 'showpiece planning' through model farms and isolated research stations.

Village power, attitudes and institutions

India has about 646,000 villages. One of the themes of this chapter is that the type of village – its size, caste structure, cropping pattern, nutrition, tenure and urban contact – affects the rates of return to various types of farm outlay, and that the urban bias of Indian agricultural planning has stopped planners from discovering these rates and adjusting planning accordingly. Nevertheless, some generalizations can be made.

The Draft Fourth Outline, like its predecessors, contains no discussion of the rural balance of power; we have seen how resources drift to big, powerful farmers irrespective of efficiency, and urban bias is relevant both to the drift itself and to the neglect of the research required to evaluate its effect on agricultural growth. Three aspects of the rural balance of power are obviously relevant to agricultural planning. Do the new institutions of co-operation and *panchayati raj* change the power structure? How far does power lie with groups or individuals hostile to economic advance, either because they fear a threat to their dominance or because they are old, set in their ways, or detached from fleshly interest by spiritual involvement? Who are the 'progressive farmers', and what political structures will increase their influence on their neighbours?

Potter (1964, pp. 53–4) has shown that *panchayati raj* in Rajasthan leads to disproportionate representation of the high castes, the richest and the landlords; and that the degree to which town dwellers are over-represented increases with the power of the democratic body. Thorner (1965) reaches similar conclusions about co-operative farming. Mrs Epstein (1964) shows how modern economic opportunities within the village also tighten the grip

2. Attitudes *can* be changed by legislation, if those affected (a) respect or fear contract law, (b) believe the legislation will be enforced. That is the difference between the effective legislation against racial discrimination in the US and the ineffective legislation against dowries in India.

of traditional ruling groups. If these groups were also agriculturally progressive, or were made so by the new institutions, democratic regret would be tempered by economic delight; but is this so? Does not entrepreneurship come from the group trying to improve its status through economic activity, rather than from the protectors of entrenched power? Bailey's (1960) account of the Boad and Ganjam Distillers in Orissa and Basu's (1964) discussion of the Subarabaniks in West Bengal suggest that this is certainly true of backward, rigid, multi-caste villages.

In many parts of West and North India, a single cultivator caste (e.g. the Marathas in Maharashtra) has a majority in most villages. This caste takes more than a proportionate share of economic decisions in the new institutions of *panchayati raj*, cooperative credit societies, etc., which, together with land reform, have improved its position *vis-à-vis* Brahmans. Research is needed to decide if this trend is economically desirable. In my experience, Marathas have more and better (though more fragmented) land than ex-untouchables; they tend to be more traditional, less experimental farmers, though perhaps superior in their use of traditional methods. Under the new institutions craftsman castes – forced into farming by population growth, and with quite good, unfragmented land recently acquired – lose power, as do the ex-untouchables. In West Bengal, Bose (1963) shows that a village with an overall majority of traditional cultivator-castemen showed faster agricultural progress than similar villages nearby, with no clear majority caste. The point is not to praise or condemn 'majority-casteocracy', but that it has little-analysed economic implications, e.g. for optimal area selection under IAAP.

While there is little knowledge of the effects of the new power structures upon economic efficiency (and less attempt to bring such knowledge into the planners' allocative decisions), more is known, from long experience, of the economic impact of traditional power structures. Within a village, many of the old economic links are still strong. In my experience, a Brahman landlord (owning about 100 acres) was faced by State legislation entitling tenants who paid more than one-fifth of their crop as rent to buy the land. He responded by shifting tenants round his land every year or two, while continuing to charge the market rent – half the crop. That way, nobody is seen to farm a piece of land long enough to establish a plausible claim to settlement. The fact that this is tolerated, e.g. that tenants do not insist on written rent receipts, suggests that most villagers accept traditional property rights. The consequent insecurity of tenure greatly strengthens the usual objection to share-rent: that tenants do less labour and much less investment than owner-occupiers.

If the Brahman's reaction and the tenants' tolerance is typical, it is damaging (not merely futile) to change the legal super-structure of property relations without doing anything to alter the 'who-whom' of power, custom and respect. The tenant and the landless labourer will continue to defer to the landlord, the merchant and the moneylender, until the Government provides *substitutes* for the trade credit, employment and contacts with officials that (as well as exorbitant rents and interest rates) come from the old rural establishment of India. It may be costly to provide such substitutes – crop insurance, loans secured against the harvest, rural labour exchanges. But it is self-defeating to act as if such substitutes existed already and to ignore the effects on agricultural legislation of the real, feudal power relations in the villages.

Traditional 'who-whom' relations survive purely legislative reform partly because the powerful have resources (land, credit) to bind the weak, but partly because Hinduism comforts the weak with promises that adherence to their justly allotted status ensures rebirth in a higher caste, and reassures the powerful that their status is the consequence of good acts in previous incarnations. Attitudes of rural people to economic change affect the optimal allocation of resources. In particular, the Draft Outline's discussion of improved attitudes helps us to see the characteristics that planners associate with 'progressive farmers', who are claimed to be an important source of growth.

Attitudes and behaviour patterns ... have to undergo as much of a fundamental change as ... when a country gets engaged in war. These changes have to be such as to maximize work, efficiency, savings, and resource mobilization. They must motivate and move the people in the direction of economic development ... There has to be a change in the attitude of the well-to-do ... towards consumption. Austerity should be encouraged not only in daily life but also extended to ... conspicuous expenditure ... on ceremonial occasions ... Taxation should be recognized as an instrument of resource mobilization ... Social displeasure should ... be brought to bear on tax evaders ... it is also necessary to stimulate in the people ... willingness to put up with reduced availability caused by ... exports ... There has to be a deliberate building up of an attitude of preference for *swadeshi* ... It is also necessary to bring about a preference for small families (pp. 36-7).

Work, efficiency, savings and resource mobilization are 'maximized' by distinct sets of policies. Clearly the planners wish to improve attitudes to all four aims. Peasant attitudes to *work* are determined by diet, especially protein; climate, especially humid heat at peak seasons; health, especially worms and dysentery; and by the yield of, and need for, effort. We have seen that the impact of diet and health on agricultural efficiency is not analysed. As for the effects of climate, the planners' view of short crops is enthusiastic, but too general to consider the regional impact on work loads – or whether these will fall when humid heat is at its worst. Yield of, and need for, efforts must vary with mechanization and size of holding; yet the benefits of IAAP are to be applied with 'no discrimination between cultivators on the basis of resources or the size of holding'. In each case, appropriate policies to change attitudes require local fact-grubbing rather than exhortation.

Economic *efficiency*, within a given structure of ownership, means that (a) each productive unit (given its location) uses its resources as efficiently as possible; (b) units are arranged in a spatial optimum – best size, location, and degree of fragmentation into plants (or plots). For the peasant to play his part in (a) by maximizing profits he needs some assurance that the reward for ambition will not be bankruptcy in bad years. For (b) the planners rightly emphasize consolidation, but overlook certain locational aspects. Farmers put more effort (weeding especially) into big plots, and into plots near home (Chisholm, 1962). This suggests the reallocation of land among villages which goes beyond the present framework of consolidation schemes. Also, consolidation of *plots* need not lead to a more efficient size of *holding*. Again, exhortation seems to be advanced as a substitute for highly localized enquiry and action.

Savings are reduced by taxing rich people, unless the Government can replace their lost saving. The planners eschew deficit finance, yet propose 'narrowing the disparities in incomes and property ownership'.

This would be no paradox if *resource mobilization* could be achieved by exhorting people to pay taxes. Pressures against this, however, are such that other States may follow Madras and abolish land revenue (Economist Intelligence Unit, 1966). The planners obviously want to reverse this trend but it is not clear how they propose to do it.[3] This enormous topic cannot be dis-

3. If drinking were penalized by high taxes instead of by evaded laws,

cussed here, except as another example of the use of 'rural attitudes' as a catch-all for a number of policy problems, calling for local inquiry into peasant response.

The well-to-do might be discouraged from consumption by making it more expensive, and savings more profitable. The Indian Post Office Savings Bank offers unattractively low interest, around 4 per cent. Profit need not accrue in ways amenable to the economic calculus; the most profitable ways for a rich farmer to use his spare cash may be to lend it at illegally high rates, to educate his sons for urban jobs and to buy status through expensive weddings. It would help if co-operatives were actively encouraged to make consumer loans and if village funds were set up for communal finance of ceremonials. Berating individuals for extravagance in supporting rural people's few enjoyments is less useful than trying to arrange alternative support (or alternative enjoyments) which are less damaging to investment finance.

Social displeasure might be brought to bear on tax evaders if police displeasure were to help it along. The village police headman is often a big farmer, or dependent upon one, and hence may not always enforce the tax legislation to the full. Kaldor (1956, p. 76) estimates that less than half Indian income taxes are actually collected.

Preference for *swadeshi* (Indian-made goods) is not helped by stores that openly stack row upon row of illegally imported luxury foods. The British and the Indians are both gifted at self-denigration; villagers' attitudes (for example) to Indian and German Petromaxes are based on pure prejudice. The tax system might again prove helpful.

'Preference' for big families illuminates two peasant attitudes: the adaptive lag and the insurance principle. Twenty years ago, a rural couple was well advised to have five children to ensure one surviving son; today, three will do. This is a great achievement of free India, yet it has not been communicated to the peasants. But the trouble lies deeper. Peasants maximize subject only to guarantees of survival, and many children mean many friends in need. This is part of the case for social security and crop insurance; in their absence, big families are one of the wasteful forms of insurance that planners must expect from villagers.

In part, all these demands for changes of attitudes are ways to

_____

more resources would be mobilized. The abolition of prohibition by two big States (July 1967) may open the way.

pass the buck; but they also demonstrate the townsman's vision of the village divided into 'progressive farmers' (with approved attitudes) and stupid, innately conservative peasants. The latter are urban myths; their distant cousins, farmers confirmed in a set of practices that guarantee a livelihood, and reluctant to learn risky new methods from neighbours or village-level workers, are a hard reality. Conversely the search for 'progressive farmers', to serve as foci for development, may be misconceived. There *are* big, rich farmers; their lessons are for others in that tiny minority. Among small farmers, there are progressive composters, weeders, storers – and they are not the same people. Each family finds, inherits, and defends 'from long experience', farming procedures that ensure survival as a landowning unit. This *survival algorithm*[4] suits the family's risk aversion, preference between income and leisure, liking for various seldom-traded vegetables intertilled with the main crop, auspicious days, and *dharma* (spiritual and caste duty). In a complex affair like farming, it may be fatal to detach and learn a practice that is 'improved' only in the context of someone else's algorithm.

Townsmen tend to berate or to legislate when confronted with rural institutions hostile to growth. Institutions have functions, and will not be readily abandoned until they are replaced by other institutions fulfilling similar functions, unless the rural environment or value-structure changes so that the peasant no longer seeks the fulfilment of these functions. Caste, for instance, has economic drawbacks; it impedes specialization of labour according to comparative advantage, it compels the duplication of wells, it slows the response to economic incentive where such response conflicts with *dharma*, and it perpetuates inequalities that reduce the enjoyment yielded by the few commodities available. Yet all this will leave the villager unmoved, as long as caste, and caste alone, provides social order, cohesion in the sense that such order is generally accepted, and (especially through single-caste factions) some social security.

Similarly, there is little point in attacks and laws against moneylenders while co-operative credit societies may not replace them as sources of consumer loans; or against the use of land to sustain cattle of little economic value, while most peasants are encouraged to worship them by the absence of alternative sources

4. In the American sense of an intellectual short cut, a calculating device, guiding the family to a set of farming tactics that ensures survival.

of draught power, transport, fuel, soil enrichment, protein or reserve capital.[5]

Many practices inimical to modernization are disguised insurance policies. Among them are: tenants' preference for share-rents over fixed rents; borrowers' preference for grain repayment over cash repayment;[6] willingness of both to pay for their preference; hoarding of marketable surpluses; reluctance to use fertilizer where water is unsure; intertillage of cereals with robust but low-value legumes; and persistence in 'improvident maternity'. Alternative sources of security, especially crop insurance schemes, might alleviate these evils. The plans for crop insurance come very late, and States are free to finance them or not, as they choose. The Central Parliament enacted a crop insurance scheme in July 1967, but we must see how and by whom it is to be administered and financed, how the States will respond, and whether the limited resources are to be concentrated on IAAP farmers (with new inputs but assured water in most cases) or on high-risk dry farmers.

Urban power and agricultural development

We have seen that farm policy is made by the towns, and to some extent for the towns. Business and trade union leaders both want low food prices. They can 'buy' them from the big landlords in return for loopholes in land reforms and in laws limiting interest rates; for low agricultural taxes; and for subsidized inputs (especially irrigation and fertilizer) for the big farmers. Such a deal is politically stable, because urban business and labour can be easily organized into monopolies and cartels; because the *powerful* rural groups are included, and the smallholders and landless labourers are deprived of their natural leaders by emigration; and because millions of small illiterate farmers are almost impossible to organize into unions.

The deal between urban élites and big farmers has been compatible with considerable rural progress; but it has meant too small a proportion of total outlays for agriculture, and it has distorted the structure of agricultural spending. Inequality within the village, and between village and town, has been worsened, and

5. A forthcoming paper by K. N. Raj will show a high rank correlation coefficient, for States, between the proportion of 'useless' cows and of pasture land.

6. This preference is nothing new, nor is the higher grain-rate of interest; see Kumar (1965, p. 615).

growth has suffered. Production of dairy products (and perhaps rice and wheat) gets too big a share of farm [investment; coarse grains (and probably pulses) get too small a share. Urban power grows as skilled graduates concentrate in the cities. Meanwhile the planned share of public investment in organized industry goes on rising.

One group within the urban élite may try to resist these trends: the planners themselves. There is reason to believe that they have been shocked into a new realization of the role and needs of agriculture. But the planners are in Delhi, and seem to have been getting weaker in 1967; and the main agricultural decisions are made in the State capitals. Moreover, planners are human; like most of the urban élite, they are not long 'emancipated from the rural morass'. They are not eager to plunge back in, despite their great and genuine sympathy for the peasant. Yet we have been driven to the conclusion, in almost every field of rural policy, that disaggregated, local-level research and action are needed. If the planners and their research staffs go back to the grass roots, they may still command the prestige to take the necessary steps. But they will be opposed by a formidable urban coalition, and by their own background and inclinations as well.

The urban alliance: the case of employment

The use made of labour is perhaps the clearest illustration: the provision of work opportunities in successive plans has shown systematic urban bias. Between the 1951 and 1961 censuses, the proportion of workers outside agriculture (30 per cent) hardly changed, yet 6·5m of the 8m extra jobs created during the Second Plan were outside agriculture. 'During the Third Plan the addition to the labour force may be . . . 17m, about a third of the increase being in the urban areas' yet the Third Plan proposed to provide 10·5m non-agricultural jobs and only 3·5m agricultural jobs,[7] though 4m seem to have been achieved. It is not easy to make sense of the concept of unemployment in India, but on any definition it is hard to believe that in 1966 only 'about three-fourths [of the unemployed] are in the rural areas'.

The same imbalance appears in the employment plans for 1966–71. The workforce is expected to rise by 23m between mid-1966 and mid-1971. It would be surprising if townward

7. *Third Five-Year Plan*, pp. 156–9. Some of the non-agricultural jobs are in the villages, but not enough to distort the comparison very much: many of these jobs are temporary dam-building, etc.

migration outweighed the effect of urban sex ratios sufficiently to put as much as one-third of the extra workers into the towns. Thus at least 15m will be in rural areas. Yet the 18·5 to 19m extra jobs to be created in 1966–71 are to include only 4·5 to 5m in agriculture. So at least 15m extra rural workers may expect – if we make a generous allowance for extra non-agricultural work in the villages – at most 6·5m extra jobs in 1966–71, while urban unemployment is intended to fall sharply.

The failure of various schemes of local works, rural works, etc., to employ the rural labour surplus is attributed to fortuitous factors by the planners, who hope to achieve an improvement if such works are 'incorporated as an integral part of the plan'. Yet the employment target for local works is only 1·5m 100-day man-years, as against 2·5m in the Third Plan (achievement 400,000). Nothing is said about voluntary and semi-voluntary unemployment due to village festivals, dysentery, worms and job restrictions based on considerations of caste impurity. Yet the jobs are waiting to be done in every village – roof repair, well desilting, composting, weeding, even washing children. Misery is caused impartially by voluntary, semi-voluntary, and involuntary joblessness. Has a mistaken transference of Western concepts of unemployment led Indian planners to concentrate exclusively on the third type?

Further, Healey (1965) has shown how employment opportunities in dam-building are restricted, and costs raised, by failure to schedule work into the agricultural slack season (chs. 9–10). The Draft Outline does not discuss this, but the proposed reduction of real outlay on major irrigation means less scope for counter-seasonal rural employment. The imbalance of new job opportunities, the decline of local works and the lack of seasonal jobs renders the planners' claim of priority for employment hard to follow, at least in the rural areas. 'Maximize growth, never mind employment, and tax the employed to compensate the jobless' could be a humane and sensible development strategy, but it is not articulated by the planners. Once more, the practical consequences of policies for the villagers do not seem to be analysed.

Conclusions

The share of agriculture in the Draft Outline of the Fourth Plan is smaller than has ever been planned before. However the data may be adjusted for devaluation or indirect contributions from other sectors, agriculture still does not seem to be getting the priority claimed by the planners.

The overall food targets are not too high, given that the vagaries of climate (and aid) render foodgrain self-sufficiency a prudent aim. But investment is insufficient to achieve these targets, especially in view of the structure of incentives, which tends to discourage farmers from growing foodgrains.

Capital–output ratios are substantially lower in agriculture than elsewhere. Agriculture uses relatively little foreign exchange and few scarce skills. It seems impossible to account for its low share of planned resources in economic terms. There is a real paradox here: high targets, high yields for extra outlay, yet low planned outlay. Moreover, incentives are so structured as to discourage the private sector from making good the deficiencies of public agricultural outlay.

The paradox is not fully resolved by the expectation of higher yields in IAAP. IAAP is advocated in the belief that peasants themselves exhaust all opportunities to improve traditional factors and techniques. This belief rests on a questionable interpretation of peasant motive. Poor farmers are too concerned with risk to behave as simple profit maximizers; rather they inherit a bundle of farm practices, some good, some bad, together constituting a survival algorithm.

To reduce agricultural risk, planners can (a) concentrate output in low-risk areas, as in IAAP; (b) select low-risk investments – irrigation rather than fertilizers; (c) insure against things going wrong – foodgrain stocks. Current planning concentrates almost exclusively on (a), but there is no evidence that this is the cheapest policy.

IAAP is inegalitarian, and in a way that may harm growth, since it reduces risk only for peasants already enjoying assured water supply. These are already the richest and most risk-free of farmers. Since risk is a bigger deterrent to the poor, and to those who suffer a lot of it, IAAP farmers are likely to raise private investment less than dry farmers, in response to a given public outlay to cut risk. The 80–85 per cent of farmers outside IAAP, already poorer than the rest, will receive lower prices if IAAP succeeds. Neither the experience of IADP districts, nor comparisons of performance by research stations and good farmers, suggests a dramatic breakthrough.

New seeds may make the decisive difference, but probably

not as quickly as the planners suggest. The new varieties have drawbacks (palatability, fodder value, risk) for which special arrangements are needed.

Selection of I A D P (Intensive Agricultural District Programme) areas was unsatisfactory; in I A A P, area selection requires more attention and analysis. Owing to the aggregative and industrial nature of economic research in India, we do not know where the expected rate of return on the package is highest. Similar criticism applies to most agricultural outlays – land reform, farm education, health and nutritional improvements, irrigation, etc.; hardly ever do we know the rates of return on scarce resources by area and crop.

The administrators and V L Ws (Village Level Worker) to carry out I A A P seem to be lacking. Their training is too centralized, their stay in one place too short and their work too clerical. A big increase in the number of such personnel will reduce their quality, and hence farmers' confidence in extension – especially when risky new inputs are being offered. For successful implementation in agriculture, the pay and status of rural civil servants, especially V L Ws, must rise.

Agriculture's persistently low share of development resources must be traced to urban bias in the Indian policy. Reward and status are higher in urban areas, even for jobs where the social rate of return is obviously much higher in villages (e.g. doctors). Policies are made under urban pressures. Research concentrates on more easily measured industrial processes.

Agricultural planning under urban bias has registered considerable achievements, but fails to grasp the villager's decision processes. It neither exploits nor changes his motivations, especially concerning status and risk; it relies too heavily on paper legislation based on contract law; and, by failing to grasp the facts of rural power, it allocates resources to the powerful, whether or not they use those resources best.

Such allocations, often through democratic institutions, also reflect the unity of motive between the townsman (who wants a marketed food surplus) and the big farmer (who sells it). This is damaging for two reasons. Firstly, the small farmer, often with higher output per acre, is deprived of resources of credit, fertilizer, etc. Secondly, the nutritional pattern of ouput is distorted. The faster growth of urban incomes, and the higher income-elasticity of demand for milk and polished rice, anyway cause the prices of such products to rise relative to coarse grains; and the *big* farmer, as he sells to the towns, switches production accordingly. If he outbids also small farmers for scarce resources, the prospects in cheap coarse grains are even more likely to be neglected. Yet it is the consumers of such grains who need extra food most. Moreover, 'big farmer bias' and present policy may (as in the past) divert the new inputs from the cereal fields to cotton and sugar.

Both past output trends (which the planners interpret too optimistically) and present input plans suggest that planned growth rates of agricultural production may not be approached by 1970-71. Extra land and labour, which accounted for over half the farm growth of the 1950s, will increase much more slowly in future. Industrial inputs to farming depend on hopeful projections for foreign exchange. Agricultural inputs depend on unrealistic assessments of the possibilities (green manure, urban compost, changing cropping pattern). The effects of the droughts of 1965-6 and 1966-7, both on inputs and on incentives, may severely damage future growth in agriculture.

There has been much more real land reform than the usual catalogue of evasion suggests, but there is still too much reliance on paper laws, and too little fieldwork to estimate the effects on output. More should be done about consolidation, especially in States where holdings (and therefore plots) are small.

The history of rural credit, too, does not support the extreme pessimism now current, but more can be done to get credit to small farmers, especially tenants. The crop loan scheme should improve this. Abandonment of accounting fictions concerning annual repayment and consumer loans would be helpful.

The allocation of agricultural outlay among *types* has been improved, but some aspects still need explaining. In view of the high and rising share of useless cattle, and of the low calorie–land ratio, the renewed emphasis on animal husbandry is hard to understand, and may be a reflection of middle-class urban diets.

There is not enough integration of social programmes into plans to raise farm output. The Education Commission's casual treatment of agricultural education is unempirical; the rate of return on different types of education, in different forms of agriculture, should be estimated. Such evidence as exists on the returns to nutritional improvement suggests that they are appreciable, especially among the ill-fed. The pattern of investment by crops (and the distribution of farm outputs, whether through compulsory procurement or through market incentives) should take more account of this, and less of the vagaries of income-elasticities of demand, overweighted as they are by growth in the better-fed urban sector.

Employment opportunities continue to favour the towns. No strategy is proposed in the published documents to correct the distributional effects of this, either by an attack on 'voluntary' rural unemployment or by counter-seasonal timing of rural investment projects; but some such strategy may nevertheless exist.

Planning under urban bias, with its excessive reliance on town demands and big farmers' supplies, has nevertheless achieved a great deal in rural India. Whatever their drawbacks, the Intensive Programme and the new seeds may seem to consolidate this achievement. In the long run, such an impression would be unfortunate. It would obscure the real needs: for intensive research, at local level, to discover the returns on alternative schemes; for rural development directed at maximum returns rather than at surpluses for low-yield urban reinvestment; and for a break with the whole ideology of premature industrialization. India's experience since Independence proves that neglect of agriculture is a recipe for slow industrialization, not for rapid economic growth.

References

BAILEY, F. G. (1960), 'An Oriya village: 2', in M. N. Srinivas (ed.), *India's Villages*, Asia Publishing House.

BAILEY, F. G. (1966), 'The peasant view of the bad life', *Advancement of Science*, December.

BASU, T. K. (1964), *The Bengal Peasant from Time to Time*, Asia Publishing House.

BOSE, S. P. (1963), *Eadpur: A West Bengal Village*, Dept of Agriculture, Bengal.

CHISHOLM, M. (1962), *Rural Settlement and Land Use*, Hutchinson.

DHAR, P. N., and LYDALL, H. F. (1961), *The Role of Small Enterprises in Indian Economic Development*, Institute of Economic Growth, Delhi.

ECONOMIST INTELLIGENCE UNIT (1966), *Quarterly Economic Review of India and Nepal*, December.

EPSTEIN, S. (1964), *Economic Development and Social Change in South India*, Manchester University Press.

FAO (1966), *State of Food and Agriculture 1966*, Rome.

HEALEY, J. M. (1965), *The Development of Social Overhead Capital in India, 1950–1960*, Blackwell.

KALDOR, N. (1956), *Indian Tax Reform*, Ministry of Finance, Delhi.

KUMAR, R. (1965), 'The Deccan riots of 1875', *J. of Asian Studs.*, August.

POTTER, D. C. (1964), *Government in Rural India*, Bell.

ROSEN, G. (1966), *Democracy and Economic Change in India*, Cambridge University Press.

THORNER, D. (1965), *Agricultural Co-operatives in India*, Asia Publishing House.

14 J. Gray

The Economics of Maoism

J. Gray, 'The economics of Maoism', *Bulletin of the Atomic Scientists*, vol. 25, no. 2, 1969, pp. 42–51.

The Cultural Revolution was explicitly about cultural change, but it took the form of a struggle for political power. The policy implications generally were less prominent than the struggle itself, and among these the implications for economic policy made a relatively late entry.

Mao Tse-tung's ideas, moreover, and the manner in which he expresses them, tend to obscure the economic implications of his theory and of the practice which springs from it. 'Politics takes command' seems at first sight a denial of the primacy of economic growth. 'A great spiritual force can be turned into a great material force' seems to be an un-Marxist insistence on the possibility of transcending by political and ideological means the constraints of economic facts and economic laws. Mao's recent attacks on 'material incentives' seem to Westerners a rejection of the most obvious and powerful means of stimulating economic enterprise. It is this sort of epigrammatic expression of the decisive importance of 'ideological revolution' which has led to the Soviet denunciation of Mao Tse-tung as a voluntarist, an anti-Marxist who believes that the human will, by some magic, can wish away objective facts, and the Soviet charge has been taken up and elaborated in the West.

It may be that Mao Tse-tung's prescriptions for economic and social change have little in them that is immediately recognizable as 'economics', but the record of the Cultural Revolution itself leaves little doubt of the importance of economic policy within it. The movement which led to the Great Proletarian Cultural Revolution began with the Communique of the Tenth Plenum of the Eighth Central Committee, September 1962, which, as far as internal affairs are concerned, dealt almost entirely with economic policy. The two great models of Maoist organization, carefully nurtured since then and widely publicized, were both economic enterprises, one industrial (the Ta Ching oilfield) and the other agricultural (the Tachai Production Brigade). From 1963 until 1965 there were growing signs, behind the ideological exhortations which filled the press, that the real preoccupations were with economic organization.

In August 1966, on the eve of the first great Red Guard parades, the Central Committee produced its Sixteen Point Directive for the guidance of the Cultural Revolution. This document simply dealt with the organization of the movement and had nothing whatever to say about its policy implications. The Kwangtung Provincial Committee of the Party immediately produced a long commentary upon it, interpreting its implications wholly in terms of economic organization and policy. It is even possible that the political struggle which began in April 1966 was finally touched off, not by Peng Chen's protection of liberal Party writers in Peking, but by his attempt to suppress Mao's instructions on the question of agricultural mechanization.

Finally, since the successful formation of the 'three-way alliance' in 1967, which brought the main struggle to an end, the fundamental disagreements between Mao and his opponents have been spelled out in considerable detail. In the last analysis they are primarily all questions of economic policy, and it is plain that Mao's ideas on economic organization are now being very generally applied.

There can be no doubt of Mao's preoccupation in recent years with problems of economic growth, therefore, and there is no obvious case for asserting that he is primarily interested in politics and ideology. It might still be true, of course, that his interpretation of the conditions necessary for successful economic growth neglected economic analysis. It is certainly true that there is nowhere in his works any detailed attention given to problems of costs, the precise definition of effective incentives and the alternative use of resources. And it is certainly not a sufficient explanation of his sketchy treatment of such themes to say that he leaves them to the technical economist. It is clear that he regards them as of secondary importance in the process of economic growth in a country such as China.

Mao's writings

To some extent Mao's apparent indifference to economic questions becomes exaggerated in Western minds because attention has so far been unduly concentrated upon his writings before 1949, conveniently translated in the four volumes of his *Selected*

Works. Other parts of Mao's writing, especially of his writing since 1949, have been neglected, including almost everything of economic relevance. His detailed analysis of the Border Region economy between 1940 and 1943 has never been translated, except for its preface. The *High Tide of Socialism in the Chinese Countryside*, 1956, which in three stout volumes of examples and commentary puts forward every idea of economic and social organization, later to be developed in the Commune movement and in the Cultural Revolution, has never been fully analysed and is usually ignored. The economic implications of Mao's 1957 pamphlet *On the Correct Handling of Contradictions among the People*, developed in a wealth of exegesis, have never been dealt with, because of the strange Western assumption that it dealt primarily with conflicts of opinion, while in fact (like any Marxist) Mao was actually preoccupied with conflicts of interest, and therefore with what are fundamentally economic questions.

It is not possible to elaborate here on Mao's economic ideas, but before considering the economic implications of the Cultural Revolution, it may help to put forward a hypothesis concerning them which may assist the reader in understanding what follows.

An examination of Mao's writings suggests three points of importance in the economic sphere:

1. Mao has always insisted that the emphasis of work in economics and in public finance must be on the increase of production. Taxation and state procurement must be subordinated to and dependent upon increased production. In this, he is not simply making moral noises, but reacting strongly against the static, tax-collecting tradition of Chinese administration (both traditional and Nationalist), against the counter-productive procurement policies of Stalin, and against the strong tendency of the cadres to inherit the worst of both.

2. He has always attached very great importance to material incentives in economic policy. In the perpetual tension throughout the history of Chinese communist administration since 1927, between economic rationality and doctrine or between economic rationality and social justice, Mao has usually been on the side of economic rationality, insisting that economic and social policies could not hope to succeed unless they were successful in raising personal incomes.

3. He has always emphasized the importance of entrepreneur-

ship at least as strongly as any economist working on the problems of India or of Latin America. This is obscured for the Western reader only by the fact that in the West 'entrepreneur' implies an individual operating in more or less free-market conditions. Mao's entrepreneurs are collectives, or more precisely individuals working though collectives. In spite of this, he meets the Western economist in the value which he attaches to willingness to innovate, willingness to take risks, and effective forethought. These are the qualities of the heroic leaders of the Tachai Production Brigade and of a thousand other economic enterprises, agricultural and industrial, which have been presented as models over the years since the 'transition to socialism' and planned economic growth began in 1953. One is of course at liberty to doubt how far the collective system of China can go in producing a high level of these entrepreneurial qualities; but there can be no doubt that maximizing these qualities within that system is one of Mao's preoccupations – perhaps his greatest and most constant preoccupation in the economic field.

In order to see how far these considerations have influenced the course and the consequences of the Cultural Revolution, one must evade as far as possible the general statements made by Mao and his supporters, and look at the problem in a concrete form. Mao addresses himself to the grass-roots: to half-educated sons of workers and peasants, to sub-literate lower-level cadres and to the still largely illiterate masses. He is therefore more concerned to express himself in memorable slogans than in statistical tables. The slogans provide texts which his local supporters then elaborate in concrete terms, largely by verbal communication. This present study is deliberately based largely upon publications in Chinese specialist journals, where one might expect that Mao's case would be put in its most sophisticated form; but even there, especially as the Cultural Revolution gathered strength, the slogan, the epigram and the mnemonic soon come to dominate what was published. It is only by taking one important practical issue and examining it that one can bring Maoist economics down to reality.

Tenth plenum policy

One key issue in the struggle which was developing over economic policy and organization after 1962 was the question of the best means to achieve the mechanization of Chinese agriculture. The

Communique of the Tenth Plenum put forward a new economic policy expressed in the formula: 'Take agriculture as the foundation of the economy, and industry as the leading factor.' This was a reaction to the agricultural disasters of the preceding three years. It looked forward not simply to giving agriculture priority in economic planning, and to the fullest possible use of industry to equip agriculture, but also to two specific policies: first, the transformation of agricultural technology by the development of mechanization, electrification, water conservancy and the use of chemical fertilizers; and second, concentration upon the creation of areas of stable high yields as a defense against the natural disasters which had so damaged the economy between 1959 and 1961.

In relation to this, the Tenth Plenum reasserted much more strongly than any previous statement the idea that class struggle must be expected to continue after the foundation of the socialist state. The context showed, and subsequent comments confirmed, that renewed class struggle was closely related to the new policy of transforming agricultural technology. The full resources of the collectives would have to be mobilized for investment in agriculture if the new plans were to be realized; the diversion of savings and labor into the private sector which had been permitted to flourish increasingly since 1959 would have to be curtailed.

Behind this decision by the Central Committee lay two issues which might (in spite of the resounding phrases in which this new consensus was expressed) give grounds for renewed and fundamental disagreement. Firstly, it is very probable that the reassertion of collectivist agriculture was not accepted with equal wholeheartedness by all the leaders. The form (the small cooperative represented by the production team, or the very large collective represented by the Commune?) was not defined, nor was the degree to which the private sector would be reduced. Secondly, nothing was said about how collective resources would be mobilized: in the form of local savings directly invested by the collective as in the Communes of 1958; or by increased taxation and procurement making possible greater central investment in agriculture by the state?

In relation to the new economic policy, the question of agricultural mechanization and how it could be achieved was of fundamental importance. The crux of agricultural mechanization is the tractor. In 1952–53, the first tractor stations appeared in China. They were operated by the state and fees charged for their services to the farmers. That some of China's leaders were unhappy from the beginning about this acceptance in China of the Soviet organization of agricultural mechanization is now revealed by quotations from remarks reported to have been made by Kang Sheng (now one of the hard-core Maoist group) in 1954 after his return from a tour of inspection of the Soviet Union:

Tractors and peasants

'Collective farms in the Soviet Union have many machines, but output is nevertheless low, and costs are high . . . ' And on the Chinese imitation of the Soviet Union's tractor stations: 'This is the problem that must be solved: how to link the tractors to the peasants . . . If tractor stations continue to be run in their present form . . . they will become disguised tax-collectors, and will hold the peasants to ransom, as the Soviet tractor stations do . . . '

Consequently, when collectivization had been rapidly completed in 1956 under pressure from Mao Tse-tung, backed by a conference representing not only the Party leadership but the provincial, municipal and regional authorities throughout China, experiments were conducted in Manchuria and in North China in permitting the collectives to run their own tractors. In March 1958 (we are now informed by Red Guard sources) at a conference at Chengtu in Szechuan, Mao Tse-tung advocated that agricultural mechanization should be carried out through the collectives themselves, buying the equipment out of their own resources and operating it on their own account. Although this decision was apparently suppressed by the Party's right wing, when the Communes were formed later in the same year, 70 per cent of the existing tractors were handed over to them.

The opposition, however, displayed their lack of enthusiasm by carrying this out in a perfunctory way, giving no help or guidance to the Communes: 'In some places a meeting was held in the morning, and the tractors were driven away in the afternoon.' For two years, say Mao's supporters, the relevant ministries did not hand down a single document nor convene a single conference to assist the Communes in handling the machinery. The Communes suffered heavy losses, and those who supported the alternative policy of providing mechanization through the state were then able to argue that the experiment had been a costly failure, not only for the Communes themselves but for the state which had to bail them out.

This Maoist story implies that the opposition was basically indifferent to mechanization of agriculture. Liu Shao-chi and Po I-po are quoted to prove this, but the quotations are obviously torn from their context and almost certainly misrepresent their views on the desirability of mechanization, as opposed to the methods of achieving it. The Maoists can nevertheless point to the fact that the business of agricultural mechanization was split among three different ministries, and generally bandied about from hand to hand in a way which does not suggest that the Liu Shao-chi administration gave the problem very high priority. Local tractor and equipment plants were apparently closed down and much of the industry made subordinate to the production of other types of motor vehicles.

Communal mechanization

The recommendation of the Chengtu Conference of March 1958 that the collectives themselves should take the initiative in mechanization was, it is claimed, suppressed until 'some people discovered it' in 1965. Mao's only victory in this issue was to secure in 1963 the establishment of a Ministry in whole and sole charge of agricultural mechanization, a measure which he had sought since 1956. It was, however, short-lived, and was perverted from its intended purpose of providing guidance to communal mechanization, to the centralized manufacture of equipment within the system of state operation now being evolved by Liu Shao-chi and Peng Chen. This was a centralized and monopolistic system, culminating in 1965 in a proposal to change the various economic ministries into trusts, of which the China Tractor and Internal Combustion Company was one. They hoped eventually that these public trusts would operate directly under the state Economic Commission, outside the control of the Party committees at all levels, and outside the control of local government bodies, and that the operations of these trusts would be judged by their profitability.

As far as the problem of agricultural mechanization is concerned, the crisis came in early 1966. Mao Tse-tung (Red Guard sources state) took up a report on the problem prepared by the Hupeh Provincial Committee, a report favorable to his own views and requested that it be given nationwide Party circulation. Liu Shao-chi refused to circulate the report, or Mao's accompanying comments, until the Central Committee had given its opinion. He gave Peng Chen the task of drafting this opinion. Peng Chen did so, and he also edited Mao's own comments, cutting out Mao's warnings against rigid centralization, and also (which was both significant and infuriating) cut out his condemnation of Soviet agricultural policy. Within days, Lin Piao's troops turned Peng Chen out of his office, and the Cultural Revolution became a struggle for political power.

Intermediate technology

A subsidiary issue was the fate of Mao's attempt to organize and guide the peasants to develop their own 'intermediate technology' by systematic improvement of existing tools. In 1958, he had called for research stations in every province. In 1959, he put forward a plan for units in every *hsien*, in which scientists, technicians, local blacksmiths and carpenters would be associated with veteran farmers in working out new tools suitable to their locality. The Liu faction took no interest in this, believing that such an intermediate technology could at best have only a temporary importance, and they persisted more and more in pursuing 'bigness, modernity, completeness and newness.'

We have, of course, only the Maoist story of these events. Although a rapid check back through the documentation of the years in question certainly shows that a muted struggle on these lines was going on, we have no access to any full statement of the opposition's case. We have to work, for the present, with what the Maoists chose to quote of it in the course of their attacks. If these quotations (which are very repetitive and sometimes contradictory) are organized into something as near to logic as they will permit, the argument is broadly as follows:

Since the peasants are unable to do the job, the State must do it. Although ownership and operation by the Commune has been implemented, actually investment is still made by the State, and operational losses are still subsidized by the State. We must equip whole *hsien* one by one. Many machines must be concentrated in one *hsien*. For ten years the State will invest a very large sum of money, and it will begin to recover it at the end of these ten years. The State will then use this sum of money to equip another area. The State will have to invest 10 to 20 billion *yuan*.

In charging fees [for the use of tractors] fields should be divided into a number of grades. The fees charged may be lower for large plots and higher for small plots. Operations should be guided by price.

The power of the trust (in capitalist countries) is very great. The capitalist experience of management of enterprises – especially of monopolistic enterprises – should be studied. The bureaus of the various ministries are to be converted into companies and become, not administrative organizations, but enterprises. Let us set up a trust [for agricultural machinery] and set up supply stations along railway lines and highways. We should not set up stations according to administrative divisions, nor should we make direct allocations to the *hsien*. All stations should be run independently of the local governments.

Our present method is for provinces, municipalities, regions and the different departments of the Central Committee to interfere with the economy. This is an extra-economic method. It is not a capitalist method, but a feudal method.

It is clear that the 'Party people in authority taking the capitalist road' were in fact, on this vital issue as well as in many others, taking the road of East European liberalization. Before we assume, however, that because Liu Shao-chi seems to be a liberal in this sense, Mao must represent resurgent Stalinism, it may be as well to quote Mao Tse-tung's opinion of Soviet agriculture written in his comments on the 1966 Hupeh proposals, and edited out by the liberals: 'The agricultural policy of the Soviet Union has always been wrong in that *it drains the pond to catch the fish*, and is divorced from the masses, thus resulting in the present dilemma.'

This, it may be noted, is more than an attack on 'Khrushchev revisionism'. Soviet agricultural policy has '*always been wrong*', and its failing – ruthless procurement – is one which Mao and his audience know very well was at its unbelievable worst not under Stalin's successors but under Stalin himself.

Mao versus Liu

The Maoist arguments against Liu Shao-chi's policy on agricultural mechanization, put into a connected argument, are as follows:

The cause of agricultural mechanization must be made to establish flesh-and-blood ties with the masses. We always advocate that revolution depends on the masses of the people and on everybody going into action, and are opposed to depending on a few people issuing orders. We should bring local initiative more into play and, under the unified planning of the central government, let the localities do more.

Collectives must depend on their own strength to achieve agricultural mechanization. Mechanization should be linked with defense against famine and should serve the people. Reliance on state investment would be 'draining the pond to catch the fish', reflecting the mistakes of Soviet revisionism. State operation of tractor stations makes it impossible for the peasants generally to grasp modern production methods and technical knowledge. In this way the difference between workers and peasants will widen and widen. The tractor stations obliged to show a profit have refused to plough for communes and teams in difficulties.

If the monopolistic agricultural machinery trust merely considers specialization in and standardization of a few products without giving any consideration to the actual needs of the rural communes – especially the areas with low output and poor communications – in what way is it different from the capitalists who 'have only an eye for gain' and 'refuse to do unprofitable business?'

Disparate views

Thus two distinct economic points of view emerge on this issue. The Liu administration seeks to get rid of political and administrative interference in economic organization; to improve efficiency by concentrating production, cutting out small inefficient enterprises, and standardizing products; to avoid wasteful investment by putting the operation of the industry on the clear and simple basis of profit and loss; to avoid wasteful use of resources by keeping the operation and repair, as well as the manufacture, of agricultural equipment in skilled hands. The means they chose to apply were those which were being experimented with in other communist countries at much the same time.

The Maoist view, however, emphasizes the following points:

1. The peasants will not take an interest in mechanization or try to exploit its possibilities fully unless and until they have the machines at their own disposal, so that they can 'regard the machines as a dependable force for the all-round development of production in a planned manner', instead of regarding them as something foreign which they call on, if at all, only when hard-pressed in the busy season. The idea that tractor stations themselves should take responsibility for directing local agricultural production is emphatically rejected.

2. Reliance on State investment for mechanization would mean, in one form or another, increased procurement of agricultural produce to pay for mechanization, through centralized institutions remote from the peasants. It would 'drain the pond to catch the fish'.

3. State operation of equipment provides no 'educational fallout'.

4. Centralized monopoly of the industry deprives the local communities of one of their most obvious lines of industrial growth:

service to local agriculture. This and the previous point are combined in the statement that the movement for the improvement of farm tools which Mao sought to maintain 'promoted local industry and handicrafts and also helped people to free their minds from superstitious attitudes and dogmatism about agricultural mechanization'.

5. Using profit as the criterion of efficiency in the operation of agricultural machinery stations will tend to concentrate development in the richer areas and leave the poorer and remoter areas untouched, thus widening the gap (already politically important) between the richer and the poorer areas of China.

6. The dependence of the peasants on mechanization provided by skilled technicians and workers from outside would widen the existing social gulf between urban workers and rural peasants.

To sum up these points, Mao is opposed to the monopolization of agricultural machinery by the state on the grounds that it would increase the state's procurement needs and add to the peasants' burden, that it would impoverish the development of the local economies by minimizing the opportunities of the peasant communities to master modern technology and to develop local industry, and that it would tend to increase rather than diminish two existing social gulfs – that between city workers and the rural farming population, and that between the richer and poorer parts of China.

Of these points, clearly the most important in his mind is the question of education through participation. 'The important question is the education of the peasants,' is one of Mao's most frequent quoted aphorisms. Applied to the question of agricultural mechanization, it means that the peasants will not accept, or fully use, *or pay for*, agricultural mechanization unless they can be brought to appreciate its full possibilities in the amelioration of their own lives. It also means that this appreciation will be developed only by inducing the villages gradually, through their own efforts toward an intermediate technology, to mechanize out of their own resources and to operate the machines with their own hands, in a milieu in which local industry, agricultural mechanization, agricultural diversification, and the education (both formal and informal) growing out of these activities, mutually enrich each other.

Perhaps the key to Mao's convictions is best provided by an account given in the *Draft History of Agricultural Taxes*, of a controversy which is said to have taken place among the Party leaders during the discussions following the end of the first five-year plan. Agricultural production and incomes had increased during the first plan. The question was whether or not procurement assessments should therefore be increased in the second plan. Such an increase would have been orthodox communist practice, on the assumption that any increased investment made possible by the increase in production should be made centrally by the state. According to the *Draft History*, written explicitly as concrete illustration of Mao's discussion of conflicts of interest among individual, collective and state in his pamphlet *On the Correct Handling of Contradictions among the People*, Mao insisted that the absolute quantity of taxes and compulsory purchases should remain the same, and the surplus accruing from increased production should be left in the hands of the collectives, to be invested by the collectives themselves.

The reason which Mao is said to have advanced for this unorthodox policy was that the peasants would learn to appreciate the nature of the relationships among individual, collective and state interests – and the crux of this was an appreciation of what industry could do for them – only if they developed and operated industry for themselves. He had already made it clear in his own pamphlet that he regarded the state bureaucracy as the biggest obstacle to the growth of an appreciation among the population generally of the basic identity of individual and communal interests which the Party's economic planning was supposed to enshrine.

This was the basic argument behind the Great Leap Forward and the Communes, and the examination made here of the problems of agricultural mechanization shows that, for Mao, the argument still stands.

Parallels in the West

Significantly, while Mao has been working out the implications of his ideas on the 'education of the peasant' as the fundamental problem of the Chinese economy, Western economists have been coming to parallel conclusions. In the decade since the Communes were established, it has become a commonplace in the West to say that the problems of economic growth in poor countries are very often not, in any obvious sense, economic problems at all, but are problems of ignorance and apathy, and of social habits and attitudes in the underdeveloped countries.

We do not deny to men who emphasize this idea the title of economists, and there is no reason why we should believe that Mao's ideas, however idiosyncratic, indicate that he has no thoughts on economics. Indeed, once the similarity of his ideas to our own is recognized, we should acknowledge that he was the first to express them. Having done so, we may understand his ideas better by noting that he is the only statesman anywhere who has made a determined and intelligible effort to transcend the 'contradiction' between economic incentives on the one hand, and fear and ignorance on the other, by policies which seek to maximize the educational effects of participation in production.

These ideas of Mao Tse-tung, expressing a concern with material incentives, a rational procurement system, and a pre-occupation with the development of enterpreneurial qualities, are obscured by his insistence on a high level of collectivism. Western views of what collectivism is and how it works are, of course, based on the depressing history of Soviet collective agriculture in the Soviet Union itself and in the East European communist countries. It is impossible to discuss Mao's economic ideas and policies intelligibly if one assumes from this history that Soviet and East European agriculture has failed simply because it is collective. There is no warrant for such a conclusion.

In the story of the failure of Soviet-type agriculture, the mere fact of collective organization is probably the least of it. Uneconomic levels of procurement, starvation of capital, starvation of talent, lack of consumer goods, direction from outside by an urban-based and urban-biased Party – almost any one of these factors is enough to account for the stagnation of agriculture. One might also add that, in comparing the Russian *kholkhoz* with the Chinese collective (cooperatives until 1958, Communes thereafter), the totally different historical situations from which they sprang has influenced their development and their possibilities. The attitude of the Soviet Party to agriculture sprang from the pre-revolutionary situation in which, as the Russian economy broke down under the strain of war, the countryside had to be dragooned into supplying the starving towns. Collectivization in Russia was a response to emergency conditions – undertaken before the threat of famine, and forced through by civil war.

On the contrary, in China Mao Tse-tung has been able to choose his moment, and every step in the development of collective enterprise in China has been taken in the wake of economic success. The movement for the organization of agriculture was launched in 1953 when the economy had recovered from the devastation of the Japanese war. It was completed in 1956 after the bumper harvest of 1955. The Communes were set up in 1958 after the record harvests of 1957. The movement to restore the collectives after the bad years of 1959–61 began with the first normal harvest in 1962, but the Cultural Revolution was launched only after a steady improvement in agricultural production from 1962–65. If there has been an element of force in the collectivization of rural life in China, there has also been an element of optimism, derived from successful experience. There has also been the long experience of the Chinese Communist Party during the Kiangsi Soviet and the Japanese War of running a rural economy, in conditions which enforced even at the outset and without institutional change a significant level of cooperative activity on the part of the rural population.

Reaction from Soviet model

It is thus possible to approach Mao's collectivist ideas and policies in a questioning, rather than a dogmatic, spirit, and to judge them on their merits. They may then be seen to represent a reaction from the Soviet model at almost every point.

The first and perhaps the most important contrast to be made concerns procurement. On this there does not appear to be much dispute in China. While the *étatist* policies of the Liu administration are opposed by Mao partly because they seem to imply an increase in procurement, it is notable that throughout the period during which the controversies have been going on, with the means of publicity at first firmly in the hands of Liu's administration and then in the hands of the Maoists, past levels of procurement are not an issue. Even at times when the most liberalizing elements in China have been able to make their voices heard, this has remained true. (This tends to confirm work done in the West on the subject.) Even those who advocated between 1959 and 1961 that the family and not the collective should be assessed for taxation and State purchases, did not go on to argue that the burden ought to be lightened. It seems to be accepted in China that procurement prices, even if they are inevitably below free market prices, cover production costs and leave a profit. The Chinese have not 'drained the pond to catch the fish'.

As far as capital for agricultural development is concerned, we have seen evidence that Mao Tse-tung prefers to encourage the collectives to invest for themselves rather than increase State investment. The funds for such investment are expected to come from increased production of agricultural produce and – not least – from successful diversification of the local economy through handicrafts, animal husbandry and afforestation, according to the possibilities of the area. Such diversification has played an important part in increasing local capital accumulation since the very beginning of the organization of agriculture in 1953.

As far as talent is concerned, and this as we have seen is to Mao the most fundamental point, he believes in diversification, work-study education, a drive for the spread of scientific attitudes through the 'democratization' of science, and – at a level nearer to coercive measures – the sending of educated youth in enormous numbers down to the villages to make their lives there. In general the maximization of education opportunities, with this in mind, will prevent the villages from being drained of talent and enterprise, and will develop latent talent to the fullest extent.

The implications of all this are that the collectives will be run by peasant cadres for the peasants, and not dominated, as in the Soviet Union, by urban bureaucrats and technicians.

Finally, Mao seeks to avoid the Soviet problem that lack of consumer goods leads to lack of incentive to market agricultural produce, by encouraging local economic diversification.

These are the features of the system of cooperative production which Mao seeks to develop, He may not be right, but it would be difficult to argue that he is irrational. The only argument which could prove his ideas irrational would be the argument that collective incentives, through the shared profits of cooperative working, must in all circumstances prove ineffective.

Class struggle

The question remains, however, that if Mao Tse-tung puts forward this essentially economic argument, based upon incentives and how to make these incentives effective by education, why then does he feel obliged to justify his policies by non-economic slogans such as 'Let politics take command', and why does he feel obliged to emphasize that a class struggle is involved?

There are two quite distinct phenomena involved in what Mao now characterizes as class struggle, and although neither of them is class struggle in the classical Marxist sense, they certainly represent certain Chinese social realities.

The first phenomenon is the crystallization in China after the revolution of a 'new class' in the sense in which this phrase has been used by Djilas, composed of Party administrators, managers and technicians. There is a wealth of evidence (from first-hand observers in China) of mandarin-like behavior by cadres, of privileged schools for the sons of cadres, and all the other depressingly predictable signs of the formation of a new and hereditary ruling class perpetuating many of the attitudes of their predecessors. This is the fundamental point of Mao's resistance to the extension of State enterprise. It is a political and social point rather than economic, but Mao draws from it the economic lesson that, if such a ruling group hardens out, it will put an insuperable obstacle in the way of the development of the abilities and sense of responsibility of the mass of the population on which economic vigor in the last analysis depends.

Halting the drain

The second phenomenon is that within the collectives some individuals (whom Mao believes to be a small minority) have the means to participate profitably in the private sector and the free market which grew rapidly after 1959. It is obvious that at Chinese standards of income and saving, collective enterprise is unlikely to succeed without the participation of the more prosperous and the more skilled. Their concentration upon individual enterprise and private profit is therefore a mortal drain on collective resources, and must be stopped. His condemnation of Soviet procurement policy can be assumed to have the corollary that the private sector in the Soviet Union was a necessity of life, when the whole economy was organized on the basis of exploiting the collective to the point where collective agricultural operations were carried on at a steady loss and maintained by sheer force. Clearly if Mao's concept of the collective was successfully applied, there would be no such necessity in China. The limitation and eventually the elimination of the private sector he therefore regards as both necessary and justified. 'Class struggle' in the countryside is directed at removing this obstacle to collective investment and enterprise.

To prevent the growth of these two social phenomena, the new class of technocrats, and the new class of private-sector operators, politics must take command. If these new cleavages in Chinese society are prevented, and the ring held for the development of collective entrepreneurship, then Mao believes that 'a great spiritual force will be transformed into a great material force': the masses of China will at last become aware of the infinite possibilities of material progress through modern technology and large-scale social organization, and will launch a massive war for the control and exploitation of nature, before which they have lived precariously throughout history. In the light of Mao Tse-tung's explicit policies, it is unnecessary to see in such slogans an excessive faith in the human will, or a romantic preoccupation with struggle for its own sake. Nor are they simply an expression of his own personality. The Chinese people may rise massively to the occasion, or they may not, but to expect them to do so is not excessively romantic.

The evidence

There exists, moreover, evidence of a sort by which Mao Tse-tung seeks to prove that he is right. It consists of the description of the experience and achievements of individual collectives. A constant stream of such descriptions has poured out since 1953. As each case gives time, place and individual names, and as in most cases the collective concerned was opened to public view as a example and seen by hundreds and in some instances thousands of peasants, it can be assumed that the descriptions do not depart too far from reality.

Taken as a whole, these exemplary cooperatives, Communes, production brigades or production teams cannot of course provide any guide to average performance nor were they intended to provide this. They represent Maoist performance at its best, they represent what the rest of China might eventually achieve, and they give an enormous amount of detail about how their results were won. They have been totally neglected by specialists on China, but no attempt to evaluate Maoism is possible without reference to them, whatever the difficulties the use of such material may involve. An analysis of this material could at least answer the question whether Maoism, in the sense discussed, exists only as an aspiration, or has reality at least here and there in China.

It is clear, however, that a Maoist economic system cannot exist only in spots. Mao's economic program involves the integration of all economic activity in China, as well as the provision of a national political framework to support the program in its first stages. During the Cultural Revolution, during which he has been careful to reveal his hand only gradually as the struggle deepened and widened to take in larger and larger sectors of

Chinese society, he has nowhere stated systematically what economic policy and organization would be. But there exists one document which can illustrate many aspects of the future. This is the Report of the Kwangtung Provincial Committee, of August 1966, in which the Maoists of South China set forth their interpretation of the meaning of the Cultural Revolution. It was never acknowledged by the Peking Maoist leadership. It represents an extreme view, and its publication over the provincial radio may indeed have played a part in the condemnation of Tao Chu, the most important southern leader in the early stages of the Cultural Revolution, on charges which included 'ultra-leftism'. If it was opposed, however, it must have been more on grounds of its call for full, immediate and therefore coercive implementation of the Maoist line than because it misrepresented the final implications of the line. The passages relevant to economic organization can be summarized as follows:

Chairman Mao's instruction exhibits to us a magnificent blueprint of communism, points out the concrete road to the elimination of the three great differences and the transition to communism. Previously, we always thought that the scientific prediction of Marx and Engels on the elimination of the three great differences was a matter of the distant future. Having studied this instruction of Chairman Mao, we feel that it is already on our agenda, and something quite tangible.

The most fundamental measure is to turn the whole province into a big school for the study of Mao Tse-tung's thinking. Workers, peasants, soldiers, students and commercial circles, and all sectors of the economy, must, in their own work posts, take an active part in class struggle, in the socialist education campaign and in the great proletarian Cultural Revolution, and criticize the bourgeoisie. Meanwhile they should also learn politics, military affairs, and culture becoming truly worker-peasant wielding both pen and sword.

All enterprises with suitable conditions should introduce in a big way the worker-peasant labor system, particularly enterprises with close relations with agriculture. Existing enterprises and those built or extended in future should, in the light of the characteristics of their trade, respectively adopt the system of rotation workers, temporary workers, seasonal workers or contracted workers with the Communes and brigades, and gradually turn a number of permanent workers into worker-peasants. In a methodical manner, remove some factories to the rural areas, particularly the existing processing industry which depends on farm and sideline products as raw materials. These should either set up processing centers or actively develop the processing industry within the collective economy. All factories, mines and enterprises with suitable conditions should engage in farm and sideline production. They should actively integrate the factory with the Communes, having the factory lead the Commune, etc., on a trial basis, thus integrating industry with agriculture.

Commercial points and networks in rural areas should hand over some of their work to the rural Communes, brigades and production teams. The basic-level finance and trade units should put into effect the system of rotation workers who will be recommended by the collective. These will include workers for commerce, food, supply and marketing, finance and tax-collection, banking and the granting of loans. All small business and peddling in basic-level commerce in the countryside of the province must be thoroughly reformed.

In future the development of state-run farming, forestry and reclamation must follow the line of joint management by the State and the Commune. Existing state-run farms, forestry and reclamation farms must also at the same time be people's Communes. All agricultural forestry and reclamation farms must diversify their economy, with agriculture as the main pursuit.

In accordance with the characteristics of the Communes which are big and public, the Communes should step by step develop into basic-level organizations with agriculture as the main pursuit and at the same time running industry and wielding pen and sword. They should, with agriculture as the main pursuit, run one or two major industrial and sideline productions in the light of local conditions; with food grain as the main crop, they should grow one or two major industrial crops. In the light of local conditions, step by step set up small farms, small forestry farms, agricultural science centers and agricultural machinery stations. Actively and methodically develop Commune industry, handicraft industry and joint management of industry and handicrafts by Commune and brigade. Every year the Communes must spontaneously and methodically send peasants to factories to be rotation workers, seasonal workers or temporary workers; to join the army; to attend various schools or training courses; to be 'political apprentices', to take part in various political campaigns, etc.

The leadership of the schools must be truly in the hands of the proletariat . . . Reform the education system of schools, resolutely implementing the principles of education serving proletarian politics and education integrating with productive labor . . . All-day schools must be methodically and gradually transformed into work-farmwork-study schools. Schools built in future must be located in the countryside without exception . . . Students should come from the Communes and go back to them, and be fostered into new-type laborers that combine mental and manual labor.

The superstructure must serve better the economic basis. Structures should be resolutely streamlined, sweeping away all ideas, viewpoints, regulations and systems that are unfavorable to the diminishing of the three great differences . . . Office cadres must go deep into the basic levels to stay at points, strengthen the mass viewpoint, and make a success of investigations and study. Cadres must particularly be made to take part in productive labor.

It is perhaps in the idea of the 'destruction of the three great differences' – among industry and agriculture, town and country, and mental and manual labor – that Mao's point of view on social and economic change is best summed up. In Karl Marx's own writings, the elimination of these social gulfs was expected to follow the creation of communism: it was a characteristic of the final classless Utopia. In Mao's thought, their elimination becomes instead the most critical step towards successful economic development in his own underdeveloped country, a step now planned in detail.

The argument in China does not, of course, involve free enterprise as one of the choices. The alternatives at present are represented by the policies of Mao and those which he ascribes to Liu Shao-chi, both communist and equally alien to Western ideas of economic organization. Westerners, fortunately, do not have to make the choice, but we have an interest in the results. If Mao Tse-tung's social and economic program should prove successful in solving the problems of ignorance, fear and social disunity which he regards as fundamental obstacles to rapid economic growth, we cannot but remember that half of the world suffers bitterly from the existence of similar obstacles, and his solution – if a solution it should prove to be – might have very wide application.

Part Five
Class Structure and the State

Previous readings have shown the necessity of bringing economics and sociology back into political economy. This becomes explicit in the readings in the present section. The political dimension of economic strategy is sharply sketched by Wallerstein (Reading 15) focusing on the state. The control of the state (i.e. not merely the government) is of the utmost importance in any contemporary society. Wallerstein locates this theme in the political economy of underdevelopment in relation to both international forces and their potential hostility, and the problems of internal social mobilization for development. Some of the points he makes find concrete expression in the analysis by Arrighi and Saul (Reading 16) of class formation in Africa. They provide an exemplary totalizing perspective with respect to the interconnectedness of economic, political and social 'factors' and the relationship between their operation in national and international terms. O'Connor (Reading 17) offers a provocative view of the Cuban revolution in relation to the historical nature of Cuban society as a distinctive case of 'developed underdevelopment'. He argues that the political revolution once established entailed a social revolution (and the class conflict this term customarily denotes, *pace* Lipton (Reading 13, p. 238) as the basis for subsequent development.

15 I. Wallerstein

The State and Social Transformation: Will and Possibility*

I. Wallerstein, 'The state and social transformation', *Politics and Society*, vol. 1, 1971, pp. 359–64.

We live in an era in which virtually all political men claim they are for the economic development of their own country and the world. Yet we know that the reality is that over the past few centuries a few countries have developed far more rapidly than the rest of the world, and that, at present, by a host of indicators, the economic gap between the more- and the less-developed countries seems to be increasing rather than narrowing despite the presumed efforts of multitudes of groups and governments.

Prima facie there seems to be a discrepancy between will and possibility. I pose this not as a metaphysical problem, but as a sociological one: under what circumstances can will and possibility be conjoined such that substantial and rapid social transformation involving economic development may take place.

If we are going to be historically concrete, the only socially meaningful units of measurement of these transformations in the modern world are nation-states. It is a state that is transformed. It is a national economy whose structure is developed, whose output is increased, whose mechanisms of internal distribution are or are not made more egalitarian. This is not to suggest that nation-states are the only, or even the most important, operating entities. There are clearly both imperial economic networks and multinational corporate structures which have a major, if not determinative, say in the global set of decisions. But, when men say they are for 'development', they are thinking of national units, and it is only when these national entities are really strong and relatively autonomous that we are likely to find a relatively high degree of economic wealth for all strata of the population.

In a formal sense, what we mean by development is first of all increase of the overall productivity of an economy to increase

* Paper presented at a special session on Sociology in the Second Development Decade, 7th World Congress of Sociology, Varna, Bulgaria, 15 September, 1970.

the surplus, and secondly expansion of its capital base, presumably by foregoing a certain amount of immediate consumption of this surplus in favor of investment. The prevailing psychological assumption of modern social science (of all its ideological schools) seems to be that, in the absence of specific social pressure to the contrary, men will tend to define their self-interest in terms of expanded personal consumption. Hence it follows that the key politico-economic problem of development is how to restrain this desire for immediate consumption.

This is particularly the case of a so-called underdeveloped country where the average consumption is below the emerging international social standard and in many areas below even a physiological minimum. For purposes of our discussion, let us simplify the picture, at least momentarily, and suggest that there are three basic groups among whom a national economic product is distributed: the workers (both rural and urban), the cadres (a global category encompassing quite disparate groups that must be treated separately in concrete analysis), and the outside world. Each participates, in varying degrees, in the production. The natural cycle of an underdeveloped country is that the pressures of the internal cadres and the external world for consumption are so great that the entire surplus is thus absorbed, leaving no significant amount for collective social investment, and hence in the long run there is no significant expansion of the social production. Of course, some of the product consumed by the outside world is invested in other countries. Also some of the product retained by internal cadres is in fact hoarded for future consumption. But from the national perspective both 'external investment' and 'internal hoarding' are ways of 'consuming' the surplus.

In the modern world, there have been two traditional modes of attacking the problem: a capitalist mode and a socialist mode. The root element of the classic capitalist solution has been reward for incentive and effort not only by greater immediate reward but, as an inducement for postponing part, never all, of the consummatory gratification, a guarantee of future still further expanded consumption. This guarantee was made by the state and took the form of both subsidy and property rights. Although capitalist ideology used the word 'risk' to describe this exercise, it was of course realised that any serious and sustained uncertainty (in short, true risk) would of course lead to a refusal of the property-owner to invest rather than to consume or to hoard.

In this classic solution, the non-cadres, the workers were presumed to work for low rewards because they had no alternative. No alternative here meant, in fact, when one pushed the analysis, no political alternative.

Thus, the workers produced because they were forced to, the cadres worked hard because they were rewarded for it (and specifically super-rewarded if they allowed part of their reward to be reinvested), the global product expanded, and the nation-state 'developed'.

The socialist argument went quite differently. It argued that underdevelopment was the product precisely of the consumption of the surplus by internal cadres and external powers, and that capitalism provided insufficient incentive for the workers to increase production. Furthermore, it was argued, the productivity of the workers was far more crucial to the expansion of production than the productivity of the cadres, since it is their 'labor' which produces the overwhelming majority of surplus-value. Hence, it followed that a socialist system which would collapse the distinction between workers and cadres, reward men's labor appropriately, and would eliminate export of profits to the external world would both raise productivity because of new incentives and allow a collective investment of a large part of the surplus, thus assuring economic development.

In their pristine forms, neither of these models of development made the role of the state machinery central to the success or failure of the model. In that sense, in theory, the models were exclusively concerned with 'economic' motivations, and the analyses were not political or politico-economic in tenor.

Yet, in fact, the political institution of the state was critical to the process of economic development whether under a capitalist or a socialist mode. The evidence on capitalist development is fairly clear today,[1] and, as for the socialist states, no one denies it.

The reason seems to me very clear. The state apparatus has been the central mechanism of decision making because only the state commanded sufficient strength (both in terms of armed force and in terms of control of the ideological machinery) to insist on specific allocations of the surplus such that a certain amount would be reserved for capital investment.

There is a further aspect to this process. Nation-states do not exist in a void; they exist in a network of nation-states. The early

1. The literature is voluminous. Some references are: Aitken (1959), Dobb (1946, ch. 5), Kahan (1967) and Veblen (1966).

economic development of Western Europe was made possible by their utilization of cheap colonial labor in the Western Hemisphere and Asia. But it was also rendered relatively easier by the absence of powerful pre-existent industrial states which had the power to intervene in their internal affairs and actively block development processes.

Developing countries in the twentieth century face an entirely different situation. They do not have external colonies to exploit and they are faced with pre-existing industrial states with the power and the will to intervene in their internal affairs. This is the problem of imperialism.

In such a circumstance, the essential problem of economic development can be posed as follows: How is it possible to install and maintain in state power a regime with the will and the possibility to transform the social structure in a way that would make possible a dramatic rise in productivity and investment, when the possibility is based on somehow insulating the government from the various pressures to consume its surplus immediately? To make the problem even more specific, the issue is less how to install such a regime than how to maintain it in power over a long period of time, perhaps thirty to fifty years, during which time sufficient capital accumulation could take place, a national economy could be erected, and national (as opposed to subnational) strata or classes could be sufficiently organized so that the state machinery is structurally resistant to outside intervention, internal secession and palace *coups d'état*.

Next, one should examine the installation and maintenance of such a regime in terms of the control of the three main sectors of surplus-distribution mentioned before – internal cadres, external world, and workers.

The most difficult aspect of limiting consumption by internal cadres is that a regime in power, whatever its ideological self-assessment, is by definition composed of a section of the cadres. Its interests are, to a very large extent, linked with the interests of the cadres as a stratum. Furthermore, its strength, at least in part, is dependent on the support of these cadres.

It can, of course, use physical force up to a point to control these cadres. This technique works for a while. A regime can rely on police force to hold the cadres in line, though this has all the disadvantages the Communist Party of the Soviet Union recognized at its Twentieth Party Congress and since. Or a regime can utilize an upsurge of working-class elements to control the cadres, as in the 'cultural revolution' in China. This method, too, has built-in limitations, as recent attempts by the Chinese political leaders to curb the excesses of the Red Guards and give more order to the political process have indicated. The use of force against its cadres by a weak regime may lead simply and directly to its overthrow, as has been the case in a number of African states in the post-independence period.

The regime can also use ideology to keep its cadres in line. Any ideological appeal to self-restraint in consumption by cadres will of course accomplish the end desired, provided the ideological pressure is firm and unremitting but not inflexible. Weber and others have described how Calvinism was thus used in the seventeenth century. Marxism has been similarly used in the twentieth century. But ideological pressure only works as long as faith persists, and the persistence of faith is itself a function of a certain degree of success combined with a certain tension due to ideological opposition plus the existence of a professional body of ideologists – usually, in modern times, within the framework of an ideological party.

Given the limitations of force and ideology to control the cadres, it is no surprise that the regime will fall back on rewards of money, status and power, including the offer of both security and perpetuity of reward. But as this happens, the surplus begins to be consumed by these very cadres; the revolution risks being 'betrayed', unless rewards of this kind can be limited.

The control of outsiders is in many ways even more difficult than the control of internal cadres. Outside powers can scarcely be 'bought off' by a weak regime; indeed, the opposite is the case. Nor has an appeal to ideological norms been historically very effective in limiting imperial interference in internal affairs. The most effective device historically has been to invest national force in political isolation which seems to have a multiplier effect. Isolation is more plausible for large nations (which are very few in number) and isolation is more possible under certain international conditions which are largely out of the control of the nation seeking the isolation. We shall specify these conditions.

Finally there is the question of controlling the workers. An increase in reward is very costly in terms of the relatively small surplus of a developing country. Increased egalitarianism, that is, reduced rewards to the cadres, may help to satisfy them, but then the regime is subject to the dangers of a revolt of the cadres. Ideological controls seem to be less effective over workers than ideologists imagine. Perhaps this is the consequence of a deep skepticism workers have learned to have about rulers.

A Senegalese sociologist has written recently that economic development can be successfully achieved only if 'the majority of the people are consciously and firmly mobilized to carry out and defend its implementation' and if its achievement 'rests principally on their own efforts' (N'Diaye, 1970, p. 6). The author says that an example of this is Vietnam. No doubt the description of the proper relation of the workers to development is true, but the question is precisely how to bring about this symbiosis between cadres and workers. It has nowhere proved easy. Nonetheless, in some countries, it has been true for a time. Such worker involvement is of course far easier in the midst of a war for one's homeland, as in Vietnam, which strengthens ideological devotion of both workers and cadres, than in less besieged times. However, whatever the ideological position, in no historical case heretofore has the element of force been absent from the control of the consumption of at least a large part of the working classes.

The will to develop is represented in the readiness of the regime to control consumption. The possibility is a function of certain natural economic and geographic factors, certain structural factors (there must be a certain technological base on which to stand) and a certain conjuncture of international events.

The major international event that can assist in development is the diversion of outside governmental and private forces to their own internal tasks. Such diversion could be occasioned by several circumstances: sharp competition among relatively equal outside powers, which neutralizes the ability of any one to intervene effectively; eruption of too many problems in the peripheral areas of an imperial network simultaneously; internal crises in the metropolitan center.

The halfway houses are many. The failures to develop are written in the historical sands a hundred times over. Development does require a 'breakthrough'. But it is a political breakthrough that in turn makes possible the far more gradual economic process. For a movement with the will to develop, to gain power is difficult. For a movement that has gained power, to retain power against counterforce is also difficult. For such a movement not to be eaten away in its will by the counter-pressures of those against whose interests they act but on whose goodwill they partially depend is the most difficult of all. And to be able to implement such a program at a specific moment in time, when the international conjuncture is favorable, may seem like a quixotic dream. And nevertheless it has been done – sometimes.

References

AITKEN, H. G. J. (ed.) (1959), *The State and Economic Growth*, Social Science Research Council.

DOBB, M. (1946), *Studies in the Development of Capitalism*, Routledge & Kegan Paul.

KAHAN, A. (1967), 'Nineteenth-century European experiences with policies of economic nationalism', in H. G. Johnson (ed.), *Economic Nationalism in Old and New States*, University of Chicago Press.

N'DIAYE, J. P. (1970), 'Comment de Gaulle a seduit l'Afrique', *Jeune Afrique*, No. 485, April.

VEBLEN, T. (1966), *Imperial Germany and the Industrial Revolution*, Ann Arbor Paperbacks.

16 G. Arrighi and J. S. Saul[*]

Class Formation and Economic Development in Tropical Africa

Excerpts from G. Arrighi and J. S. Saul, 'Socialism and economic development in tropical Africa', *Journal of Modern African Studies*, vol. 6, no. 2, 1968, pp. 141–69.

A noted economist (Perroux) has defined socialism as 'le développement de tout l'homme et de tous les hommes'. Providing the motor for a drive towards socialism there is generally to be found a conviction that man's creative potential can only be fully realised in a society which transcends the cultural centrality of 'possessive individualism' and in which a signal measure of economic and social equality, the preconditions for genuine political democracy, are guaranteed. In the best of socialist intellectual work, however, socialists have been equally interested in economic development and in the full release of the potential for growth of the productive forces in a society. Within this tradition it was perhaps Marx who most dramatically fused the concern for economic development and the concern for the elimination of class inequalities in his presentation of the socialist case. He argued that the inequalities of the bourgeois society of his day increasingly meant that the potential of the available industrial machine would not be realised: inequality and muffled productive forces thus went hand in hand.[1]

Certain class inequalities have sometimes proved to be historically necessary to foster the full release of the potential for growth of the social productive forces; this is too obvious a fact to require emphasis. But the existence either of some necessary dichotomy between 'development' and 'equality' or, on the contrary, of some necessary link between the two cannot be postulated *a priori*. It has to be ascertained empirically through an analysis of the relationship between the class structure of a society and its economic development at each historical juncture.

[*] An earlier version of this article was presented to the plenary session of the University of East Africa Social Science Conference held in Dar es Salaam in January 1968.

1. On the continued validity of a much refined Marxist critique of contemporary capitalist society along similar lines, see Baran and Sweezy (1966).

A sophisticated socialist case in contemporary Africa must therefore fuse a concern for an increased rate of economic development with a perception of the role played in the development equation by the existence and emergence of classes and groups with differential interests and access to benefits. Moreover, as will be argued in this article, one does in fact find the productive potential of African societies, and therefore their development and structural transformation, constrained by the present pattern of world and domestic economy and society; the available surplus is ill utilized – drained away, for example, as the repatriated profits of overseas firms or consumed by self-indulgent domestic élites – and the generation of a larger surplus from, for example, an aroused and mobilized peasantry discouraged. As this suggests, it is the pattern of current inequality, in particular, which tends thus to hamper a rise in productivity.

A viable socialist strategy directed towards these twin concerns will have to face dilemmas of choice in three closely related policy areas. On the level of the international economic and social system, one confronts the spectre of international capitalism and a grave inequality of financial power, realities which, as will be shown, can be major constraints on general development. On the domestic scene, one faces the problem of the relationship between 'town', the centre of administration and of such industrialization as takes place, and 'country', an interaction from which real development could spring but which all too often defines the split between unequal and unconnected spheres of a society falling short of genuine transformation. Finally, one has the problem of agricultural development itself in a rural sphere where inequalities can and do begin to emerge, although, at least in the short run, these have a rather more ambiguous impact on the pace of development than the other inequalities already hinted at. [. . .]

Class formation and economic development

The vast majority of the population of tropical Africa consists of independent producers who do not depend upon wage employment for their subsistence.[2] Any discussion of economic develop-

2. Doctor and Gallis (1966) estimate that the proportion of the labor force of tropical Africa in wage employment is, on average, 11·1 per cent. However, migrant labor, characterized by partial dependence upon wage employment for its subsistence, is included in the estimate, so that the proletariat proper accounts for a lower percentage than the above.

ment in tropical Africa must therefore begin with a general description of African pre-capitalist or, as they are more often referred to, traditional economies. This is extremely difficult, in view of their heterogeneity;[3] but some common features of particular relevance to our discussion can be singled out.

Individuals can customarily acquire land for homestead and farms through tribal or kinship rights. Only comparatively rarely is land acquired or disposed of through purchase or sale, though the commercialization of agriculture has often been followed by a marked expansion of private land ownership. The specialization of labour has generally not gone very far in traditional African economies; a relatively small range of commodities is produced and few full-time specialists are to be found. In addition, the technology is rather rudimentary from the point of view of the tools used, storage and transport facilities, the control of plant and animal disease and the control of water storage. Market exchanges were – and still are in many areas – peripheral, in the sense that most producers do not rely on exchange for the acquisition of the bulk of the means of subsistence. Thus the high dependence on the physical environment, due to the rudimentary technology, is matched by a relative independence from market fluctuations.

Social cohesion is fostered by obligatory gift- and counter-gift-giving between persons who stand in some socially defined relationships to one another, and/or by obligatory payments or labour services to some socially organized centre which re-allocates portions of what it receives. Security of subsistence is therefore generally guaranteed to the individual in two ways: through socially structured rights to receive factors of production and through emergency allotments of food from the chief and gifts from kin.

It is widely accepted that African peasants have, in general, been highly responsive to the market opportunities that have arisen through contact with European capitalism. This responsiveness has manifested itself in the labour migration system and/or in the rapid expansion of production for the market of both subsistence and cash crops. It seems that this responsiveness was made possible by the existence in traditional African economies of considerable surplus productive capacity in the

3. For a bibliography on traditional African systems, see Middleton (1966).

form of both surplus land and surplus labour-time.[4] This means that the confrontation of a traditional economy producing a limited range of goods with the sophisticated consumption pattern of an advanced industrial system led to a re-allocation of labour-time from unproductive traditional activities to the production of a marketable surplus.[5]

It has been pointed out, however, that the increase in peasant production for the market has had the character of a 'once and for all' change (though distributed over a number of years), as witnessed by the characteristic growth curve of such production; a curve, that is, rising steeply in the early phase and tapering off gradually (see Myint, 1964, and Walker, 1964). This phenomenon can be accounted for by the fact that the social structure of the traditional economies favours, by maximizing security, the adoption of a short 'time horizon' in the allocation of whatever surplus might have been produced as between consumption, unproductive accumulation, and productive accumulation.[6] In other words, peasants still largely involved in a pre-capitalist mode of production are likely to have a strong preference for present consumption and often for unproductive accumulation, which, by maintaining or strengthening social cohesion, preserves the security afforded by the traditional system. This preference is likely to be strengthened by the confrontation of the peasants with the sophisticated consumption pattern of advanced industrial systems mentioned in the previous paragraph.

It would seem, therefore, that we have two problems involved in promoting the growth of productivity of the African peasantry: (a) *the problem of creating incentives to exploit whatever surplus productive capacity in the form of surplus land and surplus labour-time may exist;* and (b) *the problem of raising the productive absorption of the surplus produced in the traditional sector in order to engender the steady growth of the productivity of labour.* The first

4. See Myint (1964, ch. 3) and also Walker (1964, pp. 111–14).

5. The adjective 'unproductive' has, of course, no negative implication concerning the rationality or the necessity within the traditional society of activities so characterized.

6. We define 'surplus' as the difference between the aggregate net output produced (net, that is, of the means of production used up in the process) and the means of subsistence consumed by the community, both referred to a given period of time. By 'subsistence' we understand goods that are socially recognized as necessities, so that they exclude what may be called 'discretionary' consumption. On the concept of the surplus see Baran (1967, ch. 2), and Bettelheim (1965). Our definition is closer to Bettelheim's than to Baran's.

problem concerns the relationship between the modern and the traditional sectors; that is, it concerns the pattern of surplus absorption in the former which is likely to maximize the incentives to increase productivity in the latter. The second problem, on the other hand, relates to the type of organization of production and institutions in the traditional sector which is likely to guarantee the desired responses to the stimuli transmitted by the modern sector. In tropical Africa the first problem seems of primary importance because population pressure on the land, though growing, is generally not yet severe, so that most traditional economies still have some surplus productive capacity. For this reason we shall focus our attention on the development potential of the pattern of surplus absorption in the modern sector.

The 'ideal type', in Max Weber's sense, of surplus absorption in the modern sectors of present-day tropical African economies is characterized by three main forms of surplus absorption: the export of profits and investment income in general; discretionary consumption on the part of a small labour aristocracy, as defined below; and productive investment, embodying capital-intensive techniques, mainly concentrated in sectors other than those producing capital goods.[7] In order to understand the relationship between these three forms of surplus absorption, it is convenient to begin by examining the causes and implications of the sectoral distribution and factor-intensity of productive investment.

The use of capital-intensive techniques of production in tropical Africa is not only the result of technological factors. Two other factors seem equally relevant: the investment policies of the modern international corporations in underdeveloped economies and the wage and salary policies of the independent African governments, which, in turn, depend upon the character of their power base. With regard to the former, the modern international corporations tend to adopt capital-intensive techniques mainly because of managerial constraints and because of their strong financial position.

Techniques of management, organization and control have evolved in the technological environment of the industrial centres and cannot be easily adapted to the conditions obtaining in underdeveloped countries. In consequence, the spectrum of

7. This 'ideal' type is analysed in greater detail in Arrighi (1969). The category 'capital goods' must be understood in a very broad sense as including all those goods which directly increase the productive capacity of the economy.

techniques taken into consideration by the corporations may not include labour-intensive techniques. An equally and probably more important factor seems, however, to be the financial strength of these corporations, which they acquire through their pricing and dividend policies in the industrial centres as well as the periphery.[8] The international corporations apply to all their branches technical methods corresponding to their capital (Perroux and Demonts, 1961, p. 46); as a result, capital-intensive techniques are adopted in tropical Africa irrespective of the situation in the territories where the investment takes place.

But capital-intensity of production is also favoured by the salary and wage policies of the independent African governments. The salary structure of the independent African states remained as a colonial heritage and, as Africans gradually entered the civil service and the managerial positions in large foreign concerns, they assumed the basic salaries attached to the posts (Lloyd, 1966, pp. 10–11). This unquestioning acceptance of a colonial salary structure brought about a huge gap between the incomes of the élites and sub-élites in bureaucratic employment and the mass of the wage workers. Thus the whole level of labour incomes, from the unskilled labourer upwards, came into question and, given the political influence of urban workers on African governments, the major employers of labour, a steady rise in wages ensued. This steady rise is also favoured by, and tends to strengthen, the capital-intensive bias of investment, discussed above. Capital-intensity generally means that labour is a lower proportion of costs, so that the individual concern is more willing to concede wage increases (especially foreign oligopolies which can pass on cost increases to the consumer). However, this reinforces the tendency towards capital-intensive (or labour-saving) growth and a 'spiral process' may ensue (Turner, 1965, p. 21).

With regard to the sectoral distribution of productive investment, besides obvious technological factors (economies of scale, advantages of operating in an industrial environment, etc.) there seem to be three main reasons for the observed under-investment in the capital-goods industries of tropical Africa. In the first place, the very bias in favour of capital-intensive techniques discussed above tends to promote the use of highly specialized

8. The concepts of 'industrial centres' and 'periphery' have been introduced by Raul Prebisch to designate the advanced industrial economies and the relatively underdeveloped countries, respectively.

machinery and consequently restrains the growth of demand for capital goods that could be produced locally. Other reasons relate more directly to the behaviour of the modern international corporations. In non-industrialized economies the market for capital goods is small; for such goods to be produced there must be good reasons to believe that the whole economy will develop in such a way as to nourish a market for capital goods (Barratt Brown, 1963, p. 419).

This fact was no serious obstacle in the nineteenth century, when competitive entrepreneurs and financial groups often undertook investment which was 'unjustified' by market conditions, thereby fostering the industrialization of less developed economies. Nowadays the great calculating rationality, care, and circumspection in approaching new developments which characterize modern corporations prevent that process from taking place. As Sweezy has remarked, it is one of the many contradictions of capitalism that better knowledge may impair its functioning. Finally, the lack of investment in the sector producing capital goods is also determined by the oligopolistic structure of advanced capitalist countries because this implies that producers of capital goods, in deciding whether to establish, or to assist in establishing, a capital-goods industry, will generally take into account the effect of the decision not only on their own and their competitors' export interests but also on those of their customers.

The lack of development of the capital-goods sector has important implications for the growth of the modern sector. For such a development, when it does occur, can perform the dual function of expanding both the productive capacity of the economy *and* the internal market. This latter function, too often disregarded, was emphasized by Lenin, who argued that the development of the internal market was possible despite restricted consumption by the masses (or the lack of an external outlet for capitalist production) because 'to expand production it is first of all necessary to enlarge that department of social production which manufactures means of production, it is necessary to draw into it workers who create a demand for articles of consumption'. Hence 'consumption' develops after 'accumulation'.[9] Thus under-investment in the capital-goods sector restrains the expansion not only of the productive capacity of tropical Africa but also of its internal market, perpetuating the dependence of the

9. Quoted in Alavi (1964, pp. 106–7).

economy on the growth of world demand for its primary products. It is not surprising, therefore, that the economies of tropical Africa have been unable to grow faster than their exports. In the period 1950–65 real product seems in fact to have grown at an average compound rate of 4·2 per cent per annum,[10] which is about 1 per cent lower than the rate of export growth.

Given the high rate of population growth, per capita real product has increased at an average rate of 2 per cent per annum in the same period. This relatively low rate of growth, combined with the effects of the 'wage-mechanization' spiral discussed above, has resulted in a decrease in the proportion of the labour force in wage employment in most countries and has been accompanied by a widening gap between urban and rural incomes.[11] It is far from correct, however, to assume that all classes in the urban areas have benefited from this widening gap. A large proportion of urban workers in Africa notoriously consists of semi-proletarianized peasants, periodically engaged in wage employment. This migrant labour force is not 'stabilized' and in general does not acquire that specialization needed in industrial enterprises which use capital-intensive techniques. These labourers *as a class*, i.e. as peasants temporarily in wage employment, cannot gain from the 'wage-mechanization' spiral we have been discussing, since higher individual incomes are matched by a reduction in their wage employment opportunities.

The higher wages and salaries, however, foster the stabilization of the better-paid section of the labour force whose high incomes justify the severance of ties with the traditional economy. Stabilization, in turn, promotes specialization, greater bargaining power and further increases in the incomes of this small section of the labour force, which represents the proletariat proper of tropical Africa. These workers enjoy incomes three or more times higher than those of unskilled labourers and, together with the élites and sub-élites in bureaucratic employment in the civil service and expatriate concerns, constitute what we call the labour aristocracy of tropical Africa. It is the discretionary consumption of this class which absorbs a significant proportion of the surplus produced in the money economy.

The third significant form of surplus absorption is the profits, interest, dividends, fees, etc., transferred abroad by the international corporations. It seems a well-established fact that foreign

10. See OECD (1967).
11. See Arrighi (1969) and Turner (1965, pp. 12–13).

private investment in less developed economies (far from being an outlet for a domestically generated surplus) has been, in the recent past, an efficient device for transferring surplus generated abroad to the advanced capitalist countries.[12] It is a highly plausible assumption that, at least with regard to tropical Africa, this transfer of surplus is bound to increase in the future, for two main reasons: the high rate of profit expected by foreign corporations and the relatively slow rate of growth of the economies of tropical Africa. It appears that returns in the order of 15–20 per cent on capital, usually on the basis of an investment maturing in about three years, are required in order to attract foreign capital to tropical Africa.[13] The implication is that, in order to offset the outflow of profits, foreign investment in the area must steadily grow at a rate of 11–14 per cent, which seems impossible of attainment in economies growing at a rate of 4–5 per cent. Thus, while the transfer of surplus has been somewhat contained during the present phase of easy import substitution, the outflow can only become more serious in the years ahead as that phase comes to an end.

We may now turn to discuss the development potential of this pattern of surplus absorption. The focus of attention must be upon the creation of stimuli to exploit the surplus productive capacity existing in the traditional economies. There are two main ways in which African peasants participate in the money economy: through periodic wage employment and through the sale of agricultural produce. It follows that the development potential of a given pattern of surplus absorption in the modern economy is determined by its impact on the demand for peasant labour and produce. From this standpoint the pattern discussed has little, if any, potential. The slow growth of the money economy and the concurrent high rate of mechanization and automation hold back the growth of wage-employment opportunities for the peasantry. More important still, the absorption of a considerable share of the surplus by the discretionary consumption of the labour aristocracy (which creates demand in the

12. In the case of the USA, for example, figures contained in the *Surveys of Current Business* of the US Department of Commerce show that total direct investment abroad, for the period 1950–63, amounted to $17,382m. against a total inflow of investment income of $29,416m. See Baran and Sweezy (1966, p. 107). Data derived from the same source show that, in the period 1959–64, US direct investment (excluding oil) in Africa amounted to $386m. and investment income to $610m.

13. See Morgan (1965).

industrial countries or in the modern economies of tropical Africa themselves), and by the transfer of investment incomes abroad, restrains the growth of internal demand for peasant produce. As a consequence the creation of stimuli to increase productivity in the rural areas is left to the sluggish expansion of foreign demand for African produce and to those 'invocations to effort' which are a prominent feature of much 'socialist' practice in Africa and to which we shall return.

The slow growth of peasant incomes and productivity has in turn a negative impact on the growth potential of the modern sector itself, since it further hampers the expansion of the internal market. It would seem, therefore, that an acceleration of economic growth in tropical Africa within the existing political-economic framework is highly unlikely and, as the phase of ease import substitution is superseded, a slow-down may actually be expected. In the light of these considerations, the current economic growth of tropical Africa may be properly characterized as 'perverse growth'; that is, growth which undermines, rather than enhances, the potentialities of the economy for long-term growth.[14]

In describing theoretically the current pattern of growth in Africa we have argued in terms of an 'ideal type', as we were bound to in an essay of this sort. The full range of historical cases will undoubtedly include exceptions which do not fit our conclusions. Yet it is interesting to note that even the Ivory Coast, model of the international capitalist road to development, is beginning to feel the pinch which accompanies that strategy; several authors have recently commented on the country's pattern of growth 'without development', without genuine self-sustaining transformation, which looks increasingly tenuous for the long run as profits begin increasingly to flow back to France and few reinforcing complementarities emerge. Indigenous sources of capital and 'entrepreneurial' ability (public or private), which might push in a more fruitful direction, are stifled by the emergent class structure and pattern of international involvement.[15]

The foregoing discussion suggests the advisability of a policy of self-reliance *vis-à-vis* international capitalism for two main reasons: (a) because of the drain on the surplus which, sooner

14. The concept of 'perverse growth' has been introduced by Ignacy Sachs (1966).
15. See Amin (1967a, 1967b) and Dobrska (1966).

or later, is engendered by dependence on foreign capital; and (b) because of the impact of foreign investment (with respect to choice of techniques and to its sectoral distribution) upon the structure of the tropical African economies.[16] It does not follow, however, that the disengagement from international capitalism is a *sufficient* condition for development. As we have seen, the emergence of a labour aristocracy, with considerable political power, was brought about not only by the pattern of foreign investment but also by the acceptance of a colonial salary structure on the part of independent African governments. The labour aristocracy will therefore continue to use its power in a state-controlled modern sector in order to appropriate a considerable share of the surplus in the form of increasing discretionary consumption. Under these conditions 'perverse growth' would continue notwithstanding state ownership of the means of production (see Sachs, 1966). In order to achieve 'real' long-term development, disengagement from international capitalism will have to be accompanied by a change in the power base of African governments.

Yet even the re-allocation of surplus from the discretionary consumption of the 'labour aristocracy' to productive investment, though a necessary condition, is not sufficient for steady long-term growth. Productive investment in the modern sector must be directed towards the creation of development stimuli in the traditional sector; that is, it must be directed to the expansion of those industries producing the capital and the consumer goods most suited to the requirements of the traditional sector. Failing this, as the history of socialist development in non-industrial environments has so often demonstrated, the growing demand for labour and produce following upon industrialization would merely lead to unfavourable terms of trade for the traditional sector, restraining the exploitation of its surplus productive capacity.[17]

The problem of creating incentives to exploit surplus produc-

16. It is surprising that apologists of foreign private investment in Africa (who consider the drain on the surplus a payment for technical assistance and finance supplied by the international corporations) have seldom paused to consider whether the managerial, administrative and technical skills supplied are suited to the requirements of the receiving economies from the standpoint of their growth potential (as opposed to some short-term effects on income and employment).

17. For an excellent discussion of problems of socialist development in a non-industrial environment, see Schurmann (1966).

tive capacity in the traditional sector is crucial because there still exist, among the peasants of tropical Africa, surplus land and surplus labour-time. The second problem involved in raising the productivity of African peasants is that of ensuring the *productive absorption of the surplus produced in the traditional sector*. Here the question of rural transformation is more starkly posed, even if difficult to answer at the theoretical level. It will involve some calculations as to whether the transformation of traditional economies is best attained through the formation of an agrarian capitalist class or the gradual absorption of the individual peasant families into larger units (cooperatives, collectives, communes): whether through the utilization or superseding of traditional forms of work cooperation: and whether through reliance upon central marketing boards or traders for the collection of produce from, and distribution of manufactured goods to, the traditional producers.

Certainly a process of very real differentiation is afoot in many parts of rural Africa. The commercialization of peasant agriculture has often been followed by a marked expansion of private land ownership,[18] and a growing division between the nascent agricultural 'entrepreneurs' (the 'kulaks', as Professor Dumont recently referred to them in Tanzania), the more marginal cash croppers, the subsistence farmers and the agricultural labourers. Increasingly these strata have differential interests with implications for rural strategy. Thus, for example, cooperatives may come to be manipulated by the more economically advanced peasants for their own benefit. If the instruments of 'generalized mobilization' become mortgaged to one particular group, the thrust of such a development policy may well be blunted.

On the other hand, it has been ably argued that at this stage in development it may be wise to 'let the kulaks run', to allow the logic of the market to *briser la famille* (as Samir Amin has put it), and to break down the attendant traditional economic constraints once and for all.[19] It is not inconceivable, of course, that links of common interest formed between emergent 'capitalist' farmers and the labour aristocracy could become a further force to sustain the present pattern of economy and society – one thinks of the symbiosis between planters and bureaucrats in the Ivory Coast. Yet much will depend upon the general framework provided by the trajectory of development in the modern sector as

18. See Chodak (1966).
19. See Amin (1965, pp. 10–17, 230–32).

to how short-run compromises with 'inequality' in the 'traditional' sector are situated and perhaps eventually controlled.

In conclusion, the first part of our analysis raises a number of questions concerning the relationship between current class formation and long-term development in tropical Africa. The growth of a labour aristocracy and the reliance on international capitalism, far from being necessary for such development, seem instead to reduce the growth potential of the economies in question, although the relationship between class formation and development, for the short run at least, is much less clear in the rural areas. It may be argued that the changes in surplus utilization, which we have seen to be necessary for real development, are not possible under present historical conditions, particularly in view of the short-term losses in economic growth and, quite possibly, in political stability that would ensue from any serious attempt at disengagement from international capitalism or reform of the power base of the African governments involved. This question, however, by no means invalidates the historical necessity of the change itself, which should therefore be of central importance in socialist debate.

References

ALAVI, H. (1964), 'Imperialism old and new', *The Socialist Register, 1964*, Merlin Press.

AMIN, S. (1965), *Trois expériences Africaines de développement: le Mali, la Guinée, et le Ghana*, Paris.

AMIN, S. (1967a), *Le Développement du Capitalisme en Côte d'Ivoire*, Paris.

AMIN, S. (1967b), 'Côte d'Ivoire: valeur et limites d'une expérience', *Jeune Afrique*, October.

ARRIGHI, G. (1969), 'International corporations, labour aristocracies and economic development in tropical Africa', in D. Horowitz (ed.), *The Corporations and the Cold War*, Monthly Review Press.

BARAN, P. A. (1967), *The Political Economy of Growth*, Monthly Review Press, reprinted in Penguin, 1972.

BARAN, P., and SWEEZY, P. M. (1966), *Monopoly Capital*, Monthly Review Press, reprinted in Penguin, 1968.

BARRATT-BROWN, M. (1963), *After Imperialism*, Heinemann.

BETTELHEIM, C. (1965), 'Le surplus economique, facteur de base d'une politique de développement', in his *Planification et croissance accéléré*, Paris.

CHODAK, S. (1966), 'Social classes in sub-Saharan Africa', *Africana Bull.*, vol. 4, Warsaw.

DOBRSKA, Z. (1966), 'Economic development of the Ivory Coast from the winning of independence', *Africana Bull.*, vol. 5, Warsaw.

DOCTOR, K. C., and GALLIS, H. (1966), 'Size and characteristics of wage employment in Africa: statistical estimates', *International Labour Rev.*, vol. 93, no. 2, February.

LLOYD, P. (ed.) (1966), *The New Elites of Tropical Africa*, Oxford University Press.

MIDDLETON, J. (1966), *The Effect of Economic Development on Traditional Political Systems South of the Sahara*, The Hague.

MORGAN, D. J. (1965), *British Private Investment in East Africa: Report of a Survey and a Conference*,

MYINT, H. (1964), *The Economics of Developing Countries*, Hutchinson.

OECD (1967), *National Accounts of Less-Developed Countries*, preliminary, Paris.

PERROUX, F., and DEMONTS, R. (1961), 'Large firms – small nations', *Presence africaine*, vol. 10, no. 38.

SACHS, I. (1966), 'On growth potential, proportional growth, and perverse growth', *Czechoslovak Econ., Pap.* vol. 7, pp. 65–71, Prague.

SCHURMANN, F. (1966), *Ideology and Organization in Communist China*, University of California Press.

TURNER, H. A. (1965), *Wage Trends, Wage Policies and Collective Bargaining: The Problems for Underdeveloped Countries*, Cambridge University Press.

WALKER, D. (1964), 'Problems of economic development in East Africa', in E. A. G. Robinson (ed.), *Economic Development for Africa South of the Sahara*, Macmillan.

17 J. O'Connor

On Cuban Political Economy

J. O'Connor, 'On Cuban political economy', *Political Science Quarterly*, vol. 79, 1964, pp. 233–47.

The thesis of this paper is that the social revolution in Cuba (1959–61) was inevitable in the sense that it was necessary for the island's further economic and social development. The national-ization and consolidation of industry, the collectivization of more than one third of Cuba's farm land, the complete reorgan-ization of the labor unions and the banking and commercial systems, and thoroughgoing economic planning, rescued the island from permanent economic stagnation.[1] For this reason, Cuban socialism can be explained and understood in the context of the social structure of the old society – not as the sour fruit of some 'abnormality' or 'conspiracy'.

A corollary of this thesis is that any ruling group which failed fundamentally to modify or replace Cuba's old economic institutions could not count on a long and stable tenure. It also follows that the political orientation of any political leader of 'liberal' or conservative persuasion who wished to retain power would have to shift more or less rapidly to the left to correspond with social reality.

The argument may be summarized as follows:

1. From a very early date the Cuban economy developed along capitalist lines. Pre-capitalist forms of economic organization –

1. The shift of the great part of Cuba's trade from the United States to the socialist countries, and the reorientation of Cuba's foreign policy, do not directly concern us here. They are questions related to the transition from capitalist to socialist economy, but they seem to have had an independent character as well. For this reason they are more simple, and at the same time more complex than the question of Cuban socialism itself. On one level of analysis, it is obvious that the United States' refusal to trade with Cuba drove the island to the Soviet Union. Looking deeper, one is com-pelled to inquire into the nature of the relationship between the United States and Cuba for clues to its deterioration. Clearly, the rapid socializa-tion of the Cuban economy contributed to the severance of ties between the two governments.

traditional, feudal or mercantile – were in no way important features of the old society. During the twentieth century, the island's economy acquired the significant characteristics of monopoly capitalism, chief among which was the cartelization of markets. Monopoly controls blanketed Cuba's social economy and blocked the fulfilment of the island's true economic potential by wasting land, labor and capital, and other economic resources.

2. Throughout the political revolution which triumphed in January 1959, a small group of men acquired and retained the initiative. These men were non-Communists, and, while forming an alliance with the Cuban Communist party in late 1958 or early 1959, consistently kept the initiative during the social revolution of 1959–61. What is more, this social revolution was rapid, relatively peaceful and defended by the vast majority of the Cuban people. These observations suggest that a social revolution of a specifically socialist character was not merely an ideological product, but a realistic and authentic response to social reality.

3. The political revolution was not marked by sharp class conflicts, and revolutionary programs drawn up before 1959 had appeal for nearly every Cuban social and economic class. Class conflicts developed out of the economic and political measures of the Revolutionary government which destroyed revolutionary unity by systematically discriminating against some classes and in favor of others and by polarizing political attitudes on the questions of elections, political parties and relations with the United States. It is said that these measures provide *prima-facie* evidence that Fidel Castro betrayed the original spirit and aims of the revolution (the betterment of the economic, social and political condition of the Cuban people) when in fact they may have been the logical outcome of an attempt to realize these very aims.

From a very early date Cuba exhibited the main features of modern capitalist economy. Unlike most Latin American economies, Cuba lacked an important subsistence sector and nearly all segments of the population were integrated into the market economy. As early as 1899 over two-thirds of the rural labor force were engaged in the cultivation of cash crops, while subsistence farming employed probably less than one-quarter of the work force.

J. O'Connor 299

By mid-century the subsistence sector had been nearly totally submerged by specialized agricultural production for export and home consumption. Throughout the countryside the propertied rural middle class gave way to foreign capital, which exploited opportunities for large-scale production, and corporate and absentee ownership. Following the sugar crises of the 1920s a fine web of relationships began to bind together agriculture and high finance; the bankers also had a finger in commerce and, to a lesser degree, manufacturing.

The great part of the island's agricultural production was organized along monopolistic lines. Output restrictions, pegged prices and other forms of monopolistic control blanketed sugar, tobacco, rice, potato and coffee farming. In the key sugar sector, mill owners, growers and wage workers all had powerful organizations. Outputs, wages, prices and the distribution of sugar earnings were determined by the mill owners or growers cartels, or by a three-cornered bargaining relationship on the level of national politics.

In industry there were 150 employers' associations of one kind or another, many of them with wide powers over their members. Compulsory 'producers' associations' dominated sugar and tobacco manufacture, and the great public utilities each had clear monopolies in their fields. As for the labor movement, it was, compared with the island's labor force, one of the largest in the world, and the central federation enjoyed unusual power over its affiliates. There was, besides, an extremely well developed 'labor aristocracy' which had sealed off a number of important labor markets from outside competition, and which was mainly responsible for the extraordinarily low relationship between labor productivity and wages.

In short, the economic institutions which we are accustomed to associate with the high-income capitalist nations overlaid the island's market system. It should be stressed that monopoly practices in Cuba's product and labor markets sprang up in the soil of a market economy. Restrictions in the rural economy were not of the type ordinarily associated with a system of traditional agriculture, and controls in the labor market were not those customary in mercantile or neo-mercantile systems. Cuba's economic institutions were capitalist institutions, historically specific to Cuba. These institutions had, by and large, a monopolistic character, as well. For this reason, they placed limits on the pace of Cuba's economic development by inhibiting the improvement of agricultural yields, wasting land, barring the wide introduction of a mixed, scientific agriculture, placing ceilings on labor productivity, and, in general, on the ability of the economy to mobilize and utilize domestic and foreign capital efficiently.

In an economy which had been stagnating since the Second World War (ignoring temporary ups and downs in the sugar market), it should be unnecessary to emphasize the implications of these limits on economic growth for the nature and scope of the Cuban Revolution.

Against this background, the character of the political and social revolutions in Cuba is more comprehensible. In the *political* struggle against President Fulgencio Batista the decisive influence was apparently the dedication of a small band of young men. From the attack by Fidel Castro on the Moncada Barracks in July 1953, throughout the guerrilla war of 1957–58, until late 1959, when the Castro group firmly consolidated political power, not a single peasant revolt ignited the Cuban countryside. Passive resistance, surreptitious aid to Castro's forces, there were, to be sure; unlike a dozen other political revolutions, however, the peasant classes failed to grasp the initiative at any point in the struggle. Early in 1959 Comandante Ernesto (Che) Guevara, Castro's closest associate, appropriately described the Cuban peasants as the revolution's 'invisible collaborators'. The labor movement, in which over one-half of Cuba's labor force was enrolled, figured even less prominently in the rebellion. It was in January 1959, after the regular army had received Castro's final blows, that the working classes shut down Havana's industry and commerce. Earlier, a general strike in April 1959 had been a total failure. The new Revolutionary government consistently retained the political initiative; the general strike in late January in the port city of Manzanillo protesting the leniency shown by the revolutionary tribunals toward war criminals was apparently the only major reversal of roles.

In the *social* revolution of 1959–61, the liquidation of Cuba's private-property system was invariably initiated by the ruling group. The peasantry did not spontaneously seize and cultivate idle lands; with a handful of exceptions, they failed to claim even the small fields in which they labored until the new government formally turned these tracts over to them. To be sure, a decree published in February denied rights to land under the coming Agrarian Reform Law to any peasant who without authorization occupied properties belonging to someone else. More significant than the existence of the law is the fact that it did not have to be enforced. Nor did the urban workers and sugar mill laborers independently occupy the factories (this was a sharp departure from the abortive social revolution of 1933); rebel army or militia units at the direction of the central government took possession of Cuba's farm land and industry.

These two sets of events – the exclusive and individualistic flavor of the political revolution and the almost bloodless social revolution – are intimately connected. The social revolution was more or less orderly because the political revolution transferred power from one relatively small group of men to another, and because the masses of Cubans at the very least passively supported the social revolution.

In this context, it is significant that Cuba's is the only specifically socialist social revolution in history which was not authored by local Communist parties with or without the backing of the Red Army. Not until 1959, when the actual fighting had ceased, did Castro's 26th of July Movement win the open backing of the Cuban party (the Partido Socialista Popular, or PSP), although this is not true of some individual Communists who sided with Castro somewhat earlier, and, as might be expected, survived the 1962 spring and summer purges of old-line Communists almost to a man. The political careers of many of the old-line Communists were painfully brief. Subject to bitter public and private attacks by the 26th of July Movement's organ, *Revolución*, during most of 1959, the party members gained footholds in the new revolutionary organizations in 1960 *after* the major expropriations (with a few exceptions, most notably the trade unions in which they had always figured strongly and in two or three important offices in the National Agrarian Reform Institute [INRA]), helped shape the mass organizations and the new party, the ORI (Integrated Revolutionary Organizations), into their image of revolutionary associations in 1961 and early 1962, only to be deprived of many of their positions in the spring and summer of that year and replaced by non-Communist revolutionary personnel.[2]

2. For the events in 1959 see Zeitlin and Scheer (1963). The role of the party in 1960 and 1961 is described in Draper (1962). In this collection of articles is also 'L'Affaire Escalante', which tries to interpret the purges at the top to North Americans. Monitoring of Cuban radio broadcasts and

In connection with the question of the source of political initiative, it is important to point out that in the history of modern revolutions the Cuban experience was unique in another respect, and departed especially sharply from the October Revolution. Irresistibly drawn to the peasantry in order to consolidate power, Lenin paved the way for the seizure of the estates. By this very measure, though, the central authority deprived itself of effective control of the land. Fifteen years passed before the rural economy was collectivized and integrated into the structure of the planned economy. The Cuban Revolution spared Fidel Castro an analogous problem, since the seeds of a planned rural economy were planted *simultaneously* with the transformation of land ownership. The fact that the Cuban farm worker and peasant never had the political initiative made possible the immediate collectivization of the cattle, rice and sugar sectors of the rural economy. The fact that the better part of these sectors was already organized into large-scale producing units which had long utilized land, labor and capital inefficiently made collectivization practical, feasible and rational.

This development distinguishes the Cuban Revolution not only from the Russian Revolution, but sets it apart from the Chinese, the Mexican and even the Bolivian experiences, as well. In Mexico the peasants at times had absolute initiative; until 1952 the Chinese leadership by force of circumstances emphasized individual ownership of the land; so did the Bolivian revolutionary group, and so it does today. The anti-feudal character of all these upheavals, though, was mirrored very faintly in Cuba, for reasons we have already discussed.

A summary of our argument to this point discloses that: non-Communist revolutionaries made a socialist revolution on an island where feudalism (or the neo-feudalism of pre-revolutionary Soviet Union, China, Mexico and Bolivia) was largely absent, but where capitalistic, monopolistic controls were prominently featured. The PSP never had the political initiative either before or during the key stages of the social revolution; the party, in

perusal of Cuban periodicals reveal that the purge had reached into the lowest levels of the ORI by mid-summer, 1962. This was confirmed by the author in August 1963, by another American, Maurice Zeitlin (1962) and by an anti-Castro writer in 'Pero sigue la Purga' (*Cuba Nueva*, 15 May, 1962). That the PSP never had absolute initiative is unwittingly suggested by the leading exponent of the 'revolution betrayed' thesis when he wrote that 'if all had been going well in Cuba for the past year, the PSP's control might well have gone unchallenged ...' (Draper, 1962, p. 209).

fact, at first even opposed those sections of the May 1959 Agrarian Reform Law which encouraged collective production of agricultural commodities. The aim of the revolutionary leadership was to get the stagnating Cuban economy off dead center to improve the social and material conditions of the Cuban people. When they turned to socialist forms of economic organizations to realize this aim, they were supported by the majority of Cubans. From all of this evidence, one can clearly make a case that socialist economic planning in Cuba was less an ideological product than an expression of hard economic necessity.

Socialism – public ownership of the means of production – sometimes emerges from class conflict, and is invariably accompanied by more or less severe political warfare between classes. Cuba was no exception. The political revolution had a distinct classless character (at least no single class had the initiative during this phase of the struggle), but sharp class conflicts developed in the course of the social revolution. The emergence of these conflicts was accompanied by dramatic changes in the Revolutionary government's political line.

Beginning in mid-1959, after the Agrarian Reform Law put Cuba and the world on notice that a thoroughgoing social revolution was in the making, the Revolutionary government began to mark off sharply the 'revolution' from the 'counter-revolution'. Departing from his previous position, Castro was the first to insist on the black-and-white nature of the struggle, an attitude that was quickly adopted by other government officials. Divisions and differences of opinion over revolutionary policy existed within the governing group – the struggle between the Castro group and the 'old' communists is one instance – but the main lines of both domestic and foreign policy were (and are) seldom questioned, or in doubt. The extreme polarization of Cuban politics after mid-1959 is well exemplified in speech after speech delivered by Cuban government leaders. In this theme, the revolution and the Cuban nation are made one and the same, as indicated by Castro in early 1960: 'To be a traitor to the Revolution is to be a traitor to the country. The destiny of our sovereignty is at stake. . . . We have decided that either we are or we are not a free country. And we are and want to be a free country.'[3]

3. Radio interview with Fidel Castro reported in Havana *Post*, 19 January, 1960.

From mid-1959 to the present, however, *genuine* cleavages in Cuban politics have been sharp and opposing opinions have been fiercely held, defining a political mood which corresponds in many ways to social and economic reality. From January 1959 on, a series of profound economic and social changes accompanied these inimical attitudes, and to a large degree were responsible for them. There were no less than *fifteen hundred* decrees, laws and resolutions during the first nine months of 1959.[4] Unquestionably, nearly every new measure – especially those affecting the property system – drew some Cubans closer to the Revolutionary government and repelled others, leaving few indifferent. At the very least, each major law (the rent reduction and price control laws, agrarian reform and the 'intervention' of the utilities are some examples) compelled the ordinary Cuban to question his own political orientation; the most sweeping of these occasioned cabinet crises, resignations, flights abroad, and their cumulative effect led to the short war at Playa Giron in April 1961. The basis for the demand to choose sides – for or against the Revolutionary government – was therefore laid by the government's early economic and political measures. To make such a demand required some confidence that a sizeable body of opinion would confirm the government's position. This suggests that the original revolutionary legislation might be likened to a whirlpool expelling odd debris, yet sucking in the hull of the ship. Be that as it may, it is certainly likely that the slogan itself, together with the heady spirit in which it was launched, contributed to a political atmosphere in which a middle position became increasingly unrealistic and untenable. Castro's personality, after all, confers on the revolution a very special flavor. When he told an audience in the summer of 1960, at the time the United States acted to bar Cuban sugar from the mainland market, 'In each cooperative we are going to build a town . . . with or without the quota. Each little town will have a school for the children of the members of the cooperative, with or without the quota . . .',[5] he conveyed a sense of boundless optimism apparent as early as the famous 'History Will Absolve Me' speech in 1953 and by which his associates were invariably impressed. Reading through his speeches and declarations one is

4. Author's estimate based on *Primer Indice Anual de la Legislación Revolucionaria*, 1ro. de Enero a 31 de Diciembre de 1959 (Havana, 1960).
5. *Trabajo Cuba* (published by the Cuban Ministry of Labor), no. 3, July 1960.

struck by the fact that the image of defeat, or even retreat, rarely, and then only reluctantly, appears. This nearly limitless confidence undoubtedly has affected Cuban politics and the island's economic development.

That the new government chose to polarize opinion around the fundamental issue of its own support cannot be fully explained by Castro's optimism, however. It had the alternative – in place of isolating, indeed outlawing, any opposition, the logical climax of the government's actual policy – that of allowing his opposition to form into functioning interest groups. From there, employing the tactics of divide and conquer, he might have thwarted any potential majority coalition. These groups or parties would probably have ranged from the 'left-opposition' of the small Cuban Trotskyite movement all the way to the moderate right of the large sugar and commercial interests (supposing that they had purged their numbers of pro-Batista elements). The leadership of the revolution, by playing one group against another, ceaselessly probing the weaknesses of each, might have retained power indefinitely.

Yet this policy seemed to have little relevance to the Cuban scene of 1959–60. Its usefulness is evident if in a crisis the ruling group cannot count on clear majority support; an example that springs to mind is British rule in India. Had the British rulers been foolish enough to imitate Castro's policy, they would have driven the opposition together, in the process probably creating a majority capable of threatening their own rule. Only a ruling group which anticipates majority support can for very long afford to alienate opposition elements so thoroughly that they are compelled to form strong working alliances. The Castro government appeared to be well along this path in the summer and fall of 1960 at the height of the first crisis with the United States.

Finally, the only dialogue between the 'revolutionary party' and the 'counter-revolutionary party' was literally at gun point. The social revolution had been consummated. Relations with the United States had totally deteriorated. And Castro, together with thousands of 26th of July Movement 'liberals' and 'reformers', had been radicalized and labelled 'betrayers'. Why did events follow this course?

Early in 1959, Castro was in every sense a popular hero whom many did not hesitate to compare with Martí. Among the island's nearly seven million people, few concealed their esteem, fewer still their respect. Even for the business community the future seemed promising. A leading business and financial organ reported that 'American concerns with Cuban interests generally did not expect the change in Cuba's government to hamper their operations.'[6] In Cuba itself, the United States embassy took an optimistic view of the long-term investment possibilities. Some firms pre-paid taxes to help Castro consolidate his new government and others planned to accelerate investment programs temporarily postponed during the fighting.[7] Business leaders in Cuba who 'as recently as one month ago were gravely concerned about the revolution' apparently had undergone a radical shift in temper.[8] Their doubts would soon return, however, for a rather elementary reason.

On the one hand, a wide range of pressing social, economic and political problems, some of which had lingered on for years and others of which were fresh, containing unknown implications, confronted the triumphant rebels. In a hundred arenas, the new government struggled to make, implement and enforce measures demanded by these problems. On the other hand, before assuming power, the Castro group had published or broadcast certain policy statements and decreed certain laws, enforced in those territories seized and occupied by the Rebel Army. Castro, the guerrilla leader, however, had embraced policies of a vague and ambiguous character; ideas were endorsed which Castro, the national politician, would later discard. The original (10 October, 1958) decree taking up the agrarian problem will do as an illustration.[9] Article 2 promised all farm operators cultivating fewer than 27·2 hectares a plot of land of at least that size free of charge. This provision was directly incorporated into the major May 1959 Agrarian Reform Law.[10] Where contiguous land was available this policy was carried out in practice. Article 6 of the

6. In a seminar at Princeton University held on 21 April, 1959, Castro himself attributed this near-unanimous support to his failure to carry out a specifically *class* war in 1957 and 1958, and to the universal fear and hatred among the Cuban people of Batista's police. Havana *Post*, 22 April, 1959.

7. Textilera Arguanabo and the Cuban Telephone Company, for example, made advance payments on their profits taxes totalling $640,000. Havana *Post*, 22 January, 1959.

8. *Wall Street Journal*, 2 January 1959.

9. *Ley No. 3 de 10 Oct. 1958*, Departamento Legal, Sección Asesoría de las Delegaciones de Zonas Reforma Agraria (Havana, 1959).

10. Law of Agrarian Reform, Article 18 in *Gaceta Oficial de la Republica de Cuba*, Edición extraordinaria especial, 3 June, 1959.

October decree, which provided expropriated landowners with compensation, was also contained in the law of May 1959, although, with a handful of exceptions, it was not complied with. However, nowhere does the early law touch on the related problems of foreign properties or the *latifundium*, obviously political questions of a profound character. The vague reference to these problems in the introduction of the October decree could only raise more questions than it could answer.[11] This is but one instance of the vagueness which seems to have characterized Castro's early outlook, and not a very conspicuous one at that. One authority has compiled a whole catalogue of others of the revolutionary's 'broken promises' (Draper, 1962, pp. 15–20).

A great many people were therefore understandably uncertain about the concrete steps the new government would take in the areas of economic development and domestic politics. The regime began to show its hand almost at once (by 'intervening' in the Cuban Electric Company, for instance), but the anti-Batista moderates whom Castro placed in the first cabinet made it a point to reassure the business community. President Urrutia himself proclaimed that Cuba needed and wanted foreign investments.

With the benefit of hindsight it is tempting to conclude that Castro's group deliberately concealed their true designs from the Cuban population and opinion abroad as a tactical move to win all the support they could possibly get. It is not intended definitively to defend or refute this view here. It will be useful, though, to suggest that this hypothesis fails to exhaust the possibilities. Castro, for example, might very well have been confused or uncertain over the concrete problems – the agrarian problem, the question of economic development, and pressing political problems such as widespread government corruption,

11. *Ley No. 3*, Por Cuanto (no. 13): 'It will be the task of the future government of the Republic to dictate an additional law to fulfill Article 90 (treating the *latifundium*) of the 1940 Constitution.' While the Cuban Constitution of 1940 established a legal basis for limiting the amount of land which an individual owned, Article 90 is similarly vague, and consequently any reference to it would be devoid of any real content. Article 90 merely 'permitted the fixing by law of the maximum amount of land to be held by a person or entity', and stated that means shall be taken to 'restrictively limit the acquisition and possession of land by foreign persons and companies and . . . to revert the land to Cubans'. (US Dept. of Agriculture, 1960).

the fragile Cuban party system, and elections – which for years had been prominent features of the Cuban scene. The rebel leader, after all, surrounded himself with as varied a group of advisers as any national politician in memory: centrist careerist politicians, Keynesian economists, ex-and-would-be-bureaucrats, sincere liberals, professional revolutionaries and amateur Marxist tacticians – there was very little advice Castro could not get if he wanted it. No less important, his own knowledge of Cuban economic and social life was apparently confined to three or four major areas. About the large class of small tenants and squatters in Oriente Province, the sugar industry and the condition of the very poor throughout the island, he certainly knew a great deal. He had never been, however, in close touch with the problems of the tobacco farmers and other more or less well-to-do Cuban rural workers (apart from the sugar growers). And on the subjects of urban industry and trade and the city working class, he had much – as it turned out – to learn. In this connection, it is interesting to point out that in his first essay on the Cuban Revolution, Theodore Draper (1960), who was later to develop the 'revolution betrayed' thesis, wrote: 'When Fidel Castro entered Havana . . . no one knew what he was going to do. It is doubtful whether he himself knew, except in the most general terms.' As a matter of fact, this actively squares with Castro's own self-evaluation, expressed on numerous occasions, but never so frankly as in the famous 'Marxist-Leninist' speech of 1 December, 1961. Two months later he characterized the revolutionary leadership in these terms: 'We were like a man with a vocation for music. But a man's vocation for music does not grant him a right to call himself a musician if he has not studied musical theory. When we started our revolutionary struggle, we already had some knowledge of Marxism-Leninism and we were in sympathy with it. But, by virtue of this, we could not call ourselves Marxists-Leninists . . . We were apprentice revolutionaries.'[12]

There is also the possibility that both opinions, the one favorable to Castro, the other, because he is made out to be a deliberate liar, very unflattering, are partially true. In this event, the 'conspirator' theory loses much of its bite; it is not hard to understand why a politician would hesitate to reveal plans which he knows may be unrealistic and never be put into action.

12. Radio interview, Moscow Domestic Service, 29 January, 1962.

Whatever the case, the fact is that his early support was extremely heterogeneous, and, for this reason, any policy would be bound to appear as a kind of betrayal to someone. No policy, though, would likely be considered a betrayal by everyone. To put it differently, few measures, and no really important ones, could possibly be universally popular; at the same time, every measure would heighten the loyalties of some of his followers. It was certain, therefore, that his universal popularity in January 1959 would be transitory. The struggle between the Association of Sugar Cane Planters and the Sugar Workers Federation over the issue of cane cutters' wages is a good example of the many class conflicts which would eventually spoil revolutionary harmony. On 15 April, 1959, the new government decreed a 15 per cent rise in the wage rates of the cane cutters. The cane planters (*colonos*) were ordered to pay the wage increases in full; they were to be reimbursed, however, by the mill owners, to the extent of one-third of the extra wage costs.[13] The *colonos* quickly voted among themselves to repeal the decree, arguing that the wage advance would make their farms 'non-operational'. Their protest was without effect. It goes without saying that the disputes which raged over the May Agrarian Reform Law and the Urban Reform Law a little later were argued strictly in class terms. And over the issues of elections and reconstruction of the Cuban political party system, and relations with the United States, it was the professional and middle classes which turned against the Revolutionary government. In the ranks of the poorer rural and urban workers and the marginal peasants there was little or no agitation for the reintroduction of the political forms and institutions dominating the Cuban scene prior to Batista's coup in 1952, nor was there great fear of the island's powerful northern neighbor.

While the economic and social measures divided the island along class lines to produce a kind of 'reactive' class conflict, there was no mass agitation for the reorganization of the Cuban economy. The interventions and expropriations of 1959–60 clearly had the *support* of the majority of Cubans (even the relatively conservative sugar growers supported the seizure of the estates); but the poorer, underprivileged classes failed to *initiate*

13. Havana *Post*, 17 April, 1959; 28 April, 1959. In January, the Association had asked the government for an advance to meet wage payments. They had not anticipated that the wage hike of the year before would be retained in 1959; Havana *Post*, 28 January, 1959, citing *Diario de la Marina*.

these actions. For this reason, an explanation of Cuban socialism which runs along the lines of pure 'class struggle' doctrine is obviously forced and overly abstract.

This admission, however, does not rule out the possibility that Castroism and Cuban socialism were built on economic – not ideological – foundations. First, one cannot characterize the Cuban Revolution as primarily anti-feudal; quite the contrary, the Cuban economy exhibited all the main features of well-developed (one is tempted to say, over-developed) capitalism. What is more, Cuban capitalism was monopoly capitalism; *for this reason, the Cuban economy failed to grow as rapidly as existing technology, savings and the supplies of labor and land permitted.* What inhibited the island's economic growth was not the absolute supplies of factors of production, but the way in which they were *organized.* Viewed in this context, it is highly suggestive that the 'ideologists' apparently failed to have the political initiative at any time; we know that the Cuban Communist party did not make the revolution, and it remains to be proved that Fidel Castro was inevitably to term himself a 'Marxist-Leninist'. Finally, we know that it was possible more or less peacefully to forge socialism in Cuba, implying that most Cubans were ready (or at least willing) to accept a socialist economy, in marked contrast to the Russian experience.

References

DRAPER, T. (1960), 'The runaway revolution', *The Reporter,* vol. 22, 12 May, pp. 14–20.
DRAPER, T. (1962), *Castro's Revolution: Myths and Realities.*
US DEPT. OF AGRICULTURE (1960), 'Agrarian revolution in Cuba', in *Foreign Agriculture,* Foreign Agricultural Service, vol. 24, no. 5, March.
ZEITLIN, M. (1962), 'Castro and Cuba's communists, *The Nation,* November.
ZEITLIN, M., and SCHEER, R. (1963), *Cuba: Tragedy of the Hemisphere,* Grove Press, reprinted in Penguin, 1964.

Part Six
The International Context – Partners in Development?

Discussions of relations between developed and underdeveloped countries often employ the notion of 'partnership' to refer to a community of interest. The working scepticism with which, hopefully, the social scientist is endowed precludes the acceptance at face-value of such a concept. In the first place, it is imperative to situate the coexistence of development and underdevelopment in a system of international inequality, not only economic but also, in most cases, political, military and ideological. Second, it is necessary to analyse, (a) this system of inequality as it defines the conditions of development for Third World countries, and (b) how such development to be effective might come into basic conflict with established centres of economic and political power. These broad questions form the context for the consideration of more specific themes such as the transfer of technology and technical assistance, discussed by Vaitsos (Reading 18), and Cruise O'Brien (Reading 19). The latter provides a rare analysis of the concrete social processes and tensions of administering aid. Girvan and Jefferson (Reading 20) show that the concept of economic integration like others discussed in this collection, possesses no unambiguous technical status. The process of international integration in contemporary capitalism operates through a network of international corporations whose decisions are guided by very different concerns than overcoming the underdevelopment of poor countries. Finally, Illich (Reading 21) challenges the cultural framework of many expressions of 'development', and in particular the value of certain 'exports' from rich countries. Whether one agrees with his polemic in its entirety or not, he urges an awareness of questions critical to pursuing the fully human meaning of development.

18 C. V. Vaitsos[*]

Bargaining and the Distribution of Returns in the Purchase of Technology by Developing Countries

C. V. Vaitsos, 'Bargaining and the distribution of returns in the purchase of technology by developing countries', *Bulletin of the Institute of Development Studies*, vol. 3, no. 1, 1970, pp. 16–23.

The intellectual tradition of most modern economists (at least in the 'Western' world) is such that they explicitly or implicitly associate the allocation of resources and distribution of returns with the market mechanism and a price system. Aside from issues that arise with respect to the degree of 'purity' and 'perfection' of the market-price system (a subject that has long been discussed), economists who accept it implicitly assume, among other things, that (a) goods, services and factors of production are 'individually owned' (by persons or firms) and (b) the parties participating in an exchange are able to assess the values of the economic units transacted. The market within which technology is being commercialized violates both assumptions related to the price system, as it is traditionally defined. Consequently, technology commercialization can best be described through other mechanisms, and one that appears most appropriate is that of bargaining. Policy makers, therefore, who concentrate on the 'price mechanism' (as taught to us by traditional economic theory) in order to maximize their country's interests when technology is being purchased, are misorienting themselves completely.

The reasons are as follows. Technology, being a form of information, is 'non-exhaustible'. Its use contrasts with the usage (or consumption) of an item which is 'individually owned', in which case the availability to others (or to the same person in the future) is at least partially reduced through wear and tear. Technology, then, is by nature 'jointly' and not 'individually' owned. The usage of information by a person or firm does not in itself reduce its present or future availability. Information is 'non-exhaustible'; the price mechanism that could satisfy the efficient transfer of 'individually' owned goods is inappropriate in this case.

* C. V. Vaitsos works in Lima, on technical assistance contract to the Andean Pact Group.

The marginal cost of using or selling an already developed technology is zero for the owner of that technology. Where cases of adaptation arise, the owner incurs certain costs which can be estimated and usually do not exceed a figure in the tens of thousands of dollars.[1] In several industries the sellers of technology to developing countries have themselves copied such technology from the originators who incurred the R and D expenses. (A systematic study undertaken in the petrochemicals industry indicated that during the period after original development when technology sales to developing countries were most likely to occur, the original producers of a product or process accounted only for 1 per cent of the total licensing. The remaining 99 per cent was divided between 'followers' of commercial producers (52 per cent) and engineering firms (47 per cent).[2] On the other hand, from the point of view of the purchaser, the marginal cost of developing an alternative technology with his own technical capacity might amount to millions of dollars. Or he might be unable to develop it, or at least think so, in which case his relative marginal cost is infinite. Given market availabilities, the price between zero or tens of thousands of dollars, and millions of dollars or infinite is, in turn, determined solely on the basis of a crude relative bargaining power. There is no price which *a priori* can be claimed to be more or less appropriate within the two limits specified.

A further consideration arises as to whether information, technology or ideas are 'owned', to start with, in accordance with the traditional definition of property. Ideas can certainly be captive either legally, i.e. patent privileges, or technically, i.e. in a case where they are kept secret, or when a potential user does not have the knowledge to absorb and use certain information. But can they be 'owned'? It has been argued that '. . . property in ideas once published is an insoluble contradiction . . . [He who argues that his ideas have been stolen] . . . complains that something has been stolen which he still possesses, and he wants back something which, if given to him a thousand times, would add nothing to his possession'.[3] Furthermore, how can 'owner-

1. For an analysis of marginal *versus* full cost considerations in the development of new as well as the sale of already developed technology that is purchased by the 'non-industrialized' world, see Vaitsos (1970).

2. Stobaugh (1970, p. 5).

3. Rentzsch (1866, p. 333).

ship' be claimed in inventions or ideas when any advancement in thought is a result of dependence on and further elaborations of previous inventions or ideas?[4] The distinction between 'ownership' and 'captivity' leads us to the following consideration. In part of the market of technology commercialization an external mechanism is interposed so as to create, artificially, a scarcity which in turn results in a price system. Such interposition is achieved through patents. 'Clearly the patent system is our attempt to include the production of inventions in the same framework of pricing as the production of other things, and to do this by creating scarcity – by limiting the use of the invention . . . So far as inventions are concerned a price is put on them not *because* they are scarce but *in order* to make them scarce to those who want to use them' (Penrose, 1951, p. 29).

The second assumption made about the price system as an efficient means of allocating resources implies that 'the parties participating in an exchange are able to assess the values of the economic units transacted'. Here again the existing market of technology commercialization not only differs from that of the price system, but also places the purchaser in a structural position of basic weakness. In the formulation of the demand for technology, or for information in general, the prospective buyer needs information about the properties, potential results, alternative offers, etc., of the item he intends to purchase. In this respect the technology market is no different from all other markets. Yet quite often, the item itself that one needs to purchase, i.e. technology, is at the same time the information that is needed in order to make a rational decision to buy it. What is needed is knowledge about knowledge, which could effectively be one and the same thing. As a result the assumed roles of an efficient market mechanism break down, at least on the part of the buyer. In evaluating contracts of technology purchase by developing countries, one is immediately struck by the total vagueness by which technical assistance is being acquired contractually. The licensor is quite generally left with complete freedom to transfer

4. 'It is little short of absurdity to call any one of the interrelated units *the* invention, and its 'creator' *the* inventor. The man who brought to a certain stage of fruition the efforts of myriad predecessors, and whom therefore we call the inventor, may have made a great contribution. But seen in its proper setting and perspective, the contribution is something less than cataclysmic' (Kahn, 1940, p. 478).

whatever he decides while the purchaser has explicit and fixed conditions with respect to payments, terms of obligations, etc. The buyer, quite often, does not know what to ask.

The properties of the market of technology transfer are therefore such that the mechanism that best describes its functioning is the process of bargaining (and not the traditionally defined market-price system). The buyer is, moreover, placed in a position of structural weakness in the formulation of his demand for information. We now have to consider why developing countries confront, in addition, other problems which further diminish their relative bargaining power and hence increase the cost of technology acquisition. I shall be briefly treating three general aspects.

1. The process of industrialization through final product import substitution of the 'late late-comers' has been such that developing countries basically confine themselves to the transformation (and not properly the production) of products that have been imported from abroad. Within this context technology purchase involves, to a great extent, know-how embodied in intermediate products and capital goods. As a result purchases of the latter are tied-in with the purchase of technology. A study undertaken in Colombia showed that all the contracts of technology commercialization that provided information on intermediate product purchases explicitly required the purchase of such products from the seller of technology.[5] In addition, even if contractual terms do not so specify, the know-how purchase often defines (sometimes quite uniquely) the origin of intermediate products. As a result the market of such products becomes monopolistic, i.e. the licensee of Pfizer Co. has to buy tetracycline from Pfizer since the latter is the only one that can export the product to a country if it owns the patent that covers the product. A licensee of Toyota has to import components from the licensor since the technology embodied in the chassis and assembling of Toyota cars requires specific Toyota components. From research in Colombia and extrapolating from a sample that included 25 per cent of the imports of 40–50 per cent of the pharmaceutical industry, it was estimated that the country paid for intermediate products in 1968 close to US $20,000,000 solely due to *price differentials* above those available in the 'international' market for the same products. Price differentials were observed in each of the sectors

5. The following discussion is based on Vaitsos (1970, pp. 10 ff). The quotation is from p. 11.

studied which included chemicals, electronics and rubber products. 'Defining as effective returns to the parent corporation the sum of reported profits of the subsidiary, royalty payments and intermediate product overpricing, the following data can be inferred from our sample of the Colombian pharmaceutical industry. *Reported profits constituted 3·4 per cent of effective returns, royalties 14·0 per cent and "overpricing" 82·6 per cent.*' In view of such overpricing the basis for costing technology and/ or capital (in case of foreign direct investment) cannot be found in royalty payments or in declared profit repatriation, but has to rest on the prices paid for intermediate products and capital goods. Tie-in arrangements resulting from contractual terms and/ or technical requirements and/or ownership ties, have properties which make the market price system a poor mechanism to distribute benefits while protecting the interests of developing countries.

2. Markets where prices are settled through bargaining, like the labor market, have generally developed explicit institutional methods and rules upon which negotiations are settled. Such methods enable the participating parties to protect their interests by the proper definition of the negotiable elements, maximum and minimum positions of bargaining, identification of areas where the other party is most or least likely to 'give in', etc. Industrialized countries, both because of the sophistication and size of their companies, and because of the existence of specialized government agencies (see MITI and JETRO in Japan) have enabled their technology buyers to negotiate with considerable knowledge and intelligence. Developing countries, however, in spite of being highly dependent upon foreign technology, have not yet shown an awareness of the critical problems involved.

To start with, a large part of foreign know-how is introduced through the establishment of foreign-owned companies. Such subsidiaries lack even a minimum negotiating position since their interests are, presumably, identified with those of their parent corporation and not with the host country. For example, it is not uncommon to encounter cases where a foreign wholly-owned subsidiary has capitalized in its books technology that originated from the parent corporation. As a result it could be (a) paying royalties, (b) reducing its tax payments through depreciation 'charges' of intangible assets, (c) having lower tax coefficients in countries where taxable profits are related to 'invested' capital, and (d) claiming higher capital repatriations in countries with exchange controls, all for the same know-how. Clearly a foreign-owned subsidiary does not need to capitalize technology since 100 per cent of its capital is already owned by its parent.

Institutional mechanisms and procedures to handle adequate bargaining of foreign-technology purchases are lacking not only in cases of parent–subsidiary situations, or with respect to the proper definition of implicit costs that result from intermediate product overpricing – an item which is usually left out of the negotiating process. Procedures are also inadequate for the evaluation of even the explicit, negotiable elements in technology purchase such as royalty payments. They are usually negotiated on the basis of sales, and not with respect to the income-generating effects of technology, such as profits for firms and domestic value-added for countries. As a result of this mis-specification of the 'economic effects' of a particular know-how purchase one encounters cases where royalty payments, which appear quite 'reasonable' with respect to sales, amount to a multiple of profits or value-added. (One result of the present system is that a country's payments on technology that originated from abroad rise proportionately with its final-product tariffs.)

The inadequacy of the present bargaining system stems partly from the lack of any adequate specifications of what is meant by technology importation. When evaluating contracts in developing countries one generally encounters the tautological definition that technological purchase implies the importation of know-how. The issue arises as to what, at least operationally, is the technology that a country is importing for a given industry, or process or product. Is it technical assistance which is transmitted through personnel, or a manual with production specifications, or a license of a patent (which clearly is not technology but the legal permission to use technology), or know-how already embodied in intermediate products and machinery, or factory layouts, or what? Each of these different types of technology importation has different potential alternative sources of supply and hence different alternative prices; each expresses different types and degrees of dependence between technology supplier and receiver; each has attached to it different types of obligations and rights for the contracting parties, etc. The type of technology needed by developing countries in their present industrial stage is amply available around the world. Therefore, the breakdown of what is collectively referred to as technology importation and the exact specification of each of its parts would make it possible to transform a market which is at present almost totally monopolistic into a competitive one. The degree of this competitiveness will depend on the amount of information a potential buyer has in the pursuit of information purchase.

3. It is not surprising that a market whose basic properties have been left so inadequately defined is also characterized by a totally inappropriate legal framework at least as far as developing countries are concerned. The contractual terms by which technology is being sold to developing countries violate the basic principles of anti-monopoly or anti-trust legislations through which developed countries attempt to protect the interests of their national economies. For example, a clause which is most common in technology sales is that of export prohibition. In the already referred to sample of nationally owned firms and joint ventures in the Colombian chemical, textile and pharmaceutical sectors, 85 per cent of the contracts studied explicitly prohibited exports of products manufactured with the use of imported technology. Also thirty-three out of thirty-five contracts that were concerned with making information available, explicitly required the purchase of intermediate products from the technology supplier. Similar clauses exist for the purchase of capital goods, hiring of key personnel, level and structure of production, price fixing for sale or resale of goods etc. Legal and administrative [6] procedures have been set up in developed countries to regulate such practices. The basic legislation that exists in developing countries with respect to the impact and ramifications of technology importation is mostly related to the limits imposed on the business practices of their own nationals and not those of the sellers of technology. For example, legislation on technology importation in developing countries is mostly identified with industrial property legislation such as patent laws. No relevant economic analysis is being pursued as to whether patents really protect the interests of the 'non-industrialized' countries, while legal systems are transplanted from developed nations whose needs and interests are totally different.[7]

6. Examples of legal procedures are Section 1 of the Sherman Act, Section 3 of the Clayton Act, article 85 (1) of the Rome Treaty, article 37 of the Price Ordnance of France, the Economic Competition Act of 1958, Netherlands, etc.; of administrative procedures: US Internal Revenue Service, Code 492.

7. '. . . Provisions [of the modern international patent system] it is

Concluding remarks

Countries do not make resource allocations on education, defense, space programs, public health, etc. on the basis of the market-price system. The particular characteristics of the 'markets' in these areas are quite distinct from the properties and image we inherited from the 'economic liberalism' of the previous century. Nations have, thus, attempted to introduce other means in order to allocate resources and distribute benefits. (Some of them, like the voting process, do not even fall within the strict definition of economic market system.) Technology importation has structural properties that make the market-price mechanism totally inadequate in the process of defending the interests of the receiving countries. Once this has been understood, a new system, long overdue, can be developed which enables developing countries to take advantage of technology.

---

evident, have altered the complexion of the patent grant from one designed primarily to stimulate domestic industry to one in which the foreign patentee has an increased chance of producing where he chooses and retaining his patent monopoly', United States Government, Committee of the Judiciary, US Senate, 85th Congress, 1st Session, study on 'The international patent system and foreign policy', Washington, 1957, p. 3.

References

KAHN, A. E. (1940), 'Fundamental deficiencies of the American patent law', *American Economic Review*, vol. 30.

PENROSE, E. T. (1951), *The Economics of the International Patent System*, Johns Hopkins Press.

RENTZSCH, H. (1866), 'Geistiges eigenthum', *Handwörterbuch der Volkswirtschaft*, Leipzig.

STOBAUGH, R. (1970), 'Utilizing technical know-how in a foreign investment and licensing program', paper delivered to the National Meeting, *Chemical Marketing Research Association*.

VAITSOS, C. V. (1970), 'Transfer of resources and preservation of monopoly rents', paper presented at the *Dubrovnik Conference of the Development Advisory Service of Harvard University*, 20–26 June, pp. 18–21.

19 R. Cruise O'Brien*

Colonization to Cooperation? French Technical
Assistance in Senegal

R. Cruise O'Brien, 'Colonization to cooperation? French technical
assistance in Senegal', *Journal of Development Studies*, vol. 8, no. 1,
1971, pp. 45–58.

Origins and structure of the programme

'It is the purpose of technical assistance programming to indicate
where the needs for foreign skills and training are most pressing,
and to design a strategy for aid to ensure that the scarce resources
are used where their yield will be greatest' (Maddison, 1965, p.
164).

Neither an assessment of the output of a technical assistance
programme nor the calculation of its effectiveness can be derived
from such a simplistic formula. The 'architects' of such programmes often do, however, treat the export of knowledge or skill as
if it were a tangible input which could have a reasonably calculable
output. The disappointment with which the ineffectiveness of
certain programmes is subsequently reviewed can perhaps be
explained in terms of a dual misunderstanding. First is the lack
of concern for the cultural and behavioural environment into
which these skills are introduced, either by technical assistance
planners or those sent out to serve on the programme. Second is
perhaps the absence of explicitly stated objectives for the general
programme, apart from the training of local cadres and the

* An earlier draft of this paper was presented to a Staff Seminar at the
Institute in February 1970, and circulated in their communications series
as 'The Limits of French Technical Assistance in Senegal'.

This article is part of a general study on the French in Senegal to be
published early in 1972 as *White Society in Black Africa*, Faber and Faber.
The evidence is based on field research in Paris and Dakar in 1966/67
including a social survey by questionnaire containing 250 interviews of
French men and women employed in the public and private sectors. Of
this total number, sixty-three were technical assistants, selected according
to a stratified quota sample of their representation in various ministries,
public services and educational institutions. Certain of the questions were
designed specifically to examine their activities and perceptions in the working environment and will be used in the text where relevant. Numbers and
basic trends in personnel allocation were updated with the assistance of the
French Secretariat of State for Cooperation in Paris in April 1971.

provision of certain skills and knowledge until local civil servants are fully prepared to take responsibility. Such general aims give no indication of the scope and purpose of the activities of individual technical assistants. To have been simply designated in an advisory capacity leaves open to interpretation the limits of discretion and authority contained in the role of the technical assistant. In consequence, this role may vary widely from post to post depending on the nature of the work and the personalities involved. And differing expectations surrounding the role may even provide a source of tension between the technical assistant and the local civil servants with whom he works. These problems are perhaps particularly evident where there is a massive personnel export to a particular country and where a significant proportion of that personnel are serving in an advisory rather than teaching capacity, as in the case of the French programme in Senegal (or the British programme in Zambia). One can learn from such extreme cases, however, in that there may be certain basic problems and propositions which are apparent and relevant to any context in which technical assistants are serving in some capacity in relation to the local administration.

There are still more than 1200 French technical assistants in Senegal in 1971, whose services are provided by a programme administered through the Secretariat of State for Cooperation.[2] About three-quarters of these are in the educational sector and the remainder in the administrative posts (see Table 1 below) where their influence, although varying widely according to personal and political factors, is disproportionate to their total numbers. The impact of the programme lies not only in the numbers of personnel but in the continuation of structures and attitudes derived from the colonial period which permeate the public service. Since the technical assistant himself often fulfils an ambiguous role, there is a natural tendency on the part of both

2. Its full designation is the Secretariat of State for Foreign Affairs in Charge of Cooperation. Previous to 1966, it was the Ministry of Cooperation. The administrative change made it part of an enlarged Ministry of Foreign Affairs to ensure that technical, economic, financial and cultural aid would be better co-ordinated. In Senegal, there are many technical assistance projects and schemes which are either financed by French funds or staffed by Frenchmen, which do not fall under the rubric of the official programme. The University of Dakar, for example, is heavily staffed and partly directed by the French Ministry of Education, and private development agencies, UN and Common Market programmes alone increase the number of Frenchmen so engaged by about 100.

Frenchmen and Senegalese to return to the more obvious patterns of behaviour established in the past, the ultimate effect of which is that a French network within the administration retains considerable influence on policy.

Table 1 **Annual totals of French technical assistance personnel in Senegal 1961–71**

	Education	*Administration*	*Total*
1961	582	861	1443
1962	723	671	1394
1963	823	557	1380
1964	896	518	1414
1965	948	551	1499
1966	983	540	1523
1967	969	551	1520
1968	959	556	1515
1969 (Jan)	880	322	1202
1971	891	318	1209

Source for 1961–66: French Aid and Cooperation Mission, Dakar 1967; for 1967–71; Sec. of State for Cooperation, Paris, 1971.

Post-colonial French policy in its first phase was not at all concerned to promote the viability of national economic structures in former African dependencies. Awarded the formal political attributes of nationhood, these countries were bound structurally and financially to the metropolitan system. Self-sufficiency was an irrelevant consideration. The maintenance of substantial French personnel in Senegal today is the calculated cost to the French taxpayer of ensuring the security of French aid and capital investment and/or of providing the necessary stability for Senegalese economic development within the franc zone and the French Community.

The continuity of French presence in the public sector may in part be explained by the extent to which Senegal's administrative and economic infrastructure was integrated into the French system in the fifteen years prior to independence. Such French projects as FIDES (*Fonds d'Investissement pour le Développement Economique et Social*) provided African states with very complex administrative structures which were based entirely on metropolitan forms and methods (Jeanneney Report, 1963, pp. 80–81).[3] The annual running costs of the system, and particularly of European personnel to direct it, became a considerable part of the colonial budget. In 1956, for example, the wages of the public sector in Senegal were 9·6 per cent of the Gross National Product, 3·2 per cent being for Europeans, while in the Gold Coast in the same year, the equivalent was 6·7 per cent and 0·7 per cent respectively (Hayter, 1966, p. 40).[4] This has had a certain effect on the present structure and finance of the Senagalese public service. Independent Senegal has retained most of the French administrative structures inherited from the colonial period and expanded into many other areas. Where local personnel sources have been insufficient to maintain these structures efficiently, personnel has been supplied from France.

Senegal has one of the highest concentrations of French technical assistants and teachers in Africa (about the same number as in the Ivory Coast and Madagascar), although she was considered to have been one of the two French West African countries (with Dahomey) which could have exported public servants to some of her less well-endowed neighbouring countries at the time of independence. The explanation for this concentration of French personnel in Senegal lies as much with explicit Senegalese policy as it does with the continuation of French influence, and the policy objectives of France toward former colonies. The determined policy of close cooperation with France, of which President Senghor is such an ardent exponent, has had the advantage of assuring minimal politica' stability in Senegal since independence. *Coopération* or *le dialogue* were the official labels for this policy in public rhetoric, but the realities of the relationship often belied the reciprocity implied in such terms.

The original agreement[5] between France and Senegal which established the technical assistance programme in 1959 made reference to the 'provision of personnel esteemed necessary for the functioning of the public services' of the Republic of Senegal. It mentioned certain prescriptions binding the technical assistants,

3. In specific terms, the Report states: 'Projects administered under FIDES gave priority to the infrastructure and provision of manpower, a long-term policy with sacrifices in the short-term. They were, above all, inappropriate to the type of aid required after independence.'

4. Citing Saxe (1960).

5. *Convention Relative au Concours en Personnel Apporté par la République Française au Fonctionnement des Services de la République du Sénégal*, signed in Paris, 14 September, 1959 by M. Dia and J. Autin, roneo copy given to me at the Senegalese *Service de l'Assistance Technique*.

such as conformity to the regulations and policies of the Senegalese government, abstention from actions which might be politically sensitive and the respect of confidentiality for information obtained in a professional capacity. Apart from this, however, there was no positive definition of the role of a technical assistant in the service of the Senegalese government, and this has not since been done at any official level. While it would have been very difficult to provide specific information and guidance on the very varied working roles filled by the technical assistants, the absence of any adequate definition of the scope and limitations of their responsibility, or the nature of reciprocal interaction between the French and the Senegalese in a professional capacity, has obviously left interpretation open to debate. This vagueness has served to enhance the power of the individual technical assistant, making the personal qualities he brings to the role (notably his knowledge and experience) assume a much greater importance. It may also, of course, engender misunderstandings between African and French colleagues unaware of the precise nature of the job – its limitations and responsibilities.

Planning for the allocation of technical assistants to various ministries, services and schools is worked out in joint Franco-Senegalese Commissions[6] on the basis of existing expatriate personnel in each area and planning for forthcoming projects. In the Senegalese administration there is a permanent department, the *Service de l'Assistance Technique*, which co-ordinates these requests and deals with ongoing personnel problems and planning relating to the programme. Most of the routine work involves the processing of personnel files and taking up the balance of repatriation and new appointments in various spheres of activity. Basic disagreements with the local office of the French Secretariat of State for Cooperation in Dakar, the *Mission d'Aide et de Coopération*, arise over a basic conflict of interest. The Senegalese wish to retain those technical assistants who have been long in service, are well integrated locally and thus of optimal effectiveness according to their consideration.[7] The most

6. These commissions meet at three-year intervals to decide the allocation of administrative personnel. The allocation in education is done annually in a joint meeting of representatives of the African countries concerned and a representative of the French Ministry of National Education.

7. Interview with the Director of the Senegalese *Service de l'Assistance Technique*, November 1966. This service is part of the *Sécrétariat-Général*, which is organized directly under the Office of the President.

experienced technical assistants are obviously nearly all ex-colonial officers, which gives a certain irony to the situation. The Senegalese are hardly alone among recipients of technical assistance in their preference for retaining ex-colonial officers as long as possible, often in opposition to personnel planners from donor countries.[8] In the Senegalese case, it is precisely these ex-colonials whom the French Secretariat of State for Cooperation are most eager to repatriate. The official French view is that it is problematic to retain personnel abroad too long because of the potential difficulties of professional reintegration when they return to posts in France (quite often the reason among other donor countries as well). Recent French policy has been to try to impose a maximum length of service abroad and to encourage maximum contracts of only two or three years for new recruits, a move which was opposed by Senegalese officials dealing with personnel programming. Education was the only sphere in which limits were actually set, although these were quite liberal: thus a maximum of fourteen years of service abroad was imposed in 1967, despite vigorous opposition from both the Senegalese government and the French teachers already in post.

While the growing preference among Paris officials for shorter contracts of service is obvious, nearly 60 per cent of those technical assistants interviewed in a total survey of fifty in 1966 had been in the colonial service, having been grafted on to the newly defined programme of cooperation in 1961. But by comparison, French technical assistants in Senegal as a professional group had less overseas residence or colonial experience than their compatriots in the private sector – employed in a wide variety of commercial, industrial and service establishments – whose continued presence in Senegal has maintained Dakar as an attractive expatriate location with more than 25,000 French residents. The location serves to explain in part the personal reluctance of many technical assistants to face repatriation to a potentially less attractive post in France with much less professional responsibility.[9]

The financial responsibility for the technical assistance scheme

8. Information provided by an official of the Manpower Planning Unit, Overseas Development Administration, British Foreign Office, February 1971.

9. Details concerning job satisfaction among technical assistants and their personal views on the programme as a whole may be found in chapter 7 of my forthcoming book (see footnote 1).

is largely French, although the Senegalese government contributes to it a stipulated proportion annually, which adds to already very heavy national spending on administrative salaries, some 47 per cent of the total annual budget (First, 1970, p. 109).[10] All technical assistants are given a base pay of about £84 per month (50,000 CFA francs) by the Senegalese government, which is about one-third of the average total gross salary. The Senegalese contribution to the salary of each French technical assistant is equivalent to the average salary for the highest rank of local civil servants. In addition to contribution to salaries, the Senegalese government provides furnished housing for expatriate personnel which is customary in many bilateral programmes. In Dakar and other major towns in Senegal, prices for such accommodation are inflated because of the demand for scarce places, and the government commitment thus becomes, in effect, a subsidy of luxury property, most of which is owned by French companies or Lebanese businessmen.

A growing number of technical assistants have been annually supplied through the scheme of *militaires de contingent* which was introduced in 1963. These are military conscripts with university degrees who substitute for their military service a thirteen-month tour in French cooperation schemes overseas. Their services were first offered free to France's former colonies in Africa, but after 1966 the same basic salary contribution was requisite for them as for all technical assistants in the programme. Their total salary (£100 or 60,000 CFA. francs) was only slightly higher than the local contribution thus providing a considerable economy for France in making up the requisite number of personnel needed by each country,

Justified by French officialdom for their youth and exuberance, the *militaires de contingent* are always portrayed as an antidote to the aura of continued colonial presence in the assistance programme: 'young men for a young country'. Since their introduction, the Senegalese have continually complained that they have inadequate experience to act in an advisory capacity. Owing to continued pressure on this matter (through the Senegalese *Service de l'Assistance Technique*) nearly all of them are now serving as teachers rather than advisers, although in this capacity also their lack of experience remains a source of discontent. The fact that their military stipend is almost covered by the Senegalese contribution, and that they are housed by the government, has deepened

10. Citing Chaliand (1966).

this discontent. Most outspoken local critics of the technical assistance programme regard the scheme as an indirect Sengalese subsidy to the French armed forces. *Militaires de contingent* were 10 per cent (150) of the total number of French technical assistants (1520) when I was interviewing in Senegal in 1967, a proportion which has been raised to more than 17 per cent (204 of a total of 1209) in 1971. In the interests of achieving economies on the programme the French government has thus continually increased their numbers, while Senegalese officials feel that they annually lose well-established and experienced civil servants for young men who only remain in the country for a short tour of thirteen months.

Since the focus of this discussion is on the French technical assistant in an administrative capacity, it will not be able to include the numerous problems to be studied in connection with the very substantial personnel input in the educational sectors, some of which are documented in a number of official publications (République du Sénégal, 1965–69) and in a study devoted specifically to the examination of one particular educational institution (Flis-Zonabend, 1968). It may suffice here just to mention that problems in the educational sector lie obviously much less in the area of role definition (and ambiguity of the technical assistant in his role), than in the structure of a curriculum which remains so heavily dominated by French models and practices with expatriate teachers doing exactly the same type of job they do in France (the highest proportion in my survey who saw *no* differences between their work in France and in Senegal). It has often been remarked that French teachers live in a more enclosed and isolated manner than any other group of expatriates. But it is difficult in this context to lay the blame for lack of adaptation in education on the individual technical assistant, or on their social habits as a group. That a French teacher brings with him, a preparation which may not correspond to the actual needs of the country, or a lack of flexibility in terms of adaptation to local cultural needs in the performance of his work is a reflection of a weakness in the definition of the programme of education by the Senegalese Ministry of Education, all too ready in many instances to retain French models.

Review of the dynamics of the programme

The first general review of the French programme of cooperation came in the Jeanneney Report of 1963. It was followed a year later by a programmative review of five years of Ministry of Cooperation activities in Africa, which finally recommended among other things an abandonment of the idea of aid as an instrument of total economic integration into the French Community and of the idea that there should be exclusive economic complementarity between France and her former overseas territories (Triboulet Report, 1964, pp. 5–8). The re-thinking of strategies contained in the Jeanneney Report was aimed at trying to change the attitudes both of African policy-makers like those in Senegal who chose to rely almost exclusively on France for personnel and aid, and French policy-makers concerned with overseas aid. Specific recommendations included a reduction in the number of French technical assistants in purely administrative posts, as a step towards more rapid abandonment of colonial structures (Triboulet Report, 1964, pp. 22, 64–5). In Senegal this generated an attempt to shift expatriates from managerial to technical posts in the administration, a distinction which proved difficult to maintain in the actual working situation. The majority of administrative personnel at this time were of course former colonial officers, and shifting their established roles and experienced methods of work was as difficult for them as for Senegalese colleagues who had come to rely upon them.

While French personnel remained in important posts in many sectors of the administration (and, in fact, their numbers increased between 1963 and 1967 as did Senegalese requests for personnel), the new policy had at least some effect on the redeployment of this personnel. First, there was an attempt to shift the emphasis from administrative to teaching posts. Second, within the administration an attempt was made to shift expatriates to certain sectors considered more technical than purely administrative – education, health and production (the last of which included several ministries – Rural Economy, Planning, Commerce and Industry). While the total number of technical assistants serving in Senegal was increased by 100 in 1964, the internal shift remained toward 'specialist' ministries or from managerial to specialist posts.

In the Ministry of Finance, however, which was considered to be one of the more managerial than technical departments, the plan to reduce expatriate personnel in the years between 1963 and

1966 was reappraised after a disappointment in the performance of their African replacements. Thus in 1966 there were again slightly more Frenchmen in this Ministry than there had been in 1963. Their proportion to local civil servants is higher in Finance than in most ministries, and several serve on the *Cabinet du Ministre*, which has since independence been directed by a Frenchman with Senegalese nationality. The consistently high concentration of Frenchmen in the Ministry of Finance has been made possible by an increase of technical assistance personnel involved in data processing (information collection and programme analysis) in that Ministry, which has also affected the Ministries of Justice and the Interior. There has thus since 1970 been a shift back of personnel from specialist ministries to the general administration, estimated now to account for about 50 per cent of the total personnel outside the educational sector (318 in January 1971). Obviously, this is only a launching period for these activities, after which more Senegalese will be trained to handle data processing. But with a view to examining some of the problems outlined in the following section, there are basic questions of involvement and authority which remain of crucial importance.

Ambiguity in the role of the technical assistant

It may be argued that the vagueness or ambiguity of the role of the technical assistant provides the latent political function of enhancing French power in the administration and that the lack of clarification is deliberate, since a clearer specification would naturally tend to restrict his area of manoeuvre in the authority structure. It is less my concern here, however, to try to examine the nature of the situation as a matter of deliberate policy than to analyse the results in the working environment. In so far as technical assistants in any administration may add to its efficiency or effectiveness, they are in a sense serving the *status quo* or the existing regime. To make the jump from this position to infer that their efforts are always in favour of French interests, however vaguely or narrowly defined, is a bit more problematic. Local French businessmen interviewed in my survey for example, were sharply divided as to whether or not the presence of technical assistants served their interests. In Senegal, it would appear in any case that the maintenance of a regime friendly to France is more certainly served by the presence of 2200 French troops

(ISS, 1970, p. 54)[11] (excluding French advisors in the Senegalese army) stationed a mile or two from the capital than 1200 technical assistants serving in a wide variety of posts throughout the country.

The actual responsibility of a technical assistant, whose function may be to 'aid', 'assist' or 'train', is ambiguous in the context of a governing organization, and in the absence of any attempt to specify his role, other factors (as we have seen), become extremely important. The personality of the expatriate, his length of experience and his relationship with the director or minister for whom he works, are among the factors which determine his influence.

Since the Senegalese administrative structure is based so closely on the French model, the latter remains the obvious reference point for activity and assessment. Two-thirds of those technical assistants serving in administrative posts (interviewed in my survey) saw no difference between the jobs they did in France and those they were doing in Senegal, which would seem to indicate that a majority were still 'directing' or 'administering' rather than 'advising'. Here lies the basic confusion of the 'staff' or 'advisory' role of the technical assistant which seems in practice to award him 'line' or executive status in the actual organization. A technical assistant accepts that the Senegalese administrative system does function differently than that to which he is accustomed and that Senegalese administrative behaviour is considerably distant from his own, but retaining the French model, he is either disillusioned by the inefficiency, under-employment and corruption among which he works, or he uses it to reassure himself that his services are indispensable.

The expertise provided by technical assistants can become a potent kind of authority in an administrative system, although it is rarely recognized as such and can be exercised with little knowledge of the environment and little responsibility for the consequences. In this situation the essential ambiguity built into the role of the advisor and his place in the organization becomes important. He may be counselling someone who is in a higher administrative position then himself, although a political appointee

11. The presence of this force is in keeping with the arrangements of the French Community, and although they have never been used actively in Senegal, they have intervened in other parts of Africa to protect the interests of pro-French regimes.

without the knowledge and expertise or the executive experience which he possesses. Is the technical advisor supposed to do only what his minister asks or may he disagree with him on the basis of his personal knowledge and experience? Does the technical advisor only prepare memoranda within the parameters of existing policy or may he initiate a new departure by suggesting a new programme or procedure? All of this seems to be unclear, and practice varies widely from place to place within the administration, depending less ultimately on role articulation in the executive organization than on the personal qualities or 'power' which the individual brings to the role.

Technical assistants (particularly the younger ones) are often developmentalists or technocrats whose advice and counsel are made on the basis of technical calculation of cost, output and effectiveness whereas local civil servants are well aware (and in some cases perhaps too well aware) of extra-administrative considerations which may ultimately influence a decision. The location of a deep well, for example, might be optimally placed near a densely populated farming area, whereas it might in the last resort be placed on the estate of a traditional religious leader whose capacity to supply votes or other political support is of importance to the minister. Such conflicts of interest exist in all countries, but they can be particularly dramatic in developing countries where resources are extremely scarce and the imperatives of the political kingdom so predominant. Here, I think, is a crucial issue with wider relevance for planning and aid administration.

Virtually all administrative decisions have political implications of some kind, even if they were formulated on a non-political basis. And it can be said that the decision made by a technical assistant to give advice 'A' rather than 'B' is in itself political whether formulated on an ideological basis or a technocratic, and ostensibly neutral basis. The influence of the technical assistant may be identified as the 'sapiential' authority he exerts in the organization. This authority, which is perhaps intended to be neutral, may in practice be determined by the experience of the given technical assistant (the technocrat), his political disposition (the ideologue) or his career interests (the Minister's 'yes-man').

There is only a fine distinction between technical assistants who are committed developmentalists and those who are progressives or socialists in the Senegalese context. Although at a national level ideological considerations are not of great importance, there are recognizable cliques of ideologues – both expatriate and African – in the administration. In Algeria, following the revolution, expatriate ideologues became known as *pieds rouges* (the successors to the settlers or *pieds noirs*), and, while a new departure in terms of European participation in that context, the Algerians found that these new Marxist advisors also provided new types of problems because of their lack of understanding of the traditional values of Muslim society (Lentin, 1966, p. 44). In Senegal their counterparts are called *pieds roses* because, although socialist in sentiment, they are generally of a more evolutionary or liberal persuasion (and often associated with liberal Catholic organizations in France). Their 'prefabricated plans for development' are not popular in many local circles.[12] While there is criticism among Senegalese civil servants of most technical assistants for not being responsible for the decisions on which they advise, there is also a fear that some may become an independent force, losing the perspective of 'assisting the nation', and directing it instead. The balance is a difficult one to maintain.

The results of ambiguity in the administration

The network of French technical assistants has become an 'administration within an administration' (or an 'administration within a non-administration'), partly because of the weakness of the Senegalese civil service. Frenchmen in each department tend to form a separate clique or team responsible to the minister or head of department. Expatriates are usually physically separated in an office or cluster of offices, often doing policy studies for which there are few experienced or qualified Senegalese civil servants. In the Ministry of Planning, for example, the expatriate planning team appeared to carry considerable latent executive authority, yet in 1967 there was no Senegalese working on the team in order to learn these skills.

Decisions from one part of the administration to another pass often from French advisor to French advisor. And decisions within a department are sometimes made among senior civil servants and their technical advisors, without the knowledge or

12. 'He (the technical assistant) must not be so impressed by his tasks as to mix in internal matters, playing the role of the *éminence grise* – in the political context. He is often involved in intrigues which influence his decisions and the way he thinks, but which do not necessarily conform to the ideal of what is good for the nation' (République du Sénégal, 1967, p. 62).

consultation of Senegalese colleagues.[13] Such a pattern of activity is obviously more rapid and efficient, and senior civil servants have come to rely on the interlocking directorate of technical assistants rather than allow major decisions to be lost in the inefficiency of the regular administrative structure. Instead of coping with the difficulties of the local administration, there remains the option of just ignoring it.

In addition to the structural deficiencies of the scheme, the difficulty of promoting personal relations between French and Senegalese civil servants inhibits the growth of a good working relationship. Because Frenchmen and Senegalese were frequently found to be mutually reluctant to share an office, each preferring to work alongside a colleague of the same race, the purpose of training the Senegalese in certain skills and techniques has in fact almost been abandoned. With little pressure from Senegalese sources, the expatriate administration within an administration persists.

It is not for lack of opportunity for discussion of these problems in Senegal that they still remain important in the working situation. For several years in the mid-1960s, annual information sessions [14] or day-conferences were held in Dakar among French teachers, technical assistants and Senegalese civil servants in which an open confrontation of such problems as the ambiguity of the role of the technical assistant, the lack of established norms of behaviour (their terminology) between French and Senegalese colleagues was frankly discussed. Concern about cultural misunderstanding, mutual suspicion generated from mutual ignorance, lack of professional contact which affected the operation of the administration and the effectiveness of education were repeated in session after session. Attendance at these meetings was on a voluntary basis and, as might have been expected, those who attended were those who would have been most likely to have raised such questions with colleagues outside of a formal discussion in any case, and therefore needed it least. It seemed to

13. This practice was cited to me by a Senegalese civil servant in the Department of Rural Administration, which contains many expatriate ideologues and Senegalese 'Diaists' (followers of the Prime Minister deposed in 1961) and is generally regarded as one of the more successful combined French-Senegalese efforts.

14. They often began with the discussion of a general theme such as local traditional society, or life in Dakar, which was intended to acquaint technical assistants with aspects of the country in which they were serving (République du Sénégal, 1965–69).

be the same group on the whole who attended year after year, and although the discussions (which were roneoed and distributed at least to all technical assistance personnel afterwards) may have provided those present with an annual catharsis, it seemed to have little effect on the general structure or predominant patterns of behaviour.[15]

'It is in effect very difficult to pass concretely from a political phase of colonization to a political phase of cooperation,' as it was aptly put by the Director of Rural Administration (République du Sénégal, 1967, p. 131). In the context of the administration there remains the basic problem of interaction between two groups which have for so long known one another in a superior-subordinate framework. The basic ambiguity of the new role of technical assistant has tended to force both Frenchmen and Senegalese into behaving in terms of the residual relationship upon which the colonial service was built – the Frenchmen direct and the Senegalese are directed. One expatriate who had served in the colonial administration used it as a justification for returning to the former situation in explicit terms:

[The present system] could only be effective if the technical assistants directed things like a colonial administration. The dialogue is ill-defined and doesn't work well. It leads to confusion.

Africans can only work with Europeans if they know that they are respected and commanded at the same time.

And Senegalese informants, when asked whether technical assistants work in good rapport with local civil servants, have variously responded:

There is a superior-inferior relationship built into the mentality of each: collaboration cannot proceed at an equal level. Since there are no 'human' relations between them, there is no professional rapport.

and

The technical assistance is a common effort within 'the family'. We have the habit of working with them from colonial experience.

The colonial framework remains obviously apparent in people's thoughts. And the tendency to return to the former structure of

15. Briefing and debriefing sessions with technical assistants have also in other contexts been relatively unsatisfactory (MacBean and Morton, 1971). Very often, obviously, the repeated frustrations which the expatriate expert or technical assistant feels exist in the working context overseas seriously affect his attitude toward the job and, despite his best intentions, his effectiveness over a certain period of time.

dependence, when faced with a new and potentially ambiguous situation, is manifest in the behaviour of certain Senegalese civil servants. While a Frenchman remains close at hand, the tendency of most civil servants is to pass the responsibility to him. Often when a special project is in progress, extra hours are put in by technical assistants while the Senegalese civil servants go home. There are two independent factors which affect this situation: differing cultural views of work and of the importance of work; and the size of the Senegalese administration. Since many civil servants are superfluous to the functioning of the administration, and much of the crucial work will be done by Frenchmen anyway, there is no compunction about missing work or arriving late, and at a higher level there may be no compunction either about the deliberate confusion of public and private funds.

Personal and family loyalties remain for the Senegalese much more important than a spirit of formalistic impersonality and reward commensurate with responsibility – which are regarded as essential to an ideal-type bureaucracy (Gerth and Wright Mills, 1958, pp. 330, 341). The confusion of norms of behaviour from a modern and a traditional context largely influences the functioning of the Senegalese administration, as it does that of many other African countries. The structure was criticized by French administrators for being weak, ineffective, heavy (a French legacy), disorganized, parasitic and anti-modern (La Palombara, 1963, pp. 10, 11).[16] The majority of technical assistants interviewed were opposed to accelerated Africanization, because of the behaviour they had observed at work. The extent to which such behaviour is inevitable in the transition from a peasant to an industrial society or perpetuated by French presence (or a combination of factors) remains an open question. French aid, as most obviously manifest in the administration, is an example of development generated from outside at the cost of the improvement of the indigenous administrative structure or an adjustment of the values of the people participating in that structure. Instead of trying to come to terms with problems general to the bureaucracies of many states in Africa, the Senegalese government has postponed the problem

16. 'Insofar as public administration systems fall short of the Weberian legal-rational model, they are said not to be modern. . . . Technical assistants have a tendency to go abroad with this (the attributes of the ideal-type) intact, while we know that the respective bureaucracies of Britain and the United States (for example), when experiencing rapid economic change, conformed to the Weberian model much less than they do today.' (1963, p. 11).

by relying on French personnel. The irresponsibility of individual civil servants and the weakness of the general structure remains.

Conclusion

The preceding analysis, which is based primarily on role relationships and social interaction between Senegalese and French expatriates in the working context, is intended to examine the limitations of heavy reliance on personnel from a former colonial power in the first phase of political independence. It is intended to underline that while there are sound reasons for relying on those who are familiar with the local context through long contact and working experience, it may nonetheless be difficult to establish a framework for the transfer of skills and knowledge or the promotion of independent action in such a working environment.

The arguments presented also seek to emphasize the need to look beyond simple numbers of inputs of personnel or manpower planning in the field of technical assistance programming. It is not sufficient to look upon the inputs of knowledge and expertise which a technical assistant may bring to his job or the inputs of expert personnel without giving close attention to non-quantifiable factors. Those which are relevant in trying to evaluate such programmes include: the mode of selection of the technical assistant, his background and the non-technical qualities he brings to the job, the type of briefing and introduction he receives to his work, the clarity of the role to be performed, the amount of training for localization contained in the job and, above all perhaps, his contact and interaction with local counterparts. It would appear that certain elements outlined in the Franco-Senegalese case may be relevant also to American and British programmes. It is perhaps all too easy to dismiss the example of the French in Senegal as an 'extreme' case of continued presence from the former colonial power in terms of capital aid and private investment as well as personnel, and to situate any faults of the programme or its performance here. While the administration within an administration or the efficient operation of a technical assistance network within a vast, expanding and inefficient local bureaucratic system may not be so obvious elsewhere, the power which an individual technical assistant brings to his role in terms of experience, expertise and efficiency still remains very generally important.

It might be advisable to take a second look at the location and activity of technical assistants, given the current practice in many

African countries of expanding the civil service with school and university graduates who might otherwise be unemployed and therefore potentially dissident to the regime in power. With the growing prospect of even more unwieldy structures than exist at present and increasing inefficiency, the few expatriates who are serving in this context may thus have even greater power and authority than had been formerly the case. This would apply as well to experts on short-term contracts as others – the temptation of senior civil servants to by-pass the formal structure for the sake of efficiency is great. And while this practice in itself is likely to incur the hostility of local civil servants, their under-employment and demoralization in their work may serve to exacerbate it.

References

CHALIAND, G. (1966), 'Indépendence nationale et révolution', *Partisans*, May–June.

FIRST, R. (1970), *The Barrel of a Gun*, Allen Lane The Penguin Press.

FLIS-ZONABEND, F. (1968), *Lycéens de Dakar*, Maspero, Paris.

GERTH, H., and WRIGHT MILLS, C., (trans. and eds.) (1958), *From Max Weber*, Oxford University Press.

HAYTER, T. (1966), *French Aid*, The Overseas Development Institute Ltd.

ISS (Institute for Strategic Studies) (1970), *Military Balance*, London.

JEANNENEY REPORT (1963), *La politique de coopération. Avec les pays en voie de développement:* Rapport d'Étude, Instituté par le décret du 12 Mars 1963, Rép. de France, Ministère d'Etat Chargé de la Réforme Administrative. Remis au Gouvernement le 18 Juillet, 1963.

LA PALOMBARA, J. (1963), *Bureaucracy and Political Development*, Princeton University Press.

LENTIN, A. P. (1966), 'La situation de la minorité européenne en Algérie', *Le Mois en Afrique* (Revue Française d'Etudes Politiques Africaines), December 1966.

MACBEAN, A. I., and MORTON K. (1971), *Draft Report on Survey of* (British) *Technical Assistance Experts*, University of Lancaster, April, roneo.

MADDISON, A. (1965), *Foreign Skills and Technical Assistance in Economic Development*, Development Centre of the Organization for Economic Cooperation and Development.

RÉPUBLIQUE DU SÉNÉGAL (1965–69), *Sessions d'information du personnel d'assistance technique*, Dakar, Ministère d'Enseignement Technique et de la Formation des Cadres, Centre National de Formation et d'Action, roneo.

SAXE, J. (1960), *The Legacy of Britain and France in West Africa*, Harvard University Center for International Affairs, October.

TRIBOULET REPORT (1964), *Cinq ans de fonds d'aide et de coopération* (1959–64). Rép. de France, Ministère de la Coopération. Rapport presenté par H. R. Triboulet, Ministre délegué, chargé de la Coopération, 9 Avril.

20 N. Girvan and O. Jefferson*

Corporate *v.* Caribbean Integration

N. Girvan and O. Jefferson, 'Corporate *v.* Caribbean integration',
New World Quarterly, Jamaica, vol. 4, no. 2, 1968, pp. 45–56.

The ends of integration

The economic integration of a region comprising a number of
politically separate units, has come to be seen by many 'poor'
countries as necessary to their economic development. The gains
from integration are normally taken to be two-fold: the realization of economies of large-scale production and of specialization
by location. This is based on a concept of economic development
which identifies its most important aspect as the growth of manufacturing industry, and its most important index as the growth of
per capita income. On the further assumption that the most
important obstacle to the growth of manufacturing is the smallness of domestic markets, economic integration becomes a
natural out-growth of development strategy. For, the argument
runs, the widening of the market which is brought about by the
freeing of tariff and quota restrictions on trade within the region,
permits higher levels of regional output, at lower real production
costs. In that sense, current ideas of the ends of integration are
conditioned by current concepts of the process of economic
development.

We wish, however, to relate the ends of integration to a concept
of economic development which is defined *qualitatively* rather
than *quantitatively*. The economic development of any political
or geographic unit is a process by which the inhabitants continuously and creatively manipulate the natural environment for the
satisfaction of the material needs. Like the Burmese economist,
Hla Myint, we place emphasis on the existence of a balance
between 'wants' and 'activities' over time in the community.
The single most important characteristic of 'poor' countries is
the widening gap, not so much between the rich countries and

* The authors are both in the Department of Economics at the University
of the West Indies, Jamaica Campus. Girvan is Chairman and Jefferson
Treasurer of New World Group Ltd.

themselves, as between the material aspirations of their inhabitants and their ability to fulfill them.

Secondly, we wish to avoid the use of average income per person as the index of development. For one thing, economies can 'grow' without 'developing' as Demas has pointed out.[1] More important, average per capita income says nothing about its distribution. Most important of all it says nothing about the degree to which the population participates in, and controls its economic life. Many poor countries have exhibited growing total and per capita incomes with a decreasing degree of popular participation in economic activity and control. Insofar as the end of economic development is a growth in human welfare then this might be called progress only for those social segments enjoying a growth in income, and even that might be questioned. We focus instead on changes in the degree of popular participation in meaningful economic activity; and in the ability of the society and its constituent productive units to organize the economy for the satisfaction of the material needs of *all* individuals.

Third, we lay stress on the role of technology in the process of development. But technology is never developed and applied in a vacuum. For our purposes, what is important is that technological development takes place within the context of an economic organization which ensures first, that it transforms whatever materials the economy has into productive resources; and second, that the gains from technological progress accrue to the national economy.

A development process defined in this way is, of course, difficult to invest with specific quantitative indices. But there will nonetheless be observable changes. For one thing, there will be a growth in the proportion of the population involved in economic activity characterized by growing output per man and rising income over time. Secondly, there will be significant increases in the degree of utilization of natural and human resources and the existing stock of technical knowledge. Finally, we would expect

1. W. Demas (1965) argued that 'enclave' economies with a highly capitalized, high-value export sector (mineral or plantation) can 'grow' without 'developing'. Development he defines as a process of self-sustaining growth, and is characterized by a substantial growth of inter-industry transactions, in the economy's capacity to respond to adverse exogenous economic changes, and in its ability to develop and apply innovations to the production structure (pp. 8–10).

to see the emergence of more rational systems of resource allocation in the most important sectors of the economy.

If the development process is seen in this way then schemes of collaboration and economic integration between politically separate units also become an important part of the development strategy, but on a somewhat different reasoning. To be sure, the pooling of markets to exploit economies of scale and locational specialization will be one of the economies of integration, but not the only or even the most important one. A second important economy will arise where there are complementarities of *input* in the use of natural and technical resources. McIntyre has called this Resource Combination. Thus, where one country has deposits of iron ore, another sources of cheap power, another the potential for natural or synthetic rubber production and another a certain stock of engineering skills; then all four could be used for the establishment of an earth-moving and transport equipment industry that none of the countries alone could have initiated. In traditional neo-classical economics, of course, such economies are realized by freeing the movement of goods, labour and capital between the countries. But later we advance reasons for believing that prevailing systems of resource allocation in Latin America and the Caribbean would tend to inhibit the realization of such economies even in the event of a liberalization of trade and factor movements.

This brings us to a third economy of integration in the context of a development process as outlined above. An attempt to rationalize methods of resource allocation from the point of view of national and regional objectives will undoubtedly encounter resistance from the existing institutions of resource allocation, which often have quite other objectives. In certain sectors, such as agriculture and distribution, these institutions may be domestically based while in others, such as mining, manufacture and finance, they are more likely to be international in character and based in the metropolitan countries. And in a world where the balance of economic and military power is heavily on the side of these metropolitan countries a development strategy of the 'poor' countries which runs contrary to the interests of the 'rich' ones may be expected to encounter enormous difficulties. Thus the pooling of the individual bargaining powers of the former may be essential to the rationalization of their *internal* production structures and constitutes perhaps the decisive reason for integration.

Within the context of such strategies of development and of regional integration, the possible gains from schemes of collaboration and economic integration between the Caribbean and Latin America may be significant. The question will be asked, why then is there so little economic contact between the two areas? It is the answer which we wish now to explore.

Latin America–Caribbean economic relations
Official trading arrangements

Apart from imports of crude petroleum and petroleum products from Venezuela and Colombia trade between the Caribbean and Latin America is minimal. On the basis of data for the latest available year for Barbados, Guyana, British Honduras, Jamaica and Trinidad and Tobago, petroleum accounted for more than 90 per cent of total imports from Latin America. In none of these countries do imports from Latin America, other than petroleum, account for more than 3 per cent of total imports. The situation in other Caribbean countries is not markedly different.

Imports other than petroleum involve only a limited range of foodstuffs and raw materials. Among these are meat from Argentina and Uruguay, timber from Nicaragua and Honduras, beans from Chile and Mexico, animal feed from Argentina and leather from Uruguay. Imports of manufactured goods are insignificant. These consist mainly of occasional purchases of machinery, transport equipment and cement from Venezuela, cotton yarn and thread from Colombia and manufactures of silver from Mexico.

On the export side Guyana has been selling small quantities of bauxite to Argentina, Colombia and Mexico, while Jamaica occasionally exports alumina to Brazil. Trinidad and Tobago is the most important exporter. She sells petroleum products to Brazil, Chile and Central America as well as small quantities of ammonium sulphate and clothing to Central America and Venezuela, respectively. But even in the case of Trinidad and Tobago exports to all of Latin America account for less than 3 per cent of total exports.

The relatively low level of trade between the Caribbean and Latin America stems in part from competing production in the two areas. This has been accentuated by preferential agreements which have tended to tie Caribbean territories to a metropolis. Almost every Caribbean country is involved in some such relationship – Puerto Rico with the United States of America; the Commonwealth Caribbean with the United Kingdom; Martinique, Guadeloupe and French Guiana with France; Surinam and the Netherlands Antilles with the Netherlands; Cuba with the Soviet Union.

Even if the preferential agreements associated with these relationships were based on a historical comparative advantage that has by now largely disappeared, while such agreements undoubtedly enable the factors of production engaged in the favoured industries to earn higher rewards than would otherwise obtain they tend to perpetuate a pattern of resource use which inhibits the ability of the economy to make much-needed adjustments. They also inhibit economic cooperation both within the Caribbean area, and between the Caribbean and Latin America.

Integration arrangements

Integration movements within the region have so far been concentrated within Latin America in the form of the Latin American Free Trade Association (LAFTA) and the Central American Common Market (CACM) which have been in existence for some years. The only Caribbean country to have attempted to link up with either of these movements has been Cuba. That country's application was rejected by LAFTA in 1962 on the ground that her economic system was incompatible with the treaty establishing the association, though the precise nature of the incompatibility was not stated.

It is instructive to look at the progress of the existing Latin American integration movements since such an exercise sheds light on some of the problems which would arise from attempts to foster Caribbean–Latin American integration through similar means.

Latin American Free Trade Association

The Latin American Free Trade Association which came into existence in 1960, embraces Mexico and the whole of South America with the exception of Bolivia, Guyana, Surinam and French Guiana. Venezuela was not one of the original signatories to the treaty but after years of hesitation she finally joined in 1966. The Treaty of Montevideo which embodies the ideals of the association expresses the belief that the widening of the market resulting from the liberalization of trade between the member countries would stimulate a better utilization of the available factors of production and facilitate the development of new enterprises. The original aim was to eliminate all duties and restrictions on 'substantially all their reciprocal trade' over a twelve year period.

The participating countries differ widely with regard to their economic character. Brazil, Mexico, Argentina and Venezuela have attained a relatively advanced stage of industrial development. Close behind, though with special characteristics of their own, come Chile and Colombia. At the other extreme are countries such as Ecuador and Paraguay. Because of this disparity in levels of development and the fear of polarization various provisions were inserted in the treaty to attempt to deal with the special problems of the less developed countries. These provisions did not calm the fears of Bolivia which has remained outside the grouping.

Trade between South American countries has always been modest partly because of the lack of a variety of saleable products and the absence of adequate communications. The Andes are a formidable barrier between the nations to the East and West. Practically no east–west roads or railways are existent. Until recently trade has also been impeded by high protective tariffs on many products in most countries and by the instability and heterogeneity of exchange rates. Despite liberalization in recent years only about 10 per cent of the LAFTA's trade is internal. Furthermore, the available data suggest that because of duplication of manufacturing enterprises throughout the area the bulk of the intra-regional commodity flows consists of the traditional exchange of foodstuffs and other primary commodities.

It is now generally acknowledged that progress towards integration within LAFTA has not been as spectacular as had been hoped. President Frei of Chile appears to have summed up the general feeling quite adequately when he stated in 1965 that 'the advance towards economic integration has been slow and cumbersome. The possibilities of making further headway under the present system of minutely detailed tariff negotiations would seem to be exhausted'.

Some observers have indicated that the slow progress is due at least partially to the lack of automaticity with regard to reductions in trade barriers. It is doubtful, however, whether the mere reduction or elimination of customs tariffs would suffice to promote expeditious integration of certain key industries such as steel, petrochemicals, pulp and paper, capital goods, motor vehicles and metal-transforming industries.

In view of the fact that the stage of easy import substitution has been passed in the more advanced Latin American countries there is urgent need for a regional investment policy designed to cope with the technically complex industries requiring large investments and a sizeable market. There is also need to define more precisely, in the light of experience, the principle of special treatment for the relatively less developed countries and the procedures to correct the dislocation that could emerge for the liberation of intra-regional trade. Institutional reform is a necessary, though by no means sufficient step if economic integration within LAFTA is to be accelerated.

The experience of the Central American Common Market has been somewhat different. This grouping which includes Costa Rica, El Salvador, Guatemala, Honduras and Nicaragua has achieved the most advanced state of economic integration between developing countries, and can offer useful lessons to countries setting out on a similar path. Beginning in 1950 as a network of bilateral free trade agreements, it had by 1958 crystallized into a multilateral free-trade area. In 1960, the basis for integrated regional development was laid down with the creation of the common market and a number of institutions and mechanisms designed to co-ordinate the activities of the five member countries.

Some indication of the success of the integration movement can be gained by observing the trend of regional trade. This accounted for about 15 per cent of the global trade of the area in 1965, compared to 3·5 per cent in 1950 and 8 per cent in 1961. At present it accounts for about 5 per cent of the gross domestic product of the area compared to 2 per cent in 1961. It is significant that the most dynamic element in regional trade has been manufactured goods indicating the strength of regional industrialization for import substitution.

The institutional infrastructure has been one of the most critical factors making for the relative success of economic integration in Central America and should be of particular interest to other developing countries contemplating integration. In this regard the pivotal institution has been the Secretariat of the Integration Treaty (SIECA). This provides co-ordinating services for the common market, as well as being the secretariat for the Economic Council, composed of the Ministers of Economy of the participating states. Other institutions such as the Advanced School of Public Administration, the Central American Institute for Industrial Research and Technology, and the Central American Bank for Economic Integration have helped to foster the development of a regional approach, and to provide important services for easing the transition towards an integrated economy.

A noteworthy feature of Central American integration is the serious attempt made to avoid inequality in the gains realized by the participating countries. It was feared that in the absence of specific controls new industries would gravitate towards El Salvador where industrial development is most advanced. As a consequence the Agreement on the Regime for Central American Integrative Industries provides that manufacturing plants requiring access to the entire Central American Market as a condition of reasonable efficiency may be designated as 'integration industries'. The products of such plants receive the privilege of immediate free entry into all five countries while any plants established outside the agreed programme would become subject to the usual duties, and receive free entry only at the end of the transitional period. No one country can acquire a second 'integration' industry until all the others have at least one.

Fiscal incentives to industries have already been unified by the Central American countries. The objective has been to prevent competition for new investment from becoming too fierce with the establishment of free trade, thus giving rise to unnecessary income losses and an uneven and uneconomic pattern of industrial development in the area.

There are many problems still to be overcome. Transport costs are high because of mountain and forest barriers which render communication difficult in some areas. Policies regarding labour mobility and the national jurisdictional status of multinational companies whose services are used in several republics still have to be worked out. Nevertheless Central America is irrevocably committed to full economic integration.

The achievement of this aim will not, however, remove the needs for Central America to forge links with larger markets outside since her regional market may not be large enough to ensure the optimum use of her forest and mining resources. At one time it was hoped that an early link between LAFTA and CACM would have been possible but the lagging pace of integration in the former has cast doubts on the possibilities of such a union in the near future.

Obstacles to Caribbean–Latin American integration

It was noted earlier that the existing low level of trade between the Caribbean and Latin America is due in part to competing production. This applies both to primary commodities and light manufactures. The situation has been aggravated by trade barriers on both sides involving both high tariffs and non-tariffs barriers. Furthermore, as McIntyre has pointed out, it might not be easy for either side to ease current restrictions on imports of light manufactured goods especially on textiles and clothing. In Central America cotton fabrics and clothing were among the commodities accorded slower rates of liberalization in the General Treaty of Economic Integration and similar treatment was extended to textiles in the programme of LAFTA.

But even if trade restrictions could be dismantled further problems would beset Caribbean–Latin American trade in the short run. In the first place, there would be the usual problems involved in breaking into a new market with different specifications and tastes. A tremendous promotional campaign would be called for. Second, high transport costs and in some cases absence of transport facilities would severely hamper the flow of trade. For example, communications with the Pacific coast in proximity to which most of the large Central American consuming centres are located are relatively underdeveloped. In South America even Guyana which borders on Brazil is virtually cut off through lack of transport facilities from the large consuming centres in the south of that country. The markets of Argentina, Paraguay and Uruguay are similarly largely inaccessible. The transport problem which, as we have seen, also affects the pace of integration within Central and South America can be solved only in the long run through massive infra-structural investment by the countries concerned. It must be stressed, however, that the full potential for trade between the Caribbean and Latin America cannot be realized merely by removing tariff barriers and improving transportation facilities. This can be done only through a deliberate process of planning aimed at exploiting in a rational way the complementary resources of the areas. In the next section we discuss some institutional factors which have so far inhibited structural integration of the two regions.

Resource allocation in the private sector

In effect, the preferential trading arrangements between each Caribbean country and its metropolitan partner reflects the historical concept of the Caribbean economies as being counterparts of the temperate countries. In the past century certain institutions of a private nature have emerged linking the Caribbean and Latin America alike even more firmly, and in a dynamic manner, with the metropolitan economies, especially the United States. These institutions are the multinational corporations.

For our purposes the salient feature of the multinational corporation (MNC) is the integration of its activities, involving segments of the economies of a large number of different countries, within the frontiers of a single decision-making machinery. The goal of the MNC is the maximization of profit in the long run, but this goal often resolves itself into a number of proximate objectives such as the maintenance of existing, and the capture of new raw material sources, and of markets; and a high rate of technological progress in the fields of process and product innovation.

The operations of MNCs may actually conceal certain *existing* economic relationships between the Caribbean and Latin America. In the previous section we mentioned the low volume and narrow range of trade between the two regions. What is not brought out by those figures is the extent to which the resources of each region reach the other in a more finished form *via* processing plants in the United States. For example in 1962 Latin America imported 60,000 tons of aluminium, the bulk of its requirements, from the United States and Canada. But the United States and Canada in turn import nine-tenths of the raw materials needed to make aluminium from the Caribbean. That is to say, North American-based multinational corporations, four in number, mine and treat bauxite in the Caribbean, and transfer the material to processing plants in the United States and Canada. Part of the output of aluminium and semi-finished aluminium products is then exported to Latin America.

On the other side, a substantial portion of Latin America's output of metal ores is exported to the United States. This is the case for such commodities as Mexican iron ore, manganese, fluorspar, lead, zinc and asbestos; Chilean copper; Venezuelan petroleum and iron ore; Peruvian copper, lead and zinc; and Brazilian manganese. In turn, these materials provide a significant portion of total US supplies, and the bulk of US imports of these materials from Latin America takes the form of imports by parent companies from their branches and subsidiaries in the area. To complete the circuit, some 37 per cent of the imports of metal manufactures, and machinery and transport equipment, by the four largest Commonwealth Caribbean territories is supplied by the United States. Thus to some extent, the resources of Latin America participate in the development of the Caribbean through the channels of the MNC and via the American economy.

The significance of this is three-fold. Firstly, it indicates that there are significant economic relations between the two regions which are hidden by the multinational corporations. Moreover, it suggests that the existing competitiveness of the production structures of the two regions is no guide to their potential complementarity. But what is perhaps most important is that the product and commodity flows are not so much between economies, as between one plant and another, within the multinational corporations and their own marketing agencies. Thus, intra-corporate commodity transfers between plants located within different countries may satisfy the formal criteria of international trade, but so far as resource allocation is concerned, the flows are of an internal character within frontiers which are institutionally, not politically, defined.

The consequence of the high degree of mobility within the company must be a certain degree of rigidity so far as intra-regional product and capital flows between companies are concerned. For example, the MNC with raw material facilities and processing capacity will not normally purchase raw materials from another producer. For in the first place, the cost of purchase from another producer will be in some sense at a market value which includes profit, while the material is obtained from their own subsidiary at production cost. Secondly, the opportunity cost of purchasing from another producer will be the lower utilization of capacity in the subsidiary. In other words, one of the elements of a profit-maximization policy for an MNC is the fullest possible utilization of capacity in all its vertically and horizontally integrated activities. The result is that while there is a premium on intra-company product and factor flows there is a rigidity in product and factor flows between companies producing similar sets of commodities, whether these companies are producing in the same region or in the same country, or not.

Thus *corporate integration* can, and often does, result in *regional fragmentation*. This fragmentation does not only occur between the two regions, as we have already suggested. The experience of the Caribbean with its bauxite industry suggests that fragmentation can take place within a given region and even within one country. Thus that part of the bauxite output of Jamaica and Guyana which is produced by Reynolds Metals, the US aluminium producer, reaches the fledgeling aluminium smelting industry of Venezuela after being shipped to the US and manufactured into alumina at Reynolds' plants. It is then re-exported to the South American mainland, in spite of the fact that Guyana borders on Venezuela, and Jamaica is also nearer to that country than the United States. Conversely, Reynolds' bauxite output in Guyana and Jamaica has not so far been available to the existing processing capacity in both countries because this capacity is owned by a different company.

It is interesting to examine in this light the experience of Latin American countries in attempting import-substitution industrialization. Countries such as Brazil and Mexico have had some success in replacing finished consumer goods. But difficulties encountered in attempting to extend this to the stages of intermediate and capital goods has meant that the pace of import-substituting growth has slackened considerably. The area therefore continues to be a major exporter of basic materials, and a major importer of capital and intermediate goods.

The reason is often held to be the fact that economies of scale are most important for capital and intermediate goods, and that the smallness of national markets in Latin America cannot support these secondary and tertiary stages of industrialization. It should, however, be noted that the standard pattern for import-substitution in the area has been the persuasion of US firms to locate plants in the area for the service of national markets. Many of these ventures are undertaken in partnership with local capital but normally the US firm (usually an MNC) supplies the technique, the brand name, the management, the physical equipment and the materials. And it is noteworthy that in 1964 of the total US exports to foreign manufacturing affiliates of US firms in Latin America, 57 per cent (US $400 million) consisted of parent-company exports to affiliates of materials 'for processing or assembly' and of 'capital equipment for investment use'! The largest items in the former category were transport equipment, chemicals, food products and electrical machinery.

Such factors suggest that the size of the markets for intermediate and capital goods is limited not only by the national boundaries but also by corporate frontiers. Thus where a country has set up three car-assembly plants under the aegis of Ford, General

Motors and Renault the 'market' for motor-vehicle components is split in three, one to each parent company; and is further fragmented by a certain degree of product differentiation and the built-in propensity (often cemented with specific contractual arrangements) for each subsidiary to purchase from its parent.

When considered in conjunction with the fact that the bulk of Latin America's exports of basic materials consists of intra-corporate flows, this factor gives us a clue to understanding the resilience of the traditional pattern for Latin America to export primary products and import manufactures. For where raw material output in Latin America is institutionally linked to processing capacity in the metropolis, and where assembly in the area is institutionally linked to supply in the metropolis, the pattern of economic activity and of international trade and capital flows assumes a degree of permanence which the liberalization of trade barriers, by itself, cannot break. For both the Caribbean and Latin America such a framework of resource allocation works so as to systematically divorce their resources from their needs, and to integrate their resources with the needs of the North American industrial complex. The limited import-substitution achieved by the two regions so far consists in essence merely of the relocation of a part of the incremental terminal assembly facilities of the MNCs within the hemisphere.[2]

It has been suggested that the most important aspect of economic development in the production structure is the continuous substitution of domestic output for imported output in incremental supplies; that this process is most important for intermediate and capital goods; and that it is marked by substantial growth of interindustry interdependence within the national economy. Clearly, the structure of the MNC with its vertically integrated links with the metropolis inhibits the growth of such industrial interdependence within the national and regional economies. Equally, this structure makes for growing inter-activity interdependence within the *corporate* economy. One of the characteristics of the growth of today's large firms is the continuous extension of the production frontier into produced inputs and elaborated outputs: the former being the equivalent of the substitution of domestic for imported output in the national economy. And insofar as the bulk of processing facilities are already in the metropolitan economy it is natural

2. For a strategy of planned integration of incremental output for the Caribbean, see Brewster and Thomas (n.d.).

that the extensions of the production frontiers will take place there.

This also helps to explain why the direction of technological progress tends not to be to the advantage of the Caribbean and Latin America. Naturally, firms and governments which face a growing dependence on foreign sources for important materials will have a strong incentive to look for substitutes more readily and reliably available. Part of the rapid emergence of synthetic materials in the United States, for example, can be seen as the substitution of domestic technology for imported natural resources. The tendency for the growth of demand for some of the regions' exported raw materials (as distinct from agricultural products) to be less than the growth of income of the consuming industrial nations can be seen as the logical result of the organization of technological research. The needs of the two regions lie rather in the direction of a larger utilization of domestic resources for the satisfaction of domestic needs. The present organization sets up a built-in incentive for the replacement of the regions' resources by metropolitan resources. Moreover in so far as it is metropolitan capacity which satisfies the bulk of the regions' needs for finished goods, and metropolitan technology which makes available the range of production possibilities, then there is also a built-in propensity for the satisfaction of the regions' needs to be based on imported resources, technological and human as well as natural.

Some conclusions

If the development strategy for both the Caribbean and Latin America is to be the use of domestic resources for the satisfaction of domestic needs in a dynamic manner, then the gains from schemes of integration between the two regions can be considered in this context. Such a strategy would be four-pronged: the rationalization of the methods of use of principal natural resources, the reorganization of technology and the use of human resources, an emphasis on the role of capital and intermediate goods industries using domestic resources and the re-orienting of economic infrastructure to service the new pattern of commodity flows. Regional integration in a general sense could be an important part of such a development strategy by pooling natural resources and thereby realizing economies of resource complementarity; by the pooling of technology, the technological research effort and the use of human technical skills, and above all, by combining economic and political bargaining power.

The precise gains from integrating the two regions could only be established after institutional changes designed to discover the actual empirical possibilities. Yet at this stage we would be sufficiently bold as to guess at some of the gains from both points of view. To the Caribbean, the potential advantages of schemes of structural integration with Latin America are immediately obvious: access to a region whose size and potential offer the chance of absorbing enormous commodity flows in volume and in range; and whose resource products, under alternative systems of resource use, might be made available to the area at lower real costs than at present.

To Latin America, the possible gains are less obvious in that the physical smallness of the Caribbean means that the latter's market may never be more than marginal to the continental output. But at the outset we can think of at least two factors which the archipelago could bring to the continent. The first is a stock of natural resources which, although narrow in range, is considerable in volume. Caribbean countries and countries bordering on the Caribbean sea contain over 90 per cent of the hemisphere's reserves of bauxite; and the world's largest reserves of laterites. Thus the area could perhaps help provide the resource base for a large continental metallurgical industry involving steel and aluminium, the world's two leading metals.

A second possible advantage to Latin America from schemes of integration with the Caribbean arises out of the fact that every major metropolitan culture is represented in the area: Britain, France, Holland, the United States and recently the Soviet Union. In the past, the metropolitan connections have reduced the area to the role of appendages to big powers. But in the future if the selective use of the fund of technology developed in the advanced world will be a necessary part of Caribbean–Latin American economic restructuring, then the Caribbean links with the metropolis in language and educational systems may be turned to good advantage, even as the traditional economic relationships are changed.

It goes without saying that it will only be possible to move from the general to the particular when specific research projects on schemes of integration between the two regions are set up.

References

BREWSTER, H., and THOMAS, C. (n.d.), 'The dynamics of West Indian economic integration'. University of the West Indies.

DEMAS, W. (1965), *The Economics of Development with Special Reference to the Caribbean*, McGill.

21 I. Illich

Outwitting the 'Developed' Countries

I. Illich, 'Outwitting the "developed" countries', *New York Review of Books*, 6 November 1969, pp. 20–24.

It is now common to demand that the rich nations convert their war machine into a program for the development of the Third World. The poorer four-fifths of humanity multiply unchecked while their per capita consumption actually declines. This population expansion and decrease of consumption threaten the industrialized nations, who may still, as a result, convert their defense budgets to the economic pacification of poor nations. And this in turn could produce irreversible despair, because the plows of the rich can do as much harm as their swords. US trucks can do more lasting damage than US tanks. It is easier to create mass demand for the former than for the latter. Only a minority needs heavy weapons, while a majority can become dependent on unrealistic levels of supply for such productive machines as modern trucks. Once the Third World has become a mass market for the goods, products and processes which are designed by the rich for themselves, the discrepancy between demand for these Western artifacts and the supply will increase indefinitely. The family car cannot drive the poor into the jet age, nor can a school system provide the poor with education, nor can the family icebox ensure healthy food for them.

It is evident that only one man in a thousand in Latin America can afford a Cadillac, a heart operation or a Ph.D. This restriction on the goals of development does not make us despair of the fate of the Third World, and the reason is simple. We have not yet come to conceive of a Cadillac as necessary for good transportation, or of a heart operation as normal healthy care, or of a Ph.D. as the prerequisite of an acceptable education. In fact, we recognize at once that the importation of Cadillacs should be heavily taxed in Peru, that an organ transplant clinic is a scandalous plaything to justify the concentration of more doctors in Bogotá, and that a Betatron is beyond the teaching facilities of the University of São Paulo.

Unfortunately, it is not held to be universally evident that the majority of Latin Americans – not only of our generation, but also of the next and the next again – cannot afford any kind of automobile, or any kind of hospitalization, or for that matter an elementary school education. We suppress our consciousness of this obvious reality because we hate to recognize the corner into which our imagination has been pushed. So persuasive is the power of the institutions we have created that they shape not only our preferences, but actually our sense of possibilities. We have forgotten how to speak about modern transportation that does not rely on automobiles and airplanes. Our conceptions of modern health care emphasize our ability to prolong the lives of the desperately ill. We have become unable to think of better education except in terms of more complex schools and of teachers trained for ever longer periods. Huge institutions producing costly services dominate the horizons of our inventiveness.

We have embodied our world view into our institutions and are now their prisoners. Factories, news media, hospitals, governments and schools produce goods and services packaged to contain our view of the world. We – the rich – conceive of progress as the expansion of these establishments. We conceive of heightened mobility as luxury and safety packaged by General Motors or Boeing. We conceive of improving the general well-being as increasing the supply of doctors and hospitals, which package health along with protracted suffering. We have come to identify our need for further learning with the demand for ever longer confinement to classrooms. In other words, we have packaged education with custodial care, certification for jobs, and the right to vote, and wrapped them all together with indoctrination in the Christian, liberal or communist virtues.

In less than a hundred years industrial society has molded patent solutions to basic human needs and converted us to the belief that man's needs were shaped by the Creator as demands for the products we have invented. This is as true for Russia and Japan as for the North Atlantic community. The consumer is trained for obsolescence, which means continuing loyalty toward the same producers who will give him the same basic packages in different quality or new wrappings.

Industrialized societies can provide such packages for personal consumption for most of their citizens, but this is no proof that these societies are sane, or economical, or that they promote life. The contrary is true. The more the citizen is trained in the consumption of packaged goods and services the less effective he seems to become in shaping his environment. His energies and finances are consumed in procuring ever new models of his staples, and the environment becomes a by-product of his own consumption habits.

The design of the 'package deals' of which I speak is the main cause of the high cost of satisfying basic needs. So long as every man 'needs' his car, our cities must endure longer traffic jams and absurdly expensive remedies to relieve them. So long as health means maximum length of survival, our sick will get ever more extraordinary surgical interventions and the drugs required to deaden their consequent pain. So long as we want to use school to get children out of their parents' hair or to keep them off the street and out of the labor force, our young will be retained in endless schooling and will need ever-increasing incentives to endure the ordeal.

Rich nations now benevolently impose a straitjacket of traffic jams, hospital confinements and classrooms on the poor nations, and by international agreement call this 'development'. The rich and schooled and old of the world try to share their dubious blessings by foisting their pre-packaged solutions on to the Third World. Traffic jams develop in São Paulo, while almost a million northeastern Brazilians flee the drought by walking 500 miles. Latin American doctors get training at the New York Hospital for Special Surgery, which they apply to only a few, while amoebic dysentery remains endemic in slums where 90 per cent of the population live. A tiny minority gets advanced education in basic science in North America – not infrequently paid for by their own governments. If they return at all to Bolivia, they become second-rate teachers of pretentious subjects at La Paz or Cochibamba. The rich export outdated versions of their standard models.

The Alliance for Progress is a good example of benevolent production for underdevelopment. Contrary to its slogans, it did succeed – as an alliance for the progress of the consuming classes, and for the domestication of the Latin American masses. The Alliance has been a major step in modernizing the consumption patterns of the middle classes in South America by integrating them with the dominant culture of the North American metropolis. At the same time, the Alliance has modernized the aspirations of the majority of citizens and fixed their demands on unavailable products.

Each car which Brazil puts on the road denies fifty people good transportation by bus. Each merchandised refrigerator reduces the chance of building a community freezer. 'Every dollar spent in Latin America on doctors and hospitals costs a hundred lives', to adopt a phrase of Jorge de Ahumada, the brilliant Chilean economist. Had each dollar been spent on providing safe drinking water, a hundred lives could have been saved. Each dollar spent on schooling means more privileges for the few at the cost of the many; at best it increases the number of those who, before dropping out, have been taught that those who stay longer have earned the right to more power, wealth and prestige. What such schooling does is to teach the schooled the superiority of the better schooled.

All Latin American countries are frantically intent on expanding their school systems. No country now spends less than the equivalent of 18 per cent of tax-derived public income on education – which means schooling – and many countries spend almost double that. But even with these huge investments, no country yet succeeds in giving five full years of education to more than one-third of its population; supply and demand for schooling grow geometrically apart. And what is true about schooling is equally true about the products of most institutions in the process of modernization in the Third World.

Continued technological refinements of products which are already established on the market frequently benefit the producer far more than the consumer. The more complex production processes tend to enable only the largest producer to continually replace outmoded models, and to focus the demand of the consumer on the marginal improvement of what he buys, no matter what the concomitant side effects: higher prices, diminished life span, less general usefulness, higher cost of repairs. Think of the multiple uses for a simple can opener, whereas an electric one, if it works at all, opens only some kinds of cans, and costs one hundred times as much.

This is equally true for a piece of agricultural machinery and for an academic degree. The midwestern farmer can become convinced of his need for a four-axle vehicle which can go 70 m.p.h. on the highways, has an electric windshield wiper and upholstered seats, and can be turned in for a new one within a year or two. Most of the world's farmers don't need such speed, nor have they ever met with such comfort, nor are they interested in obsolescence. They need low-priced transport, in a world where time is not money, where manual wipers suffice, and where a piece of heavy equipment should outlast a generation. Such a mechanical donkey requires entirely different engineering and design than one produced for the US market. This vehicle is not in production.

Most of South America needs para-medical workers who can function for indefinite periods without the supervision of an MD. Instead of establishing a process to train midwives and visiting healers who know how to use a very limited arsenal of medicines while working independently, Latin American universities establish every year a new school of specialized nursing or nursing administration to prepare professionals who can function only in a hospital, and pharmacists who know how to sell increasingly more dangerous drugs.

The world is reaching an impasse where two processes converge: ever more men have fewer basic choices. The increase in population is widely publicized and creates panic. The decrease in fundamental choice causes anguish and is consistently overlooked. The population explosion overwhelms the imagination, but the progressive atrophy of social imagination is rationalized as an increase of choice between brands. The two processes converge in a dead end: the population explosion provides more consumers for everything from food to contraceptives, while our shrinking imagination can conceive of no other ways of satisfying their demands except through the packages now on sale in the admired societies.

I will focus successively on these two factors, since, in my opinion, they form the two coordinates which together permit us to define underdevelopment.

In most Third World countries, the population grows, and so does the middle class. Income, consumption and the well-being of the middle class are all growing while the gap between this class and the mass of people widens. Even where per capita consumption is rising, the majority of men have less food now than in 1945, less actual care in sickness, less meaningful work, less protection. This is partly a consequence of polarized consumption and partly caused by the breakdown of traditional family and culture. More people suffered from hunger, pain and exposure in 1969 than they did at the end of the Second World War, not only numerically, but also as a percentage of the world population.

These concrete consequences of underdevelopment are rampant; but underdevelopment is also a state of mind, and understanding it as a state of mind, or as a form of consciousness, is the critical problem. Underdevelopment as a state of mind occurs when mass needs are converted to the demand for new brands of packaged solutions which are forever beyond the reach of the majority. Underdevelopment in this sense is rising rapidly even in countries where the supply of classrooms, calories, cars and clinics is also rising. The ruling groups in these countries build up services which have been designed for an affluent culture; once they have monopolized demand in this way, they can never satisfy majority needs.

Underdevelopment as a form of consciousness is an extreme result of what we can call in the language of both Marx and Freud '*Verdinglichung*' or reification. By reification I mean the hardening of the perception of real needs into the demand for mass manufactured products. I mean the translation of thirst into the need for a Coke. This kind of reification occurs in the manipulation of primary human needs by vast bureaucratic organizations which have succeeded in dominating the imagination of potential consumers.

Let me return to my example taken from the field of education. The intense promotion of schooling leads to so close an identification of school attendance and education that in everyday language the two terms are interchangeable. Once the imagination of an entire population has been 'schooled', or indoctrinated to believe that school has a 'monopoly on formal education, then the illiterate can be taxed to provide free high school and university education for the children of the rich.

Underdevelopment is the result of rising levels of aspiration achieved through the intensive marketing of 'patent' products. In this sense, the dynamic underdevelopment that is now taking place is the exact opposite of what I believe education to be: namely, the awakening awareness of new levels of human potential and the use of one's creative powers to foster human life. Underdevelopment, however, implies the surrender of social consciousness to pre-packaged solutions.

The process by which the marketing of 'foreign' products increases underdevelopment is frequently understood in the most superficial ways. The same man who feels indignation at the sight of a Coca-Cola plant in a Latin American slum often feels pride at the sight of a new normal school growing up alongside. He resents the evidence of a foreign 'license' attached to a soft drink which he would like to see replaced by 'Cola-Mex'. But the same man is willing to impose schooling – at all costs – on his fellow citizens, and is unaware of the invisible license by which this institution is deeply enmeshed in the world market.

Some years ago I watched workmen putting up a sixty-foot Coca-Cola sign on a desert plain in the Mexquital. A serious drought and famine had just swept over the Mexican highland. My host, a poor Indian in Ixmiquilpan, had just offered his visitors a tiny tequila glass of the costly black sugar-water. When I recall this scene I still feel anger; but I feel much more incensed when I remember UNESCO meetings at which well-meaning and well-paid bureaucrats seriously discussed Latin American curricula, and when I think of the speeches of enthusiastic liberals advocating the need for more schools.

The fraud perpetrated by the salesmen of schools is less obvious but much more fundamental than the self-satisfied salesmanship of the Coca-Cola or Ford representative, because the schoolman hooks his people on a much more demanding drug. Elementary school attendance is not a harmless luxury, but more like the coca chewing of the Andean Indian, which harnesses the worker to the boss.

The higher the dose of schooling an individual has received, the more depressing his experience of withdrawal. The seventh-grade dropout feels his inferiority much more acutely than the dropout from the third grade. The schools of the Third World administer their opium with much more effect than the churches of other epochs. As the mind of a society is progressively schooled, step by step its individuals lose their sense that it might be possible to live without being inferior to others. As the majority shifts from the land into the city, the hereditary inferiority of the peon is replaced by the inferiority of the school dropout who is held personally responsible for his failure. Schools rationalize the divine origin of social stratification with much more rigor than churches have ever done.

Until this day no Latin American country has declared youthful under-consumers of Coca-Cola or cars as lawbreakers, while all Latin American countries have passed laws which define the early dropout as a citizen who has not fulfilled his legal obligations. The Brazilian government recently almost doubled the number of years during which schooling is legally compulsory and free. From now on any Brazilian dropout under the age of sixteen will be faced during his lifetime with the reproach that he did not take advantage of a legally obligatory privilege. This law was passed in a country where not even the most optimistic could foresee the day when such levels of schooling would be provided for only 25 per cent of the young. The adoption of international standards of schooling forever condemns most Latin Americans to marginality or exclusion from social life – in a word, underdevelopment.

The translation of social goals into levels of consumption is not limited to only a few countries. Across all frontiers of culture, ideology and geography today, nations are moving toward the establishment of their own car factories, their own medical and normal schools – and most of these are, at best, poor imitations of foreign and largely North American models.

The Third World is in need of a profound revolution of its institutions. The revolutions of the last generation were overwhelmingly political. A new group of men with a new set of ideological justifications assumed power to administer fundamentally the same scholastic, medical and market institutions in the interest of a new group of clients. Since the institutions have not radically changed, the new group of clients remains approximately the same size as that previously served. This appears clearly in the case of education. Per pupil costs of schooling are today comparable everywhere since the standards used to evaluate the quality of schooling tend to be internationally shared. Access to publicly financed education, considered as access to school, everywhere depends on per capita income. (Places like China and North Vietnam might be meaningful exceptions.)

Everywhere in the Third World modern institutions are grossly unproductive, with respect to the egalitarian purposes for which they are being reproduced. But so long as the social imagination of the majority has not been destroyed by its fixation on these institutions, there is more hope of planning an institutional revolution in the Third World than among the rich. Hence the urgency of the task of developing workable alternatives to 'modern' solutions.

Underdevelopment is at the point of becoming chronic in

many countries. The revolution of which I speak must begin to take place before this happens. Education again offers a good example: chronic educational underdevelopment occurs when the demand for schooling becomes so widespread that the total concentration of educational resources on the school system becomes a unanimous political demand. At this point the separation of education from schooling becomes impossible.

The only feasible answer to ever-increasing underdevelopment is a response to basic needs that is planned as a long-range goal for areas which will always have a different capital structure. It is easier to speak about alternatives to existing institutions, services and products than to define them with precision. It is not my purpose either to paint a Utopia or to engage in scripting scenarios for an alternative future. We must be satisfied with examples indicating simple directions that research should take.

Some such examples have already been given. Buses are alternatives to a multitude of private cars. Vehicles designed for slow transportation on rough terrain are alternatives to standard trucks. Safe water is an alternative to high-priced surgery. Medical workers are an alternative to doctors and nurses. Community food storage is an alternative to expensive kitchen equipment. Other alternatives could be discussed by the dozen. Why not, for example, consider walking as a long-range alternative for locomotion by machine, and explore the demands which this would impose on the city planner? And why can't the building of shelters be standardized, elements be pre-cast, and each citizen be obliged to learn in a year of public service how to construct his own sanitary housing?

It is harder to speak about alternatives in education, partly because schools have recently so completely pre-empted the available educational resources of good will, imagination and money. But even here we can indicate the direction in which research must be conducted.

At present, schooling is conceived as graded, curricular, class attendance by children, for about 1000 hours yearly during an uninterrupted succession of years. On the average, Latin American countries can provide each citizen with between eight and thirty months of this service. Why not, instead, make one or two months a year obligatory for all citizens below the age of thirty?

Money is now spent largely on children, but an adult can be taught to read in one-tenth the time and for one-tenth the cost it takes to teach a child. In the case of the adult there is an immediate return on the investment, whether the main importance of his learning is seen in his new insight, political awareness and willingness to assume responsibility for his family's size and future, or whether the emphasis is placed on increased productivity. There is a double return in the case of the adult, because not only can he contribute to the education of his children, but to that of other adults as well. In spite of these advantages, basic literacy programs have little or no support in Latin America, where schools have a first call on all public resources. Worse, these programs are actually ruthlessly suppressed in Brazil and elsewhere, where military support of the feudal or industrial oligarchy has thrown off its former benevolent disguise.

Another possibility is harder to define, because there is as yet no example to point to. We must therefore imagine the use of public resources for education distributed in such a way as to give every citizen a minimum chance. Education will become a political concern of the majority of voters only when each individual has a precise sense of the educational resources that are owing to him – and some idea of how to sue for them. Something like a universal GI Bill of Rights could be imagined, dividing the public resources assigned to education by the number of children who are legally of school age, and making sure that a child who did not take advantage of his credit at the age of seven, eight or nine would have the accumulated benefits at his disposal at age ten.

What could the pitiful education credit which a Latin American Republic could offer to its children provide? Almost all of the basic supply of books, pictures, blocks, games and toys that are totally absent from the homes of the really poor, but enable a middle-class child to learn the alphabet, the colors, shapes and other classes of objects and experiences which ensure his educational progress. The choice between these things and schools is obvious. Unfortunately, the poor, for whom alone the choice is real, never get to exercise this choice.

Defining alternatives to the products and institutions which now pre-empt the field is difficult, not only, as I have been trying to show, because these products and institutions shape our conception of reality itself, but also because the construction of new possibilities requires a concentration of will and intelligence in a higher degree than ordinarily occurs by chance. This concentration of will and intelligence on the solution of particular problems regardless of their nature we have become accustomed over the last century to call research.

I must make clear, however, what kind of research I am talking about. I am not talking about basic research either in physics, engineering, genetics, medicine or learning. The work of such men as Crick, Piaget and Gell-Mann must continue to enlarge our horizons in other fields of science. The labs and libraries and specially trained collaborators these men need cause them to congregate in the few research capitals of the world. Their research can provide the basis for new work on practically any product.

I am not speaking here of the billions of dollars annually spent on applied research, for this money is largely spent by existing institutions on the perfection and marketing of their own products. Applied research is money spent on making planes faster and airports safer; on making medicines more specific and powerful and doctors capable of handling their deadly side-effects; on packaging more learning into classrooms; on methods to administer large bureaucracies. This is the kind of research for which some kind of counterfoil must somehow be developed if we are to have any chance to come up with basic alternatives to the automobile, the hospital and the school, and any of the many other so-called 'evidently necessary implements for modern life'.

I have in mind a different, and peculiarly difficult, kind of research, which has been largely neglected up to now, for obvious reasons. I am calling for research on alternatives to the products which now dominate the market; to hospitals and the profession dedicated to keeping the sick alive; to schools and the packaging process which refuses education to those who are not of the right age, who have not gone through the right curriculum, who have not sat in a classroom a sufficient number of successive hours, who will not pay for their learning with submission to custodial care, screening and certification or with indoctrination in the values of the dominant elite.

This counter-research on fundamental alternatives to current pre-packaged solutions is the element most critically needed if the poor nations are to have a liveable future. Such counter-research is distinct from most of the work done in the name of the 'year 2000', because most of that work seeks radical changes in social patterns through adjustments in the organization of an already advanced technology. The counter-research of which I speak must take as one of its assumptions the continued lack of capital in the Third World.

The difficulties of such research are obvious. The researcher must first of all doubt what is obvious to every eye. Second, he must persuade those who have the power of decision to act against their own short-run interests or bring pressure on them to do so. And, finally, he must survive as an individual in a world he is attempting to change fundamentally so that his fellows among the privileged minority see him as a destroyer of the very ground on which all of us stand. He knows that if he should succeed in the interest of the poor, technologically advanced societies still might envy the 'poor' who adopt this vision.

There is a normal course for those who make development policies, whether they live in North or South America, in Russia or Israel. It is to define development and to set its goals in ways with which they are familiar, which they are accustomed to use in order to satisfy their own needs, and which permit them to work through the institutions over which they have power or control. This formula has failed, and must fail. There is not enough money in the world for development to succeed along these lines, not even in the combined arms and space budgets of the super-powers.

An analogous course is followed by those who are trying to make political revolutions, especially in the Third World. Usually they promise to make the familiar privileges of the present elites, such as schooling, hospital care, etc., accessible to all citizens; and they base this vain promise on the belief that a change in political regime will permit them to sufficiently enlarge the institutions which produce these privileges. The promise and appeal of the revolutionary are therefore just as threatened by the counter-research I propose as is the market of the now dominant producers.

In Vietnam a people on bicycles and armed with sharpened bamboo sticks have brought to a standstill the most advanced machinery for research and production ever devised. We must seek survival in a Third World in which human ingenuity can peacefully outwit machined might. The only way to reverse the disastrous trend to increasing underdevelopment, hard as it is, is to learn to laugh at accepted solutions in order to change the demands which make them necessary. Only free men can change their minds and be surprised; and while no men are completely free, some are freer than others.

Further Reading

Most references are to books in English, although some articles from an enormous journal literature are also included, and several works in French. Although highly selective the following provides a cross-section of development literature.

1 General

Well-known introductory texts and general statements include the following:

P. Baran, *The Political Economy of Growth*, Monthly Review Press, New York and London, 1962.

C. S. Belshaw, *Traditional Exchange and Modern Markets*, Prentice-Hall, Englewood Cliffs, NJ, 1965.

J. Bhagwati, *The Economics of Underdeveloped Countries*, Weidenfeld & Nicolson, London, 1966.

S. N. Eisenstadt, *Modernization: Protest and Change*, Prentice-Hall, Englewood Cliffs, NJ, 1966.

B. Higgins, *Economic Development: Principles, Problems and Policies*, Norton, NY, 1968, revised edn.

W. A. Lewis, *The Theory of Economic Growth*, Allen & Unwin, London, 1955.

H. Myint, *The Economics of the Developing Countries*, Hutchinson, London, 1964.

P. Worsley, *The Third World*, Weidenfeld & Nicolson, London, 1964.

The major social science journals often contain articles on development problems; in addition there are journals specializing in particular problem-areas such as demography, education, administration and community development. There is a further species of journals devoted to (geographical) area studies, e.g. the *Journal of Modern African Studies*, with a strong development interest. An increasing number of journals specifically concerned with development include *Economic Development and Cultural Change* (Chicago); *Journal of Development Studies* (London); *Journal of the Developing Areas* (Illinois); *Development and Change* (The Hague), and *Cultures et Développement* (Louvain). Also growing in number and importance are journals published in The Third World, such as *Social and Economic Studies* (Jamaica), and *METU Studies in Development* (Turkey). Examples of the radical approach are to be found in, e.g. New Left Review (London), *L'Homme et la Société* (Paris), *Monthly Review* (New York and London), and *Science and Society* (New York).

Many of the best known journal articles have been reprinted in such collections as –

A. N. Argawala and S. P. Singh, (eds.), *The Economics of*

Underdevelopment, Oxford University Press, NY, 1958.

J. L. Finkle and R. W. Gable (eds.), *Political Development and Social Change*, Wiley, NY, 1968.

G. M. Meier (ed.), *Leading Issues in Development Economics*, Oxford University Press, NY, 1964.

G. D. Ness (ed.), *The Sociology of Economic Development*, Harper & Row, NY, 1970.

Some work by East European scholars is available in English, for example the series, *Studies in Developing Countries*, published by the Centre for Afro-Asian Research of the Hungarian Academy of Sciences, Budapest; and some publications of the USSR Academy of Sciences, Moscow; (e.g. I. I. Potekhin, *African Problems*, 1968). A number of translations are collected in T. P. Thornton (ed.), *The Third World in Soviet Perspective*, Princeton University Press, NJ, 1964.

An indispensable source of statistical abstracts, reports and trend analyses are the publications of the United Nations and its special agencies, such as FAO (Food and Agricultural Organization), and UNIDO (UN Industrial Development Organization), and various regional UN Economic Commissions. Many conferences and publications are sponsored by UNESCO. Official reports are also issued by other international bodies, governments, banks etc. For reference purposes there are some useful handbooks on Asia, Africa and Latin America which are revised periodically, as well as the quarterly country reports of the *Economist Intelligence Unit*.

2 Theories and methods

The study of Third World problems has stimulated, on the part of some at least, a new and very necessary critical awareness of the assumptions and conceptual limitations of western social science. Some discussions of development economics are cited in the Introduction (Clairmonte, 1900; David, 1967; Gerschenkron, 1962; Hahn and Matthews, 1965; Martin and Knapp, 1967; Myint, 1967; Myrdal, 1957; Seers, 1963, 1969; Wilber, 1969). In addition to the articles by Bernstein (1971, 1972) and Frank (1969), referred to in the Introduction, discussions of the sociology of development include:

R. Bendix, 'Tradition and modernity reconsidered', *Comparative Studies in Society and History*, vol. 9, 1967.

R. I. Rhodes, 'The disguised conservation in evolutionary development theory', *Science and Society*, vol. 32.

The dominant political science orientation was established by G. A. Almond and J. S. Cotsman (eds.) (1960), *The Politics of Our Developing Areas*, Princeton University Press, and consolidated in the series of synopsia following this *Studies in Political Development*, published by Princeton University Press for the Committee on Comparative Politics of the US Social Science Research Council. A characteristically sharp discussion of issues was provided by J. P. Nettl (1969), 'Strategies in one study of political development', in C. Leys (ed.), *Politics and Change in Developing Countries*, Cambridge University Press, London. An illuminating analysis of a change in preoccupation from the 'prospects of democracy' to an emphasis on order is D. Cruise O'Brien (1972),

Modernization order and the erosion of a democratic ideal, American political science, 1960–1970', *Journal of Development Studies*, vol. 8.

Obviously questions of theory and method cannot be properly considered in isolation from substantive problems, and are discussed in relation to specific issues in many of the other works given here. See, for example, the next two sections for the question of underdevelopment and issues debated among economic anthropologists.

3 The nature of underdevelopment

Useful reviews of the concept of underdevelopment are contained in:

J. Freyssinet, *Le Concept de Sous-Développment*, Mouton, Paris and The Hague, 1970, second edn.

T. Szentes, *Interpretations of Economic Underdevelopment: A Critical Study*, Centre for Afro-Asian Research of the Hungarian Academy of Sciences, Budapest, 1968.

A. G. Frank, *Capitalism and Underdevelopment in Latin America*, Monthly Review Press, NY and London, is frequently cited for the radical historical interpretation of underdevelopment, 1969, second edition, but see also –

S. Amin, L'Accumulation *à l'Échelle Mondiale*, IFAN, Dakar, Paris, 1970; and the use of this perspective in the recent work of some development economists like K. A. Griffin, *Underdevelopment in Spanish America*, Allen & Unwin, London, 1970.

Studies of colonial economy and society include:

G. Arrighi, *The Political Economy of Rhodesia*, Mouton, The Hague, 1967.

G. Balandier, *The Sociology of Black Africa*, London, 1970.

J. V. Levin, *The Export Economies*, Harvard University Press, Cambridge, Mass. 1960.

S. J., and B. M. Stein, *The Colonial Heritage of Latin America*, Oxford University Press, NY, 1970.

The concept of involution introduced by Geertz (Reading 2), principally with regard to the changes in ecology and village social structure, has been applied to other aspects of Indonesian society by W. F. Werthein (1964) *East–West Parallels*, W. van Hoeve, The Hague.

In this area, as in others, the work of historians provides an indispensable source of material if often rather restricted in analytical vision.

For references on the related theme of imperialism, see Section 8.

4 Agriculture and rural and social structure

Two good collections of readings are those edited by:

G. Dalton, *Economic Development and Social Change. The Modernization of Village Communities*, Natural History Press, NY, 1971.

T. Shanin, *Peasants and Peasant Societies*, Penguin, Harmondsworth, (1971).

These contain a number of articles relevant to the debate among economic anthropologists concerning the use of Western economic concepts in analysing agricultural organization in pre-capitalist, and underdeveloped societies. On this see:

R. Firth (ed.), *Themes in Economic Anthropology*, Tavistock, London, 1967.

E. LeClair Jr, and H. K. Schneider (eds.), *Economic Anthropology*, Holt, Rinehart & Winston, NY.

For different points of entry into this debate by Marxists, see:

M. Godelier, '*Objet et methode de l'anthropologie economique*', *L'Homme*, vol. 5, 1965, and one work of C. Meillassoux listed in his article cited in the Introduction – neither of these writers are discussed in the 500 or so pages of LeClair and Schneider. In this connexion, the convergence of the concerns of economics and anthropology, reference should also be made to

P. Hill, 'A plea for indigenous economics: the West African example', *Economic Development and Cultural Change*, vol. 15, 1966, which is reprinted in her *Studies in Rural Capitalism in West Africa*, Cambridge University Press, London.

The nature of peasant economic activity and the distortions that can arise from the categories used in agrarian censuses are themes of the instructive essays by D. and A. Thorner, *Land and Labour in India*, Asia Publishing House, Bombay and London, 1962.

The issues raised by Stavenhagen (Reading 4) are dealt with more fully in his *Les Classes Sociales dans Les Sociétés Agraires*, Anthropos, Paris, 1968.

A model of presentation and analysis of survey data is

S. L. Barraclough, and A. L. Domike, 'Agrarian structure in seven Latin American countries', *Land Economics*, vol. 42, 1966.

T. S. Epstein, *Economic Development and Social Change in South India*, Manchester University Press, Manchester, 1962 is an exemplary study of local change, and one of many village monographs by anthropologists.

J. Hinderink and M. Kiray, *Social Stratification as an Obstacle to Development*, Praeger, New York, 1970 is a comprehensive study of the effects on four villages of new patterns of cash-cropping, by Turkey's leading sociologist and a Dutch geographer.

E. H. Jaccoby, *Man and Land. The Fundamental Issue in Development*, Deutsch, London, 1970,
and
D. Warriner, *Land Reform in Principle and Practice*, Clarendon, Oxford, 1969

are surveys of agrarian problems and strategies by two people with long experience in this field (see Further Reading, Section 6).
Another well-travelled and experienced observer is the noted French economist, R. Dumont, whose writings constitute almost a genre apart, marked by an urgency and irreverence often lacking among writers on development; see, for example, *Lands Alive*, Merlin, London, 1965. *False Start in Africa*, Deutsch, London, 1966.

With regard to agricultural economics, J. W. Mellor, *The Economics of Agricultural Development*, Cornell University Press, Ithaka, NY, 1966, is a comprehensive textbook. Further discussion of certain issues can be found in two recent synopsia:

E. L. Jones, and S. J. Woolf (eds.),
Agrarian Change and Economic Development, Methuen, 1969.
C. R. Wharton Jr (ed.), *Subsistence Agriculture and Economic Development*, Cass, London, 1970.

Well-known views on agricultural development were proposed by
C. Clark, and M. R. Haswell, *The Economics of Subsistence Agriculture*, Macmillan, London, second edition, 1966,
and
T. W. Schultz, *Transforming Traditional Agriculture*, Yale University Press, New Haven, 1964.

Schultz technically oriented prescriptions have stimulated some controversy, and opposition from those with a more structural approach (for example, Beckford, Reading 6; Petras and La Porte, Reading 12).

5 Industrialization

A. Mountjoy, *Industrialization and Underdeveloped Countries*, Hutchinson, London, 1963 provokes a brief introduction; an up-to-date and much more extensive review of literature and issues, which also contains a comprehensive bibliography, is R. B. Sutcliffe, *Industry and Underdevelopment*, Addison-Wesley, London, 1971.

A sociological perspective is given in:
W. E. Moore, *The Impact of Industry*, Prentice-Hall, Englewood Cliffs, NJ, 1965.

The papers of a multidisciplinary seminar sponsored by UNESCO have been published in
B. F. Moselitz and W. E. Moore (eds.), *Industrialization and Society*, Mouton, Paris, 1963.

Useful country studies include
W. Baer, *Industrialization and Economic Development in Brazil*, Irwin, Homewood, Ill., 1965,
and
P. Kilby, *Industrialization in an Open Economy: Nigeria 1945–1966*. Cambridge University Press, London, 1969.

Small industry, particularly in Japan and India, is treated in
B. F. Hoselitz (ed.), *The Role of Small Industry in the Process of Economic Growth*, Mouton, Paris and The Hague, 1968.

Classic sources of entrepreneurial theory in economics and sociology respectively are

J. A. Schumpeter, *The Theory of Economic Development*, Harvard University Press, Cambridge, 1934,
and
M. Weber, *The Protestant Ethic and the Spirit of Capitalism*, Allen & Unwin, London, 1930.

A psychologistic reduction of entrepreneurship to a personality type is to be found in

D. McClelland, *The Achieving Society*, Van Nostrand, Princeton, 1961.

A greater sociological and historical sensitivity is displayed in a number of essays in
S. N. Eisenstadt (ed.), *The Protestant Ethic and Modernization*, Basic Books, NY, 1968.

T. C. Cochran, and R. E. Reina, *Entrepreneurship in Argentine Culture*, University of Pennsylvania Press, Philadelphia, 1962, is a study by a leading historian of American business. Recent researches conducted from the Institute of Development Studies in Nairobi are presented in P. Marris, and A. Somerset, *African Businessmen*, Routledge & Kegan Paul, 1971. On labour, a symposium with a variety of contributions is W. E. Moore and A. Feldman (eds.) *Labor Commitment and Social Change in Developing Areas*, Social Science Research Council, NY, 1960. Some historical comparisons are sketched by B. F. Moselitz, 'The development of a labour market in the process of economic growth', *Transactions of the Fifth World Congress of Sociology*, vol. 2, 1962.

Two monographs are
W. Elkan, *Migrants and Proletarians. Urban Labour in the Economic Development of Uganda*, East African Institute of Social Research, 1960; (although the nature of Kampala's 'proletarians' as analysed by Elkan cautions against the transference of such concepts without great care); and
G. Pfferman, *Industrial Labor in Senegal*, Praeger, NY, 1968.
A useful analysis of Latin American data on employment structure in relation to industrialization and social stratification is presented in F. H. Cardoso, *Sociologie du Développment en Amerique Latine*, Anthropos, Paris, chapter 3, 1969.
A. Bottomley, 'The fate of the artisan in developing economies', *Social and Economic Studies*, vol. 14, 1965, discusses an often neglected question of charging occupational structure with some illustrative data from Ecuador.

6 Development planning and strategy

K. B. Griffin and J. L. Enos, *Planning Development*, Addison Wesley, London, 1970 (from which Reading 11 is taken) is an excellent introductory text; and a number of useful articles are collected in A. O. Hirschman, *The Strategy of Economic Development*, Yale University Press, New Haven, 1958, and
I. Livingstone (ed.), *Economic Policy for Development*, Penguin, Harmondsworth, 1971.

Accounts of various agrarian reforms include –
E. A. Duff, *Agrarian Reform in Colombia*, Praeger, NY, 1968.

G. S. Saab, *The Egyptian Agrarian Reform*, 1952–62, Oxford University Press, London, 1967.

D. Warriner, *Land Reform and Development in the Middle East*, Oxford University Press, London, 1962, second edition.

See also the books by Jaccoby, Warriner and Dumont cited in section 4.

Studies of the Indian experience include –
S. C. Dube, *India's Changing Villages, Human Factors in Community Development*, Routledge & Kegan Paul, London, 1958.

J. W. Mellor *et al.*, *Developing Rural India. Plan and Practice*, Cornell University Press, Ithaca, NY, 1968.

Differing assessments of India's experience and policy are given by
F. R. Frankel, 'India's new strategy of agricultural development:
political costs of agrarian modernization', *Journal of Asian Studies*,
vol. 28, 1969,
and
J. Adams, 'Agrarian growth and rural change in India in the 1900s',
Pacific Affairs, vol. 43, 1970.

A useful comparison of India and China is to be found in
P. K. Bardhan, 'Chinese and Indian agriculture: a broad comparison of
recent policy and performance', *Journal of Asian Studies*, vol. 29, 1970.

I. and D. Crook, *Revolution in a Chinese Village. Ten Mile Inn*, Routledge
& Kegan Paul, London, 1959,
and
W. Hinton, *Fanshen*, Monthly Review Press, NY, 1959, are
sympathetic eye-witness accounts of Communist-induced changes in
Chinese villages. These need to be complemented with a more sober
assessment of overall agricultural performance, as provided by Bardhan.

Debates about industrialization strategy have often centred on import
substitution, which is the subject of a proliferating literature. A number
of recent articles are cited in Reading 11. To these can be added the
review by

H. J. Bruton, *The Import Substitution Strategy of Economic Development.
A Survey of Findings*, Research Memo No. 27, Centre for Development
Economics, Williams College, Williamsbourn, Mass, 1969.

UNIDO, *Planning for Advanced Skills and Technologies*, NY, 1969.
Some useful articles are those by

C. G. Riski on Chinese policy, which is further developed in his 'Small
industry and the Chinese model of development', *The China Quarterly*,
no. 46, 1971,
and
A. K. Sen, on 'Choice of technology: a critical survey of class debates'.

Education and manpower requirements and policies are discussed in
C. A. Anderson and M. J. Bowman (eds.), *Education and Economic
Development*, Cass, London, 1966,
and
F. Harbison, and C. A. Myers (eds.), *Education, Manpower and
Economic Growth*, McGraw Hill, NY, 1964.

P. Foster, *Education and Social Change in Ghana*, Routledge & Kegan
Paul, London, 1965, is a good monograph which gives some idea of the
view from the secondary school.

K. Griffin (ed.), *Financing Development in Latin America*, Macmillan,
London, 1971, is prefaced by the assertion that even highly technical
questions of planning cannot be considered in isolation from the processes
of decision-making in the class and power processes structure.

Despite an early and provocative essay by
M. Bronfenbrenner, 'The appeal of confiscation in economic development',
Economic Development and Cultural Change, vol. 3, 3, 1955, expropriation
and naturalization have been largely ignored by development economists
(however much they have filled newspaper headlines). See, however, the
case study by

M. O. Faber, and J. G. Potter, 1971, *Towards Economic Independence. Papers on the Nationalization of the Copper Industry in Zambia*, Cambridge University Press, London, 1971.

Useful contributions to the theory and analysis of social planning are Economic Commission for Latin America, Social Affairs Division, 1966. 'Social Development' and 'Social Planning': A Survey of Conceptual and Practical Problems in Latin America, *Economic Bulletin for Latin America*, vol. 9; and R. Apthorpe (ed.), *People, Planning and Development Studies: Reflections on Social Planning*, Cass, London, 1971, which contains a good essay on African rural planning by the Editor.

Part of the literature evaluates particular plans in terms of the desirability of their goals and methods, and/or their implementation. An example which contains detailed analysis is
A. H. Hanson, *The Process of Planning. A Study of India's Five-Year Plans, 1950–64*, Oxford University Press, London, 1966. Various aspects of Turkey's first five year plan (1963–67) are examined by S. Ilkin and E. Inang (eds.), *Planning in Turkey*, Faculty of Administrative Sciences, Middle East Technical University, Ankara, 1967. Papers – both general and case-studies – of a 1969 conference on *The Crisis in Planning*, held at the Institute of Development Studies (Sussex), are in press, to be published by Sussex University Press.

Organizational and administrative aspects of policy implementation has given rise to a large literature. Representative of the main orientation is R. Braibanti (ed.), *Political and Administrative Development*, Duke University Press, Durham, NC 1969, which includes statements by a number of social scientists with experience as consultants to the US government. The full analyses of such issues must take account of the nature of bureaucracy and the state in Third World countries. More a bridge between the concerns of this and the next section is to be found in the idiosyncratic and interesting work of F. W. Riggs, *Administration in Developing Countries*, Houghton Mifflin, Boston, 1964. Underlying Riggs' system of neologistic definitions is a concern to locate administration in an understanding of the total social structure of underdevelopment.

7 Class structure and the state

Many writers have discussed class structure and the nature of the state in Third World countries, but a systematic theoretical approach is still lacking.

Political scientists have emphasized the question of élites, which receives a full and representative treatment in
D. Apter, *The Politics of Modernization*, University of Chicago Press, 1965. The relationship between élite and 'mass' is a concern of the difficult book by J. P. Nettl, *Political Mobilization*, Faber, London, 1967, which nevertheless contains some sharp insights. This theme is explored more concretely by a number of the contributors to G. Ionescu and E. Gellner (eds.), *Populism*, Weidenfeld & Nicolson, London, 1969.

It is to be remembered that the anti-colonial and nationalist movements in Asia and Africa were an important context for the emergence of indigenous élites. An early (pre-Independence) and still illuminating work is
T. Hodkin, *Nationalism in Colonial Africa*, New York University Press, 1957. A host of other books on this subject include

G. McT. Kahin, *Nationalism and Revolution in Indonesia*, Cornell University Press, Ithaca, 1952.
J. S. Coleman, *Nigeria: Background to Nationalism*, University of California Press, Berkeley, 1958.

S. G. Haim (ed.), *Arab Nationalism*, University of California Press, Berkeley, 1962.
See also P. Worsley, *The Third World*, cited in Section 1.

For studies of the sociologically more elusive 'middle class', see International Institute of Differing Civilizations, *Development of a Middle Class in Tropical and Sub-tropical Countries*, INCIDI, Brussels, 1956.

J. J. Johnson, *Political Change in Latin America: the Emergence of the Middle Sectors*, Stanford University Press, Stanford, Calif., 1958.
B. B. Misra, *The Indian Middle Classes*, Oxford University Press, London, 1961.

The relationship between a 'middle class' of small and medium businessmen and bureaucrats and development is difficult to define. The social weakness and political ineffectiveness of a business group engaged in usually dependent mercantile activity has often been pointed out for the Middle East, for example see
C. Issawi, 'The entrepreneur class', in S. N. Fisher (ed.), *Social Forces in the Middle East*, Cornell University Press, Ithaca, 1955, and A. Mottinder, 'How the Arab bourgeoisie lost power', *Journal of Contemporary History*, vol. 3, 1968.

This has led some to speak of a 'new middle class' of development-minded technocrats, professionals and military officers. A more sophisticated presentation of this theme than is customary is to be found in
M. Halpern, *The Politics of Social Change in North Africa and the Middle East*, Princeton University Press, 1963.

Again, attention is focused on the state which is often regarded as the major instrument of development in Third World countries, with its actual or potential ability to mobilize resources. This idea is held by many with different view-points (including those who advocate some form of capitalist development). The role of the 'strong state' is emphasized in the vast survey directed by G. Myrdal, *Asian Drama*, 3 vols., Pantheon, NY, 1968.

An interesting study of the problems of implementing a particular programme, Indian community development, is contained in
R. Bendix, *Nation Building and Citizenship*, Doubleday, NY, 1969.

S. C. Dube, 'Bureaucracy and nation-building in transitional societies', *International Social Science Journal*, vol. 16 (special issue on leadership and economic growth), conveniently summarizes a number of familiar observations, including the tension between administrative and political élites. Works on bureaucracy by Rigg and Braibanti (eds.) were cited in the previous section.

Studies which attempt to locate bureaucracy in the broader framework of class analysis include
A. Abdel-Malek, *Egypt. Military Society*, Random, 1968.

R. Fitch, and M. Oppenheimer, *Ghana. End of an Illusion*, Monthly Review Press, NY, 1966.

The military, in fact, seems to be the state institution which is often as determinant in one sense as it is inconclusive in others. The sanguine view of the military as a force for modernization is to be found in the comparative study by
M. Janowitz, *The Military in the Political Development of New Countries*, University of Chicago, 1964,

and in the collection of case studies edited by

J. J. Johnson, *The Role of the Military in Underdeveloped Countries*, Princeton University Press, 1962,

More critical assessments – from very different perspectives – are those by
S. E. Finer, *The Man on Horseback*, Pall Mall, London, 1962, and
R. First, *The Barrel of a Gun*, Allen Lane, London, 1970.
The former employs a set of criteria of (civil) political culture; the latter draws on the theory of neo-colonialism (see next section).

In the advanced Latin American countries analysis of the military phenomenon has to take account of a more complex class structure which includes a national capitalist class. The latter is discussed in the interesting essays by C. Furtado, *Diagnosis of the Brazilian Crisis*, University of California Press, Berkeley, 1965, written on the eve of the 1964 military intervention.

With regard to revolutionary societies, there is a masterly analysis of China by F. Schurmann, *Ideology and Organization in Communist China*, University of California Press, Berkeley, 1968. This second edition contains a discussion of the Cultural Revolution. On Cuba, further to the article contained in this collection, there is the very useful book by
J. O'Connor, *The Origins of Socialism in Cuba*, Cornell University Press, Ithaca, 1970.

Supplementary works on class and state in Cuba are those by
J. M. Alier, 'The peasantry and the Cuban Revolution from the spring of 1959 to the end of 1960', *St Anthony's Papers*, no. 22, Oxford University Press, London, 1970, and M. Zeitlin, *Revolutionary Politics and the Cuban Working Class*, Harper & Row, NY, 1970 (second edition).

The economic and social bases of class formation and change are discussed in a number of works given in sections 4 and 5 above. With regard to class organization and political action, books on urban labour include
V. Alba, *Politics and the Labour Movement in Latin America*, Stanford University Press, Stanford, California, 1968, and I. Davies, *African Trade Unions*, Penguin, 1966.

Recent years have seen a great interest in peasant political action.
Frantz Fanon, *The Wretched of the Earth*, Penguin, 1967, contains some penetrating sociological insights and has become a contemporary classic. Nevertheless it remains a call to revolution rather than a systematic analysis of the conditions under which peasant revolution will take place (the reasons for this are given in
P. Geismar, *Frantz Fanon*, Grove Press, NY, 1969.

More analytical discussions by Marxists include
H. Alavi, 'Peasants and revolutions', in *The Socialist Register 1965*, 1965, and E. J. Hobsbawm, 'Guerillas in Latin America', in *The Socialist Register, 1970*, 1970 (both edited by R. Miliband and J. Saville and published by Merlin Press, London).

E. R. Wolf, *Peasant Wars of the Twentieth Century*, Harper & Row, NY, 1969, examines the cases of Mexico, Russia, China, Vietnam, Algeria and Cuba. A rather different work, outstanding in its scope and achievement, is B. Moore Jr, *The Social Origins of Dictatorship and Democracy*, Allen Lane, London, 1967. J. Womack Jr, *Zapata and the Mexican Revolution*, Thames & Hudson, London, 1969, is a most sensitive and illuminating historical monograph.

8 The international context

International economics and politics are fields which have given rise to a voluminous and technical literature. International relations constitute a vital context in which the stated intention to aid development, and the means proposed to do this, have to be assessed in the light of foreign policies which reflect the interests of nation states.

L. Pearson *et al.*, *Partners in Development*, Praeger, NY, 1969, a report sponsored by the World Bank, advocated improving the quantity and effectiveness of aid (and foreign private investment) within the terms of the existing system. See also the recent works of R. F. Mikesell, *The Economics of Foreign Aid*, Aldine, Chicago, 1968, and G. Myrdal, *The Challenge of World Poverty*, Pantheon, NY, 1970, and the contributions to the symposium edited by C. Legum, *The First UN Development Decade and its Lessons for the 1970s*, Praeger, NY, 1970.

The politics of the organizations through which much aid and technical assistance is channelled are discussed in
R. W. Cox (ed.), *The Politics of International Organizations*, Praeger, NY, 1970.

J. Bhagwati (ed.), *International Trade*, Penguin, 1969, and G. M. Meier, *International Trade and Development*, Harper & Row, NY, 1963, are by well-known economists in this field.

Various aspects of international business practice are discussed in the useful symposium edited by
C. P. Kindleberger, *The International Corporation*, MIT Press, Cambridge, Mass., 1970.
The very pertinent case of the oil industry is dealt with in two good recent studies –

E. D. Penrose, *The Large International Firm in Developing Countries: the International Petroleum Industry*, MIT Press, Cambridge, Mass., 1968.
M. Tanzer, *The Political Economy of International Oil and the Underdeveloped Countries*, Beacon Press, Boston.

M. Kidron, *Foreign Investments in India*, Oxford University Press, London, 1965, is a critical study with a mass of empirical data.
Withdrawing foreign private investment as an aspect of aiding development is raised by
A. O. Hirschman, *How to Divest in Latin America and Why*, Essays in International Finance no. 76, Dept. of Economics, Princeton University, 1969.

The political economy orientation of these last five works suggests a connection (which, however, remains to be made more explicit), with the work of sociologists like

G. M. Lagos, *International Stratification and Underdeveloped Countries*, University of North Carolina Press, Chapel Hill, 1963.

J. P. Nettl and R. Robertson, *International Systems and the Modernization of Societies*, Faber, London, 1968.

In this context reference can also be made to the ambitious but somewhat messy book by I. L. Horowitz, *Three Worlds of Development*, Oxford University Press, NY, 1966.

The most comprehensive framework for studying international relations remains that aspired to by the Marxist theory of imperialism.

T. Kemp, *Theories of Imperialism*, Dobson, London, 1967, is a useful discussion of the classic texts, but hedges very much on the inadequacies of Lenin's theory. J. O'Connor is more critical in 'The meaning of economic imperialism', in

R. Rhodes (ed.), *Imperialism and Underdevelopment*, Monthly Review Press, NY and London, 1970. This also contains an excellent long essay by G. Arrighi on 'International corporations, labour aristocracies, and economic development in tropical Africa'.

Recent works on imperialism by Marxists which more or less imply the themes of dependence and neo-colonialism include –

H. Magdoff, *The Age of Imperialism*, Monthly Review Press, NY, and London, 1969.

P. Jalee, *L'Imperialisme en 1970*, Maspéro, Paris, 1970.

D. Horowitz, *Imperialism and Revolution*, Penguin, 1971.

See also Frank and Amin, cited in Section 3.

Acknowledgements

Permission to reproduce the following Readings in this volume acknowledged to the following sources:

1 University of California Press
2 University of Claifornia Press
3 Consejo Latinomericano De Ciencias Sociales
4 *Sociologica Ruralis*
5 Cambridge University Press
6 Institute of Social and Economic Studies, Jamaica
7 Weidenfeld & Nicolson
8 University of California Press
9 Oxford University Press Inc.
10 Asia Publishing House
11 Addison-Wesley Publishing Co. Inc.
12 Monthly Review Press
13 Oxford University Press and Royal Institute of International Affairs
14 Random House Inc.
15 Politics and Society and Professor I. Wallerstein
16 *Journal of Modern African Studies*
17 *Political Science Quarterly*
18 *Bulletin of the Institute of Development Studies*
19 *Journal of Development Studies*
20 *New World Quarterly*
21 New York Review of Books Inc.

Author Index

Subject Index

Agriculture
  and mechanization, 234, 257–65
  and employment, 247–8
Agricultural development, 142–3,
  248–52
Alliance for Progress, 319

Booker Brothers, 123–6
Bureaucracy
  in Africa, 289
  in China, 269
  in Senegal, 325–6, 335–9

Cadres, 280–81
  in China, 272–3
Capitalist development, 26–7, 33–7,
  73–7, 299–301
  see also Colonialism,
    international corporations
Caste, 180–81, 245
Central American Common
  Market, 247–8
Class conflict, 173, 310–11
Class formation, 90, 95, 295–6
  see also Industrialization
Class structure
  in Indian villages, 240–42
  in Iranian villages, 156–63
Colonialism, 74–6, 85, 87
  in Java, 52–5
  see also Capitalist development,
    plantation agriculture
Community development, 93–4
Comparative statics, 22, 83
Consumption, 278–82, 357–364

Dependence, 76–9
Development economics, 16–18,
  97–9
Development models, 59–60
  and Soviet model, 262, 266–8
Dualism, 51, 54, 84

Education, 362–4, 365–6
  and technical assistance, 330

Entrepreneurship, 90
  see also National bourgeoisie

Imperialism, 73–4, 280
Import substitution, 219–21, 352–4
  in Latin America, 63–4, 67, 69
Industries
  automobiles (Chile), 224–5
  pharmaceuticals (Colombia),
    318–19, 321
  steel (India), 188–9
  textiles (India), 177–88
Industrialization, 216–19
  and class formation, 198–9
  and employment, 221–3
  and underdevelopment, 40–42
  value added in, 226–30
  see also Capitalist development,
    import substitution, international
    corporations, investment,
    technology
Interdisciplinary studies, 18–21,
  24–5
International corporations
  and corporate integration, 131–2,
    351–3
  and investment policies, 288–90
  and technology, 228, 354
  and transfer of resources, 291–2
  see also Plantation agriculture
Investment
  and allocation, 208–14
  and foreign control, 65, 294
  by Ghanaian farmers, 103–6,
    111–13
  sources of, 207–8
  see also International corporations,
    surplus

Labour, 281–2
  in agriculture, 81, 107–11
  and migration, 93, 291
Labour aristocracy, 291, 294, 300
Land tenure, 91
  in Iran, 161–3

Latin American Free Trade
Association, 345–7

Military regimes, 70
Money economy
 introduction of, 89–90, 286–7
 see also Capitalist development,
 colonialism

National bourgeoisie (Latin
 America), 71, 79, 197–8, 203–4
 see also State capitalism

Peasant attitudes, 238–9, 242–6
Plantation agriculture, 118–22
 and capital specificity, 136–9
 and land use, 139–41
 and production objectives, 133–6
 and risk considerations, 141–2
 see also Colonialism,
 underdevelopment
Price-system
 in international economy, 229

in planning, 214–15
and technology, 315–20

Regional integration, 341–4, 354–5

Social evolution, 23–6
Socialism, 279, 284–5, 304–5
State capitalism, 68
Strikes, 185–7
Subsistence agriculture, 86–7, 286
Surplus, 278, 287–8, 294–5

Tate and Lyle, 126–9
Technology, 342, 354–5
 and Law, 321

Underdevelopment, 25, 42
 and plantation agriculture, 143–50
 see also Capitalist development
United Fruit Co., 129–30
Urban-rural relations, 235–7, 246–7,
 273